T0312103

An Economic and Social History of the Netherlands, 1800–1920

An Economic and Social History of the Netherlands, 1800–1920 provides a comprehensive account of Dutch history from the late eighteenth to the early twentieth century, examining population and health, the economy, and socio-political history. The Dutch experience in this period is fascinating and instructive: the country saw extremely rapid population growth, awesome death rates, staggering fertility, some of the fastest economic growth in the world, a uniquely large and efficient service sector, a vast and profitable overseas empire, characteristic 'pillarization', and relative tolerance. Michael Wintle also examines the lives of ordinary people: what they ate, how much they earned, what they thought about public affairs, and how they wooed and wed. This is the only single-authored book currently available in English on this crucial period of Dutch history, and it will be of central importance to Dutch specialists, as well as to European historians more generally.

MICHAEL WINTLE is Professor and head of the Department of European Studies at the University of Hull. He has also taught at Utrecht, Victoria (Canada) and Amsterdam. His research interests are in the modern social and economic history of the Low Countries, European identity (especially the visual representation of Europe) and European industrialization. He has published widely on the history of the Netherlands. Recent books include *The Idea of a United Europe* (2000) and *Culture and Identity in Europe* (1996).

An Economic and Social History of the Netherlands, 1800–1920

Demographic, Economic and Social Transition

Michael Wintle

CAMBRIDGE
UNIVERSITY PRESS

CAMBRIDGE UNIVERSITY PRESS
Cambridge, New York, Melbourne, Madrid, Cape Town, Singapore, São Paulo

Cambridge University Press
The Edinburgh Building, Cambridge CB2 8RU, UK

Published in the United States of America by Cambridge University Press, New York

www.cambridge.org
Information on this title: www.cambridge.org/9780521782951

First published 2000
This digitally printed version 2007

A catalogue record for this publication is available from the British Library

Library of Congress Cataloguing in Publication data
Wintle, Michael J.
An economic and social history of the Netherlands, 1800–1920: demographic,
economic, and social transition / Michael Wintle.
    p.   cm.
Includes bibliographical references and index.
ISBN 0 521 78295 3
1. Netherlands – Economic conditions.   2. Netherlands – Social conditions.
3. Demography – Netherlands – History.   4. Netherlands – Population – History.
5. Netherlands – Statistic, Vital.   I. Title.
HC323.W56 2000
306'.09492–dc21   99-086453

ISBN 978-0-521-78295-1 hardback
ISBN 978-0-521-03739-6 paperback

For Sjoukje

Contents

Contents

Plates

Figures

Tables

Acknowledgements

The material for this volume has been collected over a period of more than twenty years, and I have been writing and revising various parts of it, on and off, for nigh on a decade. During that time I have been fortunate enough to earn my living teaching and researching modern European history, especially that of the Netherlands; I owe much to the stimulating environments in both the classrooms and the common-rooms of the universities in which I have been happily employed over the years. These include Ghent, Utrecht, Victoria (Canada), Amsterdam, and especially Hull, which has been my academic home base since 1977, and which has always provided a steady stream of students ready and willing to share my exploration of the subject-matter of this book. Countless individuals have assisted me towards a fuller understanding of Dutch history: they are too numerous to mention by name, but they know who they are, and I have much enjoyed and appreciated their help. The same goes for the anonymous referees who commented on drafts of this book. I am pleased to record my thanks for awards from the University of Hull's research funds, which have given me time and space to bring the project to fruition. My colleagues in the Department of European Studies, especially Philip Morgan and Jacky Cogman, have been endlessly stoical and supportive, especially during the lengthy final stages, and I could not have completed the project without their help. Finally, my preoccupation with Dutch history, and with this book in particular, has always been generously indulged by my family, and to them I am deeply grateful.

General introduction

Those from outside the Netherlands generally know very little about the country's history between the time of Napoleon and the Second World War. The Revolt of the Netherlands and the Golden Age of the Dutch Republic are familiar territory, but to most foreigners there is a veil of mystery – even nonentity – drawn over the country towards the end of the eighteenth century, marked perhaps by the resounding defeat of the Dutch and their economic pretensions in the Fourth Anglo-Dutch War (1780–84). Since the Second World War the Netherlands has become better known again, as a formidable if small economic force in an integrating Europe, and as a reputed haven of permissiveness and licentiousness: everyone knows Amsterdam.

That Dutch history has been obscure in the nineteenth and early twentieth century is hardly remarkable: it was not the cradle of industrial revolution, there were no violent political revolutions, nor any nationalist uprising for unification. Other countries have suffered similar historiographical fates: what do most of us know of the once-great Spain, or Portugal in the same period, to say nothing of Denmark and the rest of Scandinavia? Nonetheless, this book sets out to bring the Dutch back into the limelight in this internationally rather forgotten period, and to show to the non-Dutch-speaking world that the Netherlands had a fascinating and instructive history at this time, just as much as it did in the heady days of the Republic, or has done in the economic boom since the Second World War. Dutch economic and social historians themselves have long been aware of the rewards of this era: most of that extremely prolific profession works on the period since 1750 or even since 1850, rather than on the Golden Age.

This book is therefore a social and economic history of the Netherlands in the modern period, but that title needs some further specification. 'The Netherlands' refers to the Kingdom of the Netherlands as it is now constituted, but with some additions: during the period of French domination from 1795 to 1813 the present country was heavily influenced by France and at times subject to direct rule from Paris; from 1815 to 1830 it was united in one state with what is now Belgium; there were considerable border changes around what has since become the independent Duchy of Luxembourg; and the Netherlands possessed an enormous overseas empire, much of which survived and thrived throughout the nineteenth century right up to the Second World War.

As for timing, the period covered here concerns what might be called the 'long' nineteenth century. Comprehensive coverage is offered between 1813 and 1914, the dates of the Netherlands' escapes from past occupation by one foreign emperor and from potential domination by another. However, the frame of reference is very much wider, for the reason that the book seeks – principally in the nineteenth century – an explanation for the characteristics of Dutch society in the more familiar later twentieth century. This approach might be branded teleological, or even triumphalist, but in truth it amounts to little more than a frank recognition that the questions historians ask of their material in the past are substantially governed by their society's concerns in the present. This does not mean that anything which did not lead directly to the present situation should be ignored. On the contrary, what has been discarded is often as interesting as what has been embraced, for the 'constituting other' is as important to the make-up of the identity of a person, group, nation or state as are the essentialist characteristics which are recognized as fundamental. This is therefore an approach to history which is almost universal, if not universally admitted. It can be elaborated into a major epistemological framework, such as modernization theory, but in truth it is equally valid if portrayed as a straightforward wish to illuminate the present with a knowledge of the past. In the simplest terms, then, the Netherlands is today a crowded, prosperous and relatively tolerant country: how did that come about?

Deciding where to start and finish is always an issue for the historian: on the principle of ever-continuing causation, one should start with pre-history. However, in practical terms, the French period (1795–1813) is accepted in this volume as an important hiatus, with full recognition of the simultaneous continuities, especially in demographic and economic matters. A recent major work on the economy of the Republic, by Jan de Vries and Ad van der Woude, has concluded that the period 1780–1815 marked the death of the 'first phase of modern economic growth' in the Netherlands,[1] and Jonathan Israel's rather less radical approach to the same subject has also accepted that the economic power of the Republic was winding down in the eighteenth century, and died a death in the French period.[2] Although the nineteenth-century economy was certainly

[1] De Vries and Van der Woude, *Nederland*, 763–89.
[2] Israel, *Dutch primacy*, 11; and Israel, *The Dutch Republic*, 998–1006.

based on the events and structures of the previous period, the advent of a unitary state to replace the federal structure of the Republic makes the closing stages of the French period an intelligent place to start the history of the modern period. Nonetheless, there will be frequent reference here to the later eighteenth century and indeed the earlier Republic, especially in economic and socio-political matters.

As for the end-point, the case is even less clear-cut. It is the contention of this work that a transition to a modern society – the modern Netherlands – had been substantially completed in a demographic, economic and socio-political sense by 1914, and that is why the comprehensive coverage will tail off around that time. However, it would be foolish to deny that many of the developments had some of their most important changes still to come at that time – one could mention the decline in the birth rates, the rise of the great Dutch multinationals, or the welfare state – and so in many areas this 'history' will include taking the analysis well beyond the First World War, and in some cases past the Second.

Nonetheless the extended nineteenth century remains the focus. De Vries and Van der Woude have claimed that modern economic growth was achieved in the Republic;[3] that claim is contentious, but all would agree that it had to be achieved again (or perhaps for the first time) in the nineteenth century, in Kuznets' sense of sustained growth in national income per capita, accompanied by major population growth and structural change across all sectors in the economy. This was the century of the 'demographic transition'; in social history, the nineteenth century was the one of integration and location of the Dutch people in the wider national community, of emancipation, democratization, and the beginnings of modern mass education and the welfare state. Of course these developments continued after 1914, but – as will be demonstrated in the following chapters – the fundamental structural die had been cast in the nineteenth century.

In 1988 three 'Young Turks' (as they styled themselves on the day) issued a clarion call for some direction in the researching and writing of the economic and social history of the Netherlands, a manifesto they entitled, *Dutch history as deviation*.[4] Its authors were worried about foreign historians 'cherry-picking' Dutch history, and called for a more programmatic approach to historical work, based on investigating the ways in which the Dutch have proved themselves unusual: in their

---

[3] De Vries and Van der Woude, *Nederland*.
[4] Davids, Lucassen and Van Zanden, *De Nederlandse geschiedenis*. It was by no means universally welcomed on the day or subsequently (see Kossmann, *Een tuchteloos probleem*, 77), but launched an important research project which eventually resulted in the publication of Davids and Lucassen, eds., *A miracle mirrored*.

'pillarized' socio-political system, for example. The year before, the proceedings of a major historiographical review conference at the University of Utrecht had cast doubt on certain aspects of Dutch historical work, with an especially stinging attack on the practice of economic history, from Richard Griffiths.[5] It was a time of self-doubt in the profession throughout the Western world: with all the specialization and proliferation of the 1960s and 1970s, the discipline seemed to have lost some of its direction. In the event Dutch history, and economic and social history in particular, has gone from strength to strength, with increasing amounts of very high quality work being produced, and even some attempts at synthesis rather than further fragmentation. The debates and controversies in Dutch history will be outlined here where appropriate, for they often point to the heart of the issue, and reflect unerringly what the Dutch themselves have thought about their past (and their present) at various stages.

The acknowledged master of political and cultural history, Ernst Kossmann, remarked in his Oxford edition of *The Low Countries 1780–1940* that Dutch culture had – with the exception of theologians – produced very few writers of constructive synthesis, especially among historians.[6] This was perhaps a little rich coming from one who was engaged in writing precisely that kind of constructive synthesis himself, and the deficit has certainly been radically reduced in recent years, with large numbers of book-length studies as well as the customary proliferation of excellent essays and articles. But in economic and social history it is still the case that there have been very few attempts at synthesis. The standard work on the modern period remains that written by I.J. Brugmans in the 1950s;[7] despite being severely dated in many respects, it is still the only comprehensive single-authored work covering the whole subject, and it remains today an invaluable source of information. (It is also uncanny how much of Brugmans' analysis has been vindicated in recent years.) There have been edited collections which attempt the task of covering the whole modern period, for example in the multi-volume national history, *General history of the Netherlands*, which appeared in the late 1970s and early 1980s. Some of the contributions were exemplary, especially those by Theo van Tijn on social history, but inevitably the coverage and quality was uneven. That was also true of an edited volume on *Dutch society since 1815*, appearing in 1985,[8] which contained a particularly useful synthesis on demography (of which grateful use is made

---

[5] Published as Griffiths, 'Economische ontwikkeling'.
[6] Kossmann, *The Low Countries*, 259–61.   [7] Brugmans, *Paardenkracht*.
[8] Van Holthoon, ed., *De Nederlandse samenleving*.

in the early chapters of this book).[9] In economic history, Jan Luiten van Zanden evidently possesses all the skills of research, synthesis, and more, in order to produce a masterly and comprehensive synthesis on the nineteenth century, but has not yet chosen to do so.[10] So the fact remains that, since the labours of Brugmans forty years ago, we have no general socio-economic history of the Netherlands in the modern period, in either Dutch or English.

This book does indeed aim to provide a single-author interpretation of a wide field over an extended period in the way that Brugmans did, and that Kossmann did for political and cultural history, but is certainly not as comprehensive or methodical in its coverage of the traditional territory of socio-economic history as Brugmans' work was. On the other hand, however, it is in some senses rather broader. It offers a triptych of demography, the economy, and society, with rather more attention to the first subject than is usually given. In the final part on social transition, the lens is also focussed more widely than has often been the case. This is not a political history, but politics regularly features in these pages, both in terms of economic policy (a traditional stamping ground for the economic historian), but also in terms of political reform and organization, democratization, participation, and identity formation. There is a drive here to integrate political history with social and economic history, while the latter remains the prime focus. Considerable attention is paid to religion, and to colonial affairs. This is, then, an intentionally broad portrait of the Netherlands over an extended time period, with very few exclusions. There is scant diplomatic or military coverage (though both are mentioned repeatedly), but otherwise most fields are represented.

With such a wide canvas, many details have inevitably been left indistinct. The bibliographical appendix of works referred to in the notes is already quite large enough, but represents only a fraction of the profession's production over the last generation. The sources for this book have been secondary; the employment here of archival sources is limited to an occasional apposite quotation in order to illustrate a general point. This is a book based on the primary researches of others (including my own at other times). The geographical coverage is of the nation as a whole, although the urban areas of the West tend to predominate, as they do in all Dutch historiography above the regional level. On the other hand, one of the extraordinary features of modern Dutch history is the surprising

---

[9] Van der Woude, 'Bevolking en gezin'. A similar multi-author edited volume on the economic and social history of the early twentieth century appeared in the form of Den Hollander et al., eds., *Drift en koers*.

[10] Indeed he has recently done so in English for the twentieth century: Van Zanden, *The economic history*.

regional diversity in such a small country; that diversity, and its eventual demise before the advance of the centralization and state-building of the last two centuries, frequently forms a starting point for the investigation in the subsequent chapters. Often I have taken the advice of the 'Young Turks' and adopted as entry point an unusual feature of the Dutch experience compared to their neighbours:[11] their extremely rapid population growth, their awesome death rates, their staggering fertility, their large and efficient service sector, their overseas empire, their 'pillarization', their relative tolerance. But by way of balance there is also an attempt to pay attention to the ordinary in the Netherlands: what people ate, how much they earned, what they thought about public affairs, how they wooed and wed. And equally there is, I hope, evident in these pages a determination to place the Dutch in their European context. The word 'Sonderweg' is not used of Dutch history as it is of German, but many historians implicitly adopt a comparable agenda: this book aims to show that while the Dutch were interesting and unique in certain ways, their place is firmly within the maritime core of industrializing Northwest Europe; their uniqueness is meaningless removed from that environment, and their attributes shared with their neighbours far outweigh their idiosyncrasies.

The layout of the book is straightforward. There are three parts, on demography, the economy, and society. The twelve chapters all cover the same long period of time of at least a century. However, there is no division in chapters or sections by time period, which is the more conventional treatment.[12] Instead, each chapter takes a theme, a mode of transition, and follows its twists and turns through a hundred years and more, seeking out the periodicity of change and inertia. The objective is to present the reader in the Netherlands and further afield with an image of the period as whole, in its several aspects. The extended nineteenth century was one of fundamental change in all sectors of the life of the Dutch community; by 1914 most of the major developments which were to shape the country of today had already taken place, or were well on their way.

[11] Davids, Lucassen and Van Zanden, *De Nederlandse geschiedenis*, 8–9.
[12] In Brugmans, *Paardenkracht*, for instance.

Part I
Demography, and the health of the nation

1   Demographic indicators

1.1   Population increase and vital statistics

One of the most eloquent indicators of the state of an economy is the physical well-being of its population. The demographic history of the Dutch in the modern period has some distinctive characteristics, while remaining clearly rooted in the mainstream pattern of European development. The European population increased approximately fourfold between 1750 and 1950, from 144 million to 574 million. There was considerable variance in the rate of increase across the regions of Europe, and the Netherlands tended to fit into the pattern of faster growth which characterized some of the northern European nations like the United Kingdom, Scandinavia, northern Germany and the Low Countries.[1] Between the beginning of the nineteenth century and the outbreak of the Second World War, the world population is estimated to have grown by a factor of 2.4, the European by a factor of 2.9, while the Dutch managed to expand their numbers by a factor of no less than 4.4.[2]

Indeed, a whole string of more subtle demographic indicators than the gross population increase show the Netherlands to have been something of a demographic maverick: not only did it possess one of the highest growth rates, but it also has had some of the highest birth rates and the lowest death rates in the world, and in the twentieth century its life expectancy has also been among the highest. All this has meant that the Netherlands is now the most densely populated country in the OECD area.[3] Two factors lie at the root of this prominence of the Netherlands within the European pattern: the rapidity and extent of the decline in mortality since the middle of the last century, and the relatively late and gentle decline in fertility rates.[4] The Dutch population started growing earlier, and applied the brakes to its growth much later than most of its

---

[1] Tuma, *European economic history*, 202–3.   [2] Heere, 'De tegenwoordige', 4.
[3] At 390 persons per km^2 in 1971 (Table I.1), and 432 in 1987 (Wintle, 'The Netherlands economy', 356). Heeren and Van Praag, *Van nu tot nul*, 76–7; and Van Heek, *Het geboorte-niveau*, 190–1.
[4] Engelen and Hillebrand, 'Vruchtbaarheid', 248.

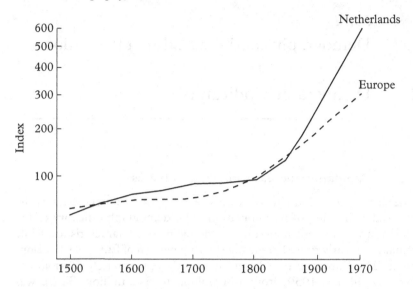

Figure I.1 The Dutch and West European population, 1500–1970; index (1800 = 100).

Source: Goodman & Honeyman, *Gainful pursuits*, 20; and Mitchell, *European historical statistics*, 3–8.

European counterparts. The details of and reasons for this state of affairs will form the principal themes of this chapter.

Population in the Netherlands (present borders) increased from just over 2 million in 1795 to 5.1m. at the turn of this century, and then to 15.4m. in 1994 (Figure I.1 and Table I.1). The annual rate of increase stayed well below 1 per cent per annum until the 1870s, when it leapt from 0.82 per cent in the 1860s to 1.21 per cent p.a. in the next decade (see Table I.1). Thereafter the annual rate of increase continued to rise until the 1930s, since when it has subsided. How can we explain what has been called this 'bizarre demographic development'?[5] The first objective is to determine what happened in the 1870s to allow the population to 'take off' in such a fashion.

Aggregate birth rates in the Netherlands (Table I.2) fluctuated around the mid-thirties per thousand population between 1815 and the 1870s, and then entered a long decline which has only been briefly interrupted by the 'baby-boom' after the Second World War. In other words, if we are seeking an explanation for the rise in the Dutch population which began to accelerate from the 1870s onwards, the birth rate alone is not

[5] Drukker, *Waarom de crisis*, 249.

Table I.1. *Population in the Netherlands at census counts, 1815–1971, with sex ratio and average annual rate of increase.*

Year	Total × 1,000	Males × 1,000	Females × 1,000	Sex ratio F/M	Total population index (1830=100)	Population per km²	Average annual rate of increase
1830	2,613	1,278	1,335	1.045	100	80	
1840	2,861	1,401	1,460	1.042	109	88	0.95
1849	3,057	1,499	1,558	1.040	117	94	0.76
1859	3,309	1,629	1,680	1.031	126	101	0.82
1869	3,580	1,764	1,815	1.029	136	109	0.82
1879	4,013	1,983	2,030	1.023	152	122	1.21
1889	4,511	2,228	2,283	1.024	173	139	1.24
1899	5,104	2,521	2,584	1.025	192	154	1.31
1909	5,858	2,899	2,959	1.021	224	180	1.48
1920	6,865	3,410	3,455	1.013	263	211	1.72
1930	7,936	3,943	3,993	1.013	304	244	1.56
1947	9,625	4,838	4,878	1.008	368	296	1.25
1960	11,462	5,754	5,802	1.008	439	352	1.47
1971	12,709	*6,465	*6,493	*1.004	486	390	0.99

Sources: CBS, as reported in Van der Woude, 'Bevolking en gezin'; and Bos, 'Long-term demographic development'.
* Figure for 1969.

very helpful. If the birth rate were determining the size of the total population, then we would expect the latter to fall heavily from the 1870s onwards, whereas what in fact happened was an unprecedented rise. Birth rates (and fertility rates) may conceal all manner of vital information about the dynamics of the Dutch population, especially at local and regional level, but as far as the national rise in population is concerned, the explanation lies for the main part with other factors. Theoretically, it is possible that the population increase came about from the 1870s onwards as a result of in-migration, with the number of immigrants outstripping the emigrants. Again, migration holds the key to a number of vital issues, but not to the total population increase in the nineteenth century: there was a slight immigration surplus early in the nineteenth century which then reversed into one of emigration (not large), which lasted until the First World War and beyond (Table I.3; see below, section I.6, on migration). We are left, then, with the death rates.

Death rates in the Netherlands (Table I.2) fluctuated around a slightly declining trend from the time of Waterloo to the time of the Paris Commune in 1870, and then went into free fall. With a blip for the First

Table I.2. *Birth rates, death rates, infant mortality rates and marriage rates in the Netherlands, ten-year intervals, 1840–1955.*

Period	Marriages	Births	Deaths	Deaths under 1 year per 100 births
	(per 1,000 average annual population)			
1840–49	7.3	33.1	26.3	18.2
1845–54	7.7	33.0	26.1	18.8
1850–59	7.9	33.8	25.5	19.5
1855–64	7.9	33.8	26.1	19.9
1860–69	8.2	34.7	24.9	19.8
1865–74	8.2	35.5	25.0	20.7
1870–79	8.1	36.2	24.5	20.4
1875–84	7.6	35.8	22.6	19.1
1880–89	7.1	33.5	21.3	18.3
1885–94	7.1	33.5	20.3	17.0
1890–99	7.3	32.7	18.7	16.0
1895–04	7.5	32.1	17.0	14.7
1900–09	7.5	30.9	15.6	13.0
1905–14	7.4	29.1	13.9	11.1
1910–19	7.4	26.9	13.0	9.7
1915–24	8.1	26.2	12.5	8.3
1920–29	8.0	25.1	10.5	6.6
1925–34	7.5	22.6	9.5	5.2
1930–39	7.6	21.0	8.8	4.2
1935–44	7.7	21.0	9.5	4.0
1940–49	8.4	23.9	9.9	4.2
1945–54	8.9	24.0	8.5	3.3
1950–55	8.4	22.0	7.4	2.3

Source: CBS.

World War and rather more than a blip for the Second (see Figure I.2), they have continued to fall ever since. In aggregate terms, then, the main reason at national level why the Dutch population rose, and rose rapidly after the 1870s, was a fall in mortality. In brief, relatively few people were dying, rather than more babies being born: the Dutch were living longer.

Life expectancy did indeed rise rapidly (Table I.4). In the 1840s a Dutchman could be expected to reach the age of thirty-six on average; women would live slightly longer, to about thirty-eight and a half. By the 1920s, these figures had leapt to sixty-two and sixty-four respectively, and then rose further, nearly doubling in little more than a century. The major acceleration in this improvement of prospects began – as we are coming to expect – in the 1870s; a detailed study of Utrecht has confirmed that there was no improvement at all before 1860.[6] But the concept of an average

[6] Mandemakers and Boonstra, eds., *De levensloop*, chapter 3.

Table I.3.   *Migration surplus/deficit in the Netherlands, 1815–1909 (× 1,000).*

Date	Population growth	Birth surplus	Deduced migration balance	CBS-calculated migration balance	Overseas migration balance
1815–19	79	92	−13	—	—
1820–29	301	211	90	—	—
1830–39	237	215	22	—	—
1840–49	196	202	−6	−9.3	−12.4
1850–59	252	261	−9	−10.3	−15.8
1860–69	271	346	−75	−66.8	−23.8
1870–79	433	449	−16	−13.0	−2.8
1880–89	498	566	−68	−67.0	−34.9
1890–99	593	675	−82	−82.0	−56.0
1900–09	754	841	−87	−85.0	−84.1
1840–1909	2,997	3,340	−343	−333.4	−229.8

Source: Stokvis, 'Nederland en de internationale migratie', 72.

Figure I.2 Mortality rates in the Netherlands, 1816–1975, quinquennial averages, deaths per thousand population per annum.

Source: Van der Woude, 'Bevolking en gezin', 30.

Table I.4. *Life expectancy at birth in the Netherlands, male and female, 1840–1952.*

Period	Males	Females
1840–51	36.2	38.5
1850–59	36.4	38.2
1860–69	37.2	39.1
1870–79	38.4	40.7
1880–89	42.5	45.0
1890–99	46.2	49.0
1900–09	51.0	53.4
1910–20	55.1	57.1
1921–30	61.9	63.5
1931–40	65.7	67.2
1947–49	69.4	71.5
1950–52	70.6	72.9

Source: CBS.

life expectancy at birth is of course a spurious one: the most likely fate to befall the Dutch newly born in the nineteenth century was one of death before reaching the age of twelve months. Once the infant had passed its first birthday, chances of survival improved slightly, and after the age of five they began to look quite rosy.[7] But with extremely high death rates for most of the nineteenth century, a worryingly prominent role was played by infant mortality. At national aggregate level, with death rates at over twenty-five per thousand per annum for nearly all of the period up to the 1870s, something like 20 per cent of those deaths were of infants under the age of one year (Table I.2). Locally, these mortality rates could rise to and remain at truly awesome levels, so much so that it is difficult for Western historians today to imagine life under such conditions.

National death rates were above twenty per thousand for almost the whole of the century, and only began to come down after the 1870s (Table I.2); by far the worst areas, especially in the middle of the century, were the coastal provinces of Groningen, Friesland, Noord- and Zuid-Holland, and especially the infamous Zeeland.[8] Zeeland had mortality rates of up to thirty-eight per thousand per annum in the period before the 1870s, and in some of its villages the statistics took on proportions that can only be described as horrific. In the forties and fifties of the last

---

[7] Van der Woude, 'Bevolking en gezin', 35. On infant mortality and its eventual decline in the nineteenth century in the town of Tilburg, see Van der Heijden, *Het heeft niet willen groeien.*

[8] Heere, 'De tegenwoordige', 6–7; and De Vooys, 'De sterfte'.

century, in Wissekerke, the rate was no less than forty-seven, and in Wolphaartsdijk it actually reached the psychologically devastating level of fifty.[9] For most of the nineteenth century the regional differences in the death rates of the Netherlands, which were considerable, are largely to be explained by variances in the child and infant mortality rates. In summary, the death rates were high until the 1870s, then declined rapidly, and after 1914 were not exceptional in comparison with other European countries. From that point on there was little regional variation.[10] Three questions pose themselves: why were the rates so high, why did they vary so much from province to province, and what brought them down so rapidly after 1870?

The 'demographic transition'

These are questions about what has come to be called 'the demographic transition': the switch from a population which maintained relative stability, with high death rates compensated for by high birth rates, to a society where population growth was relatively restricted again, but now with low death rates cancelling out low birth rates. The watershed period, with both birth rates and death rates plummeting, was usually a period of enormous population growth, for while fewer children were being born, the decline in mortality proceeded much faster, with the result that the new survivors outstripped the now unborn with great rapidity.[11] The theory of the demographic transition has been much disputed, but still determines most of the parameters of discussion and research; there is evidence that fertility rates were often anything but passive in the 'transition', and we shall study them in detail here, but it is still the rapid rise in population and fall in the death rate which continues to attract much of the attention of historians.[12]

1.2 Explaining the decline in mortality

Three general sorts of explanations have been put forward for the fall in mortality in the nineteenth century: those which concern the food supply, those which stress improvements in medicine and health care,

---

[9] De Vooys, 'De sterfte', 236. See also De Man, *Bijdrage tot de kennis*; De Man, 'Het sterftecijfer'; and Broes van Dort, *Bijdrage tot de kennis*. For a general summary of these discussions about Zeeland, see Wintle, *Zeeland and the churches*, 41–3.
[10] Van der Woude, 'Bevolking en gezin', 35–8.
[11] The classic formulation of this analysis was in 1945: Notestein, 'Population'.
[12] Note, for example, the recent inaugural lecture of one of the Netherlands' foremost demographers: Van Poppel, *Statistieke ontleding*. Other texts are very numerous; a good introduction in English is Petersen, 'The demographic transition'.

and those which deal with the improving public-health environment. Few would dispute the importance of improvements in the quantity and quality of food to the health of the population. If we accept a classic Malthusian situation in a country like the Netherlands which did not undergo an iron- and coal-led Industrial Revolution, then a massive increase in the food supply would permit and even cause an expansion of the population, by improving the diet of Dutch men, women, and particularly children, and thus by keeping them alive longer. It can be objected that the Dutch agricultural sector, and the commercial sector which connected the Netherlands to other sources of agricultural supply, were far from primitive and had been highly developed for several centuries, and that therefore the food supply was not in the least inelastic: the Malthusian concept of a direct and inevitable relationship between domestic farming and the level of the population simply did not pertain in the Netherlands of the nineteenth century. The food supply will be dealt with in more detail in chapter 2; meanwhile it is clear that the doubling of the population in the nineteenth century must have been affected by an increasing availability of better food. For example, the introduction of the potato to European diets is accepted as having acted as an important extender of life from the late eighteenth century onwards,[13] and the impact of the agricultural golden years of the 1850s and 1860s, lasting into the 1870s, with harvests and yields at unprecedented levels, cannot have failed to exert an influence on the decline in mortality from the 1870s onwards. The import of increasing quantities of cheap grains from the world's wide-open spaces from the 1870s onwards further continued this trend of there being larger amounts of cheap food available to the people of the Netherlands. This, then, was an enabling factor: economic expansion, especially in agriculture and trade, permitted the population to grow, as well as being at least partially caused by that growth. However, the 'Malthusian' explanation seems to operate more as a background factor, and less as a direct cause for the rapid decline in mortality, especially from 1870 onwards.

There is an attraction in the directness of taking an approach which embraces medical advances as the great cause of the defeat of disease, and indeed medical historians of earlier generations have tended to ply their trade as one which charts the gradual but increasing success of medicine in the battle against mortality. Smallpox was one of the greatest killers, and especially of children; Peter Razzell in particular has suggested that the role of the introduction of inoculation and even more of vaccination against it was critical in bringing down death rates in England.[14] There

[13] De Meere, *Economische ontwikkeling*, 114.
[14] Razzell, *The conquest*; and Razzell, *Edward Jenner's cowpox vaccine*.

was a spate of laws across Europe making smallpox vaccination compulsory after the epidemic at the beginning of the 1870s, including one in the Netherlands in 1872, which seems to fit perfectly with the decline of infant and general mortality from that point.[15] Further, one can point in the Netherlands to a law of 1865 which limited quackery in medicine by introducing compulsory training for physicians, and to the radical improvements and professionalization of hospitals in the course of the nineteenth century.[16] These medical improvements certainly had an impact, although the effectiveness of vaccination has been heavily disputed; the problem is generally one of timing. The effects of most of the advances in the nineteenth century were probably limited to the upper classes, and only in the present century did medicine progress far enough to alter dramatically the death rates of ordinary families.

Without dismissing these explanations related to the food supply and to medical advances, it remains to assess the virtues of the third category: that of various environmental changes, man-made and otherwise, which improved the condition – and the length – of life in the Netherlands in the last century. They covered a wide range: one of the most important must have been that a number of potentially lethal contagious diseases had declined in their effectiveness against the human race, such as the bubonic plague.[17] There are discernible trends in long-term biology which point to the decline in the virulence of certain diseases in the nineteenth century; unfortunately we know too little about these developments to be categorical. On the other side of the equation, immune systems seem to have become stronger against these diseases, and that is readily understandable in terms of the increase in quality and quantity of the food supply: an adequate and regular diet helped build up the kind of constitution which could shake off attacks from endemic diseases like fevers or even smallpox. The process of industrialization meant that, over time, personal hygiene could improve: such articles as soap and cotton underwear became mass-produced and therefore cheap and available to virtually all people.[18] The public-health reforms engineered by Edwin Chadwick in England from the 1840s onwards came later in the Netherlands, but then so did the large-scale industrialization and urbanization which made the reforms so vital, with the result that the Dutch were able to benefit quite directly from such environmental improvements as sewers and running water.[19]

[15] See Rutten, '*De vreeslijkste aller harpijen*'; and section 2.3 below.
[16] Brugmans, *Paardenkracht*, 427–8; and Verdoorn, *Het gezondheidswezen*.
[17] Noordegraaf and Valk, *De gave Gods*; and Baudet and Van der Meulen, *Kernproblemen*, 133.
[18] Lee, ed., *European demography*, 15.
[19] Petersen, *Planned migration*, 22.

It is wise to assess the causes of declining mortality in terms of a matrix of factors which combines all three types of reasons: medical, agricultural and environmental, with an emphasis on the last category. An authoritative study on the health of the town of Utrecht attributed the fall in the death rate, and especially in infant mortality, to a combination of factors, including the vaccination law of December 1872, the increasing popularity of buttermilk (which reduced the occurrence of salmonellas), the improved quality of the care of the poor and sick as a result of the overhaul of the system of local government and the Poor Law, and a generally improving and modern mentality.[20] There was therefore a multiplicity of factors at work.

But two of the factors in particular command more specific attention in the case of the Netherlands: the condition of the water, and the attitudes of the Dutch to breastfeeding. The key to the problem appears to lie in the very substantial regional differences in the death rates – especially the child mortality – which existed between the various parts of the Netherlands.

Water and mortality

The figures in Table I.5 show where the danger areas were. The high rates before the 1870s were to be found in the west of the country: these are the low-lying, damp or even wet Holocene clay-soil areas.[21] Much of the land in these parts had been reclaimed from sea or river; some of it was poorly drained, and even waterlogged for much of the year. The problem was particularly acute in the worst area, the province of Zeeland, but applied to most of the coastal, western half of the Netherlands which is at or under sea-level (very roughly equivalent to the sea-clay area, shown in Figure I.3). Polders surrounded by dikes are meant to drain naturally, and usually a mud-flat was not encircled with a dike until it had become high enough to drain itself at low water. However, in the course of the centuries the sea-level had risen, and auxiliary pumping became necessary. Before the days of steam pumps this meant that certain areas were characterized by marshy or boggy conditions or even by open water, which was poorly circulated and thus prone to stagnancy, and also affected by salination and thus brackish. These conditions are not good for producing drinking water, but they also form the perfect breeding ground for the larvae of the mosquito which carries and transmits malaria: the *Anopheles maculipennis atroparvus*, or short-winged variety. This insect breeds in salt or brackish water, which makes the Netherlands

[20] Bosschaert, *De stad Utrecht*, 80–1.
[21] Van der Woude, 'Bevolking en gezin', 57.

Table I.5 *Death rates in the Netherlands and its provinces, five-yearly periods, 1816–1975 (per 1,000).*

	1816–20	1821–25	1826–30	1831–35	1836–40	1841–45	1846–50	1851–55	1856–60	1861–65	1866–70	1871–75	1876–80	1881–85	1886–90	1891–95
Groningen	21.4	21.0	32.1	21.0	21.6	22.0	26.3	22.7	25.8	21.8	21.7	23.0	20.4	17.9	17.4	17.2
Friesland	20.3	21.1	33.0	23.1	21.0	21.2	25.6	20.2	25.3	22.7	19.8	20.9	19.3	17.7	17.7	16.7
Drenthe	20.7	19.2	25.2	20.5	22.1	21.7	27.3	20.2	20.2	21.9	22.1	20.6	19.9	19.6	19.7	19.8
Overijssel	25.7	24.0	26.4	24.2	24.1	24.0	26.5	22.4	24.2	23.6	24.1	24.1	22.4	21.5	21.4	20.9
Gelderland	22.9	21.0	22.2	22.7	22.4	22.6	23.9	20.5	22.4	22.5	22.5	22.8	20.4	19.3	19.6	19.7
Utrecht	27.3	26.0	28.7	30.0	27.8	25.9	32.8	26.4	27.6	25.1	29.0	27.8	24.3	23.1	22.0	20.9
N-Holland	31.6	32.0	37.5	34.3	31.9	30.1	36.7	27.2	30.7	25.3	26.8	26.7	24.6	23.1	20.9	18.5
Z-Holland	31.6	29.3	31.7	33.7	29.5	30.0	36.8	30.8	31.0	29.4	30.3	30.9	26.5	24.5	22.3	20.5
Zeeland	37.0	33.7	38.0	34.4	30.9	31.5	34.7	30.9	31.5	28.6	26.2	26.4	22.4	19.3	18.8	18.7
N-Brabant	23.6	21.1	23.4	25.4	22.4	21.7	23.2	21.7	23.4	23.4	22.8	24.3	22.8	22.4	22.1	22.4
Limburg	—	—	—	—	—	22.9	23.7	23.3	22.7	22.4	22.2	22.9	21.7	20.3	19.0	20.8
Netherlands	'27.0	'25.7	'28.0	'25.8	'25.8	25.6	29.7	24.9	26.7	24.8	25.0	25.5	23.0	21.6	20.6	19.7

	1896–1900	1901–5	1906–10	1911–15	1916–20	1921–25	1926–30	1931–35	1936–40	1941–45	1946–50	1951–55	1956–60	1961–65	1966–70	1971–75
Groningen	15.0	14.8	13.0	12.3	13.5	9.9	9.8	8.9	8.9	10.7	8.3	8.0	8.4	8.7	9.2	9.2
Friesland	14.8	14.4	13.1	11.9	13.0	10.5	10.4	9.8	9.9	11.1	9.1	8.6	8.7	8.9	9.4	9.6
Drenthe	16.9	16.4	14.9	13.5	14.5	10.3	10.2	8.8	8.5	10.1	7.5	6.8	7.1	7.2	7.8	8.2
Overijssel	17.9	17.0	14.7	12.7	13.9	10.5	9.9	8.7	8.7	10.3	8.0	7.2	7.4	7.5	7.8	8.0
Gelderland	17.4	16.4	15.0	13.3	14.1	11.3	10.7	9.5	9.5	12.6	8.3	7.8	7.6	7.9	8.3	8.2
Utrecht	18.1	16.7	14.4	12.9	13.6	10.5	9.7	9.2	9.3	12.4	8.4	7.8	8.0	8.2	8.3	8.1
N-Holland	16.4	14.7	12.9	11.7	12.6	9.8	9.5	8.7	8.9	11.8	8.0	7.8	8.1	8.4	9.0	9.1
Z-Holland	17.6	15.7	13.7	11.8	12.7	9.4	9.2	8.4	8.5	11.2	7.5	7.4	7.6	8.0	8.5	8.7
Zeeland	16.8	15.2	13.8	12.7	12.9	10.2	9.7	9.3	9.8	11.7	9.1	9.2	9.0	9.3	9.7	9.6
N-Brabant	20.1	19.6	17.9	16.6	16.5	12.7	11.5	9.8	8.9	10.8	7.8	6.9	6.7	6.8	6.8	6.8
Limburg	18.3	18.6	17.3	16.0	15.0	11.5	10.4	8.9	8.6	10.8	7.5	6.9	6.8	6.8	7.0	7.4
Netherlands	17.3	16.2	14.4	12.9	13.6	10.4	10.0	8.9	9.0	11.4	8.0	7.5	7.6	7.8	8.2	8.3

Source: CBS, reported in Van der Woude, 'Bevolking en gezin', 30.
* Excluding Limburg.

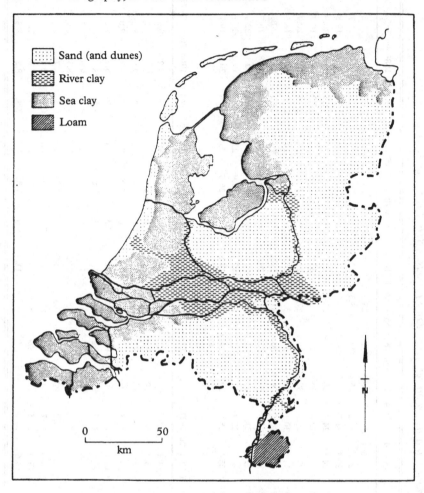

Figure I.3 General soil map of the Netherlands.

coastal area one of the most infested by malarial fevers in northern
Europe, at least until the widespread availability of quinine. The long-
winged variety breeds in fresh water, and is considerably less malarious.[22]
This disease in various forms was virtually endemic in the Netherlands
until the 1870s, and there is a clear link between the areas of land
reclamation, salination, malaria and high mortality in the early part of the
nineteenth century.[23] However, there were other problems afoot: as H.

[22] Swellengrebel and De Buck, *Malaria*, 6, 26–8, 119. See also Brouwer, 'Malaria'.
[23] Hofstee, *Korte demografische geschiedenis*, 66–7 and 69–72; on Zeeland see Wintle, *Zeeland
and the churches*, 42–3.

Brouwer has observed, one of the provinces worst affected by the high mortality was Zuid-Holland, which suffered little from salination problems. There the culprit was again the water, but this time it was the drinking water.[24]

Some Dutch tap-water nowadays comes from collection plants in the dunes, and is of excellent quality; much of the rest, although chemically safe, is so heavily treated because of its origins in some of Europe's most polluted rivers that its taste is quite repellant. For much of the nineteenth century not only was the taste dubious, but the hygienic quality of the drinking water was deplorable. The contemporary nineteenth-century accounts of the local drinking water supplies make sobering reading, and the damning reports are by no means limited to industrial towns: they also cover market towns and villages, and even the open countryside. It should be borne in mind that the really lethal municipalities mentioned above, like Wissekerke and Wolphaartsdijk, were about as rural as it was possible to get in the western part of the Netherlands. Reports speak of fetid open sewers full of decomposing faeces, putrid canals full of rotting fish and industrial effluent, great open dung-pits adjacent to the water, and foul-smelling dank bogs and marshes.[25] In most of the western Netherlands, there was an almost complete lack of sweet, swift-running water; salination and poor circulation rendered much of it stagnant, and (as we have seen) a breeding ground for insects. In his masterly survey of the demographic history of the Netherlands since 1815, Van der Woude concludes that in the west of the country, up to the 1870s, malaria and bad water were principally responsible for the horrendous mortality rates, especially the ones for children.[26]

These appalling public-health circumstances began to improve from the late 1860s onwards. Quinine became widely and affordably available, and one of the main sources of supply was the Dutch East Indies. By 1930 it was supplying 97 per cent of the world market. Pharmacists succeeded in producing quinine in the Netherlands in 1832, but production was not commercially viable until well after the mid-century. Eventually, it was instrumental in bringing down the fatalities caused by malaria.[27] From the 1850s onwards steam pumps began to replace windmills in existing polders in some of the river areas, increasing the circulation and regulating the level of the water in the polders and drainage ditches; in the 1860s this practice became more widespread in the coastal provinces, and grew as the century progressed. These developments had important

---

[24] Brouwer, 'Malaria', 156–7; and Van der Woude, 'Bevolking en gezin', 57.
[25] Caland, *Beschouwingen* (1857); and Broes van Dort, *Bijdrage tot de kennis* (1861).
[26] Van der Woude, 'Bevolking en gezin', 58.
[27] Algera-Van der Schaaf, 'Quinine cultivation'; Headrick, *The tools of empire*, 71–2; Headrick, *The tentacles of progress*, 230–7; and Swellengrebel and De Buck, *Malaria*, 26–8.

consequences for agricultural production, as the water content of the heavy alluvial soils could be properly regulated, but also had considerable effects on the general health of the local population.[28] At the same time, in the last quarter of the nineteenth century, the medical reports began to be heeded, and the supply of drinking water improved, partly because of piped water for urban areas, and partly because of better drainage and some elementary control of pollution.[29] All this, together with medical improvement and enhanced quantity and quality of diet, went some way to improve the atrocious conditions found in the west before the 1870s.

Breastfeeding and mortality

Nonetheless, water does not provide a total explanation: piped water had reached only the larger towns by 1900. In the Zeeland case, it was only the towns of Middelburg and Vlissingen,[30] but the countryside of that infamous province saw its mortality rates drop from as early as the 1860s. It then witnessed a sharp relative fall to rates around the national average within twenty years (Table I.5). Steam pumps must have played a role, but Van der Woude concludes that the other crucial factor was diet.[31] Given the fact that the regional differences in mortality in the main concerned children, and infants in particular, it is relevant to examine the changes in infant diet in the nineteenth century.

The incidence and duration of breastfeeding has formed the subject of several research projects in the Netherlands,[32] since the beginning of this century, and indeed it is clear that the medical profession was aware even in the last century that breastfeeding was to be preferred to bottle-feeding infants, with a view to their chances of survival. There was indeed an inverse relationship between the incidence and duration of breastfeeding and the infant mortality rate, and this was generally true across Europe.[33] The content of the bottle-feed was generally lacking in nutrition, and was often made up with water which was potentially lethal. There was a major campaign launched, amounting to a veritable civilization offensive, dedicated to spreading the word among Dutch peasants and workers.[34] One of

---

[28] Van Zanden, *De economische ontwikkeling*, 236–7. On steam power, see section 5.2 below.
[29] See Vogelzang, *De drinkwatervoorziening*; Jansen and De Meere, 'Het sterftepatroon', 203–10; and Lintsen *et al.*, ed., *Geschiedenis van de techniek*, vol. II, pp. 76–7. For a detailed account of the coming of piped water to Tilburg, see Van der Heijden, *Kleurloos*.
[30] Vogelzang, *De drinkwatervoorziening*, 4.
[31] Van der Woude, 'Bevolking en gezin', 58–9.
[32] Vandenbroecke, *et al.*, 'De zuigelingen- en kindersterfte'; and Van Eekelen, *Naar een rationele zuigelingenvoeding*.
[33] Van Eekelen, *Naar een rationele zuigelingenvoeding*, 218–19; Lee, ed., *European demography*, 17.
[34] Van Eekelen, *Naar een rationele zuigelingenvoeding*, 213 and 220–3; and Van der Woude, 'Bevolking en gezin', 59.

the most celebrated campaigners was active – according to his own version of events – right at the beginning of the century, in 1809, in no less a personage than the King, Louis Napoleon, brother of the French Emperor and installed as monarch of the satellite Kingdom of Holland between 1806 and 1810. During a royal 'progress' through the towns and villages of the south-west of his domain in May 1809, Louis recalled in his memoirs that,

The King [Louis] remarked with pain and surprise, that many of the country-women, instead of bringing up their infants on their first and natural food, gave them cow's milk and pap; and enjoined the ministers of religion, to use all their efforts to remove this abuse. He interrogated many of the Zeeland women respecting this custom; and perceived with astonishment, that it was become a system among a people, whose women are almost without exception excellent mothers and faithful wives. The magistrates avowed the inutility of their endeavours to alter this practice. The women of Zeeland are accustomed to wear a sort of half-veil of very fine linen, which falls over the back part of the head and the temples, but does not descend lower upon the face than the forehead, where it is fixed by a slip of gold, which the married women wear on one side of the forehead, and the unmarried on the other. Without infringing on this custom, the King ordered, that those women who suckled their infants should alone be permitted to wear a complete circle of gold on the forehead; and that three rich ornaments of this kind should be distributed annually to the three mothers, who should have suckled the greatest number of infants.[35]

No doubt the story improved with the telling, and the spectacle of the foreign-born king quizzing the buxom matrons of Zuid-Beveland about their suckling habits raises a smile, but it is clear that interest was shown in the subject at the highest level. And indeed the king had something to be concerned about: figures two years later for Zeeland, in 1811, show the province to have had infant mortality figures of 375 per thousand live births: a truly chilling level.[36]

Later in the century the medical and social elite was still just as keen to encourage breastfeeding amongst a recalcitrant peasantry whose women-folk had to work, often far away in the fields, and who therefore left the feeding of the children and infants to older children, and ancient grand-mothers.[37] Many a pamphlet was issued by local worthies condemning the state of the dry-nursing profession as ignorant and even dangerous, and urging improvements, as well as the extension of breastfeeding itself.[38] In their investigation into the nature of and regional differentiation in infant mortality in Belgium and the Netherlands, Vandenbroeke, Van Poppel and Van der Woude concluded that variation in the incidence

[35] Bonaparte, *Historical documents*, vol. III, pp. 111–12.
[36] Vandenbroecke, *et al.*, 'De zuigelingen- en kindersterfte', 482.
[37] Blok, *et al.*, ed., *Algemene geschiedenis der Nederlanden*, vol. XII, pp. 141–2.
[38] E.g. *De verbetering van den bakerstand* (1851).

and duration of breastfeeding was the most important variable explaining the differing levels of mortality, backed up by the quality of the local water given to the infants when they were weaned.[39] In a subsequent study, Van Poppel examined the correlation between membership of the Roman Catholic Church and high mortality, and concluded that much of it had to do with a reluctance to breastfeed on the part of Roman Catholic women, especially in the south of the country.[40] The peak in infant mortality occurred nationally in 1873, a year which is generally seen as the zenith of the economic boom of the third quarter of the century in the European economy; the relative decline in the demand for labour thereafter, especially in agriculture, ensured that more women remained at home to suckle their young, and the first factory act of 1874 began to exclude children from factories and to keep them and their mothers at home, which may also have led to more breastfeeding.[41]

So much, then, for the negative side of the demographic transition in the Netherlands: the appalling death rates of the earlier part of the nineteenth century reached their peak in the 1870s, and were caused mainly by ecological factors to do with the water supply, together with the inability and reluctance of mothers to breastfeed their babies. Mortality began to decline around 1870, and did so for a complex matrix of reasons, some of them (for example the improved food supply, and to some extent improved medical technology) increasing the resistance of the population to the ravages of disease and labour, and others diminishing the lethal characteristics of the environment, like the water and the atmosphere. But what of the positive components of the demographic matrix: births, fertility and marriage?

1.3   Marriage and fertility

In aggregate terms the birth rate declined, from higher than thirty-eight per thousand population per annum after the Napoleonic Wars, to twenty-one in the 1930s (Table I.2). But what of regional variation within the national aggregate: what can this side of the demographic coin tell us about the changes undergone in Dutch society in the last two centuries?

Table I.1 shows the gender division of the Dutch population in the last 200 years; as is usual, there has been a slight preponderance of women over men. Marginally more male children were born than female ones, but a higher mortality and a higher emigration rate among men resulted

[39] Vandenbroecke, et al., 'De zuigelingen- en kindersterfte', 484–5.
[40] Van Poppel, 'Religion and health', 244–52.
[41] Vandenbroecke, et al., 'De zuigelingen- en kindersterfte', 489–90. See also Van Poppel, *Trouwen*, chapter 2.

in the slight prevalence of women.[42] This prevalence, however, declined to only about eight per thousand by the Second World War.

As for marriage, the Netherlands falls into the European marriage pattern of relatively late wedlock, with some not marrying at all; this is thought to relate to the need to establish a means of support before launching into matrimony. Nationally, nuptuality was relatively stable for the duration of the nineteenth century, with between seven and nine marriages per thousand population taking place per year (see Table I.2), with between 13 and 15 per cent of people remaining unmarried, and with the marriage age around twenty-eight or twenty-nine for men, and twenty-six or twenty-seven for women.[43] The age at marriage fell slightly around the 1860s,[44] and began to drop faster in the twentieth century; the marriage rate began to increase after the Second World War.[45] Peaks in the marriage rate are perceptible in the 1820s, in the 1850s and 1860s, and after 1900, all readily identifiable with end of war or with economic boom.[46] There were some important regional variations, which were broadly coincidental with religious distribution. Thus marriage was at a later age and less frequent in much of Catholic Brabant, Limburg and Gelderland; in the western, urban Noord-Holland, and in northern Protestant Friesland, Groningen and Drenthe, people married earlier and more frequently. Remarriage was also more likely in the west (mixed but predominantly Calvinist) than in the south (Catholic). The explanation lies partly perhaps in the dogmatic content of the faiths concerned, but also in the availability of partners for marriage in the different regions, for there were considerable variations in the male–female ratio across the country, as a result of migration movements.[47] We shall examine the regional characteristics which can be discerned in nuptuality and marriage age[48] more closely when we come to deal with marriage fertility below.

The decline in the birth rate began in the later 1870s (see Table I.2), and slightly postdated the fall in death rate.[49] The drop was as crucial to the demographic transition as was that of the death rate: the fact that the two rates fell together meant that eventually the Dutch population achieved relative stability, but the fact that the birth rate fell more slowly and later than the death rate accounted for the enormous surge in the

---

[42] Van der Woude, 'Bevolking en gezin', 23–4.
[43] Heeren and Van Praag, *Van nu tot nul*, 99.   [44] Van Poppel, *Trouwen*, chapter 5.
[45] Van der Woude, 'Bevolking en gezin', 47; and Heeren and Van Praag, *Van nu tot nul*, 93–115 (essay by F. van Poppel).
[46] Hofstee, 'De demografische ontwikkeling', 45.
[47] Van Poppel, *Trouwen*; for the regional variations in m/f rations, see pp. 218–20 and 271.
[48] Hofstee, 'De demografische ontwikkeling', 46–7.
[49] Knippenberg, 'De demografische ontwikkeling', 59–60.

total population between 1815 and 1950. After the Second World War the birth rates continued to decline, but only fell really rapidly after 1964, which eventually brought them into line with the rest of Europe: before that date, Dutch birth rates had been high, and slow to fall.[50] The questions which beg of the development in birth rates, therefore, are why they started to decline in the nineteenth century, and why they declined more slowly than in most other European countries. The same applies to marital fertility figures, which are a much more sophisticated and nuanced indicator of reproduction behaviour than the crude birth rate. The birth rate is affected by the proportion of married women of child-bearing age in a given population, by the illegitimacy rate, and by the marital fertility rate, that is, the number of live legitimate births for each thousand married women of child-bearing age (usually taken as under fifty years of age).

1.4   Regional differences

Table I.6 shows the average fertility rates for each province in the Nether-lands for quinquennial periods between 1850 and 1914. In the course of that period, the national average moved from 304 births per annum for every thousand women of childbearing age in 1850/54 up to a peak of 310 in 1875/79; thereafter it fell decisively to 228 in 1910/14. The rate continued to fall thereafter, and reached 173.5 in the late 1930s: the steepest decline dates from the 1890s.[51]

But far more interesting are the local figures. In the 1850s, the highest rates were to be found in the south-west of the country, in the provinces of Zuid-Holland, Utrecht and Zeeland. By the time of the 1880s, the high-rated provinces had increased in number: not only were the original three well above average, but they had been joined by the two southern provinces of Noord-Brabant and Limburg. By the time of 1910/14, the original three most fecund provinces of Zuid-Holland, Zeeland and Ut-recht had dropped to average levels, while Limburg and Noord-Brabant had radically increased their fertility and had become clear leaders of the field: meanwhile Drenthe and Gelderland had entered the league as well above average in the fertility ratings. One of the major commentators, John Buissink, expressed these considerable differences in the 1850s in terms of birth control.[52] Provinces with a marital fertility rate of more than

---

[50] Knippenberg, 'De demografische ontwikkeling', 68.
[51] Deprez, 'The Low Countries', 275. Deprez prints a longer series of fertility rates than the ones presented in Table I.6 here; it is from mixed sources, but is convenient for long-term national estimates. The more accurate data in Table I.6, taken from Buissink's work, are more suitable for the provincial analysis.
[52] Buissink, 'Regional differences', 365.

Table I.6 *Marial fertility. Average annual number of legitimate live births per 1,000 married women under fifty years of age in the Dutch provinces and the kingdom by successive five-year periods, 1850-1914.*

	1850-54	1855-59	1860-64	1865-69	1870-74	1875-79	1880-84	1885-89	1890-94	1895-99	1900-04	1905-09	1910-14
(a) Absolute figures													
Groningen	285.7	275.7	272.0	279.2	285.5	294.2	270.3	266.4	263.5	258.8	252.2	236.0	212.9
Friesland	276.4	266.4	267.6	282.5	281.3	278.9	249.9	249.0	241.6	233.3	226.9	209.6	193.5
Drenthe	273.7	274.8	273.8	269.0	275.0	282.7	270.3	277.7	285.5	286.5	286.6	275.0	258.2
Overijssel	285.2	276.5	281.7	284.2	284.5	290.8	281.8	286.6	284.7	285.0	278.0	256.2	229.8
Gelderland	289.5	286.9	293.3	294.3	289.1	301.8	301.7	299.5	292.9	294.7	284.6	270.9	246.9
Utrecht	323.8	306.7	310.5	311.7	310.0	322.7	317.9	321.4	307.8	299.7	269.2	237.6	231.8
N-Holland	301.1	277.7	284.7	284.3	280.1	295.2	289.3	282.0	261.4	243.5	226.4	202.3	181.1
Z-Holland	343.6	314.6	319.7	322.6	324.7	330.1	321.6	314.3	296.1	283.8	273.2	250.0	223.7
Zeeland	339.6	313.0	328.0	332.2	339.0	331.0	304.2	303.4	296.5	288.5	226.4	202.3	212.0
N-Brabant	307.0	287.4	304.6	317.8	324.8	336.1	330.8	330.0	329.6	337.9	346.0	328.5	308.5
Limburg	285.6	289.3	295.9	305.8	314.5	330.7	320.3	319.4	322.9	334.8	341.4	328.8	314.3
Netherlands	304.2	289.8	296.1	300.6	302.7	310.2	299.5	296.9	286.6	280.2	271.1	250.5	228.5
(b) Index: Kingdom = 100.0													
Groningen	93.9	95.1	91.9	92.9	94.3	94.8	90.3	89.7	91.9	92.4	93.0	94.2	93.2
Friesland	90.9	91.9	90.4	94.0	92.9	89.9	83.4	83.9	84.3	83.2	83.7	83.7	84.7
Drenthe	90.0	94.8	92.5	89.5	90.8	91.1	90.3	93.5	99.6	102.3	105.7	109.8	113.0
Overijssel	93.8	95.4	95.2	94.5	94.0	93.8	94.1	96.5	99.3	101.7	102.5	102.3	100.6
Gelderland	95.2	99.0	99.1	97.9	95.5	97.3	100.7	100.9	102.2	105.2	104.9	108.1	108.1
Utrecht	106.5	105.8	105.0	103.7	102.4	104.0	106.1	108.3	107.4	107.0	104.8	101.7	101.4
N-Holland	99.0	95.8	96.2	94.6	92.5	95.2	96.6	95.0	91.2	86.9	83.5	80.8	79.3
Z-Holland	113.0	108.5	108.0	107.3	107.3	106.4	107.4	105.9	103.3	101.3	100.8	99.8	97.9
Zeeland	111.7	108.0	110.8	110.5	112.0	107.7	101.5	102.2	103.4	103.0	99.3	94.8	92.8
N-Brabant	100.9	99.2	102.9	105.7	107.3	108.3	110.4	111.2	115.0	120.6	127.6	131.1	135.0
Limburg	93.9	99.8	99.9	101.7	103.9	106.6	106.9	107.6	112.6	119.5	125.9	131.2	137.5

Source: Buissink, 'Regional differences', 367.

290, like Utrecht, Zuid-Holland and Zeeland, were not employing any restrictions on fertility at all. They were, in another way of measuring these things, close to the highest attainable fertility in Western societies where records have been kept: that achieved by Hutterite women in North America.[53] The figures for Zuid-Holland in the early 1850s mean that every married woman would on average give birth every three years between the age of marriage and the age of fifty: that represents, as can easily be imagined, little attempt at contraception. The middle group, with fertility rates between 270 and 290 in the 1850s, including all the other provinces, would be practising some limited form of birth control, most usually in the form of abstinence from sexual intercourse, or *coitus interruptus*, but only on a small scale by limited numbers, and with sporadic effects. Only when the rates dropped below 270 does Buissink consider that there was evidence of modern birth control in widespread practice: this only happened after 1900 in the Netherlands as a whole, and even at provincial level was still limited just to Friesland in the early 1880s.[54] However, in incidental cases, the voluntary limitation of the chances of conception within marriage is as old as society, and it was certainly far from unknown to the Dutch in the nineteenth century. The Neo-Malthusian League was campaigning for an increase in (rather than a launch of) contraception in the 1880s,[55] and Van Poppel concludes in one of his comprehensive studies of differential fertility that some limited form of contraception was being practised across the nation before the 1870s.[56]

An early analyst of these problems was E. W. Hofstee, who argued that each region in the Netherlands experienced the following phenomenon: a rise in birth and fertility rates, followed by a fall. This was undergone first by the northern and western coastal provinces, and then by the central provinces, and finally by the inland southern provinces, in a gradual movement across the country from the coast to the south-east between about 1850 and about 1950. His explanation was that 'proletarianization' gradually entered the country from the coastal area, diffusing slowly across the country until its effects had reached as far as southern Limburg. Proletarianization resulted in a rapid rise in demographic activity: the marriage age dropped, and birth and fertility rates soared. This was followed, within a generation or two, by a more modern and moderate approach.[57] This 'thesis' dictated the course of debate for a generation,

---

[53] Deprez, 'The Low Countries', 247.
[54] Buissink, 'Regional differences', 365; and Table I.6.
[55] Van Houten, *Maatschappelijke en wettelijke stelling*, 226–45 (essay by J. D. Brouwer, 1883). See also Röling, *'De tragedie'*.
[56] Van Poppel, 'De differentiële vruchtbaarheid ... sociale status', 244.
[57] Hofstee, 'De groei van de Nederlandse bevolking' (1968); Hofstee, 'De demografische

but was perhaps somewhat insular. Hofstee seemed to pay little attention to what was happening across the borders, to the north in Germany and Scandinavia, or to the south in Belgium and France: did these areas also experience a 'diffusion' of modernization?

Hofstee's critics usually built their case on religion. Hofstee's observations of regional differentiation are more or less accepted; however, the explanation, these critics argue, is to be found in the surprising variety of denominational affiliation in the Netherlands, notably the difference between the Catholic south (Brabant and Limburg) and the Calvinist north. The religious make-up of the Netherlands is quite complex, and will enter several of the socio-economic debates dealt with in other chapters of this book; Table I.7 shows the national data at census points from 1815 to 1899. The distinctive features are as follows: there is a monolithic Roman Catholic concentration in the southern two provinces of Noord-Brabant and Limburg (for the location of the provinces, see the map in Figure II.2), while the remaining Catholics – well over half of them – are dispersed throughout the northern provinces, more or less evenly, but with some concentrations in a horizontal band running across the centre of the country, and especially in Noord-Holland. Meanwhile, Dutch Calvinists are spread quite evenly throughout the provinces north of the great rivers, with a concentration in the north-east of the country (Friesland, Groningen and Drenthe). In addition, there is a band or 'bible-belt' of Calvinist orthodoxy running from Groningen through to the Zeeland islands. This distribution, together with the characteristics exhibited by the various denominations, is held by certain critics of Hofstee to be responsible for the variation in demographic behaviour. Almost any set of population statistics will show that Catholics and orthodox Calvinists have larger families, and always have done, than liberal or mainstream Protestants, Jews, the minor (non-orthodox Protestant) sects, or atheists and agnostics.[58] These same denominational affiliations are also axiomatic in determining the age at marriage, which is central to high fertility rates in the Netherlands.[59] The orthodox Calvinist and Roman Catholic denominations have been the most successful in resisting the onslaught of secularization, and it is this concept of resilience in the face of the erosion of institutionalized religion that is fundamental in explaining the regional differences in marriage age and fertility.[60]

---

ontwikkeling' (1974); Hofstee, *De demografische ontwikkeling* (1978); and Hofstee, *Korte demografische geschiedenis* (1981).

[58] E.g. Van Heek, 'Het Nederlandse geboortepatroon', 97.
[59] De Vooys, 'De regionale verscheidenheid', 229–30.
[60] Buissink, 'Regional differences', 372–4; and Van Heek, *Het geboorte-niveau*, 190–2; Wintle, *Zeeland and the churches*, 213.

Table I.7 *Religious affiliation in the Netherlands, 1815–99.*

Census date	Population	Roman Catholics	Old Catholics	Dutch Reformed (NHK)	Orthodox Calvinists (Geref.)	Lutherans	Baptists	Remonstrants	Jews	Others	No religion	Census date
1815	2,177,768	*838,000 38.31%	4,775 0.22%	*1,207,000 55.48%	0	*57,000 2.62%	30,169 1.38%	4,191 0.19%	*36,800 1.69%	1,143 0.05%	—	1815
1829	2,613,487	1,014,682 38.82%	4,426 0.17%	1,554,888 59.12%	0	—	—	—	46,397 1.77%	3,094 0.11%	—	1829
1839	2,860,559	1,095,138 38.28%	5,478 0.19%	1,704,275 59.57%	—	—	—	—	52,245 1.82%	3,423 0.12%	—	1839
1849	3,056,879	1,166,256 38.15%	5,668 0.18%	1,676,682 54.84%	40,308 1.31%	62,537 2.05%	38,575 1.26%	4,909 0.16%	58,626 1.91%	3,318 0.09%	—	1849
1859	3,309,128	1,229,092 37.14%	5,394 0.16%	1,827,894 55.24%	65,728 1.98%	64,539 1.95%	42,162 1.27%	5,326 0.16%	63,790 1.92%	5,203 0.16%	—	1859
1869	3,579,529	1,307,765 36.53%	5,287 0.15%	1,967,110 54.96%	107,113 2.99%	68,067 1.89%	44,227 1.23%	5,486 0.15%	68,003 1.89%	6,471 0.18%	—	1869
1879	4,012,693	1,439,137 35.86%	6,251 0.15%	2,196,599 54.74%	139,903 3.48%	71,815 1.79%	50,705 1.26%	9,678 0.24%	81,693 2.03%	4,659 0.11%	12,253 0.31%	1879
1889	4,511,415	1,596,482 35.38%	7,687 0.17%	2,204,948 48.88%	370,268 8.21%	83,879 1.86%	53,572 1.18%	14,689 0.32%	97,324 2.15%	16,481 0.36%	66,085 1.47%	1889
1899	5,104,137	1,709,161 35.07%	8,754 0.17%	2,480,878 48.61%	418,685 8.18%	92,897 1.81%	57,789 1.13%	20,811 0.41%	104,180 2.04%	14,803 0.29%	115,179 2.25%	1899

Source: Census data, taken from De Kok, *Nederland op de breuklijn,* 292–3.

* Figures are approximate

— Indicates that members of the denomination were included in the nearest column to the left which contains an entry (e.g. in 1839 the census included Orthodox Calvinists, Lutherans, Baptists and Remonstrants in the figures for Dutch Reformed).

1.5   The Dutch demographic experience

To return to the original set of questions about Dutch demographic history in the modern period: why has the Dutch population grown more rapidly than in most other European countries? Why were the death rates so high to begin with, and then what caused the very rapid and deep fall in mortality after the 1860s? What role did birth rates (or marital fertility) play in this? What caused them to decline more slowly than in other countries, and what caused them to increase at certain stages in certain areas? Is the explanation to be found in the very considerable variation between the regions of the Netherlands which is apparent in virtually all these indicators, certainly up to the 1950s?

The reason for the rapid growth is statistically clear: death rates fell. At about the same time, aggregate birth and fertility rates fell too, but less rapidly, so that the population grew. The reason that the Netherlands' population grew faster and longer than elsewhere in Europe is that the birth rates were slower in catching up with the declining death rates.

The issues affecting Dutch mortality were these: the fact that the Netherlands had some of the worst death rates in Europe before the 1870s was due to the lethal effects of the drainage and drinking water systems in the coastal areas of the country, which affected the whole of the local population, both urban and rural, but particularly young children, through fevers and respiratory diseases, and to diet, exacerbated by the low incidence and duration of breastfeeding. Things began to improve after the 1860s when the water-management situation was brought under control, gradually, by means of steam pumps to improve circulation and by piped drinking water. This both eliminated many of the hazards, and improved the diet and therefore the resistance of the population to those hazards. This second development (improved resistance) was much augmented by the onset of more sustained economic growth after 1850, increasing in tempo after the 1880s: better quantity and quality of diet was crucial to the abatement of mortality.[61] The regional differentiation in the death rate is largely explained by the water conditions before about 1880; thereafter the rates in the coastal provinces declined, and reached average European levels by about 1900, except in the south, in Limburg and Noord-Brabant, which took at least until 1930 to reach the average level of around nine deaths per thousand population per annum. Explanations for this later differentiation, after the water situation was on the mend, vary considerably, indicating that there were a number of factors at work. Van der Woude points to the

---

[61] See chapter 2 on diet, and Part II on economic growth.

economic situation in the south at the time, especially in industry: there was population growth but there were stagnating real wage levels, and increasing urbanization with very few new public services to cope with its problems.[62] The Hofstee answer would be in terms of a later penetration of a 'modern mentality' to these inland areas; Van Poppel has added qualified support to this by pointing to the Roman Catholics' reluctance, especially in the southern provinces after 1880, to breastfeed their children and to have anything to do with the advances of medicine and sanitation.[63] The evidence points, therefore, to a combination of environmental, economic and ideological factors, with ideology increasing in relative importance as time went on.

The same is true of birth and fertility rates: there is a complex interaction of widely differing factors explaining the temporal and spatial variations in these rates. The first of these factors was the death rate itself, especially the falling infant mortality. With so many more children surviving, it rapidly became clear that far fewer conceptions were going to be required in order to arrive at the same sized family. This realization, it is true, would be associated with the kind of mentality and view of family planning that we hold nowadays, but the effect of cascading death rates in the last quarter of the nineteenth century cannot have passed unnoticed. Biologically, as well as temperamentally, there was also a connection between falling death rates and falling birth rates: the increasing survival of infants meant that breastfeeding was carried on longer, which prolonged the temporary relative infertility which accompanies lactation. As more mothers nursed their babies longer (partly because they had been taught to, and partly because their offspring stayed alive longer), they were able to have fewer babies.[64]

Rises in fertility rates and falls in the marriage age, as they moved across the country, were also related very closely to changing and improving economic circumstances as the economy shifted from deep malaise in the 1830s and 1840s to agricultural boom after 1850 accompanied by industrialization especially after 1880. With the decline in mortality and the potential for increased numbers of more youthful procreators, the debate about births rapidly translates into one about who was limiting births: birth rates came down, but slowly, and in some areas even more slowly than others. Towards the end of the century, and increasingly as the twentieth century advanced, voluntary restriction of the numbers of births became the norm. This was partly due to the technology of artificial contraception; partly it was due to a willingness on the part of Dutch men

[62] Van der Woude, 'Bevolking en gezin', 59–60.
[63] Van Poppel, 'Religion and health', 251–2.
[64] The close statistical relation between infant mortality and birth rates is explored in Van der Woude, 'Bevolking en gezin', 60–1.

and women to depart from the exhortations of their religious leaders, who advocated large families.[65] The keenest advocates were the clergy of the orthodox Calvinist denominations and the Roman Catholic Church; the members of these two groups were also the ones who listened longest and most obediently to their clerical leaders. This circumstance, of the religiosity of certain Dutch groups and in particular the Catholics, was responsible for the slowness and lateness of the decline in Dutch birth rates, and therefore for the continued growth in the population as a whole, thus making the Netherlands one of the most densely populated countries in the world today.[66]

1.6   Migration

Internal migration

Generally speaking, there was very little inter-provincial movement of people before the mid-century, and not very much before the 1870s. The data are poor before 1850, but there seems to have been minimal movement in or out of the outer provinces such as Groningen, Friesland, Zeeland, Noord-Brabant and Limburg.[67] There was naturally some incidental movement, for instance into Rotterdam, which was beginning to expand in this period, and there was seasonal migration for harvest work and suchlike.[68] The major changes began to occur from the 1870s onwards, which was of course the decade when most of the changes in Dutch demography of the nineteenth century began to occur.[69] From that decade agricultural labourers apparently began to migrate on a larger scale, to the towns, and on a seasonal basis as well, for example as teams of flax workers; farm personnel from the sandy areas inland began to appear for harvest work on the large clay farms near the coast.[70] Figures for inter-provincial migration show clear deficits on the part of the rural provinces from the 1880s onwards, while only Noord- and Zuid-Holland, and the mining province of Limburg, were net beneficiaries. (Utrecht had mixed fortunes, alternatively gaining and losing.[71]) This restless stirring

[65] On family size, see below, section 12.4.
[66] This conclusion is also reached in Van der Woude, 'Bevolking en gezin', 65–7.
[67] Deprez, 'The Low Countries', 245–6; Heeren and Van Praag, Van nu tot nul, 222–4; Hofstee, Korte demografische geschiedenis, 97 and 140; and Kooij, 'Stad en platteland', 98–103, which provides some figures collected by Hofstee for this early period.
[68] De Meere, Economische ontwikkeling, 40–2. On seasonal migration, see below, section 12.5.
[69] Knippenberg and De Pater, De eenwording, 82–6.
[70] Van der Wielen, 'Sociale toestanden', 446–7. They were probably replacing more traditional seasonal migrants from Germany and Belgium.
[71] Ter Heide, Binnenlandse migratie, 466–7.

of the rural districts from the 1870s was the first symptom of the demographic pressures coming from the overall rise in population in that decade. In the 1880s heavy migration from the rural areas, including the sea clays, began to be a structural feature, part of it to the cities, and part abroad, to the USA, Germany and elsewhere. Inter-provincial migration seems only to have reached a significant level, therefore, when demographic pressures were applied in the 1870s to a situation which was previously more or less stable. The pressures came from population increase, and from a simultaneous agricultural crisis which began in the late 1870s and continued into the 1890s.[72] This kind of migration from (and occasionally to) rural areas towards the end of the century was a contributor to the decline or erosion of the village community, not only in the Netherlands, but on a wide front across Europe.[73]

Urbanization

One form of internal migration which demands special attention is the movement to the towns – or, indeed, away from them. For in the first half of the century there was no Dutch urbanization, but rather de-urbanization, or ruralization. The Netherlands was an extremely urbanized country in comparison with its neighbours, and had been for several centuries, but from 1800 to 1850 urban growth was only incidental, directly associated with isolated local economic opportunities. Contemporaries like the agriculture specialist H. J. Koenen were aware of the fact that the countryside rather than the towns had seen better economic fortunes prior to the 1850s,[74] and while the steepest decline of the towns (defined as having more than 5,000 inhabitants) had been in the French period, they continued to stagnate from 1815 to the 1840s, indicating an urban crisis, especially in the west. The eastern and southern towns were by no means so badly affected.[75] In the second half of the nineteenth century, nearly all towns in the country grew at faster rates than did the country as a whole.

There arises a problem of definition. In the sense of not living in a farming community, the figure of 5,000 for a town (used in the preceding paragraph) is quite serviceable. However, the Dutch constitution of 1815 defined things differently, with eighty-seven settlements in the Netherlands specified as towns (*steden*) on the basis of a legal charter rather than

---

[72] De Vries, *Landbouw en bevolking*, chapters 5, 6 and 7; Van der Wielen, 'Sociale toestanden', 450.
[73] Shorter, *The making*, 48–50.   [74] Koenen, *De Nederlandsche boerenstand*, 100.
[75] De Meere, *Economische ontwikkeling*, 34–6; Van der Woude, 'Bevolking en gezin', 27–8; Horlings, *The economic development*, 322–4.

size: these towns maintained their share of the population until the 1870s, and then began to decline in relative terms. In the Municipality Act of 1851 the legal distinction between town and rural settlement was dispensed with, and everywhere became a municipality.[76]

In terms of large towns, rather than non-villages, the Netherlands was the leading urbanized nation of Europe in 1801, with 11.5 per cent of its population living in cities of more than 100,000 inhabitants, and a further 13 per cent living in towns of more than 20,000. In 1851 she was beginning to lose ground to England as the leading urban nation, especially with regard to really large cities (over 100,000), and had fallen well behind on all fronts by 1901; on the other hand the Dutch continued to be considerably more urbanized than their continental neighbours like France and Germany throughout the century.[77] The number of really large towns in the country was small: Rotterdam, The Hague and perhaps Utrecht, with Amsterdam towering above them all. The capital had 221,000 inhabitants in 1795, which actually fell to 211,000 in 1840, but then rose to 325,000 in 1880, and further doubled to 661,700 in 1920. Rotterdam was only half the size for most of the nineteenth century, with 78,100 inhabitants in 1880.[78]

In many ways the most interesting phenomenon in modern urbanization is the growth of the really huge conurbations, and the Dutch have a classic example in the *Randstad* (Ring City), the horseshoe of linked cities dominating the west of the country today.[79] But the capital led the way in the nineteenth century: it was the only city in 1800 within what was to become the United Kingdom of the Netherlands with more than 200,000 people, and the threshold of 100,000 was only reached by Brussels in 1830 (the year in which it became a capital city itself), Rotterdam in 1850, The Hague in 1860, Utrecht in 1890, and Groningen and Haarlem in 1920.[80] Industrial towns like Enschede, Almelo, Tilburg, Eindhoven, Helmond and Maastricht grew predictably rapidly as the century drew on. But many towns saw steady rather than break-neck growth: sleepy provincial administrative centres, market towns and old merchant crossroads saw their population expand steadily, but not at the same rate as the really large cities. Dordrecht, for example, had 17,800 inhabitants in 1795, 20,700 in 1840, and 26,600 in 1880; only thereafter did its growth pick up speed, to nearly 50,000 by 1920.[81] On the other hand, the

---

[76] Van der Woud, *Het lege land*, 64–6.   [77] Kooij, 'Stad en platteland', 95.

[78] Ramaer, 'Middelpunten', 209. See also Taverne and Visser, eds., *Stedebouw*, especially pp. 174–9.

[79] See Schmal, ed., *Patterns*, especially chapter 8, on the *Randstad*.

[80] Van Houtte, *Economische en sociale geschiedenis*, 225.

[81] Ramaer, 'Middelpunten', 209; see also Koopmans, *Dordrecht*, on the staid progress of this provincial town in the nineteenth century.

relentless expansion of such towns in the last quarter of the century, both at home and abroad, was eventually the saviour of Dutch agriculture. With urban demand for food, and especially fresh food, the Dutch swung into market gardening in a major way, and it has remained a feature of their farming sector ever since.[82]

International migration

There was an immigration surplus in the Netherlands in the first half of the nineteenth century (Table I.3), most of which was represented by Germans: Dutch real wage levels were not particularly attractive at that time (see sections 4.2. and 7.4), but there may have been more employment available than in parts of Germany.[83] After 1849 the statistics are more readily available. There were roughly 70,000 foreign-born people resident in the Netherlands at any given moment between 1849 and 1899, after which the total went up rapidly, to 169,000 by 1920. The 1849 figure was equivalent to about 2 per cent of the population, declining slightly to 1.5 per cent in 1899. More than half of these foreigners were German (about 40,000), and about a quarter were Belgians.[84]

Emigration from the Netherlands to overseas destinations has attracted a good deal of scholarly attention, partly because of the quality of the data available, but in fact it was a modest affair in the nineteenth century.[85] Only 380,000 Dutch men and women emigrated from the Netherlands between 1820 and 1920.[86] This put the Dutch on a par with Denmark, Switzerland and Sweden, rather than with major emigrating nations like Germany, Scotland, Norway, and especially Ireland.[87] Only the crisis-ridden famine year of 1847/48 was really significant, when 1.7 per cent of the population actually left the country, fleeing from the potato blight and from political turmoil,[88] but otherwise the Dutch outflow was modest. Migration overseas began to take on significant proportions in the 1840s, and in most years thereafter between 1,000 and 5,000 souls sailed from

[82] Bouman, 'De tuinbouw', 390–1; Van der Wielen, 'Sociale toestanden', 450; on the move to horticulture towards the end of the century, see below, section 6.2.

[83] De Meere, *Economische ontwikkeling*, 37–40.

[84] Van Holthoon, ed., *De Nederlandse samenleving*, 73. On immigration to the Netherlands, see also the special issue, *Tijdschrift voor Geschiedenis* (1987). On social aspects of immigration, see below, section 12.5.

[85] Most of the major texts are by Robert Swierenga, e.g. Swierenga, ed., *The Dutch in America*, and are cited in the notes below. See also Lucassen, *Dutch long distance migration*. This section also draws on Wintle, 'Push-factors'; and Wintle, 'Positive and negative motivation'.

[86] Swierenga, ed., *The Dutch in America*, 16. This estimate refers to all emigrants, not just those to the USA, but probably seriously underestimates the landward migration, especially to Germany.

[87] Swierenga and Stout, 'Socio-economic patterns'.   [88] Stokvis, *De Nederlandse trek*, 5.

Dutch ports. The average annual rate of overseas emigration in the century after 1820 was 72 emigrants per 100,000 population.[89] The periodicity is displayed in Figure I.4, which graphs the annual fluctuations in the numbers of overseas emigrants from 1840 to 1920: it shows that the four main exodus periods were the decade following the potato blights of the later 1840s, the years between 1865 and 1873, the 1880s and early 1890s, and the decade between 1903 and 1913.[90] At the same time the numbers of Dutch men and women in the surrounding countries of Europe increased as well, mainly in Belgium and Germany: in 1849 there were 58,700 living across the border, increasing to 100,400 in 1889, and 142,800 in 1920. This represented about 2 per cent of the population over the whole period.[91] In addition there were substantial numbers of soldiers recruited to the armed forces in the Dutch East Indies; some 35,000–40,000 men died there in the course of the nineteenth century, though many of them had not been born in the Netherlands.[92]

As for destinations overseas, there was a catastrophic craze for Surinam in the mid-1840s, a flirtation with Argentina in the late 1850s and again in the 1880s, a mini-exodus to South Africa in the 1880s and 1890s, and some interest in Canada and a considerable outflow to Germany in the early years of the twentieth century. Large numbers also went to the Dutch colonies (though many returned as well). However, the majority of permanent emigrants were bound for the United States of America.[93]

Concerning the push factors which led the emigrants to take the plunge, Robert Swierenga's studies have made clear that most Dutch emigration was from rural areas, and that most of it was from the sea-clay grain-farming areas, like Zeeland and Groningen, where agricultural modernization was eroding the position of the small farmer and farm labourer. About a third of emigrants came from the sandy soils, and only 14 per cent from the dairy areas. Most emigrants were of farmer or farm-labourer status, and what they were after was land. Religion was also important as a push factor: many studies have pointed to the role played especially by the *Afscheiding*, the orthodox Calvinist Secession of 1834, in stimulating the nineteenth-century Calvinist waves of emigration, although we should always bear in mind that in fact 'Catholic emigrants far outnumbered the much more publicized Seceder emigration'.[94] There is also some evidence that not religious persecution by the state but

[89] Swierenga, '"Exodus Netherlands"', 518–20.
[90] See Figure I.4; and Swierenga, ed., *The Dutch in America*, 27–30.
[91] Stokvis, 'Nederland', 72.   [92] Lucassen, *Dutch long distance migration*, 25–6.
[93] Brugmans, *Paardenkracht*, 200; Petersen, *Planned migration*, 55; Van Winter, 'De Nederlanders' 87. See also Stokvis, 'Nederland'.
[94] Swierenga, ed., *The Dutch in America*, 38.

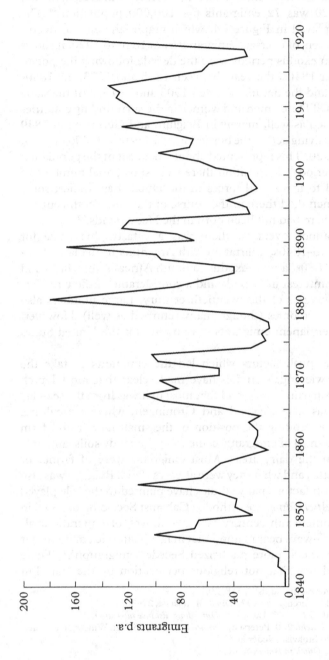

Figure I.4 Index of annual numbers of emigrants from the Netherlands to North America, 1840–1920.

Source: Swierenga, "Exodus Netherlands, Promised Land America", 524.

religious friction between Catholics and Protestants may have operated as a push factor out of the Netherlands.[95] We know further that there were forms of 'community emigration', that most emigrants were part of small but growing young families, and that the target areas in the United States were very specific indeed, concentrated mainly to the east of Lake Michigan.[96]

A final point needs to be made about the motivation for emigration, and it has to do with the periodicity of departure, especially overseas. Emigration is often the result of hardship and persecution or strife. But it can also occur when times are good, or when there is some form of socio-economic renaissance, and it is often effected by those who are not economically underprivileged and are not necessarily part of an ideological or political minority.[97] Motivation for emigration was (and remains) a mixture of positive and negative factors. Figure I.4 shows four main exodus periods from the Netherlands to the United States. It seems clear that economic deprivation had much to do with the first and third waves, in the 1840s and the 1880s, for these were decades of agricultural crisis. However, Hille de Vries has made the point that the heavy emigration from the Dutch agricultural sector in the period 1880–1914 was caused not so much by the deprivation resulting from agricultural crisis of the 1880s and 1890s itself as by the agricultural restructuring which the crisis engendered.[98] And the second and fourth waves of emigration – the late 1860s, and the decade before the First World War – were times of great success in agriculture and for the economy in general, and this too could be a reason for emigration. Having decided to go, the aspirant emigrant often waited for a favourable moment to sell out at the top of the market. Emigrants were land-hungry, but few were destitute. Moreover, the pull factors reinforced the role of these positive push factors leading to emigration: there were land booms in the United States from 1847 to 1857, and from 1865 to 1873, which clearly affected the timing decisions of those emigrants who were in a position to take advantage of the circumstances. The politician and publicist Baron B. Sloet tot Oldhuis (1808–84) recognized in 1866 that emigration was by then no longer driven by religion, but by farmers' frustration at not being able to profit fully from the generally favourable economic climate, because of bureaucratic, fiscal, legal and class restrictions in the old country.[99]

---

[95] Wintle, 'Push-factors', 530–2.
[96] Swierenga, '"Exodus Netherlands"', 523–7.   [97] Wintle, 'Push-factors'.
[98] De Vries, 'The labour market', 78–9 and 96–7; see also De Vries, *Landbouw en bevolking*; and Galema, *Frisians to America*.
[99] 'Over de oorzaken'.

Migration evaluated

In summary on migration, activity was modest until the 1870s, with the exception of a boom in emigration to the United States generated by the harvest failures of the late 1840s. The population pressure in agriculture after that decade seems to have been the driving force, with many thou-sands moving from the sand to the clay, from the rural areas to the towns, and from the clay to the United States; many of those who left for Germany came from the poorer soil areas in the east of the country. Similar numbers also left towards the end of the century for German and Belgian industry, and immigration was probably at a low level compared to earlier and later periods. Overall, these movements were modest. With the exception of the disastrous year of 1847/48, domestic and interna-tional migration was marginal to the economy compared to many other West European countries. It provided a safety valve for economic stress (for example in the sea-clay farming areas) and religious dissent (in the 1840s, and possibly in the 1880s); meanwhile, incoming foreign labour and internal migration, whether temporary or permanent, certainly ad-ded a flexibility in the labour supply which was valuable. But in the end, the modest scale of migration was an indication that life in the Nether-lands, while often no bed of roses, was no worse than in much of the surrounding environment: in short, the Dutch were very much a part of the North-West European mainstream.

1.7   Conclusion

The Dutch demographic performance is certainly worthy of study, even if not actually 'bizarre'. A number of issues have been raised in this chapter which point forward to the future sections on the economy and the social composition of the Netherlands in the long nineteenth century. In terms of timing, the 1870s was the critical decade of change for most of these demographic matters, and the pace of change accelerated from that point well into the twentieth century. The national population grew in the first half of the century, but the towns generally stagnated, and, compared to later exertions, demographic activity on all fronts was modest. After the mid-century, economic changes, especially in agriculture but also in manufacturing, were stimulating demographic change: in some areas there were augmented economic opportunities of which people took demographic advantage, while in others (like the sea-clay farming areas) structural problems in the economy increasingly led people to vote with their feet or with their demographic behaviour. Simultaneously, of course, population changes were helping to drive the economic transition. Finally, we have already noticed the critical importance of religion in this small country, and more particularly of diversity in religion. We have also remarked upon the apparent success of the moralizing civilization offensives towards the end of the century in favour of large families. The question begs as to why the Dutch were apparently so affected by religion, and how that religiosity was transformed into demographic behaviour in such a pronounced way. These lines of enquiry will lead us to examine the economic development of the country in Part II, and the evolution of Dutch vertical pluralism, or *verzuiling*, in Part III. Meanwhile, we need first to investigate the physical condition of the people of the Netherlands, in their health, their environment and their diet.

2 The condition of the people: public health, diet and nutrition

2.1 The public health environment

In chapter 1 the condition of the people of the Netherlands came under examination in terms of that population's demographic behaviour; now the focus will narrow to a rather closer range: the questions asked will concern the immediate environment of the Dutch people in the long nineteenth century, and the ways in which their daily lives were affected by these health-related matters. What was life like a hundred years ago, and what were its preoccupations? Were people terrified of death and disease, and which diseases were they most likely to contract? What was their attitude to food? What did they eat? What did they drink? What was the cultural backdrop to food? When did these things change, and why? As well as seeking established patterns, we shall also be looking for changes, and, in that some of the changes were steps in a direction leading to our own society of today, we shall be concerned with the 'modernization' of Dutch society. We shall also be seeking to amplify some of the demographic analyses offered: how did the population come to live longer, causing the numbers of people to rise, more labour to be available, and more demand to be generated?

The health-related environment at the beginning of the nineteenth century is difficult to gauge exactly, because of the lack of benchmarks, but there can be little doubt that conditions were atrocious by the standards of today. Fevers were more or less endemic, especially in the coastal provinces and river areas, and the water for drinking and for washing food utensils was potentially lethal. Food was often in short supply, and what there was might be less than nutritious or even half-rotten. There were regular epidemics of influenza, measles and smallpox, and there was widespread chronic illness of both the digestive and respiratory systems.[1]

Part of the problem was of course the waterlogged countryside itself: 'autumn sicknesses' were also known as 'reclamation illnesses', amounting to a fiercely contagious cocktail of fevers and agues which were quite

[1] De Meere, *Economische ontwikkeling*, 80–92.

capable of carrying off more than half of the local population, as they indeed did in the village of Bleiswijk (371 out of 700) in 1779–81. When these outbreaks occurred, the communities were simply isolated and the disease left to run its course, often resulting in a very high death toll: 969 died in Hillegersberg in the same three years.[2]

Pollution was more or less unrestricted for most of the nineteenth century. Even in provincial towns the industrial effluents from such processes as bleaching or dye extraction were simply dumped into the canals. Quite apart from the effect on the water supply, there were complaints in the town of Goes that the gas (hydrogen sulphide) given off by this kind of liquid waste was eating away the good citizens' brass doorknobs![3]

There are any number of incidental reports of this sort which make up an impression of a thoroughly lamentable physical environment for public health at the beginning of the nineteenth century. The problem is to gauge just how deficient it was, and whether it was getting worse or better. The mortality rates examined in chapter 1 probably provide the clearest indicator of the effect of the environment on public health: rates of up to fifty per thousand per annum were no less than frightening. But death was only the final blow: a great deal of deprivation could be undergone before life finally ebbed away. Another indicator which can show us the relative development over time of the health of the people is the average height of the population, which is directly related to its physical well-being.

The height of the population is adequately represented in the figures for the heights of military conscripts, for which data have been, with some lacunae, meticulously preserved. They are presented in the form of the percentages of those called for medical examination who were then rejected for the purposes of military service because they were too short: the critical height was 157 cm. from 1817 to 1862, and thereafter 155 cm. The figures are available for the whole of the Netherlands from 1842, and for certain regions from 1821 onwards.[4] From the earliest extant records in the 1820s up to the end of the 1850s, the percentage of Dutch males aged nineteen years who were rejected actually increased. That is to say, more and more of the population were considered physically unfit even for cannon-fodder, until after the mid-century. From 1857 onwards the percentage of rejects declined gradually, until the end of the century when

---

[2] Van Lieburg and Snelders, 'De bevordering', 60, 115–17.

[3] Broes van Dort, Bijdrage tot de kennis, 62–70. On pollution, see also Van Zon, Een zeer onfrisse geschiedenis.

[4] The methodological work on these statistics is quite thorough, and is summarized at De Meere, Economische ontwikkeling, 48–9. See also Brinkman, 'The representativeness'. See also below, section 7.4, where military records are used as an indication of the standard of living.

the system changed. De Meere concludes that the main reason for the improvement was an increasing supply of cheap food, which fundamentally affected the physical health and well-being of the population. Only after the 1870s did the percentage of rejected conscripts drop back to the levels of the 1820s; expressed in another way, it could be said that between about 1830 and 1870 people's health and diet were relatively deficient.[5]

After 1870 matters really do seem to have improved: two local studies of public health in the provincial towns of Utrecht and Groningen point to better public-health facilities like clean water, hospitals, multi-purpose clinics, better and more food, vaccinations, improved care of the poor, and the elimination of certain salmonellas by the increasing popularity of buttermilk.[6] That is not to say that by the time of World War I all was well with public health: the municipal water supply was still poisoning droves of people in the German town of Hamburg in the 1890s,[7] and there is no reason to think the Dutch were much better off. The public-health environment is still today, a century later, regularly marred by catastrophes. But at some time after the mid-century in the Netherlands there began to be an improvement in public health, and by the 1870s some elements of the environment at least were beginning to achieve an acceptable level, which is not to deny that there was still a very long way to go. These trends are borne out by the figures detailing the physique of conscripts, and by the death rates, which also began to take on less horrendous proportions from the 1870s.

2.2   Medical services

The regulation and professionalization of the medical professions played their part in this improvement. Hospitals are a case in point. In the early nineteenth century a Dutch hospital was not a place where one would go in order to be made well: rather it was a place to die. 'Hospitals' were institutions for caring for those who could no longer care for themselves, and whose relatives could no longer care for them extramurally. They were perhaps akin to our wards for the terminally ill, or geriatric wards. In the case of public hospitals it was the concern of cost-conscious officials to keep sick people out of these institutions, at home, for as long as possible, and to delay admittance to the very last moment. Change set in during the course of the century, however, and by about 1900 hospitals were at least

---

[5] De Meere, *Economische ontwikkeling*, 100–9.
[6] Kooij, 'Gezondheidszorg', especially pp. 147–51; see also Kooij, *Groningen*, chapter 5. For Utrecht, see Bosschaert, *De stad Utrecht*, 80–1.
[7] See Evans, *Death in Hamburg*.

beginning to look like the investigative and curative institutions we now know.[8]

Equally importantly, nurses and doctors underwent a professionalization process, starting with the formation of exclusive medical clubs at the end of the eighteenth century, like the Amsterdam Society for the Advancement of Natural Science, Medicine and Surgery, of 1790, designed to elevate the profession of physician from that of glorified barber to respected academic. Another example was Rotterdam's Batavian Society of 1769, also concerned with the professionalization of science.[9] The qualifications for nurses and doctors were formalized gradually,[10] and a new breed of practitioners of 'social medicine', the public health reformers or 'hygienists', rose up and grappled with the problems of the industrializing urban society of the Netherlands.[11] Perhaps the best example was Samuel Senior Coronel, who was successively municipal medical officer in Middelburg (1853) and Amsterdam (1860), and was thereafter active in Leeuwarden (1867). He was a prolific publicist, and produced a number of seminal studies, rich in medical and empirical social detail, of the public health environment of his time. He and his like-minded colleagues believed passionately that the physical environment was directly responsible for the pathetic condition of many of the working people of the country, and that it was impeding economic growth. He was an indefatigable campaigner for good housing, clean drinking water, refuse collection, nutritional improvements and a factory inspectorate.[12] Many a town – Rotterdam for instance – underwent zoning and other forms of town planning in the nineteenth century, so that slaughterhouses, rubbish dumps and mass cemeteries could be sited away from residential and business areas (or at least the more respectable ones).[13] These efforts had begun to make their mark by the 1870s, and certainly by the end of the century this professionalization and extension of the influence of the academic medical profession was having its effect.

Early in the century there had been little regulation of medicine: the 1818 Act governing the profession allowed so many variations and permutations that there was little cohesion to the system. The use of drugs and medicines was also unregulated and very variable: abuse of laudanum

---

[8] For the hospitals in Groningen see Kooij, 'Gezondheidszorg', especially p. 105; for case studies of particular hospitals see Van Lieburg, *Het Coolsingelziekenhuis*; and Van Lieburg, *Bronovo*.

[9] See Van Berkel, *et al.*, *Spiegelbeeld*, especially pp. 12–26; and Van Lieburg and Snelders, 'De bevordering'.

[10] For example, a law in 1865 against quackery. Brugmans, *Paardenkracht*, 427–8; and Kooij, 'Gezondheidszorg', 141.

[11] See Houwaart, *De hygiënisten*.

[12] See Bergink, *Samuel Senior Coronel*; and De Bruin, 'Dr. Coronel'.

[13] De Mare and Vos, eds., *Urban rituals*, 144–60.

and other opiates was common, often stimulated by over-use as a pre-scribed medicine in childhood. The trade in opiates was a free one, without restrictions; indeed it brought the Dutch government a hand-some sum in the opium poppy plantation concessions on Java, amounting to ƒ7.25m. in 1900.[14]

In 1851 there were 2,409 physicians practising in the country, which made for a ratio of one to every 1,228 inhabitants, comparing very favourably indeed with figures of about 1:2,400 in the 1980s. Indeed, the Dutch figures compared very favourably with most other places in Europe, where the ratio was usually higher than 1:2,000. There was discussion at the time of what was seen as the overprovision of medical men in the Netherlands, especially in the coastal provinces of Noord- and Zuid-Holland, Zeeland, and (to a lesser extent) Friesland, Groningen and Utrecht. In only one province, Limburg, did the ratio get above 1:2,000 in 1866. The reason for the relative concentration in the coastal areas was thought to be demand-led: richer folk lived there, and because of the malaria and other water-related diseases they tended to require more medical treatment.

However, many of the 2,409 physicians in 1851 were not academically trained, and were known as 'surgeons' (*heelmeesters*), having followed an 'inferior' course in the clinical schools. The liberal Dutch governments of the third quarter of the nineteenth century tackled this problem head-on, and the 1865 Act regulating the training of physicians was specifically designed to reduce the numbers of less qualified practitioners. The number of physicians of all descriptions rose sharply until the 1860s, and then declined until the mid-1880s, owing to the phasing out of the trade of 'surgeon'. After 1867, when the last clinical school closed in Amster-dam, no more surgeons were trained. In 1867 there were still 1,308 of them practising in the country; by 1878 the figure had dropped to 894. Academically trained doctors, meanwhile, held their own and indeed increased their numbers slightly, from 1,054 to 1,062 in the same eleven years.[15] This process of professionalization undoubtedly forced many traditional and useful healing skills out of circulation; by the same token, much of the work of trained doctors was probably dubious by today's medical standards. Nonetheless, in a country where, with the exception of Limburg, the provision of medical services was unusually dense, the quality of the service in terms of the systematic and academic training of its providers was refined and improved from the 1860s onwards.[16]

[14] Büch, 'Proeve', 68–72. On the thriving Dutch opium trade, based on Indonesia and Turkey, see Schmidt, 'Three decades'; and Schmidt, *From Anatolia to Indonesia*, 90ff.
[15] Verdoorn, *Het gezondheidswezen*, 116–26.
[16] See also *Geneeskundig Jaarboekje voor Nederland* (1865), 181–2; and De Bosch Kemper, 'Statistiek', 16–17.

2.3 Cause of death

The Netherlands generally has quite good demographic data for the nineteenth century, but it is not particularly favoured in the department of cause-of-death statistics. Good figures for the nation are available from the 1870s onwards; before that the data are incidental, although there is good long series for Amsterdam from 1774 onwards.[17] So we can be quite categorical about the end of the nineteenth century and the twentieth; before that the statistical evidence is only selective. Even then there are difficulties. As much as in any branch of codified knowledge and communication, medical semantics have undergone enormous changes from the moment they began; the objective definitions of a 'cold', a 'fever', 'flu' or an 'ague', or even of specified conditions such as malaria, typhus, malnutrition or poor eyesight, have changed so much over the last 200 years that we must be very careful indeed about comparing, for example, numbers of victims of 'intermittent fevers' in 1800 and 1900.[18] Methodological problems abound, and our conclusions must of necessity be broad and subject to modification as research progresses.

These difficulties, together with the relative youth of the social history of medicine as a sub-discipline, have meant that until recently little was said about such matters, and even that was generalized. J. A. van Houtte, the eminent Leuven historian, noted in his standard work on the economic and social history of the Low Countries that while epidemics of contagious diseases like cholera declined (the last major outbreak was in 1866), as did tuberculosis of the lungs, cancer was on the increase as a cause of death, as would be expected with the rising percentage of older people in the population.[19] It was recognized that some of the diseases referred to in the official reports were very complicated, such as the so-called 'swamp fever' (*moeraskoorts*), which was probably a cycle of diseases in certain conditions, starting with influenza and malaria in the spring, digestive organ disorders (especially in infants) in mid-summer, and respiratory diseases at the end of the season.[20] Hofstee was interested in the regional differences in the Dutch mortality rates, and investigated those cause-of-death figures which were available in the course of his enquiries. His data for the third quarter of the nineteenth century on provincial figures for certain diseases, like fevers, dysentery, disorders of the respiratory and digestive systems, and underdevelopment, were crucial in highlighting the enormous differences manifest at that time

[17] See Jansen and De Meere, 'Het sterftepatroon', 181–2 and *passim*; and Hofstee, *De demografische ontwikkeling,* 116–17.
[18] Swellengrebel and De Buck, *Malaria*, 9–15, on the changing meaning of 'malaria'.
[19] Van Houtte, *Economische en sociale geschiedenis*, 221. Epidemics attract comment in nearly all the standard works.
[20] Petersen, 'The demographic transition', 340.

between the various regions of the Netherlands. Hofstee dealt thoroughly with the local physical conditions which could account for these dispari-ties, such as salinity and poor drinking water, even though his own preference was for an explanation which emphasized local mentality traits being responsible for these demographic characteristics.[21] The economic historian J. A. de Jonge saw the decline in the death rate in the Nether-lands after 1870 mainly as a question of the decreasingly deadly effects of cholera, typhus and in particular tuberculosis, a development he at-tributed mainly to the increase in the amount and quality of food con-sumed by the Dutch.[22] A study of nineteenth-century Dordrecht found that cholera epidemics peaked at times of high food prices.[23] Some very specific studies of certain diseases in the modern period have been made, notably of smallpox and malaria, to which we shall refer in more detail below, in looking at the effects of epidemic disease on Dutch society. But because of the complex and methodologically difficult nature of the data, these issues to do with illness and cause of death have best been dealt with at local level. Two exemplary studies exist, one of the town of Groningen in the period of early statistical documentation, from 1870 to 1914, and one valuable though hardly typical series on Amsterdam, running from 1774 to 1930.[24] These studies address the questions outlined above, deal in considerable detail with the local situation, and, satisfyingly, come to quite similar general conclusions which we can extend as a hypothesis to the nation at large.

In both these cases it is clear that, although in certain peak years there were highly dramatic epidemics of contagious diseases like measles and smallpox, the steady killers – year in, year out – were the relatively unglamourous disorders of the digestive and respiratory systems. In Amsterdam in the extended period from 1774 to 1883, it is calculated that diseases of the digestive organs, including certain fevers, carried off no less than 45 per cent of the people who died, and that disorders of the respiratory systems were responsible for another 25 per cent. In the later period, from 1883 to 1930, the percentage of deaths caused by diseases of the digestive organs was still 29 per cent, and the figure for respiratory disorders had hardly dropped at all, at 23.5 per cent.[25] In Groningen, too,

---

[21] Hofstee, De demografische ontwikkeling, 117–50 and 208–9. Hofstee's main source on cause-of-death figures was the study dating from 1882 by Evers, Bijdrage.

[22] De Jonge, De industrialisatie, 260–1. His data on cause of death run from 1869–73 to 1909–13.

[23] Koopmans, Dordrecht, chapter 2, especially pp. 57–9.

[24] Respectively, Kooij, 'Gezondheidszorg' (a revised version also appeared as chapter 5 of Kooij, Groningen); and Jansen and De Meere, 'Het sterftepatroon' (these data were also used as the basis for the chapter on nutrition and mortality in De Meere, Economische ontwikkeling, 80–92).

[25] Jansen and De Meere, 'Het sterftepatroon', 188–9.

the steady killers from the 1870s to the First World War were diseases of the respiratory and digestive organs. In the eight years up to 1914 in Groningen, 6 per cent of deaths were from contagious epidemic sicknesses, which had declined from about twice that level around 1870. Tuberculosis carried off some 12 per cent, as did cancer, while heart disease and disorders of the nervous system and senses accounted for another 7 per cent each. The respiratory system claimed 14 per cent, the digestive organs 11 per cent, and the urinary and genital organs 5 per cent. Six per cent were stillborn, leaving 21 per cent of deaths caused by other factors. The main killers, then, were tuberculosis, cancer, and diseases of the respiratory and digestive organs; these last two were in considerable decline by 1914, when the up-and-coming causes of death were cancer and heart disease.[26] As these complaints of old age increased, the rate of infant mortality declined at the same time. Much later, in the 1960s, in the Netherlands in common with most other Western societies, by far the most important cause of death was heart and blood-vessel disease, followed by cancers.[27] We have here in fact a typical example of social modernization: this aspect of the human life-span can be documented as it acquired successively more of the attributes of the modern society that we know today.

The Amsterdam cause-of-death data provide more of these details. The decisive decline in mortality in the last decades of the nineteenth century, which played the crucial role in the rise of the population as a whole, was caused principally by a decline in the effect of diseases of the digestive system, including malarial fevers; Jansen and De Meere calculated that the reduction in the effect of those illnesses was responsible for no less than 62 per cent of the reduction in the death rate in Amsterdam between about 1850 and 1900. The decline in disorders of the respiratory system was responsible for 23.7 per cent of the drop in mortality, while the contagious diseases which combined skin conditions and fevers accounted for only 3.2 per cent of the decline, with the other 11 per cent being attributed to the decline in the effectiveness of other causes of death. The effects of the decline of tuberculosis were not dramatic in Amsterdam, as they have been shown to have been in England in a similar period.[28]

The question begs, of course, as to the reasons for these changes in the patterns of sickness and cause of death. Some of them are obvious, or have been uncovered in the general demographic exposition of mortality in chapter 1: the food supply, the water supply and the water environment. The food supply was probably the principal reason for the increase

[26] Kooij, 'Gezondheidszorg', 147–8.   [27] Heeren and Van Praag, *Van nu tot nul,* 161–4.
[28] Jansen and De Meere, 'Het sterftepatroon', 189–93 and 211–17.

in the population at large, and in particular it is likely that improvements in the amount and quality of infants' food, for instance by the use of boiled cow's milk, helped to reduce the terrible levels of infant mortality prevalent around the mid-century.[29] De Meere and Jansen have argued strongly that the introduction and widespread take-up of the potato as the staple of Dutch diet was crucial to the reduction in disorders of the digestive and respiratory systems, which as we have seen were in turn the main reasons for the decline in mortality as a whole.[30] The water supply was also significant for changes in the cause of death: water-borne typhus was much reduced in Groningen after the 1860s, as a result of an improving water supply.[31] We saw in chapter 1 how the drinking water situation and the drainage conditions of the land in the west of the country critically affected the death rates in the nineteenth century.

There is some evidence that inoculation or vaccination against small-pox had an effect in Amsterdam in the early years of the nineteenth century before 1814,[32] and we shall examine the effects of epidemics and the fight against them on the death rates and cause of death below. The weather was often a crucial factor, in combination with others: it affected the insect population, and the levels of food production. In the death peaks of 1808, 1826–27 and 1845–48, the weather was invariably a contributing factor, not being cold enough in winter to kill the mosquito larvae, turning sultry in the summer months to increase the problems with the water supply, and exacerbating farmers' difficulties.[33] A hot dry August could play havoc with public health in a crowded environment like Amsterdam, and often did.[34] But it is hard, overall, to avoid the conclusion that the dominant factors in changing the health of the nation, and therefore the pattern of causes of death and of the level of mortality in general, were epidemics and the food supply.

Epidemics

The two factors were of course themselves related: as the food supply and standard of nutrition increased, vulnerability to epidemics decreased. A very great many epidemics occurred in the Netherlands in the nineteenth century, and had dire effects on mortality until the 1870s at least. The

---

[29] Lintsen, *et al.*, eds., *Geschiedenis van de techniek*, vol. I, pp. 274–7.
[30] De Meere, *Economische ontwikkeling*, 111; and Jansen and De Meere, 'Het sterftepatroon', 210.
[31] Kooij, 'Gezondheidszorg', 148.
[32] Jansen and De Meere, 'Het sterftepatroon', 185; and De Meere, *Economische ontwikkeling*, 112.
[33] De Meere, *Economische ontwikkeling*, 80–91.
[34] Jansen and De Meere, 'Het sterftepatroon', 197.

most feared diseases were cholera, smallpox, measles, scarlet fever and diphtheria; malaria also operated epidemically as well as endemically, with extreme effect on the mortality figures in certain regions. The peak years in the mortality rate before 1900 were invariably related to epidemics.[35]

Cholera was by far the most feared of the contagious diseases, although in objective demographic terms it did not actually carry off very many victims. There were three really serious outbreaks in the nineteenth century: in 1832–33, in 1848–49 and in 1866, which carried off 10,106, 22,078 and 18,074 victims respectively. Perhaps the same number again caught the disease but did not eventually die of it. These figures amounted to about 2.3 per thousand population in 1832–33 (total mortality was about 25 per thousand), and about 6.24 per thousand in 1866.[36] There were other lesser outbreaks some of which were dangerous, for instance in 1855, especially in Amsterdam.[37] Nonetheless, in demographic terms cholera was not as serious as it was psychologically terrifying, and in so far as it was a killer, it was killer of the poor and overcrowded.[38]

Measles and scarlet fever were dangerous diseases, with regular death peaks which carried off large numbers, especially of children: 1794, 1797, 1817, 1833 and 1847 were all measles years in Amsterdam at least, with a significant effect on the mortality figures. Scarlet fever struck damagingly from time to time: in Rotterdam in 1778–99 and in Amsterdam in 1834, for example.[39] Malaria was endemic, in the coastal area with its salination problems in the ground water, as we saw in chapter 1, but on many occasions the outbursts reached epidemic proportions.

The 'swamp fevers' which drove off the invading English army of 1809 were almost certainly malarial. On 30 July 1809 an army of 40,000 men and 6,000 horse invaded the south-western isle of Walcheren in an attempt to cut off the harbour of Antwerp which was vital to Napoleon. They overran large areas of the islands, though they did not take the crucial town of Vlissingen, but within a few months the army had been thoroughly defeated – not by the French (or the Dutch), but by the fevers, which scythed down the soldiers in their thousands.[40] Another major year

[35] Jappe Alberts and Van der Steur, *Handleiding*, 144; Büch, 'De verziekte revolutie', 193–9; Wintle, 'Push-factors', 532–3.

[36] Van der Zee, 'Armoede', 247–9.

[37] Jansen and De Meere, 'Het sterftepatroon', 220; and Wintle, *Zeeland and the churches*, 162–3 and 199, n. 125.

[38] Van der Zee, 'Armoede', 204; see also 't Hart, *Utrecht en de cholera*.

[39] Jansen and De Meere, 'Het sterftepatroon', 197–200; and Van Lieburg and Snelders, '*De bevordering*', 119.

[40] Van Empel and Pieters, *Zeeland*, vol. II, pp. 495–6; *Letters from Flushing*; and Wintle, 'De economie van Zeeland', 97–9.

for malaria in the country was 1826, and the famine years of 1846–47 were exacerbated by a malaria epidemic in the summer of 1846,[41] made worse by a bout of Spanish flu at the same time.[42]

But the most familiar kind of deadly epidemic in the early part of the nineteenth century was the smallpox outbreak, often called the children's illness in Dutch (*kinderziekte*) because of its devastating effect on the young; 1817, 1858 and 1871 were particularly lethal years for smallpox, the last one leading to the introduction of compulsory vaccination for children in the Netherlands. In the cities of Amsterdam, Rotterdam and The Hague during the latter part of the eighteenth century, smallpox epidemics were frequent (every three or four years), but by no means everyone who had not previously had the disease was infected, and infection did not always mean fatality. Away from these large towns, smallpox was a relatively minor problem, accounting for less than 5 per cent of mortality. Apart from running away, or other self-inflicted forms of isolation and quarantine, there was little one could do about smallpox until the discovery of variolation, which involves infecting oneself with a small amount of matter taken from another person who actually has the disease. Few people outside the upper classes took advantage of this rather gruesome opportunity. During the French period, however, more statist forms of government were often keen to impose 'improvements' for the good of the population, and Jenner's vaccination technique (using matter derived from cows with a related disease, cowpox) was the perfect vehicle for state interference. The Dutch Jenner was Levy Salomon Davids, who introduced the technique, and on the strength of a decree of 1808 the new Dutch unitary state moved towards a 50 per cent vaccination rate by the end of the Napoleonic period. (The vaccination rate or index is calculated as the number of vaccinations performed on all age groups as a percentage of live births each year.) The state campaigns were extremely successful, and were continued by the government of King Willem I after 1815. In the major cities in the west, the disease was demographically insignificant after 1810. Across the country, the numbers of deaths from smallpox, particularly amongst children, whom it affected most directly, were radically reduced and remained so throughout the nineteenth century, and after legislation in 1872 which coincided with the last major smallpox epidemic the disease was largely eliminated from the statistics.[43]

Many of these epidemics were regional rather than national in their effect, but that both in fact and in the public imagination they were a

---

[41] Jansen and De Meere, 'Het sterftepatroon', 186 and 198.
[42] Büch, 'De verziekte revolutie', 194.
[43] Rutten, *'De vreeslijkste aller harpijen'*; see also Wintle, *Zeeland and the churches*, 161–3.

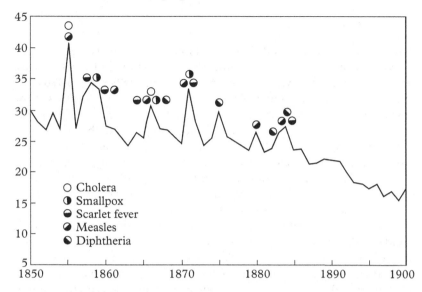

Figure I.5 The occurrence of major epidemics and the death rate in the Netherlands, 1850–1900.

Source: Jappe Alberts and Van der Steur, *Handleiding*, 144; Schuurbeque Boeye, *Het bevolkingsvraagstuk*, 12; and Wintle, 'Push-factors in emigration', 533.

major likely cause of death is beyond dispute, although the actual deaths were probably confined mainly to peak years of excessive mortality. Figure I.5 shows the peaks in the declining death rate between 1850 and 1900, and the association of the various major epidemics with the mortality peaks.

It is unlikely that the Dutch suffered much more from epidemics of contagious diseases than other nations, with the possible exception in northern Europe of malaria, but the impression they made is witnessed by the importance of these illnesses in the imagery of swearing in Dutch. If the Germans tend to swear in terms of excrement, and the English in terms of fornication, the Dutch do so in terms of terminal illnesses, and particularly of contagious ones. *Pokken, klere, tering, kanker* (derogatory adjectives deriving from the words for smallpox, cholera, tuberculosis and cancer) are some of the most common of Dutch descriptive expletives, even today; one might well say that a nation's taboos – even those of the English – are neatly mirrored in its cursing vocabulary and imagery.

Harvest failures

Apart from epidemics and their effects on the mortality peaks in the nineteenth century, before the impact of vaccination and other medical and environmental advances took effect after the 1860s and 1870s, the other main influence on mortality and indeed on cause of death was the food supply. Massimo Livi-Bacci has argued that there are few provable links in the long term between the food supply and the size of the European population, partly because the data are not good enough for the proof, but also because of the quite startling adaptability of the human system to changes in the level of nutrition. He would, however, concede that nutrition and the food supply can be crucial in the short term, before this kind of adaptability has time to develop.[44]

This is most noticeable in the case of major failures of the harvest which could and did cause widespread malnutrition and an upsurge in the death rate, as it did most famously in Ireland of the 1840s, but also indeed in the Netherlands in the same decade. There were periodic harvest failures in the Netherlands, for example of grain in general in 1817, and throughout the later 1870s, compounding the sorry influence of the onslaught of the general agricultural crisis.[45] The potato crop failed occasionally, for example in 1816, the mid-1840s and 1905.[46] Locally there were crop failures occasioned by frost, fungi and insects: in 1852 hailstones 'the size of bottles' destroyed virtually everything they hit in the fields of Walcheren.[47] This kind of local disaster could prove serious, but nonetheless was mitigated in demographic terms by the fact that, in a well-integrated economy, food could be brought in from outside to help deal with the crisis. The real catastrophe loomed when all food production in the region, nation and even continent was blighted by some affliction, and the supreme example of that was the potato crop failures of the 1840s.

In 1845 the Dutch potato crop was attacked by the fungus *Phytophthora infestans*. The blight had probably entered Europe from North America early in the decade, but it was not until the exceedingly wet summer of 1845 that the full effect was felt. The fungus is carried very rapidly by wind and mist across potato fields, infesting the leafy tops; precipitation carries it down to the tubers below ground, and heavy rain (as there was persistently in the summer of 1845) will result in the destruction of the entire crop, which simply rots. The edible potatoes grown in the clay soils of the west were worse hit than the rougher factory ones grown further

---

[44] Livi-Bacci, *Population*, xii–xiii and *passim*.
[45] Brugmans, *Paardenkracht*, 142; and Van Zanden, *De economische ontwikkeling*, 250.
[46] Van Tijn, 'De negentiende eeuw', 201; Bouman, *Geschiedenis*, 261.
[47] Geschiere, *Het leven*, 54.

inland on the sand for starch and flour. Yields that had amounted to more than 180 hectolitres per hectare in 1844 plummeted to less than 50 hl. per ha., and in the worst-hit provinces were as low as 15. The Netherlands was by no means the only country affected, for the whole of Europe suffered, with especially tragic consequences in Ireland and in Belgian Flanders, but the Netherlands was estimated to be the most potato-dependent country in Europe after Ireland. Although yields improved again from 1847, the blight continued to affect the harvest for several years, and indeed it was followed by a similar infection of the rye crop, the other staple diet of the poor in the Netherlands, especially those in rural areas.[48]

The effects of the famine on human behaviour in 1845–47 were direct, albeit acting in concert with other factors. The price of food rose and shortages were reported. Hugely increased numbers of beggars were seen, some singly – up to thirty a day calling at farmhouses in Schoondijke in the south-west – and some in gangs, marauding around the countryside. Food riots took place in towns throughout the west of the country, most notably in Delft. The provincial governments rapidly took measures to protect peace and property against the threat of violence, and 5,322 people emigrated overseas in 1847, partly to escape the disasters at home. One source estimates that there were 53,000 deaths because of food shortages in the period 1846–49.[49] More detailed analysis of the awful events of these years makes clear that in order to achieve such a devastating demographic effect, other factors had to be combined with widespread harvest failure, such as the epidemic of malaria and diseases of the digestive system which occurred in the sweltering summer of 1846.[50] Nonetheless, it is clear that sudden food shortages occurred often enough to be a source of fear and worry, that they led to extreme behaviour in at least some of the populace, and that in combination with weather and weakness from infectious disease they led to significantly increased mortality.

2.4   The food supply

The food supply, then, was one essential part of the matrix which affected the health of the nation, and the rest of this chapter will be devoted to the quantitative and qualitative aspects of that subject. What did the

[48] Bergman, 'The potato blight', 393–5; and Milward and Saul, *The development of the economies*, 186.
[49] Hofstee, *De demografische ontwikkeling*, 212; see also Bergman, 'The potato blight', 404–13; Van Otterloo, *Eten en eetlust*, 15; Willemse, 'Orde en rust', 12, 15; *Provinciaal Blad van Zeeland* (1845), item 100, 27 Sept.; Lintsen, *et al.*, eds., *Geschiedenis van de techniek*, vol. I, pp. 44–5; Stokvis, *De Nederlandse trek*, 5 and 11–12.
[50] Jansen and De Meere, 'Het sterftepatroon', 186.

Dutch eat (and drink)? How much food was there? What did it cost? How much did the Dutch consume? What were the levels of nutrition? And how did these things alter over time? Can they account for the decline in mortality, especially among children, which was so marked towards the end of the last century? The hypothesis, then, is that improved levels of nutrition increased longevity both directly and – more importantly – by increasing resistance to illness in general, especially to contagious diseases.

The Netherlands' most important source of food was its own domestic agricultural production: in the reign of King Willem I (1815–40) it has been estimated that the country was more or less self-sufficient.[51] That domestic production rose prodigiously in the course of the next hundred years or so, as a result of intensification of the agricultural economy and the introduction of new food crops with a much greater capacity to provide nutrition, but also because of the weather, which was generally improving in terms of temperature from 1800 to 1875, and of rainfall from 1800 to 1830 and from 1850 to 1870.[52] A number of commentators noticed the felicitous conditions in the 1850s, 1860s and early 1870s, when the climate in general seemed benevolent, crucial in an age of agriculture before the widespread introduction of artificial fertilizers.[53] After the 1870s other factors took over: any number of forms of agricultural technology and intensification began to take effect, so that yields per hectare of rye, for instance, rose steadily from about 1 tonne in 1870 to more than 3 tonnes in 1970.[54] Indeed husbandry improved right throughout the nineteenth century, but the weather may have played a role too in providing the extra food required by a rise in population from 2 million in 1800 to 4 million in the 1870s.[55]

J. L. van Zanden has arrived at some production estimates for Dutch agriculture, and perceives little growth in the first half of the century: labour productivity declined, as population growth more than cancelled out increases in production. The rest of the century, however, saw real growth in production, especially after 1880. The gross agricultural product rose by 155 per cent in the space of the hundred years between 1810 and 1910, which was only just behind the rate of growth in population. The number of people rose by 0.99 per cent each year over that century, while the domestic agricultural product (not all of which was food, of course) rose by 0.94 per cent. The growth accelerated as the century wore

[51] Brugmans, *Paardenkracht*, 162. During the time of the Republic it was probably not; the change may be explained by agricultural improvements and changing trade patterns in the later eighteenth century.
[52] Labrijn, *Het klimaat*, 109–11.   [53] Petersen, *Planned migration*, 30.
[54] Bakker, *Major soils*, Figure 30 on p. 52.
[55] Van Houtte, *Economische en sociale geschiedenis*, 220.

Plate 1 Vincent van Gogh, *The potato-eaters*, Nuenen near Eindhoven, lithograph, May 1885. The diet was frugal and life was hard.

on, and, most tellingly, the crop with by far the fastest growth in production was the potato.[56]

The potato: of western European nations only the Irish are more closely associated with the noble tuber than the Dutch – an image aided of course by Van Gogh's haunting portrayal of *The potato-eaters* (Plate 1). Indeed, the Dutch played a major role in diffusing the rule of the 'spud' as it spread through the old world after being introduced from the new one. The Spanish found it in Peru in the 1530s and brought it back to Europe as a botanical curiosity, where it reached the Netherlands around 1550. It required no special equipment or conditions and was easy to grow; it took only four months to mature from seed. But most prodigious were its huge yields both in bulk and nutritional value: a farming family plus some livestock could live off a couple of hectares, and by 1700 it was a common crop in the more densely populated parts of Europe. (Maize, also from South America, played a similar role in southern Europe.[57]) By

[56] Van Zanden, *De economische ontwikkeling*, 110–12 and 200–3.
[57] Langer, 'American foods', 52–5.

the 1720s the potato had become a major element in the Dutch diet, and from 1770 it increased its share of the market. By 1800 it was the staple food, having elbowed the traditional bread (and herrings) into a poor second place.[58]

The price of food

But what of the price of food? If there was more food around, but it was vastly more expensive, then the beneficial effects would have been few. Prices of food products have been collected by many historians over the years, and although there are all manner of methodological problems concerning the history of prices, a general indication of food prices over time will be sufficient for the purposes of this analysis. Van Zanden has developed a set of indices of agricultural product prices for four moments in the modern period, for around 1810, 1850, 1880 and 1910, and they are reproduced in graph form in Figure I.6. This shows grains (wheat and rye, for bread) remaining quite steady in price until the 1870s, and then coming down appreciably by the time of the First World War; meat was eaten on a regular basis by very few, but for the record, pork increased slowly in price in the first half of the century, then rapidly in the third quarter, and then declined between the 1870s and the First World War. Most important was the movement in the price of potatoes: the prices rose sharply up to the mid-century, then remained stable, and after 1880 declined significantly in line with cereals.[59]

In general, then, food became more expensive in the first half of the century, then stabilized and then decreased, with the decrease accelerating by the end of the century, significantly reducing the problems of the expense of basic food. General price series confirm this impression: nominal wholesale prices in the Netherlands crashed after the astronomical levels of the French period, and then began to climb slowly towards the mid-century. After the 1850s there was a gradual decline which accelerated after the 1870s, and continued to the turn of the century, when relative stability reigned until the disruptions of the Great War. A cost-of-living index, from the Central Bureau of Statistics and others, confirms that prices declined from a high around the 1870s until the end of the century, and then remained quite steady for a decade.[60] There is a whole range of price series available which confirm these general trends,

---

[58] Van der Maas and Noordegraaf, 'Smakelijk eten', 213–15; Van den Broecke, *Beschermd*, 89; and Pot, *Arm Leiden*, 95.
[59] Van Zanden, *De economische ontwikkeling*, 110. See also section 7.4 below, on per-capita demand and consumption.
[60] Van Stuijvenberg and De Vrijer, 'Prices', 707–9.

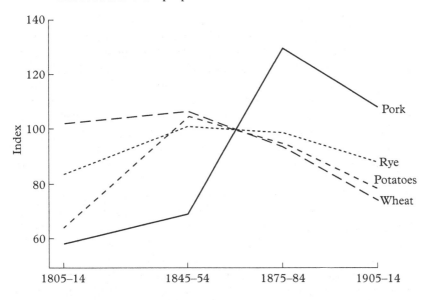

Figure I.6 Agricultural product prices, 1805–1914.
Indices of average prices in four ten-year periods for wheat, rye, potatoes, and pork (100 = mean of 1845/54 and 1875/84).

Source: Van Zanden, *De economische ontwikkeling*, 110.

from institutions like orphanages, hospitals and prisons, which kept purchasing records over long periods;[61] the details point to differences in price levels between the various regions of the country, though not in price trends, which were similar all over the nation. In bread the regional differences in price were particularly striking even as late as 1890, when a survey was carried out. Apparently the variety in price, which made bread and other essentials much more expensive in the coastal provinces, especially in Holland, Zeeland and Utrecht, survived for several decades after the differential local taxes which had originally caused them had been abolished.[62]

There were times, of course, like the late 1840s, when the price of food suddenly increased beyond all expectation, as a result of harvest failure; the same had happened during the French Revolutionary and

[61] For example, various prisons, 1870–92, and the institution 'Meerenberg', 1852–93 (see *Jaarcijfers* (1892), 51 and 54–5); and an orphanage in Harderwijk, 1555–1855 (see *Staatkundig en Staathuishoudkundig Jaarboek*, 8 (1856), 345–6).
[62] Altena and Van der Veen, 'Een onbekende enquête'; Van Zanden, 'Kosten van levensonderhoud'.

Napoleonic Wars, and would occur again during the World Wars of the twentieth century. In the 1840s, as the price of the staple potatoes went through the roof, the value of real wages dropped sharply and food crises resulted.[63] The real (deflated) price of food is of course directly related to wage levels, and a good indication of the relative position is provided by the percentage of income spent by working families on food. A general sample of the available figures shows clearly that Dutch families were spending less and less of their budgets on food as the century progressed, which indicates either that they were earning a great deal more, or that food was becoming significantly cheaper and more available, or both. In 1850 about 70 per cent of income was spent on food in ordinary families; by 1900 this had declined to 50 per cent, by 1950 it was 39 per cent, and by 1974 only 26 per cent. Combined with the likelihood that most people almost certainly ate more in 1950 than a century earlier, this certainly indicates a radical drop in the real, income-related price of food.[64] The changes in the relative price of food in the Netherlands, then, consisted of a rise in the first half of the nineteenth century, followed by relative stability between 1850 and the 1870s, and then a decline thereafter until the First World War. The most obvious reason for this progression is the general increasing prosperity and economic development, slowly filtering down to the lives of ordinary people, but certain events accounted for catalytic improvements along the way.

One such catalyst was the change in the way taxes were levied. Liberal reforms of the mid-century, including the new constitution of 1848, and the *Gemeentewet* (Municipality Act) of 1851, made radical changes: now rates were to be the same everywhere, with only restricted opportunities for the levying of local excises.[65] The liberals then took on the various national excises: those on meat (except for beef) were abolished in 1852, fuel excises were abandoned in 1863; all local excises had gone by 1865. By far the most significant was the removal of the excises on milling grain, which occurred on 13 July 1855, and which resulted in immediately cascading bread prices. A kilogram loaf of fine white bread cost 47 cents in Haarlem in 1855, and just 34 cents a year later, after the abolition of the milling excise; in Amsterdam there was a decline of 50 per cent in bread prices in the 1850s.[66]

---

[63] Stokvis, *De Nederlandse trek*, 11–12; see also Jacquemyns, *Histoire de la crise*, 262–5, on the situation across the border in Belgian Flanders. See also section 7.4 below, on real wages.

[64] Den Hartog, 'De beginfase', 336, using data from various sources; and Horlings and Smits, 'Private consumer expenditure', 24–5.

[65] Roovers, *De plaatselijke belastingen*, 52–86. For the effects of these excises on wage levels, and as an object of government policy, see below, sections 4.1 and 5.3 respectively.

[66] Van Otterloo, *Eten en eetlust*, 43; and De Meere, *Economische ontwikkeling*, 108.

Figure I.7 Wheat prices at Arnhem in the nineteenth century, guilders per hectolitre, 9–year moving averages.

Source: Brugmans, 'Economic fluctuations', 152.

2.5   The Dutch diet

What, then, did the Dutch actually eat? There are two sorts of evidence to this issue: the qualitative or descriptive, and the quantitative or statistical, the former giving us information about taste and subjective opinions on food, and the latter – if the figures are reliable – telling us objectively about actual consumption, from which it should be possible to extract information about nutrition levels as well. We shall examine the descriptive sources first.

For most of the nineteenth century the Dutch diet was characterized by a remarkable diversity: it is simply not possible to be categorical about what the average Dutchman and his family ate, for no two families ate the same.[67] In the 1830s workers ate mostly bread and potatoes, but also would occasionally have some fruit and vegetables (albeit sometimes verging on the rotten), some milk or buttermilk, and some fish. They would hardly ever have meat, except perhaps at slaughtering time in November.[68] A comprehensive piece of descriptive research into the diet of the people of Zeeland in the 1870s concluded the same: potatoes were the staple, but fish and shellfish in the ports, vegetables in season,

---

[67] See Lintsen, *et al.*, eds., *Geschiedenis van de techniek*, vol. I, pp. 40–1; and Teuteberg, ed., *European food history*, 56–70, section on the Netherlands.
[68] Van der Zee, 'Armoede', 208–10.

pulses, and even a little meat and some dairy products sometimes adorned the diet of even the meanest families (while the better off did very well).[69] Pancakes made of the cheapest flour and skimmed milk were popular in some areas. Bread was widely consumed, but in a great and complex variety of quantities and types according to region: traditional wheat-growing areas would have nothing to do with 'turf' (the much cheaper and equally nutritious rye bread). Areas like Groningen, on the other hand, which grew plenty of wheat, but which had originally concentrated more on rye in the eighteenth century, were quite happy to eat it.[70]

Nevertheless, this picture of variety and diversity, which prevents us from being categorical about what people ate in the middle of the nineteenth century, should certainly not be presented in any way as a rosy picture, either in terms of nutrition, or in terms of dietary or culinary delights. Most of the population probably suffered from a light but chronic form of malnutrition for most of the nineteenth century,[71] and although nearly everyone would have known what fruit tasted like, and would occasionally have a small piece of cured pork or the odd herring if he or she were lucky, these were rare treats for most people below the level of the middle classes – which was of course most of the populace. For with very few and very occasional embellishments, the diet of the Dutch in the nineteenth century consisted of some bread, and a very great deal of potatoes.

Potatoes formed the staple diet in the absolute sense that very little else was eaten.[72] They were often served up three times a day, seven days a week.[73] And we are not talking about *pommes-de-terre au gratin*, or even *pommes frites*; we are talking of plain, unadorned, boiled potatoes. The Dutch still eat a quantity of potatoes nowadays, but they are served with meat and vegetables, with the potatoes themselves swimming in a rich meat gravy and often mashed with winter vegetables; in the common household of the nineteenth century, it was just the spuds on their own. Salt might be added, or perhaps vinegar; a little cheap, thin gruel made from flour and mustard with water might be used to moisten it. The main meal was at midday, when the tubers were peeled and freshly boiled; at

---

[69] Fokker, 'De volksvoeding'.
[70] See Voskuil, 'De weg naar luilekkerland'; and Lintsen, *et al.*, eds., *Geschiedenis van de techniek*, vol. I, p. 95.
[71] Lintsen, *et al.*, eds., *Geschiedenis van de techniek*, vol. I, pp. 42–3.
[72] From among the multitude of contemporary references to potatoes being the main or even the only component of the poor's diet: Baart, *Westkapelle*, 120 (referring to c. 1870); and Broes van Dort, *Bijdrage tot de kennis*, on Goes (referring to c. 1850). Burema's authoritative national survey of the descriptive literature concurs: Burema, *De voeding*, 317–19.
[73] E.g. in Groningen: Paping, '*Voor een handvol stuivers*', 243.

supper the leftovers were served as a mash, and the next day's breakfast was warmed up from what was left over from the night before – but again without fat or any other adornment.[74]

Potatoes can be delicious, but the incredible monotony of this diet is quite appalling to our pampered palates today. Even the bread which was eaten was unadorned, and if anything were spread on it, then it was more than likely to be – inevitably – a little leftover mash. Eating can have had few of the social and cultural connotations that it does now, and must have been more of a necessary bodily action performed unthinkingly in order to remain functioning physically, rather akin to drinking water or even to passing water or moving the bowels. Again, Van Gogh's image of *The potato eaters* speaks volumes (Plate 1). Not that people were necessarily disgusted by their potatoes: if you have to live off one food-type, in terms of nutrition and even taste, the potato is a pretty good bet. The father of social medicine in the Netherlands, Samuel Coronel, could simply not understand it when he saw young children and infants of the urban working classes tucking into their potatoes with gusto and even sucking on them for comfort as if they were soothers or dummies.[75]

Liquid refreshment

And what did the populace drink? The middle and upper classes drank all sorts of interesting imported wines and spirits, but the poor's habits were less complicated. To wash down their meals and to quench their thirst they drank water – the quality of which was generally appalling, as we have seen, until the end of the nineteenth century. They used the water to make a weak brew of the coffee brought into the harbours by the colonial traders, or chicory as a cheaper substitute: coffee became virtually a national drink in the nineteenth century. Tea was also popular, and in certain areas, like the Zaanstreek near Amsterdam, and in Zeeland, so was hot chocolate.[76] Milk was too valuable a commodity to be drunk by ordinary people, except in the form of dairying's by-product, buttermilk.[77] And then, of course, there was alcohol.

There were only two alcoholic drinks consumed in any quantity, that is by any number of the populace: beer, and *jenever*, the renowned Dutch gin. Beer was often seen, by those who thought in those terms, as the lesser of the two evils. It was expensive, and was even praised by moral-

---

[74] Van Otterloo, *Eten en eetlust*, 16–31. See also Jobse-Van Putten, *Eenvoudig maar voedzaam*.

[75] Coronel, *Middelburg*, 241–2.

[76] Schuurman, *Materiële cultuur*, 102; and Voskuil, 'De verspreiding'.

[77] Van der Zee, 'Armoede', 212–13; and Van Otterloo, *Eten en eetlust*, 30.

izing campaigners as a good alternative to the dire perils of gin-drinking. Beer had some nutritional value. The indigenous Dutch beer of the nineteenth century was pretty poor stuff by all accounts, being cloudy, tasteless and of short shelf-life.[78] It was very much a Roman Catholic drink, being consumed heavily in the southern provinces of Brabant and Limburg, and indeed in the Catholic parts of mixed provinces.[79] After the 1880s the commercial market was taken over by German-style bottom-yeasted pilsner beers, which produced a beverage which was clear and hoppy, and which kept reasonably. Top-yeasted beer continued to be brewed on a small scale for local or even auto-consumption, especially in the south of the country. The per-capita consumption figures are interesting: from about 33 litres per capita per annum in the 1870s, they rose to around 40 litres by 1900; by the time of the later 1930s, they had fallen dramatically to a mere 14 litres per head of population.[80]

Jenever consumption at the start of the nineteenth century was prodigious: it was double the equivalent levels in France, Germany and Britain in the 1830s.[81] As Figure I.8 shows, in the early 1830s some 10 litres of strong liquor at 50 per cent pure alcohol was consumed each year in the Netherlands for every man, woman and child. It fell to about 7 litres in the late 1840s, but rose again to its old levels by the 1870s. Then a decline in consumption set in, which after the 1890s became a cascade. It was down to 5 litres per head by World War I, and was a mere 1.46 litres in 1936/37. This was a really radical change in the behaviour of the Dutch.[82] Adding all major alcoholic drinks together (spirits, beers and wines), and translating the units into litres of pure alcohol per head per annum, the pattern is a similar one. Consumption was high at 6 to 8 litres between 1800 and 1840; in the 1840s and 1850s it fell to 4 or 5. It then rose again to reach a peak of 7 litres just before 1880, when the rate began to drop, and then to plummet after 1900 to well under 2 litres in the late 1930s. (From 1960, consumption soared again to the highest levels ever recorded – 9 litres of pure alcohol for each and every member of the population every year – around 1980.[83]) There seems to be clear evidence here in the later nineteenth and early twentieth centuries of a classic bourgeois civilization offensive which actually worked: the Liquor Act of 1881 severely limited the number of licensed premises where strong drink could be sold, and

---

[78] Büch, 'Proeve', 81; and Lintsen, *et al.*, eds., *Geschiedenis van de techniek*, vol. I, pp. 172–92.
[79] Wintle, *Zeeland and the churches*, 121–30.
[80] Brugmans, *Paardenkracht*, 472; Lintsen, *et al.*, eds., *Geschiedenis van de techniek*, vol. I, p. 192.
[81] De Meere, *Economische ontwikkeling*, 97–8.
[82] 'Verbruik van veraccijnsd gedistilleerd 1913'; Brugmans, *Paardenkracht*, 472; Büch, 'Proeve', 71.   [83] Van der Stel, *Drinken*, 69 and *passim*.

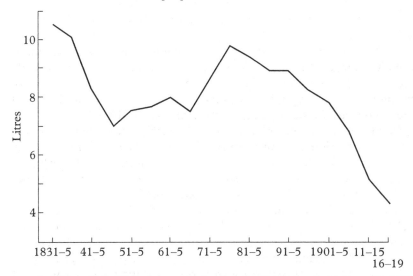

Figure I.8 Spirits consumption in the Netherlands in litres @ 50% alcohol, per head of population, 1831–1919.

Source: 'Verbruik van veraccijnsd gedistilleerd 1913', 3.

although cheap American grain eased the supply side of this industry, government excise policy applied a 600 per cent increase to *jenever* between 1840 and 1900.[84] For purposes of comparison, this steep fall in the consumption of alcohol was also recorded in Belgium.[85]

Estimated food consumption

Before arriving at final conclusions here, it is necessary to extend the mainly qualitative evidence examined so far on food and drink habits by reviewing the available statistical evidence on consumption.

The sources for the period up to 1852 are patchy, but can offer us some clear indications of the trend in per-capita consumption of the various principal products. After 1852 the official statistics take over: in 1895 and 1920 the Central Bureau for Statistics (and its forerunner) published estimates of consumption of the various articles from 1852 to 1918, which have formed the database for several studies;[86] since the

[84] Van Zanden and Griffiths, *Economische geschiedenis*, 11–12; Den Hartog, 'De beginfase', 349–50, 353.
[85] Van den Eeckhout and Scholliers, 'De hoofdelijke voedselconsumptie', 297–301.
[86] *Onderzoek naar het verbruik* (1895); and 'Onderzoek naar het verbruik' (1920). Figures for alcohol consumption 1831–1919 were published by the CBS in 'Verbruik van veraccijnsd gedistilleerd 1913'.

First World War the statistics have been readily available from official sources.

In the period before 1850, consumption of food items was stagnant or even declining:[87] the consumption per capita of meat and wheat steadily reduced, while that of rye (the poor man's grain) increased.[88] There are no figures for consumption of potatoes on a national scale, but local indications are that the potato was the saviour of the Dutch in a very difficult time from the last decades of the eighteenth century onwards, with consumption continuing to rise in the 1830s and 1840s.[89] So the population was reducing its intake of food in the form of relatively luxury articles like wheat-bread and meat, while expanding its intake of potatoes and rye, the cheapest forms of nutrient available.[90]

The per-capita consumption of all food items increased in the second half of the century, with the sole exception of buckwheat; potatoes increased, but the cereals increased more, reducing the Dutch dependence on the tuber and introducing more variety into the diet. There was a relative increase in wheat usage over rye, indicating a swing in bread preferences, and protein foods like meat and pulses saw especially large increases, as did the consumption of stimulants and luxuries like tobacco and especially sugar: the per-capita annual consumption in 1852 of sugar was 2.7 kg, but had increased to 9.9 kg by the end of the century. The consumption of many of these articles actually doubled over the half-century after 1850.[91] Average annual meat consumption nearly doubled between the 1840s and the 1930s.[92] The increasing use of potatoes levelled off after 1860, but remained high until 1920, when at last diversification meant that the potato no longer formed the monolithic diet of the Dutch.

The process of diet diversification was a slow one, starting around 1860 and continuing until after the First World War; by 1900 the Netherlands as a nation still ate little meat, existing mainly on potatoes and bread.[93] Rising levels of domestic demand for agricultural products reflected this increase too, especially between 1850 and 1880.[94] As we have seen,

[87] Van Zanden, *De economische ontwikkeling*, 139–40; Horlings, *The economic development*, 229–30.
[88] De Meere, *Economische ontwikkeling*, 93–7; Knotter and Muskee, 'Conjunctuur', 160–3; and De Beer, 'De levensstandaard'. Some of the statistics are published in De Bosch Kemper, 'Statistiek', 33–5; and *Staatkundig en Staathuishoudkundig Jaarboek* (1854), 74–6.
[89] De Meere, *Economische ontwikkeling*, 95–6 and 111; Bergman, 'The potato blight', 391.
[90] A local study of Groningen confirms this: Paping, '*Voor een handvol stuivers*', 258–9 and 382.
[91] Lintsen, *et al.*, eds., *Geschiedenis van de techniek*, vol. I, p. 232; Baudet and Van der Meulen, *Consumer behaviour*, 80. See also Van der Meulen, 'Nederlanders'.
[92] Koolmees, *Symbolen*, 42 and 46.   [93] Van Otterloo, *Eten en eetlust*, 45–7.
[94] Van Zanden, *De economische ontwikkeling*, 141 and 224.

though, the consumption of alcohol, as shown in Figure I.8, fell like a stone from the 1880s onwards. For whatever reason, Groningen was by far the heaviest consumer of strong liquor amongst the Dutch provinces.[95]

Nutrition levels

Translating these figures for per-capita consumption of various food articles into nutritional values expressed in calories is fraught with difficulties, and the results must be viewed with considerable suspicion, especially for the nineteenth century. Rough indications are all that is feasible. If we accept that about 2,500 calories per head are required each day to keep the population even minimally fed, then before 1850 that average was probably just about reached, consisting mainly of potatoes and (rye) bread. Given that this is an average, and in the knowledge that the middle and upper classes would have consumed considerably more than 2,500 calories per day, then it is clear that many in the lower orders often did not manage to consume enough to keep them from being lightly malnourished.[96] Nutrition levels probably declined from the late Republic up to about 1810, what with the deprivations of the French period,[97] and a recent study concluded that in nutritional terms existence before the mid-century was 'frankly precarious'.[98] After 1850 up to the time of the First World War there was an improvement in consumption, and another set of estimates reckons that per-capita daily consumption had risen by then to just under 2,800 calories, with an average daily intake of some 75 grams of high-protein food like meat, fish, cheese or pulses. This was still bordering on malnutrition, on the eve of the First World War.[99] Even during the Second World War (before the onset of the Hunger Winter of 1944–45), average consumption levels were generally between 3,000 and 4,000 calories.[100] Again for purposes of comparison, figures from Flanders are broadly similar.[101]

Bringing all this qualitative and quantitative evidence together, the picture is one of change, but of slow change. A. P. den Hartog has defined 'modern' food consumption as being characterized by variety, allowing a degree of individuality in taste, containing substantial amounts of industrially processed food, showing little seasonal variation, not being

---

[95] 'Verbruik van veraccijnsd gedistilleerd 1913', 3.
[96] De Meere, *Economische ontwikkeling*, 92–8.
[97] De Vries and Van der Woude, *The first modern economy*, 230.
[98] De Beer, 'Voeding', 224–5.
[99] Baudet and Van der Meulen, *Consumer behaviour*, 95.
[100] Trienekens, *Tussen ons volk en de honger*, 472–3.
[101] Vandenbroecke, 'Voedingstoestanden', 140; and Van den Eeckhout and Scholliers, 'De hoofdelijke voedselconsumptie', 287–8.

auto-produced to any important degree, with a considerable distance between the producer and consumer, and less alcohol. The kinds of factors which stimulate the achievement of this modern pattern of consumption are increasing prosperity, urbanization, technological advances which permit cheaper and more hygienic food (refrigeration, preservatives, margarine), farming changes which increase the supply of food, improved distribution networks (advertising, brands, modern shops), and an increasing intervention by government to maintain standards of hygiene and provide services like clean water, electricity and gas for cooking, and transport for perishables.[102] After 1850 some of these factors were in evidence in the Netherlands, gradually making themselves felt and resulting in an improving and more 'modern' food consumption pattern. With the exception of food shortages in the First World War, and the dreadful winter of 1944/45, there has been little widespread hunger in the twentieth century, and we have seen how the variety of food increased while infant mortality and the number of rejected conscripts decreased. Regional differences in consumption were also on the decline, as a function of the improving transport infrastructure. The process was by no means complete by 1900, nor even by the First World War, but it was well on the way.[103]

2.6   Working conditions

Of the many other possible factors affecting public health, such as housing, clothing, heating, dampness and the like, we shall look only at working conditions. In the manufacturing sector, factory conditions were for the most part grim enough to affect health directly. In agriculture hours were long and the work very heavy, especially on the clay soils, but it was in factories and unregulated sweat-shops that the real horrors of the nineteenth century lurked. The expectations generated by reading the novels of Dickens, or indeed Dutch literary equivalents like Jacob Cremer's *Factory children* (*Fabriekskinderen*, 1863), may err on the side of sensationalism, but probably do not grossly misrepresent reality.[104] Hours were long – from twelve to twenty a day. Textiles were probably the worst industries: flax shops were permeated with a thick dust reckoned to be extremely unhealthy, and textile mills in general were unheated, damp and dark.[105] A campaign was fought from the early nineteenth century

---

[102] Den Hartog, 'De beginfase', 335–50.
[103] Van Otterloo, *Eten en eetlust*, 18 and 48–50.
[104] On this 'social literature' see Van der Heijden, *Werkmansboekje*, 9–12.
[105] The general picture is provided by Van der Zee, 'Armoede', 224–34; De Vrankrijker, *Een groeiende gedachte*, 71–2; and for rural areas in Van Zanden, *De economische ont-*

onwards to improve the conditions in factories by legislation, and it was led by Dr Coronel, who made a crusade of the causation links between bad working conditions, bad health and economic underperformance. Studies flowed from his pen, the most influential amongst them being his *Health science applied to factory industry*, published in 1861.[106] In it he argued passionately for reform of working conditions in the Netherlands, making use of copious amounts of empirical data which he himself had collected. In a more specific study about calico-weaving he thundered against the deforming posture adopted by the weavers and drew attention to the workers' constant rheumy eyes and infected throats (for which they took chalk and *jenever*).[107] Glass factories and grinderies were particularly unhealthy places, and pottery workers suffered from the effects of lead-bearing chemicals in the glazes.[108] Any trades where chemicals were involved, like bleaching, dyeing, tanning, and early forms of the chemicals industry, were potentially dangerous to health.

Often it was the women and children who were most affected, though the work of Coronel and his colleagues showed that no-one was left untouched. Women were meant to work shorter hours than men in factories, though in the middle decades of the nineteenth century they often did not,[109] but it was usually the labour of children which caught the headlines and led the campaigns. The most horrendous case was of infants aged $4\frac{1}{2}$ years working fifteen-hour days in a rope works in Moordrecht, and no doubt that was exceptional, but around the mid-century it is clear that very large numbers of children aged from about nine to fifteen were working full twelve-hour days in factories, with the most severe consequences for their health.[110] Surveys carried out in 1841 and 1860 showed without doubt that large numbers of youths and young children were employed in all provinces in virtually all trades and industries.[111]

The campaign to curtail the ill-effects of unregulated working conditions fell foul of the liberal ethos of the third quarter of the nineteenth century, which was not keen to interfere, but Coronel and his allies continued to lobby. Their work eventually influenced the progressive liberal Samuel van Houten (1837–1930), who finally succeeded in passing a Child Labour Act as a private bill in 1874, which was almost

---

wikkeling, 201 and 217. See also Minderhoud, 'De landbouwindustrie', 423; and Schilstra, *Vrouwenarbeid*, 57, etc.

[106] Coronel, *De gezondheidsleer.*   [107] Coronel, 'De ziekten', 497–503.

[108] Brugmans, *Paardenkracht*, 406–7.

[109] Schilstra, *Vrouwenarbeid*, 49; and Blok, *et al.*, eds., *Algemene geschiedenis der Nederlanden*, vol. XIII, p. 297.

[110] Brugmans, *Paardenkracht*, 191–2. On the harsh world of children's work, see the comment and references in Peeters, *et al.*, eds., *Vijf eeuwen gezinsleven*, 142ff.

[111] Vleggeert, *Kinderarbeid*, 44–5, 66–7; and for a full account of the surveys, see Gorter and De Vries, 'Gegevens omtrent de kinderarbeid'.

completely ineffective and without sanctions, but which was a historic milestone – the first – in the now enormous edifice of Dutch labour law. In the mid-1880s an enquiry showed that children under twelve years were still widely employed in industry, despite it being forbidden by the 1874 Act. A Labour Act was passed in 1889, outlawing work except in the home and in agriculture for the under-twelves, and limiting women and youths of between twelve and fifteen years to eleven hours a day. The inspectorate which was set up published reports in the 1890s which showed that child labour by the under-twelves had by then disappeared. The legislation continued slowly: in 1911 a fifty-eight-hour week was introduced for women and under-sixteens, and a number of regulations were brought in for individual industries before the First World War, notably for the miners in 1906, limiting them to eight and a half hours underground. There was a very elementary general Work Safety Act in 1895.[112] These pieces of legislation and regulation were important really only in so far as they marked the start of social legislation, but in the context of public health they ensured that at least the worst systematic widespread dangers to personal health had been recognized and had begun to receive attention by the time of the turn of the century.

2.7   Conclusion

By the time of the First World War, then, in which the public health of the non-belligerent Netherlands probably suffered less than any other country in Europe, a number of factors for change were in operation which had already altered the health of the nation unrecognizably from that existing before 1850, and which were well on the way to turning the country into the modern society in demographic and public-health terms that it is today. Those factors included the prevailing sanitary and environmental conditions, the medical services, the diet and nutrition of the populace, and its working conditions. Underpinned by a general increasing prosperity reaching down at least to some degree to most orders in society, this permitted fundamental changes in the kinds of illnesses and diseases which troubled and killed the Dutch, changes which eventually meant a substantial reduction in the death rates and an increase in life expectancy. In chapters 1 and 2 we have examined the demographic and public-health elements of this process in some detail; in the following part of the book we shall be concerned with the economic aspects of that underlying increase in general prosperity.

[112] Bergink, 'Samuel Senior Coronel', 756–62; and Brugmans, *Paardenkracht*, 408–11.

Part II

Economic transition

Introduction

Of the triptych of demography, economy and society in the Netherlands in the modern period, all three are unusual, interesting and instructive. But nowhere is there more to excite interest than in the economy. In a nutshell, since the late sixteenth century this has been one of the most successful economies in the world. It has been amongst the top in terms of per-capita product or income, but never underwent an industrial revolution of the kind which typified the experience of its neighbours Britain, Belgium, parts of France, and Germany. The Netherlands, which formed perhaps the world's first modern economy,[1] was characterized by internationally renowned agriculture, and prodigious trade and transport, with a tidy but relatively modest manufacturing sector, and managed to keep up with the world leaders in economic development. How was this achieved?

We examine the Dutch economy in the long nineteenth century in some detail below, in order to come to some conclusions about the economic process undergone, to understand more about the structure of the Dutch economy in this crucial period, and to be able to draw some modest lessons about more general models of economic growth, development and industrialization. Although many regional examples will be brought into focus, and (as with demography) special attention will be paid to the internal diversity of this small country, the examination is primarily concerned with the macro-economy of the Netherlands as a whole. In chapter 3 we sift the available evidence on national economic development since the seventeenth century, and take account of the extended historiographical debate on industrialization (or the lack of it) which has smouldered for some fifty years now. This debate has been well trodden, and is perhaps nearly exhausted, but retains our interest because it is concerned with the timing and manner of the 'transition' between economic pre-eminence in the seventeenth century and a successful

---

[1] See De Vries and Van der Woude, *Nederland 1500–1815*.

post-industrial economy in the late twentieth century. Chronology and periodization will be the key themes in this chapter.

In chapter 4 we move to an analysis of the three conventional factor inputs on the supply side of the economy: labour, land and capital. However, this is by no means an exclusively quantitative approach, and the development of the various crucial sectors (finance and banking, energy) is closely plotted, along with an investigation into the reasons for the state of affairs concerning each factor input. In chapter 5 we stay with the supply side, but move away from the traditional three factor inputs, to influences which affect the efficiency or the organization of the economy: the role of entrepreneurship in the developing Dutch economy, then technology, and finally government policy. At regular junctures international comparisons will be made, both quantitatively and qualitatively, in order to locate the Netherlands firmly in its all-important European and global context.

Chapter 6 leaves aside the aggregate supply and demand approach, and offers a sectoral analysis of the Dutch economy over the extended century. In line with recent trends in research, special attention will be paid to the service sector. In chapter 7 we transfer our investigation to the demand side of the economy, where relatively little research has taken place to date (though there have been encouraging signs in recent years). 'Demand' serves more as a framework than as a strict definition of subject matter: the background question is always to do with the extent and nature of that side of the economy, but where appropriate the discussion ranges more widely. The role of the colonies in the Dutch economic experience is examined and summarized, and we ask what effects the prodigious population growth had on economic development. Then we take what indicators we can find for (aggregate) per-capita home demand: various estimates of real income and consumption are dealt with in an attempt to establish the periodicity of the dynamics of domestic demand and its stimulus to the economy as a whole.

Finally in this part of the book devoted to the economy, chapter 8 presents the conclusion of the preceding debates, and moves to an overall explanation of the relative success this small economy has enjoyed for the last two centuries. The object of the exercise is twofold. First, it is to make clear once and for all that there was very little wrong, relatively speaking, with the Dutch economy in the nineteenth century, and that its pathway to the wealth and prosperity of the late twentieth century was as serviceable as anyone else's and often considerably better. Second, we wish to explain the governing characteristics of that growth and relative success, in terms of its internal structures and dynamics, its stimuli from within and without, its strengths and weaknesses, and the reasons for its resilience.

3   Economic performance and industrialization: the Dutch debate

3.1   The Dutch compared to their neighbours in terms of GNP

There is no doubt that in the mid-seventeenth century, at the height of the economic, political and cultural influence of the Dutch Republic, the Netherlands was a very wealthy and very prosperous country indeed. In the early modern period, the Dutch were an economic success-story, with clear water between themselves and other nations.[1] However, what happened next? The conventional wisdom is that the Republic's economy became less dynamic after 1650–70, and the ageing but still standard work on the economy of the Republic in the eighteenth century, by Johan de Vries, is entitled *The economic decline of the Republic*.[2] Something seems to have gone wrong: instead of moving on from such a promising start to further economic glories in the late eighteenth and nineteenth centuries in the form of industrialization, the Netherlands floundered. Instead of forming a modern capitalist economy, the Dutch failed to graduate to modern industrial society. The Dutch economy was branded a failure, then, in the modern period. The *doyen* of Dutch economic historians of the previous generation, Peter Klein, pronounced that Dutch income per capita had probably not risen at all between 1700 and 1860, and although this was little more than an informed guess in 1973, it represented the general view.[3]

But things must be seen in a proper perspective; the Dutch have clearly been the victims of their own success in the seventeenth century, and while other countries 'coming from behind' may have undergone more dramatic economic progress, the Dutch have remained amongst the leading economic nations of the world. The country is part of the industrial and economically advanced core of maritime northern Europe,

[1] That is not to deny the many similarities between the Dutch success and that of previous and subsequent economic power-houses: Davids and Lucassen, eds., *A miracle mirrored*, 432ff.
[2] De Vries, *De economische achteruitgang*.
[3] Klein, 'Het bankwezen', 135.

together with Britain, France, Germany and Belgium.[4] That the Netherlands has held its place amongst this world-leading group is clear from
what we know of GNP per-capita figures. Dutch data available to historians until recently have been poor, but a team based at Utrecht University
and led by J. L. van Zanden has been engaged in reconstructing the
national accounts for the nineteenth century.[5] The results which have
been published to date from this ambitious and impressive project (to
which frequent reference will be made below) are now quite definitive,
although some adjustments are still being made to the data, and a full
international analysis of their implications still awaits us.[6] The findings do
not distort the general picture derived from the data used by Bairoch in
the 1970s: without any doubt, the Netherlands has been one of the richest
countries in the world since 1800.[7] The global differentials in GNP per
capita have been substantial and increasing since 1815, but the Netherlands has clearly been amongst the leaders.[8]

Moreover, this wealth seems to have been relatively equally distributed,
and it is not the case that the Dutch economy was more skewed than
others to favour only a tiny percentage of its population. According to the
researches of Jan de Meere, in the first half of the nineteenth century there
was a slight decline in the inequality of distribution, followed by a rise in
inequality between 1850 and 1880, and subsequently a significant decline, which has continued more or less to this day, with an interruption
for World War I.[9] More recent work on income distribution has suggested
that although certain regions (like Amsterdam) may have experienced a
rise in inequality early in the nineteenth century, in the country as a whole
distribution remained remarkably even before 1900. One of the reasons
was the erosion of regional differences as the economy integrated, and
another was the gradual economic growth experienced by the Dutch, as
opposed to rapid spurts.[10] The demographic evidence since 1800 presented in Part I suggests a continuing improvement in the health of the

[4] Thomson, *Europe since Napoleon*, 235–6.
[5] From 1990. See Smits, Horlings and Van Zanden, *The measurement*; Smits, Van Zanden
and Van Ark, 'Introduction'; and Burger, 'Dutch patterns'.
[6] See Smits, Horlings and Van Zanden, *The measurement*. Their analysis of domestic growth
patterns is due to appear shortly: Smits, Horlings and Van Zanden, 'Sprekende cijfers!' A
useful comparison has been drawn with Belgium on the basis of the new data: Horlings
and Smits, 'A comparison'.
[7] His preliminary findings were published in Van Zanden, 'Economische groei'.
[8] Bairoch, 'The main trends', 7–10.
[9] De Meere, *Economische ontwikkeling*, 76. This pattern is in line both with Kuznets's
expectations of the performance of a modernizing economy, and with developments in
England, France and the United States: see De Meere, 'Long-term trends'. However,
local studies indicate regional variance: in Groningen, inequality increased between 1770
and 1860. Paping, '*Voor een handvol stuivers*', 199.
[10] Soltow and Van Zanden, *Income and wealth inequality*, chapters 5 and 7, especially pp.
173–4.

Table II.1. *Estimates of real per-capita national product for selected European countries in 1970 US Dollars, 1850–1910.*

	1850	1860	1870	1880	1890	1900	1910
UK	660	804	904	979	1,130	1,269	1,302
Belgium	534	637	738	832	932	1,013	1,110
Denmark	489	487	563	617	798	850	1,050
Switzerland			589	715	750	895	992
Germany	418	481	579	602	729	868	958
Netherlands	481	522	591	707	768	840	952
France	432	474	567	602	668	784	883
Italy		451	467	466	466	502	548

Source: Crafts, 'Patterns of development', 440.

nation, which benefited proportionately the poor more than the rich, and the Dutch have always enjoyed exceptional levels of transfer payments in the framework of one sort or another of welfare system, which has alleviated some of the poverty at the lower end by redistributing substantial sums of income.[11] Amongst the 'industrialized' countries of the world, the Dutch have consistently been in the top ten in terms of GNP per capita during the twentieth century (indeed in the top six until the 1960s), lagging significantly behind only the USA and Canada.[12] Even in absolute terms, it has the sixth largest GDP in the EU, and cannot be dismissed in any sense as a micro-economy, like Luxembourg, or even Switzerland. Around the year 2000 it is home to well over 15 million people, and indeed its prodigious population growth actually conceals economic growth rates in the economy in non-per-capita, absolute terms which can only be described as phenomenal. So in the twentieth century we are talking about one of the world's most successful economies. But what of the critical nineteenth century, the century of 'industrialization'?

For purposes of comparative analysis, some of the best data publicly available at this time are those assembled by Nick Crafts, for the specific purposes of international comparison in the era of industrialization.[13] These data are plagued by all kinds of problems, of course, but their general impression is not seriously disputed. Crafts' figures are reproduced in Table II.1, together with a graph covering the leading European nations in the years 1850–1910 (Figure II.1).[14]

---

[11] See section 10.3 below, on the welfare state. [12] Bairoch, 'The main trends', 10.

[13] Crafts, 'GNP in Europe'; and Crafts, 'Patterns of development'.

[14] The period 1913–21 is covered in detail in Van der Bie, '*Een doorlopende groote roes*'; and a useful international comparison of GDP per capita from 1913 onwards appeared in Van Ark and De Jong, 'Accounting for economic growth'.

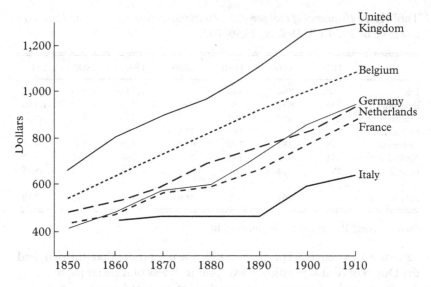

Figure II.1 Estimates of real per-capita national product for certain European countries, 1850–1910, in 1970 US dollars.

Source: Crafts, 'Patterns of development', 440.

In terms of real GNP per capita, the UK has led since the early nineteenth century, shadowed at a respectful but not enormous distance by Belgium. Until 1900 the third place was taken by the Netherlands, when it was marginally overtaken by Germany, and with France very close behind that. Crafts concludes, having assembled the data, that economic growth was a general European phenomenon in the nineteenth century, by no means confined to Britain and its industrial understudy, Belgium. Growth accelerated in the period 1870 to 1914, but steady advances before that were also booked. The Netherlands, says Crafts laconically, 'may be in some need of rehabilitation' – though to be fair the picture is not wildly different from the one which emerged from Bairoch's data a decade previously, except that Bairoch actually placed the Netherlands at the top, above the UK, in 1830.[15] On the basis of Crafts' data, the Netherlands was the third, after the UK and Belgium, to reach the threshold of $550 per capita, and the fifth to reach $900. Certainly the '"glamorous" cases of industrialization', like the UK and Belgium, had no monopoly of per-capita growth in product or income.[16]

[15] Bairoch, 'Europe's gross national product'. See also Maddison, *Dynamic forces*, which puts a special focus on the Netherlands, and places it high in the rankings since the early nineteenth century.
[16] Crafts, 'GNP in Europe', 397–8; Crafts, 'Patterns of development', 446–7.

Another set of data on GNP, based on Maddison's estimates and the early results of the Dutch national accounting project, presents a similar picture. After 1850, the Dutch were in third place or thereabouts in Europe, and maintained growth rates per capita much in tune with the other main rivals. Before 1850, Dutch growth was less competitive, and whereas (according to this set of figures) around 1800 Dutch GNP per capita was well in excess of the UK's ($548 as opposed to $493 in 1805, in 1970 $US), the Netherlands had been overtaken by the UK and by Belgium by 1850.[17]

So the Dutch economy was a world leader by the middle of the seventeenth century, and has remained in that class ever since. By 1700 large parts of the west of the country were already capitalized, agricultural processing economies, importing their staple foods from elsewhere, like the Baltic, and using their land instead to produce labour- and capital-intensive cash crops for a national and international market.[18] At the same time, the trading and shipping sector was legendary – decimated by the French occupation, the British blockade and the Continental System, it is true, but still a tradition and basis on which to build – together with the possession of a vast colonial empire in the East and West Indies.[19] And linked to that trade there was a traffic industry sector, importing raw materials, performing skilled processes on them of high added value, and re-exporting them in finished or more finished form. The Dutch economy, it seemed, had it all.[20]

3.2   Industrialization and the Dutch debate

And yet, there was no classic 'industrialization'. At best it was weak, and late. This issue has obsessed Dutch economic historiography since the War, and for a time the matter became blown out of proportion. The Netherlands may have been extremely wealthy, but what it did not have, and never had, was a Manchester, a Ghent, a Liège or a Birmingham. There had been no 'Industrial Revolution' to speak of, only false starts and disappointments. Not only could the Dutch not compete in this

---

[17] Van Zanden, 'Economische groei', 68–9. For the debate on Dutch national accounting in the nineteenth century to date, the main works also include: Van Stuijvenberg and De Vrijer, 'Prices'; Van Stuijvenberg, 'Economische groei', 72–4; Derksen, 'De groei'; Boissevain, 'De omvang'; Rijken van Olst, 'De ontwikkeling'; Bos, 'Economic growth'; Teijl, 'Nationaal inkomen'; De Meere, 'Long-term trends'; Blok and De Meere, 'Welstand'; Griffiths, *Achterlijk?*; Bos, *Brits-Nederlandse handel*.
[18] The classic study is De Vries, *The Dutch rural economy*.
[19] Some East Indies shipping survived, but not a great deal: Eyck van Heslinga, *Van compagnie naar koopvaardij*.
[20] Van Zanden, *De industrialisatie in Amsterdam*, 11.

respect with the British, but, most galling of all, neither could they do so with the Belgians, who had actually been part of the United Kingdom of the Netherlands as Dutch subjects from 1815 to the time of the Belgian Revolution against the Dutch in 1830. They had gone on to experience a quintessential Industrial Revolution, the first on the Continent of Europe and second only to Great Britain in the world. Just as historians collected complimentary remarks made by foreigners about the Dutch Republic,[21] they took a morbid fascination in the remarks made about stagnation in the nineteenth century, especially during the decade of the 1840s, when the country was held to be 'an impoverished and in some respects demoralized nation'.[22] The leading historians of the day of both young and old generations talked in terms of 'a stagnant pond' (Brugmans),[23] or of 'backward production methods . . . [in] an Asian-type country' (Van Tijn).[24] In the last decade or so the profession has come round to the view that industry-led development is not the only kind of development, and, as the national product figures show, the Dutch fared very well without any pronounced list to the side of manufacturing.[25] The regret and guilt has now left the tone of historical writing, but even now the question remains; why did manufacturing industry play such a modest part in the highly successful Dutch economic experience?

A modest manufacturing sector

There was of course a certain amount of manufacturing industry in the Netherlands throughout the nineteenth century, and certain specific parts of it were dazzlingly successful. The food-processing industries, linked for instance to colonial products (especially sugar-refining in Amsterdam),[26] or to dairy products later on, were veritable models of how to expand and modernize an industry over time. The cotton textile industry in the Twente region of the country, sheltered until the mid-century by a protective colonial regime in need of outward-bound freight, saw enormous expansion of production, full mechanization, huge profits (25 per cent p.a.), aggressive marketing, new outlets and diversification.[27]

---

[21] The classic example is Swart, *The miracle.*
[22] Van den Bosch, *et al.*, 'Rapport', 36; my translation. For foreign comments, see for example an Englishman, in 1842: Laing, *Notes of a traveller*, 6–25. However, by no means *all* such accounts were negative: for foreign views of Dutch agriculture, see Wintle, 'Modest growth', 19–20.
[23] Brugmans, 'Nederlands overgang', 79.
[24] Van Houtte, *et al.*, eds., *Algemene geschiedenis der Nederlanden*, vol. X, p. 295.
[25] For example, a summary of the historiographical debate: Van Zanden, 'Industrialization in the Netherlands'. See also Horlings, *The economic development*, 28–37.
[26] Van Zanden, *The rise and decline*, chapter 8.
[27] See the flagship example of the S. J. Spaniaard company of Borne, documented in Fischer, *Fabriqueurs en fabrikanten*; and Fischer and De Peuter, 'Winstontwikkeling'.

Nonetheless, the sector was not large compared to typical industrializing nations. The occupational census figures, displayed in Table II.2, show that in 1849 the Netherlands had less than a fifth of its workforce in manufacturing, as opposed to nearly a third in Belgium; even by 1909 the Netherlands still only managed a quarter.[28] Looking further afield, taking the occupation census figures for a wide range of developed countries between 1880 and 1910, on this yardstick the Netherlands puts in a moderate but not distinguished performance: she has higher scores for industry than Austria, Norway, Sweden and the United States, but the 'secondarization of the workforce' was well behind that reached in the UK, Belgium, Germany, Switzerland, Australia or New Zealand.[29] Other measures which give us some indication of the degree of capitalization, mechanization, efficiency and productivity of Dutch industry are statistically problematic, but they are not encouraging. Looking at the size of firms, for example, in 1825 96 per cent of skilled workers were located in firms with no more than ten employees; by 1889 this had dropped only to 75 per cent, though by 1909 it was down to a more respectable 55 per cent.[30] There was only modest mechanization in the form of steam engines, and but a small coal import surplus until the end of the century.[31] There was, then, an industrial sector, but no 'glamorous' industrialization (Crafts' term) and certainly no Industrial Revolution.

Timing and take-off

Some time and energy have been spent trying to locate a 'take-off' point in Dutch economic development, and a number of attempts have been made to apply a Rostovian developmental model to the Dutch scenario. Rostow's 'take-off' or third stage is a short period of no more than thirty years, during which modern economic growth becomes more or less self-sustaining. Its conditions are an increase in investment from less than 5 per cent to more than 10 per cent of national income, major advances in production in one or two manufacturing industries, and socio-political changes in support of the economic growth. Rostow located this stage for Britain in the period 1783–1802, for France in 1830–60, for the United States in 1843–60, for Germany in 1850–73, for Japan in 1878–1900, and for Russia in 1890–1914.[32] For Belgium the 1830s was the critical decade. Using various statistical measures, Dutch historians struggled to date the Dutch version of take-off, and not surprisingly there was a wide

---

[28] For further analysis of the occupation figures, see chapter 6 below.
[29] Schiff, *Industrialization*, 29–32.
[30] Van Tijn, 'De negentiende eeuw', 238 and 251; and 'De industrie', 64.
[31] See below, section 5.2, on technological advances.
[32] Rostow, 'Rostow on growth', 411–13.

Table II.2. Sectoral distribution of the economically active population in the Netherlands (and Belgium), 1807–1971.

The Netherlands, percentages and absolute figures

Sector	1807	1849	1859	1889	1899	1909	1920	1930	1947	1960	1971
Agric./fish. %	42.8	43.8	37.5	32.9	30.8	28.3	23.6	20.6	19.2	10.7	6.3
× 1,000	375	552	468	541	592	640	641	656	747	447	288
Extraction %	0.2	0.2	0.2	0.9	0.8	1.0	1.7	1.6	1.4	1.5	0.4
× 1,000	2	2	2	15	16	23	45	50	54	61	20
Manufact. %	19.1	19.0	20.7	22.5	24.0	24.9	27.2	26.9	27.9	131.9	25.9
× 1,000	168	239	258	370	461	563	738	855	1,082	1,329	1,192
Building %	6.6	4.8	5.4	6.9	6.8	6.8	6.8	8.0	7.4	9.1	11.4
× 1,000	58	60	67	113	130	154	185	254	289	379	523
Trade/finance %	7.2	6.4	6.7	9.3	11.4	11.9	12.8	14.8	14.2	16.1	23.3
× 1,000	63	81	84	153	219	269	348	472	550	670	1,073
Transport %	4.5	4.5	5.5	6.8	5.5	7.0	8.0	7.5	6.6	7.0	6.1
× 1,000	39	57	69	112	106	158	218	240	257	291	280
Other services %	18.9	17.9	21.5	19.3	18.9	19.0	18.9	19.5	21.4	21.5	22.0
× 1,000	165	226	268	317	363	428	513	621	831	897	1,011
Other %	0.7	2.8	2.6	1.5	1.8	1.0	1.1	1.0	1.4	2.3	7.5
× 1,000	6	34	32	25	34	23	30	33	56	96	346
Total workforce × 1,000	876	1,261	1,249	1,646	1,921	2,258	2,718	3,181	3,884	4,170	4,605
Total population × 1,000	2,163	3,057	3,309	4,511	5,104	5,858	6,865	7,936	9,625	11,462	12,709
Participation rate %	40.5	41.2	37.7	36.5	37.6	38.5	39.6	40.1	40.4	36.4	36.2

Belgium, percentages

Sector	1846	1890	1910	1947
Agric./fish.	50.9	32.0	23.9	12.4
Extraction	2.4	4.9	6.0	5.6
Manufact.	31.8	30.4	35.4	37.7
Building	2.0	3.3	5.6	5.3
Trade/finance	3.4	11.1	8.7	14.2
Transport	0.8	1.5	5.7	7.3
Other services	8.7	16.8	17.8	17.5
Other	0	0	0	0.2

Sources: Mitchell, *European historical statistics*, 51 and 57; and for 1807, Horlings, *Economic development of the Dutch service sector*, 333.

spectrum of estimates.[33] The authoritative research was undertaken by J. A. de Jonge, and published in his dissertation in 1968, which was an exacting quantitative analysis of the manufacturing sector from 1850 to 1914.[34] He calculated that Rostow's investment coefficient criterion was reached between 1880 and 1914, but that there was no Dutch version of the Rostovian strategic 'leading sector' industry.[35] Subsequent historians have tended to fall into line with this analysis, agreeing that there was no explosive Rostovian take-off, and no Rostovian leading sector, but that industrial production and sophistication increased towards the end of the century, concentrating in the decade of the 1890s, when the Dutch were fully able to take advantage of the world trade boom.[36] However, even by the time of the First World War, despite the emergence of a few 'niche' industries which were later destined to become mighty multinationals, the Netherlands could hardly be called 'industrialized' in the sense that Britain, Belgium and Germany were. It was a developed and wealthy economy, with an industrial sector which was respectable, but modest.

This account, partly in the form of a historiographical introduction to the debate on economic growth and industrialization, has indicated where the critical issues lie. First, there is the pattern and timing of development: we know that the Dutch Republic was prosperous in the seventeenth century, and that the Kingdom of the Netherlands has been prosperous in the twentieth century. What was then the pathway, shrouded in the age of questionable statistics, which connected those two high-points, and how did it affect the Dutch experience of industrialization? Second, were there any particular weaknesses or strengths of the economy? What of agriculture, and most particularly, what was the role of the service sector in Dutch development? These issues underpin the Dutch experience, but they can also cast light more generally on typologies of 'industrialization' and economic development.

3.3   Between two peaks? Transition from the Golden Age to the EEC

On the first point, the pathway leading from the economic glories of the mid-seventeenth century to the mid-nineteenth century, there has traditionally been considerable speculation.[37] The debate centres on the prog-

---

[33] A good summary is provided by Van Stuijvenberg, 'Economische groei', 59–62 and 72–4.
[34] De Jonge, *De industrialisatie*.
[35] De Jonge, *De industrialisatie*, chapter 17; also reproduced as De Jonge, 'De industriele ontwikkeling', especially pp. 76–83.
[36] E.g., Nusteling, *De Rijnvaart*, 401–4; and De Vries, 'Economische groei', 125–6.
[37] For an account, see, e.g., Van Zanden, 'The Dutch economy'.

ress of the Dutch economy in the first half of the nineteenth century, which has generally been seen as moribund – witness the apocryphal quotation attributed to Heinrich Heine, to the effect that, if anything happened to the world he would go to the Netherlands, because it was fifty years behind everywhere else, which sums up the traditional historiography on that period. At the same time, a similar view is generally held of the eighteenth century: one of decline, or at least stagnation. Much is confused by the use of Gregory King's estimates, in about 1690, of Dutch national income at about half the level reached by 1850;[38] this means that, despite the generally agreed stagnation between 1670 and 1850, national income per capita managed to double.[39] The issue remains important because the evident stagnation of the economy for at least a large part of the period 1670–1850 was succeeded by growth rates which were amongst and parallel with the highest in the world: what took place to galvanize the Dutch economy out of stagnation (albeit at a relatively high level) into break-neck growth? In order to answer that question, we need to know where to look, which is why we need to know when the growth started.

Traditionally, historians had not even bothered to look before 1850, but around 1980 Richard Griffiths and others set out to prove – quite convincingly at the time – that there was healthy economic development between 1830 and 1850, and quite possibly before that;[40] he received support from Jan de Vries, who posited that there must have been major growth in the first half of the nineteenth century, because the economy had not only stagnated from 1675 to 1813, but actually declined or contracted, for the most part before 1750.[41] Recent work by De Vries and Van de Woude posits decline to 1815, and then real per-capita growth from 1815 again, and England drawing level with the Republic around 1790.[42] Thanks to the work of the national accounts team, we now have a much clearer picture of the development of the economy in that crucial period of the first half of the nineteenth century. Provisional figures indicate that the traditional picture holds true, of negligible growth from 1800 to 1850, which implies of course that Dutch per-capita income was far in advance of that of all other countries in 1800, unless all those other economies, including Britain's, were stagnating as well.[43] It would also indicate that we should be looking for triggers of sudden but sustained

[38] Bos, 'Economic growth', 3–4; De Vries, 'The decline and rise', 155–8.
[39] De Vries, 'The decline and rise', 168; Riley, 'The Dutch economy'.
[40] Griffiths, *Industrial retardation*; Griffiths, *Achterlijk?*
[41] De Vries, 'Barges and capitalism'; De Vries, 'The decline and rise', 167–79; Brinkman, *et al.*, 'Lichaamslengte', 70.
[42] De Vries and Van der Woude, *Nederland 1500–1815*, 810–18.
[43] Van Zanden, 'Economische groei', 68–9; Van Zanden, 'The Dutch economy', 271.

growth around the time of the 1840s and 1850s. Two suggest themselves. One is the raft of economic policies brought in by liberals of one type or another in most developed countries in the decades after the 1840s, of which indeed a fine example is provided by the Dutch liberal victors of the 1848 constitutional revision, led by Johan Rudolf Thorbecke (1798–1872). The other is the Dutch colonial empire, which just at this time began earning huge sums of money for the home economy, first for its government through the infamous Cultivation System, and then after the 1860s in privatized form for most of the entrepreneurial and capitalist part of the Dutch population.[44] These are traditional kinds of explanations of growth, and and they seem to have been vindicated by the findings of the Utrecht group; however, the work of Griffiths, De Vries *et al.* has shown that there was certainly a degree of dynamism in the Dutch economy several decades before the mid-century.

Finally, another way of approaching the same problem is to attempt to establish the general economic climate or prevailing economic situation at various periods since about 1800. For general purposes before 1900 in the Netherlands, grain prices are as effective an indicator as any other, and there are a number of primary printed sources we can draw on, as well as some modern re-computations.[45] Figure I.7 shows wheat prices at Arnhem for the nineteenth century in nine-year moving averages, while Figure I.6 shows the evolution of the prices of a range of separate agricultural products for the same period. On this basis, and without too much attention to the exact timing of the turning points in the business cycle, the general pattern of development in the Dutch agricultural economy as shown in the graphs, and the pattern of economic circumstances in general both in the Netherlands and in Europe as a whole, was as follows.[46]

The French Wars at the beginning of the nineteenth century caused dislocation and shortages (with fat profits for anyone with anything to sell, like the farmers in Groningen),[47] the second quarter of the nineteenth century was one of painful recovery, the third quarter was boom time, and the final one was slump until the very last years of the century. Then a further boom led into World War I, which was an immensely successful period for the Dutch economy, and the 1920s were a resound-

---

[44] See below, section 5.3 on economic policy and section 7.2 on the colonies.
[45] The classic contemporary series include one recorded in the town of Arnhem, used in Brugmans, 'Economic fluctuations', 152; and also *Overzicht van marktprijzen*. A series estimating the value of the Dutch harvest from 1851 to 1895 was printed in *Verslag van den Landbouw* (1894–5), 129, and it follows the Kondratieff line precisely. Series compiled by modern scholars include Van Zanden, *De economische ontwikkeling*, 110; Knibbe, *Agriculture*; and Pilat, *Dutch agricultural export*.
[46] Wintle, 'Modest growth', 21.   [47] Paping, '*Voor een handvol stuivers*', 216.

ing continuation of the same.[48] (Depression characterized the 1930s, and war the 1940s; the third quarter of the twentieth century has been the biggest boom the world has ever known. Since the mid-1970s problems have beset the entrepreneur, but more recently things are looking up.) It is quite remarkable to observe, in this admittedly superficial summary, the similarity in the patterns of the two centuries under review.

Especially in the nineteenth century, this was a cycle which affected the fortunes of entrepreneurs (including small ones) within a general economic scenario. Life for most people was always hard, and the trends in health and the standard of living did not always follow the long-term business cycle.[49] But as a set of background circumstances in agriculture and other sectors like trade and manufacturing, especially for an open trading economy like the Netherlands, the picture is unequivocal.

3.4   Conclusion

In the journey between the prosperity peaks of the seventeenth and twentieth centuries, the evidence from the national accounts project suggests that the turning point came around 1850, so that triggers for sustained growth should be sought in that period. The importance of the long-term international business cycle for the Netherlands has been noted, with structural depressions characterizing the 1830s and 1880s, and booms in the 1860s and 1900s. In these terms it is logical to look in the 1840s and 1850s for a transition to modern economic growth which was able to survive the setbacks of the last quarter of the century and ride the recurring *hausse* from the mid-1890s onwards. Armed with this knowledge of the tilt of the playing field, we may now progress to examine the various aspects of the economy in the Netherlands in more detail.

---

[48] Van Zanden, *The economic history*, 93–105.
[49] See section 7.4, below.

4   Factor inputs: labour, capital, materials

4.1   Introduction

We now move to an analysis of the inputs to the Dutch economy, over the course of the next two chapters. The inputs to the economy are divided as follows. In chapter 4, we deal with the traditional tripartite separation between labour, capital and materials. In looking at labour we shall examine the changing size of the Dutch labour force, its skills, its cost, and regional variations in that cost. Under capital we shall concentrate on financial capital, and take as a point of departure the traditional argument that Dutch industry was starved of funds in the nineteenth century. It will then be possible to arrive at a conclusion on the role played by the factor capital, in all its aspects, in the economic development of the country. At the end of chapter 4, we shift attention to materials, a category which includes land, minerals, and particularly energy sources, as well as other raw materials.

Chapter 5 contains an account and analysis of a number of other influences on the supply side of the economy, to do with what early economists called the 'organization' of the prime factors dealt with in chapter 4. Some of these organizational influences are now sometimes referred to as 'residuals', and they have to do with the efficiency and organization of the economy. We have isolated three categories for the purposes of inventory and analysis: entrepreneurship, technology and government policy. These categories are indispensable in the analysis of the fortunes and dynamics of the Dutch economy in the nineteenth century. A number of standard explanations of Dutch performance form the starting point of the investigation; for instance, that Dutch entrepreneurs were inadequate coupon-clippers unable to meet the challenges of industrialization, that Dutch technology was backward, and that government policy was wanting, especially before the mid-century. The framework provided by these arguments is not slavishly adhered to: they are but an entry point into laying out what precisely occurred in these aspects of the economy, and producing a balanced account of the relative and collective importance of the various inputs and influences.

4.2   The factor labour

Table II.2 gives figures for the registered and waged economically active population in the Netherlands, and its sectoral distribution. Here we shall consider the dynamics of the labour force as a whole; its sectoral distribution will be discussed in a later chapter.[1] The series covers the years 1849 to 1971, and is calculated from census data; the 1807 figures are added from the recent work of Edwin Horlings,[2] and some sectoral distribution figures for Belgium are supplied to facilitate international comparison. There are any number of difficulties in working with such figures, for they tend systematically to underestimate the participation of women (and children) in the labour force, the sectoral divisions present serious problems of classification, and unpaid work or work paid in kind are often ignored. As the nineteenth century progressed, many children withdrew from the labour force because of education, and eventually the older generation did too, as pensions were introduced. Conscription could distort the impression given by occupational census figures.[3] However, they have the advantages of being based on data collected by contemporaries at the time for the purpose we share (analysis of the workforce), and of giving some degree of international comparability. It is therefore possible to derive certain important conclusions from the data as they stand.

The growth of the labour force

The registered working population increased roughly in line with the population as a whole. As became clear in chapter 1, the Dutch population increased very rapidly indeed, especially after 1870, and thus so did its labour force.[4] However, there are some nuances to be observed. Despite a substantial increase between 1807 and 1849 (by 44 per cent in forty-two years), the interval between the censuses of 1849 and 1859 witnessed negative growth in the Dutch labour force (a decline of 12,000 persons or 1 per cent in ten years), at a time when the population as a whole continued to grow by 8 per cent in the decade.[5] Certainly the early

---

[1] Section 6.1 below.
[2] Horlings, *The economic development*, 333.
[3] On these methodological issues, see Armstrong, 'The use'; and on the Netherlands in particular, Smits, 'The size and structure', 84–5. On conscription's effects, see Lucassen and Zürcher, 'Conscription', 405–6.
[4] See Table I.1, and the commentary above in section 1.1.
[5] There may well have been some deficiencies in the 1849 data.

1850s must have been a difficult time for working people, following hard on the heels of the 1840s, with its crop failures, food shortages and waves of emigration. Otherwise, however, the rise in the labour force kept pace with the very rapid rise in population. The participation rate, or the percentage of the total population registered in the workforce, hovered around 40 per cent (Table II.2). In the 1850s it dropped from 41.2 to 37.7 per cent, and further to 36.5 in 1889, but then recovered gently to 40.1 per cent in 1930. (Later in the twentieth century the 'greying' of the Dutch population was beginning to show itself by 1971, with the participation rate having fallen to 36.2 per cent.)

Given these rapid rates of growth in the registered labour force, no structural labour shortages seem to have occurred in the economy as a whole. Indeed, in his study of the labour market in Amsterdam in the second half of the nineteenth century, Ad Knotter concluded that there was an oversupply of labour in all sectors,[6] which accords with the generally high rates of people on poor relief. This is particularly remarkable in view of the extreme shortage of domestic labour during the heyday of the Republic, as evidenced by the abundant presence of foreign labour in the United Provinces.[7] However, there must have been imbalances, or more particularly shortages, on a local basis, in certain sectors, and from time to time. A recent study has identified a shortage of labour after 1865 in agriculture, which lost significant amounts of labour to the burgeoning manufacturing sector; the replenishment of the fertility of the soil with animal manure was very labour intensive, and therefore the productivity of agriculture suffered, with the result that the sector languished until the early 1880s.[8] However, such local and temporary (or even seasonal) labour shortages could often be resolved by import from elsewhere, especially in a port-metropolis like Amsterdam. Indeed, it has been argued that certainly until 1850 the Netherlands remained in many ways a merchant capitalist economy, which thrived by being able to use very cheap labour; where that did not exist in the home economy, it was either imported from elsewhere, or employed elsewhere and its fruits imported.[9] In the case of the economy of the metropolitan provinces of Holland,[10]

[6] Knotter, *Economische transformatie*, 252 and *passim*.
[7] Lucassen, 'Labour and early modern economic development'; and Lucassen, 'The Netherlands, the Dutch'.
[8] Knibbe, *Agriculture*, 133–4.
[9] Van Zanden, *The rise and decline*, especially chapters 1 and 7; and Van Zanden, *De economische ontwikkeling*.
[10] A note on 'Holland': in the Middle Ages and the period up to the Batavian Republic of 1798, Holland was a county and then a province, with considerable autonomy. It was the dominant region in population, economics and politics of the federal state of the Dutch Republic. For this reason 'Holland' and 'the Netherlands' were (and are) often confused, though the former was actually only one small part of the latter. In 1814 Holland became

this mechanism was effected well into the nineteenth century (though rapidly decreasing) by the use of immigrant labour, forced labour in the East Indies, slave labour in the West Indies and subsidized labour in proto-industry (where the cost of industrial labour was met partly from agriculture), and by seasonal migrant labour which flooded into the North Sea coastal area to work in a variety of sectors right up to the close of the nineteenth century.[11] As a result, despite occasional bottlenecks, the labour market did not suffer from shortages, owing to the rapidly rising domestic population and the harnessing of various kinds of affordable labour from elsewhere.

The quality of labour

If labour was generally available, there remains the question of its quality. Dutch historians used to be much concerned with the economic effects of mentality and social attitude, and contemporary Dutch accounts were certainly full of abusive remarks about the lazy, drunk, immoral and feeble workers. However, contemporary accounts of the lower classes in any country written in the early nineteenth century by the upper classes are likely to have been derogatory, and indeed many such accounts still are today. Is there any evidence that the Dutch workforce was deficient in quality? It is certainly true that the Dutch suffered from appalling mortality levels until after the 1870s, mainly because of the contaminated water supply,[12] and endemic disease may have reduced the physical strength of the workforce. This may have had its economic ill-effects, especially in agriculture on the sea-clay soils, where the work was particularly heavy and physically demanding. Furthermore, the consumption of liquor was substantial until the end of the century, by which time the Dutch bourgeois civilization offensives were getting the better of the demon drink, at least for a while.[13] It is, however, hard to establish that these things were worse in their effects in the Netherlands than elsewhere. Low nutrition levels seem not to have affected labour output unduly.[14] In a more positive sense, the education level of Dutch workers was quite high when internationally compared,[15] and any drunkenness was probably a symptom of un- and underemployment rather than a cause.

a single province of the new Kingdom of the Netherlands under Willem I, and at the constitutional revision of 1840 it was split into Noord-Holland and Zuid-Holland. The two provinces have continued to dominate the country, and so the identification and confusion between provinces and country persists, especially among foreigners. 'Holland' is used in this book only to refer to the provinces.

[11] Van Zanden, *The rise and decline*; and Lucassen, *Migrant labour*.
[12] See above, section 1.2.   [13] See above, section 2.5.
[14] De Beer, 'Voeding'.   [15] See below, section 10.2, on education.

The cost of labour: nominal wages

And what of the cost of labour? If labour was freely available and quite well educated, what of the price which an entrepreneur had to pay for it? There is little doubt that in many areas, and certainly in the first half of the nineteenth century, Dutch labour was expensive: it was the contention of Joel Mokyr that the price of labour was the most significant differential between the industrial performances of Belgium and the Netherlands before 1850. The adequate supply of labour, then, had not resulted in making it cheap. Wages had been high in the eighteenth century,[16] there were still complaints of the same in about 1800,[17] and they remained at the same level for the first half of the century, indeed until the 1860s.[18] In agriculture in the coastal provinces, but also in industry across the country and in Leiden in particular, inland in Overijssel, and elsewhere, the evidence we have is of rigidity in nominal wage rates before 1850.[19]

Research into wage levels is still in progress in the Netherlands, but the overall picture is emerging with some clarity now. Van Zanden's research into the agricultural economy – which after all concerned about half of the populace – found that nominal wages did indeed stagnate or even decline slightly from 1810 to 1850; his findings are produced in Table II.3. Between 1850 and 1880 there was a rise in nominal wages of some 50 per cent, which then doubled to more than 100 per cent by 1910.[20] (The implications of that nominal rise on *real* wage levels we shall examine in chapter 7.) Research into industrial wages from 1850 to 1913 shows that they also grew steadily in value, by something approaching 100 per cent, with rather slow progress in the 1850s and 1860s, rapid escalation in the 1870s (2.3 per cent p.a.), a slump towards stagnation in the 1880s (0.3 per cent p.a.), succeeded by healthy rises from 1890 onwards (about 1 per cent p.a.).[21] Local circumstances will certainly have caused variations, but, in the economy as a whole, nominal wages did very little at all until 1850, and then rose gradually, with spurts in the 1870s and after 1890. The critical question is, however, whether Dutch rates were higher than those current in neighbouring (and competing) countries.

---

[16] Carter, *The Dutch Republic*, 131.   [17] Wright, *Free trade*, 78–9.
[18] Ridder, *Een conjunctuur-analyse*, 195, reports wage stability in the 1850s as well.
[19] For the Wilhelminapolder model farm in Zeeland, Kuperus, 'Honderd jaar', 135; in agriculture on the sea clays, Van Zanden, *De economische ontwikkeling*, 209; in agriculture generally, Van der Wielen, 'Sociale toestanden', 433; in Overijssel, Slicher van Bath, *Een samenleving*, 605; in industry in various towns, Kint, 'Industriële lonen'; and in Leiden, Pot, *Arm Leiden*.
[20] Van Zanden, *De economische ontwikkeling*, 117.
[21] Burger and Vermaas, 'Dutch industrial wage', 114–15.

Table II.3. *Wages in agriculture. Estimates of average daily wage (summer) in Dutch agriculture (1810–1910), in cents.*

	Cents				Indices (1810 = 100)			
	1810	1850	1880	1910	1810	1850	1880	1910
Drenthe	60	60	93	126	100	100	155	210
Overijssel	54	54	81	141	100	100	150	262
Gelderland	48	48	80	124	100	100	167	259
N-Brabant	57	50	83	136	100	88	146	238
Limburg	49	49	83	136	100	100	169	277
Groningen	65	79	110	143	100	122	169	220
Friesland	82	70	100	151	100	86	122	185
Zeeland	86	65	100	142	100	75	116	165
Utrecht	75	75	100	139	100	100	133	185
Z-Holland	88	88	125	165	100	100	142	187
N-Holland	80	80	136	187	100	100	170	234
Netherlands	65	62	97	145	100	96	149	222

Source: Van Zanden, *De economische ontwikkeling*, 117.

In the Republic, right up to the 1790s, Dutch labour was nominally more expensive than in Flanders and Germany, though not in comparison with England: English wages had overtaken their Dutch equivalents around 1750. The wages in the Holland area were considerably higher than those inland, in the eastern part of the Netherlands. The wage levels in Holland had been high throughout the eighteenth century; their rapid rise had occurred long before, in the heyday of the Golden Age economy, before 1670.[22] During the first half of the nineteenth century the Dutch rates continued to exceed those of her neighbours, with the exception of England; in 1850 that was still the case, with the differentials between the Netherlands and her continental neighbours being quite small, and only England way out in front. The low growth in wage rates in the Netherlands between 1850 and 1870, compared to rates in France, Germany and Belgium, meant that by 1870 the Netherlands was no longer a high-wage economy, and the price of her labour was reasonable by international standards (it had long been cheap compared to England).[23] If there was a problem with wages, then, it was eroded by 1870 and not very substantial after 1850. What caused the Dutch wages to be high in comparison with elsewhere before the mid-century, and how damaging was it to the economy?

[22] De Vries and Van der Woude, *Nederland 1500–1815*, 707 and 710.
[23] Burger and Vermaas, 'Dutch industrial wage', 114 and 127.

Regional wage differentials

In order to answer that question, notice needs to be taken of the regional variance in nominal wages, even in such a small country. The figures produced by Van Zanden for agricultural wages, reproduced in Table II.3, display a wide range of local differentiation, from 48 cents a day for summer work in 1810 in Gelderland, up to 88 in Zuid-Holland; the range was still present a century later in 1910, with 124 cents paid in Gelderland, 165 in Zuid-Holland, and as much as 187 in Noord-Holland.[24] The same wide variance in the price of labour in farming was observed in a survey of 1800 (10 stuivers a day in Gelderland; 1 or 2 guilders of 20 stuivers each in Zeeland), and the cost of labour varied considerably in industry as well.[25] The differential between the maritime and landward provinces had increasingly been a feature of the eighteenth-century Republic,[26] and a report published as late as 1951 on regional differences in the country showed clearly that although the gap had been narrowed, there was still even then no question of a national wage.[27] In many ways the critical phase was in the early nineteenth century, when the Netherlands remained 'unindustrialized' compared to her neighbours, and in 1819 there was a survey of industry carried out which provides us with a clear picture of the differences across the country in nominal wages, recalculated by Richard Griffiths[28] and shown in Figure II.2. It demonstrates that while adults worked in industry for around 60 cents a day in the inland provinces of Noord-Brabant, Limburg, Gelderland, Overijssel and Drenthe, their counterparts in the maritime provinces were paid around 70 or 80 cents, with those in Noord-Holland receiving almost 110 cents a day. Thus high wages were indeed an issue in the Netherlands, but only in certain parts of the country (the coastal provinces). Why was labour so expensive in those areas?

Explanations for and effects of high wages

Industrial wages were high in the west of the Netherlands because of high taxes – particularly local excises – which in turn were necessary to service the enormous national and municipal debts incurred in the eighteenth century by financing other people's wars, and to pay for the

---

[24] Van Zanden, *De economische ontwikkeling*, 177; and Table II.3.
[25] Van Nierop, 'Een enquête', 105 and 317.
[26] De Vries, 'Regional economic inequality', 190–3.
[27] *Het vraagstuk der gemeente-classificatie*, especially Chapter 5, entitled, 'Opmerkingen aangaande de historische ontwikkeling der regionale loonverschillen', apparently by E.W. Hofstee.
[28] Griffiths, *Industrial retardation*, 57.

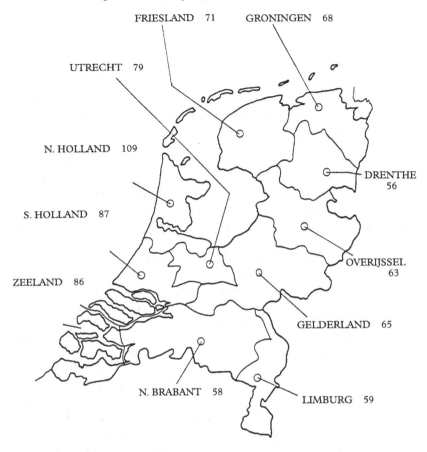

FRIESLAND 71 GRONINGEN 68

UTRECHT 79

N. HOLLAND 109

DRENTHE 56

S. HOLLAND 87

OVERIJSSEL 63

ZEELAND 86

GELDERLAND 65

N. BRABANT 58 LIMBURG 59

Figure II.2 Estimates of average daily adult wage (cents), 1819.

Source: Griffiths, *Industrial retardation*, 57.

relatively generous systems of poor relief which operated in the Netherlands. In addition they were high because the opportunity costs were
high, in Dutch agriculture and trade, both of which had been very
productive of labour since the early seventeenth century, allowing higher
wage levels.[29] In the coastal provinces the municipal debts and the taxes
to service them were higher, and in agriculture there the productivity of
the clay soil was far greater than that of the inland sand, which allowed

[29] Griffiths, 'The role of taxation'; Mokyr, 'Capital, labor', 287–94; and Griffiths, *Industrial
retardation*, 57–62.

higher nominal rewards for labour in the west.[30] On the other hand, it is not the case that *real* wages differed very much, or that the workers in the west enjoyed a better life than those in the east: local taxes and other costs, especially on bread, meant that the regional wage differences were eroded in real terms.[31]

In summary, labour was plentiful from domestic and other supplies, and was relatively well educated, but was expensive, especially in the western provinces before 1850. The reason for the high wages was not high incomes which might have generated domestic demand, but a higher cost of living.[32] Wage levels in the west had been high since the seventeenth century, so it was by no means a new phenomenon; since 1750 the level of British wages had been much higher than in the Netherlands, remaining so throughout the nineteenth century, so that was nothing new either. Nonetheless, before 1850 entrepreneurs could hardly be blamed, all other things being equal, for taking their business to Belgium, France or Germany (if indeed they did so): labour was cheaper there, though the differences were probably modest.

There has been some criticism of the wages argument, on the grounds that wages varied considerably from town to town, and fluctuated wildly, and that the cost of labour was in any case not always the main concern of the industrialist.[33] Concerning the period when Dutch wage levels were relatively high, it would be anachronistic to talk of a single market for labour, let alone a perfect one. Before 1850, and to some extent thereafter, there was a series of micro-economies, between which there was anything but an unimpeded flow of labour or entrepreneurs: transport and information systems were simply not efficient enough to permit that.[34] Research continues into wage levels, and it may yet modify our view of the importance of the price of labour to Dutch economic development. For now, though, despite continual challenges and discussions, the argument first launched by Mokyr and Griffiths, to the effect that expen-

---

[30] A technical economic study, Van Zanden, 'Regionale verschillen', concludes that in agriculture wage levels were determined by productivity, which was in turn determined by the fertility of the soil and the amount of capital (i.e. land and cattle) invested in each worker (Van Zanden also concludes that local poverty levels were irrelevant); this confirms the opinion of Hofstee expressed more than forty years previously, who put down regional wage differences mainly to soil differences: *Het vraagstuk der gemeenteclassificatie*, chapter 5, pp. 30–4.

[31] Van Zanden, 'Kosten van levensonderhoud'; translated as Van Zanden, *The rise and decline*, chapter 7. One of the reasons for the high cost of bread in the coastal areas was the restrictive practices of the bakers' organizations.

[32] See below, section 7.4.

[33] E.g. Kint and Van der Voort, 'Economische groei'; and Myrdal, *Economic theory*, 30–1.

[34] Van Zanden, 'Regionale verschillen', 284.

sive labour, amongst other things, made western parts of the Netherlands an unattractive location for modern industry before 1850, has stood the test of time. We move now to look at the significance of a second factor input into the Dutch economy: capital.

4.3   The factor capital

Capital is undoubtedly central to economic growth and development in 'capitalist' economies, but it is not clear exactly *how* important. It is difficult to demonstrate a close relation between growth rates and levels of capital formation, although efficient capital markets are clearly helpful, and investment has usually risen before periods of growth spurts.[35] This is one of the central tenets in the growth theory of W. W. Rostow, whose principal instrument for detecting modern economic growth was, as we have seen, the investment coefficient; the main reason for the importance of financial capital is its role in financing new technology and its application, upon which much of modern economic growth is based. However, the issue is fraught with problems: an adequate supply or presence of capital in an area does not mean that it will be applied to technology in industry or to the furthering of economic growth at all. And capital markets in Europe in the nineteenth century were often so dislocated that low interest rates cannot automatically be taken to have meant easy credit.[36] An increase in wealth or income does not necessarily lead to an increase in savings or investment; investment does not always mean growth; capital investment, capital stock and capital accumulation do not necessarily develop in the same or related ways, and to get wealth transformed into productive capital requires a capital market and transfer mechanism which can take centuries to develop, and still then be limited in its area of competent operation.[37]

Capital stock

Until recently we knew relatively little of aggregate capital investment in the Netherlands; some patchy work on industrial investment by De Jonge, published in 1968, formed the only attempt at systematic data.[38] The project to reconstruct the Dutch national accounts has, however, paid some much-needed attention to this area, and work by

---

[35] Milward and Saul, *The development of the economies*, 519.
[36] Bos, 'Van periferie', 76.
[37] See for example Meier, *Leading issues*, chapter 1.6; and Groote, *Kapitaalvorming*, 48.
[38] De Jonge, *De industrialisatie*, chapters 15 and 17.5.

Table II.4. *The structure of private property and the assumed rate of return on the various components of wealth, 1807– c. 1910 (%).*

Category of wealth	1807	1831/32	1843/44	c. 1855	c. 1865	c. 1880	c. 1895	c. 1910
1	35	39	38	38	42	39	31	32
2	19	13	22	19	14	6	6	5
3a	–	–	–	–	2	5	8	14
3b	19	21	12	15	14	22	28	21
4		28	28	28	28	28	37	28
Total	100	100	100	100	100	100	100	100

1 Real estate; gross returns excluding the land tax.
2 Domestic securities; government loans.
3a Shares and bonds of Dutch firms from 1865 onwards.
3b Foreign securities.
4 Other moveable property.

Source: Verstegen, *National wealth*, 102.

W. Verstegen on income from capital, and by P. Groote on investment in the infrastructure, has brought us a great deal further.[39] The income from capital is estimated to have risen from ƒ142m. in 1807 to ƒ648m. in 1910, with very slow growth in the first half of the nineteenth century, rapid growth in the third quarter, a relative slump in the fourth, and a swift recovery from 1895, thus generally following the line of the long-term cycle outlined above. Table II.4, adapted from Verstegen's work, shows that the share of the various investment sectors in that capital income was dominated by real estate, at around a third; foreign assets (including the colonies) moved between 14 and 28 per cent; domestic securities and government loans reached a peak of 22 per cent of private wealth in the 1840s, but declined thereafter to around 5 per cent by the end of the century; while domestic enterprise amounted to less than 2 per cent before 1865, but rose rapidly to 5 per cent in 1880, and 14 per cent by 1910. Only after 1895, then, did domestic industry generate significant amounts of wealth in the Dutch economy.[40] Groote has constructed a database of capital formation in the Dutch infrastructure (including

[39] Verstegen, 'National wealth'; and Groote, *Kapitaalvorming*; these built on the early estimates of Van Zanden, *De economische ontwikkeling*; and Van Zanden, 'Economische groei'.
[40] Verstegen, 'National wealth', *passim*, especially pp. 102–3; and Bos, 'Vermogensbezitters', especially p. 570.

transport, communications, drainage, underdrainage, land reclamation and dikes) for the whole of the nineteenth century, and his research has led to the following periodization of investment: there was investment stability or even stagnation before 1850, followed by a rapid rise from 1852 to 1865 (coinciding with the construction of the basic railway network). From 1866 to 1888 there was a sustained high level of investment in all forms of infrastructure, especially those connecting the country with Germany, followed by a fall in capital formation, caused mainly by the depression in agriculture, from 1889 to 1902. Leading up to the First World War there was yet another growth spurt, this time concentrating on light infrastructure and communications. The investment in the infrastructure averaged 1.2 per cent of GDP p.a. over the period 1800–1913, and was rather low in comparison with neighbouring countries, despite the high liabilities the Dutch faced with their water defences.[41] Another detailed study into the contribution of physical and human capital to economic growth in the Netherlands has calculated an investment ratio, estimated at 7.5 per cent in the 1850s rising to 17 per cent by 1913; the late 1870s and the years around 1900 were investment peaks in machinery, buildings and infrastructure. The powerful growth of investment in buildings from the 1870s, and in machinery from the 1890s, was perhaps 'the most important driving force behind the growth of GDP'.[42] De Jonge's original researches into industrial investment in the period 1850–1914 showed that savings figures for the Dutch economy had risen from about 5 per cent of national income before about 1880 to more than 10 per cent after 1900, which was sufficient cause for him to confirm a Rostovian take-off in that period.[43] To estimate capital stock in industry he used the surface areas of steam boilers as an indicator, and concluded that there was substantial growth right at the end of the nineteenth century.[44] The contribution of agriculture to the nation's capital stock, by transfer of rents, should not be forgotten, especially in the prosperous third quarter of the century, when those transfers of accumulated capital may have amounted to 5 per cent of total national income.[45]

---

[41] Groote, *Kapitaalvorming*, 61–70.
[42] Clemens, *et al.*, 'The contribution', especially p. 187.
[43] De Jonge, *De industrialisatie*, 304–5. De Jonge was using earlier estimates by the economist J. B. D. Derksen.
[44] De Jonge, *De industrialisatie*, 308–10; there is some confusion because of the difficulty of distinguishing between replacement and extension of this kind of capital stock. See also Klein, 'Het bankwezen', 141.
[45] Van Zanden, *De economische ontwikkeling*, 359.

Capital starvation?

Thus what we know of financial capital, savings, investment and capital stock in the nineteenth century leads us to believe that there was a good deal of capital about, that it grew very slowly if at all until the mid-century, and thereafter took on dynamic growth, especially in manufacturing industry right at the end of the century. Much of this capital was not, however, invested in Dutch economic enterprise, and therefore the question arises of whether Dutch industry may have been starved of it. One study has argued that, because the Belgians had a sophisticated early industrial banking system in the *Société Générale* (1822) and the *Banque de Belgique* (1835), this was the critical differential between the two countries.[46] Mokyr was of the view that capital markets were very poor as far as the supply of funds to industry was concerned,[47] and in the more traditional literature, capital starvation is assumed to have held back Dutch industry.[48] But a study of the Dutch financial markets in the second half of the eighteenth century and in the French period shows that there was plenty of finance available, that the interest rates were low, that the brokerage system was quite capable of getting the money through to domestic industry, that Dutch investors were not at all afraid of a risk, and were not necessarily averse to manufacturing industry. The problems of Dutch domestic industry at this early stage, therefore, were to do with not being able to produce competitive goods, rather than with capital starvation.[49]

Financial institutions

Many of the financial mechanisms and conventions of capital markets and banking have been taught to the rest of the world by the Dutch. The system which grew up during the Republic and was in place by the later part of the eighteenth century was based on a nation-wide network of brokers and financial advisers, who collected the available financial capital from their local patrons, who were *rentiers*, merchants, insurers, bankers, industrialists, widows, institutions and various foundations. The system was highly efficient, and as a capital-rich country the Netherlands could meet the demand for enormous loans floated on the Amsterdam stock exchange to bail out foreign governments and to pay for foreign wars. The shocks of the French period were severe, with as much as 40

[46] Kint and Van der Voort, 'Economische groei', 152.
[47] Mokyr, 'The industrial revolution', 377.
[48] A review of that literature is provided in Griffiths, *Industrial retardation*, 41–3.
[49] Riley, *International government finance*, chapter 9, especially pp. 225 and 231.

per cent of the value of Dutch capital being wiped out as a result of annulment, repudiation and inflation,[50] but the system was still securely in place throughout the nineteenth century. In fact the Amsterdam capital market of the nineteenth century has recently been pronounced sound as a bell, and as much as any entrepreneur could wish for. The same national network of brokers linked up to the *Beurs* or Exchange in Amsterdam, where the system of 'prolongation' or money-lending linked to securities on the Exchange was so efficient that it actually retarded the development of other financial institutions like banks, right up to World War I. No evidence was found of capital starvation in any sector, and the firms which failed for lack of funding were probably bad firms.[51] In the twentieth century the Dutch have built on their expertise, and have linked up effectively with the world's financial centres in London and elsewhere.[52]

Interest rates

The final nail in the coffin of the capital starvation thesis, alongside the plentiful supply of funds and excellent financial institutions, is the persistently cheap price of that financial capital in the Netherlands. Interest rates were traditionally low: from around 5 per cent in the Republic, they had fallen to as low as 3 per cent in 1790, and at the end of the long nineteenth century in 1910 they were still only around the 3.5 per cent mark.[53] In more detail, the on-call or *prolongatie* rate on the Amsterdam Exchange hovered around 3–4 per cent for the first half of the century, rose a little in the 1860s and 1870s, and had subsided gently to its old level of around 3 to 3.5 per cent by 1900. Even in peak years it seldom went above 5 per cent. The yield on government bonds was perhaps half a per cent higher before 1860, but followed the on-call rate exactly thereafter.[54] The short-term rates were lower even than in London.[55] Rates of return on investment varied according to the sector and type of activity, but real estate was the only sector to bring in a steady 6 per cent for the whole of the nineteenth century, rising to 8 per cent around the turn of the twentieth. Government bonds declined in their return rates from 6 per cent in the 1830s to just 3 in the 1890s. Most tellingly, perhaps, the rate of return on investment in Dutch domestic enterprises was around 4 per cent in 1865, rising to more than 5.5 by about 1880, but subsiding to

[50] Riley, *International government finance*, especially pp. 243–6.
[51] Jonker, *Merchants, passim*.
[52] 't Hart, *et al., A financial history*, chapters 6 and 7.
[53] Van Zanden, 'The Dutch economy', 279.
[54] 't Hart, *et al., A financial history*, chapter 5.   [55] Jonker, *Merchants*, 266.

about 5 per cent at the close of the century.[56] Not only were interest rates modest, but industry was able to turn a profit for the investors. If there was a fiend which dogged Dutch industrialization, capital starvation was not the culprit.

The destination of capital

But if there was so much money around in the Netherlands, where did it go to? Where was it employed, and was it usefully employed? We have seen in Table II.4 that well over a third of Dutch capital was invested in real estate until 1895, when it fell back a little to just over 30 per cent. For the first half of the century large amounts of capital were held in government bonds; the percentage of Dutch capital in state paper declined after 1855 from about 20 per cent to about 5 per cent by the end of the century, because the government was relieved of the need to issue new loans by the balmy effects of the colonial regime's profit transfers, after the national finances had been sanitized in the 1840s. Instead, some of that capital went into domestic enterprise, as we have seen, and much of it into foreign securities, with the opening up of private enterprise in the Dutch East Indies. Government borrowing began to attract rather more capital again towards the end of the century, to pay for burgeoning public services, especially in the municipalities.[57]

The Netherlands had always been an exporter of financial capital – not least to England.[58] In the eighteenth century Dutch capital found its way into the English National Debt, but also into other foreign securities such as American and French government loans, and infrastructural works in Spain, Russia and the Caribbean; domestic interest rates were low, and foreign investments were therefore attractive.[59] There was a strong tradition of investment in the West Indies and Guyana plantations in the eighteenth century, but these investments were on the whole injudicious and loss-making after the financial crash of 1773.[60] Investment abroad

[56] Verstegen, 'National wealth', 87 and 102.
[57] Verstegen, 'National wealth', 102; Bos, 'Vermogensbezitters'; earlier estimates in De Jonge, *De industrialisatie*, chapter 15, pp. 305–8 have been more or less confirmed.
[58] See the classic works, Carter, ed., *Getting, spending*; and Wilson, 'Dutch investment'; see also Hill, *Reformation*, 245; and Flinn, *The origins*, 42–3.
[59] Carter, *The Dutch Republic*, 131 and 141; Wright, *Free trade*, 58–9. On Dutch investment in American railways, see Veenendaal, *Slow train*.
[60] The Dutch holdings remaining in the West Indies colonies in 1815 were enumerated by the government's Director General of Trade and Colonies, Johannes Goldberg; the data are found in ARA, Goldberg, no. 181; the names of Zeeland notables are prominent. The unfortunate nature of these investments was established in Van de Voort, *De Westindische plantages*; and Van de Voort, 'Dutch capital'; the severity of the losses is moderated by new work reported in Van Zanden, *The rise and decline*, chapter 5. Neither were the Curaçao estates profitable in the nineteenth century: see Renkema, *Het Curaçaose plantagebedrijf*.

continued into the nineteenth century (see Table II.4), despite an attempt between 1816 and 1824 on the part of the government to outlaw it,[61] and after the mid-century it outstripped the National Debt as a destination for Dutch investment.[62] Periods of redemption of the domestic debt, such as the third quarters of both the eighteenth and nineteenth centuries, led to an exodus of funds seeking foreign securities.[63] In 1865, 89 of the 116 stocks quoted on the Amsterdam Exchange were foreign, and a decade later the figure was 188 out of a possible 237.[64] The wills of any number of wealthy Dutch men and women testify to this penchant for investment abroad: one example is of the liberal parliamentarian Daniël van Eck (1817–95), who died leaving a considerable fortune, including substantial amounts in Hungarian, Austrian, Portuguese, Russian, American and other foreign securities, and many in the Dutch East Indies.[65] With the demise of the government monopoly on economic activity in the East Indies after 1860, there was a massive rise in private Dutch investment there, and some huge fortunes were made. One example – though hardly typical – is the Deli Company, which in 1869 planted tobacco on the eastern coast of Sumatra. It paid out a dividend on average of no less than 59 per cent each year for the next thirty years. Not a few companies paid out on a similar scale for half a century and more.[66] It has been calculated that by 1938 nearly 2 billion $US of Dutch capital was to be found in the colonies, which amounted to some 40 per cent of total Dutch foreign investment at that time.[67] In the twentieth century the Netherlands has continued its ancient tradition and has remained a major player in the foreign investment markets, despite its relatively small size. Over the period from 1920 to 1985, she has been third or fourth in the world of international investment, especially through the mechanism of Holland-based multinational companies, outstripped only by the US and the UK, and jockeying for third position with France and Germany, and, from 1973, with Japan.[68]

This long and continuing tradition of investment abroad did not necessarily imply, however, that domestic investment was adversely af-

---

[61] Brugmans, *Paardenkracht*, 175. On the substantial capital export at the beginning of the nineteenth century, see Wright, *Free trade*, 11; and De Wit, *De strijd* (p. 346), who estimated it at ƒ650m. in about 1820.

[62] Bos, 'Vermogensbezitters', 569.

[63] 't Hart, *et al.*, *A financial history*, chapter 4.

[64] Brugmans, *Begin van twee banken*, 66.

[65] See ARA, Van Eck, no. 14. This kind of private investment is confirmed by Van den Broecke, *Financiën*, 159.

[66] Baudet and Fasseur, 'Koloniale bedrijvigheid', 330.

[67] Baudet, 'The economic interest', 241. In 1939 Dutch capital accounted for three quarters of total foreign investment in the East Indies (Hall, *A history* (1981), 834; Baudet, 'Nederland en de rang van Denemarken', 439).

[68] Gales and Sluyterman, 'Outward bound'.

fected. In the 1890s, for example, when domestic demand for capital rose and was met, export of funds continued to climb to new heights, and 'it is hard to see where the supposed preference for foreign securities could have hit home investment'.[69]

'Investor mentality'

At the beginning of the nineteenth century, the Dutch investor was probably a cautious animal, but not overcautious. The broker network system meant that the investor seldom knew a great deal about the business he entrusted his capital to. There were two types of investments: there were safe, low-yield ones for the bulk of the capital, consisting of real estate (land, or bricks and mortar) and government paper at home, whether at national or local level. Second, some of the fortune might often be set aside for more racy and potentially lucrative ventures: marine insurance, loans to business, and foreign government bonds.[70] The pattern continued throughout the century: this is confirmed by perusal of the wills and probate inventories of a number of the prominent and middling citizens of the provinces of Utrecht and Zeeland, where there was a concentration of investors, but which were by no means metropolitan. A study of twenty-five of the largest fortunes among those who died in Utrecht in 1879 revealed that more than half of their considerable wealth was in securities, with the rest in real estate and loans. A substantial proportion of the securities was held abroad by then, because of higher rates of return.[71] In Zeeland, where things were perhaps more conservative, throughout the century most of the elite's capital would be placed safely in the government stock of the day at low interest; a few thousand guilders would go to local causes, and some would go abroad to 'risky' ventures.[72] Government paper and real estate together continued to account for well over half of all private property until the final quarter of the nineteenth century, and real estate still represented a third in 1910 (Table II.4). Wealth was geographically concentrated in the western provinces,[73] which meant that much of the real estate was in buildings. This was specifically not an economy or culture of landed gentry and nobility. Such people existed, especially in the east and north of the country, but they wielded little political power, and never had done so in the merchant society of the Dutch Republic. When rich merchants bought their retirement homes in the country, there were no estates

---

[69] 't Hart, et al., A financial history, 113.
[70] Riley, International government finance, 63–7.   [71] Maris, 'De beleggingen'.
[72] This remark is based on as yet unpublished research into wills and probates in Zeeland.
[73] Van Dijk, Wealth and property, 4 and 27.

attached: just a house and garden. The 'gentry' of the rural provinces often owned some land in small parcels, and bought lordships of the manor (*heerlijkheden*) to enhance their status with a title and to give them a pretence of attachment to the village where their country house stood, but their money was mainly in government stock and other securities. Land was bought and sold avidly, and there was much absentee landlordism, but the investors were usually the town-based bourgeoisie rather than a landed aristocracy or squirearchy.[74] Far from the aristocratic models of Britain, Iberia, eastern Europe and pre-revolutionary France, Dutch wealth was urban, and it was subsidized by the countryside. Income from securities and bonds was not subject to tax at all until income tax was introduced in the 1890s, and because the tax on land was one of the principal taxes on wealth up to that time, 'in effect the population of the countryside was providing the tax revenue in the nineteenth century which the government then transferred as interest and redemption payments to the stockholders of the west of the country'.[75] Macro-economically, then, there was plenty of financial capital, and although there was a degree of conservatism in its investment, the existence of the broker network and the willingness to take risks with a portion of one's capital do not point anywhere near the direction of capital starvation for Dutch economic development. In the words of Joost Jonker, author of a recent study of the Amsterdam money market, 'there is no evidence at all of bottlenecks in the supply of finance to trade and industry'.[76] From the point of view of the entrepreneur, though, what were the available sources of funds to increase or improve economic activity? Where could one go to get the wherewithal to set up a new workshop, factory, office or company?

Prolongatie

Short-term capital was available for trade and trade-related activities via the 'on-call' or *prolongatie* system centred on the Amsterdam Exchange. 'Deposits channelled into the *prolongatie* system by provincial cashiers and stockbrokers' fed into this 'hub of the Amsterdam financial system', and formed 'the main source of credit for anyone in business'.[77] The money was collected into a pool of deposits and lent out, with securities traded on the Exchange as collateral. Terms were easy, and, until it collapsed during the First World War, it was a highly efficient and flexible

---

[74] See three studies of absentee land ownership in the nineteenth century: De Vries, 'Absenteisme'; Wintle, '"Dearly won"'; and Moes, 'Absenteïsme'.
[75] Bos, 'Vermogensbezitters', 576. My translation.
[76] Jonker, *Merchants*, 274.   [77] Jonker, *Merchants*, 273 and 267.

system of borrowing short-term money in business. The disadvantage was that its very efficiency meant that the available spare funds were snapped up into a rather fragmented system, which prevented banks and joint stock companies centralizing savings and setting up very close links between the financial sector and industry, as was the case in Belgium and Germany. However, in the Netherlands the *prolongatie* system provided funds for all but the very largest firms.[78] There were very few of those about until the very end of the century, and they had little difficulty in obtaining funds from other sources.

Traditional sources of finance

Amongst the traditional sources of finance in business there had always been self-financing, private personal loans, and the local solicitor. In the Dutch cotton industry in the Twente region of the province of Overijssel, the huge mid-century expansion, mechanization and factorization was financed internally out of profits, and so was the explosion of Dutch shipping lines at the end of the nineteenth century.[79] If profits were not enough, then there were personal loans from friends and family: it is estimated that, after 1850, 16 per cent of the national wealth consisted of private loans to individuals. Any perusal of probates and wills confirms the reasonability of that estimate: individuals lending the odd thousand to each other, and larger sums, were an important part of the functioning of the economy.[80] And in spite of the extent of capital export, funds from abroad could sometimes help out Dutch enterprise. For example, the Bathpolders project to reclaim considerable amounts of agricultural land in the Scheldt estuary from the 1850s onwards was funded entirely from England,[81] and several Dutch railway companies and banks in the second half of the century made ample use of German investment.[82]

Most enterprises in the Netherlands were small or medium in size, and employed limited amounts of plant and machinery: their requirements for financial capital were similarly modest, and because their needs were often related to stock or materials which were traded, they could make use of the commercial credit system which functioned so well. Beyond that, Dutch entrepreneurs were more likely to obtain the necessary funds in the form of loans from family, friends and colleagues, sleeping partners, or the local lawyer, who would take deposits from his clients and pass them

---

[78] Jonker, *Merchants*, 269; the problems caused by the on-call system to attempts to set up commercial banks are covered in Wijtvliet, *Expansie*.

[79] Baetens, *et al.*, eds., *Maritieme geschiedenis*, 124; and Wintle, 'Shipping'.

[80] Verstegen, 'National wealth', 88; Jonker, *Merchants*, 271.

[81] Geuze, 'Bij een eeuwfeest'.   [82] De Vries, 'De problematiek', 46.

on into the *prolongatie* system, or directly to local entrepreneurs in the form of short-term loans.[83] The local man of law was often a key figure, providing the oil in the gearbox or the mortar in the façade of the local economy, by channelling funds from those who had temporary surpluses to those who had the need.

Government funding

A further source of funding for economic enterprise in all countries has been the state, especially if the industry concerned has anything to do with military capability. Navies and armies have been at the cutting edge of technology from the time of Alfred the Great to that of Ronald Reagan. In the modern period, Dutch military spending has not been a great catalyst for industrial development, but strategic considerations in a wider sense certainly have, especially in the first half of the nineteenth century. King Willem I was known as the Merchant King (*Koopman Koning*), and has even been called a mercantilist;[84] during his reign from 1814 to 1840 he certainly exerted strenuous efforts to assist certain branches of industry with government financial help. His major creations in this respect were the Fund for National Industry (*Fonds voor de Nationale Nijverheid*), set up in 1821, and the *Société Générale*, or Netherlands General Society for the Promotion of National Industry (*Algemeene Nederlandsche Maatschappij ter bevordering van de Volksvlijt*), founded in 1822, and still a major force in the financial life of Europe today. The Fund for National Industry diverted income from the customs service and placed it in domestic industry in Willem's United Kingdom, which embraced both the Dutch and Belgian provinces; between 1823 and 1830, ƒ7.28m. was distributed in the form of low-interest loans by this government-run industrial bank, but 75 per cent of it went to the southern or Belgian provinces, which broke away from the Netherlands in 1830.[85] However, a number of engineering firms in the north, like Roentgen's in Rotterdam and Van Vlissingen's in Amsterdam, together with the textile industry in Twente and even some agricultural projects in Groningen, were beneficiaries of this scheme. It did not long survive the King's tenure of the throne, however, and by 1841 it had ceased to function, to be closed down formally in 1846.[86] The *Société Générale* had a similarly short life as far as the northern provinces were concerned, although

[83] De Jonge, *De industrialisatie*, 299–300. These traditional forms of credit, especially in the rural south of the country, are described in Van den Eerenbeemt, *Ontwikkelingslijnen*, 70–90; and Van den Eerenbeemt, *Bedrijfskapitaal*.
[84] E.g. in Brugmans, *Welvaart*, chapter 4; and in Broeze, 'Laat mercantilist'.
[85] Griffiths, *Industrial retardation*, 44.   [86] Zappey, 'Het Fonds'.

Willem's crown domain provided ƒ30m. of the ƒ50m. founding capital; again, most of the loans and contributions went to southern industry.[87] The final panel in the King's tripytch of industrial funding by the state was the Netherlands Trading Company (*Nederlandsche Handel-Maatschappij*) or NHM, founded in 1824. It was to outlast him, and still survives in a way as a banking concern (as does the *Société Générale*), in this case part of the ABN-AMRO giant. It was in a sense a partial refoundation of the Dutch East India Company, and was the monopoly agency responsible for the trade between the Netherlands and the East Indies colonies. It was not part of the government, but enjoyed a very close relationship with the state and with the King in particular. Willem I used the company as a secret banker to bail out the government in the 1830s without involving parliament, and also to effect government policy in trade and industry. In its early years, in the 1830s and 1840s, it was heavily involved in the support of the domestic cotton textile industry in Twente and other regions, in order to provide return freights for the colonial trade. Its support came in the form of guaranteed orders at protected prices, financial guarantees against loss, and also capital advances to entrepreneurs in the textile industry.[88]

After Willem I's abdication in 1840, and especially after the accession of the liberals to power after 1848, the state was much less directly involved in the provision of financial capital to domestic enterprise, until well into the twentieth century. The infrastructure of canals, railways, trams and (later on) roads was heavily supported by the state, and this generated industrial activity with the use of government capital, but outside these huge projects there were no funding schemes for industry from the government after the interventionist stand of Willem I had been replaced by more *laissez-faire* attitudes.[89]

Limited companies

The standard means of financing industrial enterprise was later to become the limited company, whether public or private. Statistics covering the number and capital of such firms were collected: there were just fifty-two limited companies registered in Dutch industry in 1861–62.[90] In 1850–51 the figure for all economic sectors in the whole country had been

[87] Tamse and Witte, *Staats- en natievorming*, 207–14.
[88] Brugmans, *Paardenkracht*, 74, 90 and 114; Van Popta, 'Staatsschuld', 169–71; the classic study is Mansvelt, *Geschiedenis*.
[89] For government investment in railways and trams, see Groote, *et al.*, 'Dutch rail- and tramways'.
[90] A series for industry in the second half of the nineteenth century is collected in De Jonge, *De industrialisatie*, 235; see also p. 299.

just 137, and even by 1899 that figure had only risen to 431.[91] In the twentieth century the number and capital of limited companies took off,[92] but from the period up to the First World War the conclusion drawn by De Jonge was that the limited company figures indicated 'an extremely modest demand for capital'.[93]

Banks

Neither were banks of very much help in providing capital for industrial activity. The commercial world of trade and shipping had an excellent credit system (outlined above), and we have noted that the system was so efficient that it may actually have hindered the development of modern banks in the Netherlands.[94] There is no evidence that banking provided the kind of boost to economic development, and especially to industrial development, that it did in several other European countries, notably Germany.[95] Klein asserted that the mid-century innovations in Dutch banking had completely failed to bridge the gap between industry and finance, and that the banks had been no help whatsoever to domestic industrialization before 1895.[96] There were indeed valiant attempts to set up *Crédit Mobilier* banks in the 1850s on the French model, providing long-term industrial loans secured by shares, but the government actually rejected the schemes on the advice of *De Nederlandsche Bank*, as inviting speculation. They were perhaps proved right by the episode of the General Company for Trade and Industry (*Algemeene Maatschappij voor Handel en Nijverheid*), a *Crédit Mobilier* institution dedicated to supporting industry. It was set up in 1863 mainly with foreign capital: within a year there was scandal surrounding the company's speculation in its own shares, the chairman fled the country, and liquidation procedures were begun. There were other small-scale attempts to set up credit unions in the 1850s and 1860s, and all these attempts encountered no obstacle whatsoever in finding subscribers to the founding capital (the *Rotterdamsche Bank* was oversubscribed fifty-eight times at its foundation in 1863).[97] So in spite of considerable improvements in the banking sector after the mid-century, Dutch enterprise was not especially assisted by this fresh influx and availability of finance, for the most part because there was very little demand from that sector.[98] There appears to have been very

[91] Brugmans, *Paardenkracht,* 88; and Van den Eerenbeemt, *Ontwikkelingslijnen,* 86.
[92] See Tinbergen, 'Kapitaalvorming', especially the table on p. 15.
[93] De Jonge, *De industrialisatie,* 300.	[94] Jonker, *Merchants,* 269.
[95] The classic study is Cameron, *et al., Banking.*
[96] Klein, 'Het bankwezen', 141–2.	[97] Brugmans, *Begin,* 56–84 and *passim.*
[98] Brugmans, *Paardenkracht,* 267–8; confirmed more recently by 't Hart, *et al., A financial history,* chapter 5, especially pp. 102 and 113.

little wrong with the Dutch banking sector; indeed, it was 'admirably suited to its purpose'.[99]

In agriculture, especially on the heavy and productive maritime clays, finance was also an important part of the economic activity based on relatively large units with substantial capital equipment. This was reflected in the general eagerness to deal in such land,[100] and by the excellent profits which could be made on a judicious investment.[101] It was always asserted, especially on the clays, that agriculture needed extra capital in order to modernize, but it may well have been the case that those who wanted to modernize had enough capital of their own, or direct access to it, and that those who did not care to modernize expensively (the great majority of farmers) did not want to take on new credit. There were attempts, many of them by the philanthropist P. J. Bachiene (1814–81), to set up mortgage-based credit arrangements for farmers in the 1840s, which came to very little,[102] and Willem I saw to the founding of a mutual credit society among the gentlemen farmers of Groningen province, in 1823, called the Company of Landowners (*Maatschappij van Landeigenaren en Vastbeklemde Meiers*), but it had few members and achieved little. There were finally a number of agricultural mortgage banks set up in the 1850s, again on the French model, but the impact was modest, because of modest demand.[103] Not until the effects of the 1880s agricultural crisis were felt by nearly every farmer in the land (outside the horticultural sector) was there a sustained rise in mass demand for agricultural credit. That demand was answered in the main by the co-operative movement, in the form of tiny local farmers' credit associations, of which there were some 1,300 by 1941, structured either as co-operatives or as mutual societies. These were then organized into national banks, which eventually grew into some of the biggest banking concerns in the country (today's RABO Bank, for instance). The first agricultural co-operative was set up by sugarbeet farmers in Aardenburg on the left bank of the Scheldt river in 1877, but the 1890s was the decade of the co-operative farmers' credit union. Exploitation of small farmers had been rife by means of advances offered by suppliers and middlemen, and the agricultural intensification demanded by the crisis, especially in the form of artificial fertilizer, made it necessary for even the small farmer to increase his working capital.[104] The crisis also generated a rapid fall in the

---

[99] 't Hart, et al., A financial history, p. 122.
[100] On absentee landownerhip, see above, pp. 100–1, on investor mentality.
[101] Van Zanden, De economische ontwikkeling, 359.
[102] See Bachiene, Over een Nederlandsche hypotheekbank.
[103] Sneller, 'Anderhalve eeuw', 70–2.
[104] See Huysmans, 'Het landbouwcrediet', 375–8; Hoogland, Landbouwcoöperatie, especially pp. 79–86; and Van Zanden, De economische ontwikkeling, 273–80.

price of land, so that the capital value of farmland – the largest component of capital stock in farming – was declining steeply from the 1870s to the late 1890s.[105] It was another case of the financial system being adequate on the whole, and responding to change when demand expanded at the end of the century.

The role of capital in the Dutch economy

Rather than *supply* of financial capital, it was unquestionably a problem of *demand*; until the 1890s there was little need for new institutions like industrial banks – and to that extent it was similar to the situation in Britain.[106] There did exist some demand from industry for additional capital, but it was restrained, and the complaints about capital starvation tended to come from firms which were probably a poor investment.[107] The needs of Dutch industry were modest for most of the century,[108] although a new wave of economic activity after 1890 made domestic enterprise hungry for more capital.[109] The Dutch financial sector was highly efficient, even if it was geared towards commerce; it was quite prepared and able to finance industry as well, and ready to take a risk if the prospects of dividends were good.[110]

A generation ago, the economic historians adopted a neo-classical model of the Dutch economy in the nineteenth century, and paid a great deal of attention to supply-side factors, not least capital. The supply of capital was not found to be wanting, and the reproaches of earlier historians against conservative capitalists who stifled vigorous industrial development were rejected wholesale, and rightly so. In the words of James Riley, on the situation at the very beginning of the century, 'The problem was neither a disinclination nor an inability to invest in industry, but the possession of only one abundant resource, and that one not yet capable of redressing deficiencies and higher costs in other pertinent resources'.[111] The analysts have agreed since then that there was little wrong with the apparatus, and that there was plenty of money about. For the last four centuries, with only a few very short interruptions, the Netherlands has been characterized by plentiful finance, good financial institutions, large-scale capital export, low interest rates, and a stable currency. In the sense of finance flowing into industry, really important changes occurred only after 1890, when the factor capital really became a catalyst for industrial

---

[105] Venema, 'Proeve', table facing p. 844; and Wintle, '"Dearly won"', 71–9.
[106] Bos, 'Kapitaal'; and Bos, 'Industrialization', 43–9; see also Brugmans, *Begin*, 132–3.
[107] Bos, 'Vermogensbezitters', 569.   [108] De Jonge, *De industrialisatie*, 312.
[109] 't Hart, *et al.*, *A financial history*, 118–22.   [110] Jonker, *Merchants*, 274–5.
[111] Riley, *International government finance*, 247; Bos agrees: Bos, 'Van periferie', 78.

growth.[112] However, much of the debate has been overshadowed by the quest for that elusive Dutch industrialization, and if we look at the economy as a whole, we have already noted that the recent authoritative study, by A. Clemens, has concluded that growth in capital stock was the driving force of the economy after 1850. That capital stock consisted of physical capital in particular, such as machines, buildings and infrastructure, but also human capital: investment in machinery (in industry) only became relatively important after the 1870s.[113] The educational level of the workforce was relatively good, though *growth* in human capital was rather slow, perhaps because of limited secondary education, while technical education programmes only came on stream right at the end of the century.[114] In summary, capital in the sense of funds for industry was never a serious problem, and capital in the wider sense, of infrastructure, buildings and human resources, was a major force in the economic growth which was taking place throughout the period, especially after the mid-century.

4.4   Factor inputs: materials

The final factor of production in the Dutch economy to be considered, after labour and capital, is materials, including raw materials, energy or fuel costs, and land. Materials have featured heavily in the discourse of historians in their attempts to explain the performance of the Dutch economy in the nineteenth century: the Netherlands' lack of coal and iron, for example, has often been used to explain the slow development of heavy industry.[115] We shall examine the details of the situation, dealing first with the mineral deposits.

Mineral deposits

The Netherlands is not particularly well endowed with what is usually understood by mineral deposits, with the exception of course of natural gas (see Figure II.3).[116] Until the discovery of the huge field at Slochteren in the province of Groningen in 1959 – one of the largest known deposits in the world – very little gas was produced. As for oil, there is an oilfield in the extreme east of the country (Schoonebeek), and a number of small fields in the province of Zuid-Holland; some 2.6 million metric tonnes

---

[112] De Jonge, 'De industriele ontwikkeling', 91.
[113] Clemens, *et al.*, 'The contribution'.
[114] Burger, 'Dutch patterns', 168–9; and De Jonge, 'De industriele ontwikkeling', 91–2.
[115] E.g., Bos, 'Industrialization', 35–43.
[116] The following paragraph draws on *Atlas*, sheet II-6.

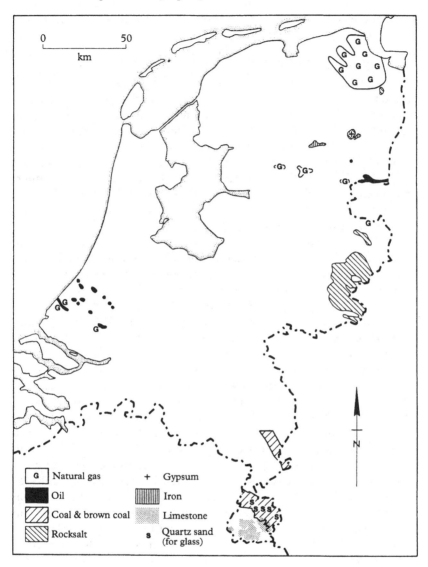

Figure II.3 Mineral deposits in the Netherlands.

Source: *Atlas van Nederland,* sheet II-6.

were produced annually by the 1960s, but production was negligible before 1945.

Coal is found only in the province of Limburg, and for the most part only in its southern half. The area forms part of the long range of basins running from northern France through Belgium and into Germany. It could be said that the Netherlands only shares in this resource (and most of its other minerals) because of the political accident of retaining the area around Maastricht after the Belgian Revolution of 1830. Surface mining in the area had been known for centuries, and a few small pits were worked in the nineteenth century, but excavation only began in earnest around 1900. At the start of the First World War the Limburg mines produced only 7 per cent of coal consumed in the Netherlands:[117] the domestic supply, therefore, was limited to say the least, especially when compared with neighbours Belgium, Germany and Britain.

The Netherlands also has modest deposits of rocksalt, used in the production of soda and other chemical industries. It is found in the east of the country, and has been worked by brine-pumping since 1918. There is a gypsum deposit in Drenthe, but it is not worked. Some minor amounts of iron ore ('bog iron') were available across the country in very small patches; they were of some significance before about 1850, but the only one left now is in the province of Drenthe. There is very little stone in the Netherlands except for limestone, again confined to Limburg: it is used for cement and fertilizer. Also in Limburg are found some brown coal (lignite) deposits, which are now exhausted. Again in the extreme south there is located some high-quality quartz sand used in glass-making (much of which is exported). Much more plentiful and widespread are sand, gravel and clay, used for building materials of many sorts. Brick-works have existed in most parts of the country for centuries, especially along the major rivers, where there was plenty of clay, and good transport, and where the land was too prone to flooding for productive agriculture.

Before the second half of the twentieth century, peat was the only really plentiful natural deposit with a direct economic use as fuel. The deposits were lowland peat in the provinces of Noord- and Zuid-Holland and Friesland, which has now been dug out almost completely, replaced by lakes or polders. In the east and north of the country there was and still is high moor peat, above the water table, which generated a major industry in the nineteenth century and was an important source of fuel, though very little is cut nowadays. It has been convincingly argued that this great thermal resource, with the lowland peat so close to the industrial and commercial centres of the Republic, was crucial to the economic success

[117] Bos, 'Industrialization', 37 note 51.

of the Dutch Golden Age. However, it is also accepted that the comparative advantage had been eroded (and to an extent dug out) by the end of the seventeenth century.[118] Other forms of fuel naturally available included a kind of turf dug from the marshes outside the sea dikes, known as '*darink*' or '*derrij*': at times it was excavated widely enough to worry the polder boards that the sea defences might become dangerously weakened.[119] There was some timber, but very little after the Middle Ages except in the south,[120] and although there were reports of burning cattle dung for domestic warmth,[121] there was not much else in the form of industrial fuel.

Land

So Dutch natural endowments in the form of mineral deposits do not amount to very much, and would amount to virtually nothing if it were not for southern Limburg, gas and peat. However, one of the traditional triumvirate of the factors of production, along with labour and capital, was land. If one includes in the equation the soil, the water and the wind, those essential features of the Dutch landscape, then there are very valuable natural endowments indeed.

Nearly all of the Netherlands is flat (except in southern Limburg), and nearly all of it is usable as farmland, except that part which is under water. Owing to its geological formation as ex-seabed and river delta, its alluvial clay soils, especially the maritime ones, are heavy to work but very fertile. (The only deposits of the gardener's perfect soil, loam or *Löss*, light but fertile, are limited – once again – to the southern part of Limburg.) Even the sandy soils of the east and the bulk of the south of the country are generally flat and have supported agriculture for centuries; with the coming of artificial fertilizers late in the nineteenth century, and cheap imported animal feed, they have become the scene of highly intensive farming and animal husbandry. These productive soils are well watered too; being located, as Napoleon is held to have remarked, at the spot where some of the major rivers of his empire entered the sea, they were seldom dry. It is true that there were few if any possibilities for harnessing water-power to drive machinery, for there was a near-total absence of the fast-flowing rivers which favoured the north of England and the Belgian

---

[118] De Zeeuw, 'Peat'. De Zeeuw's figures have been reworked by Unger, 'Energy sources', who shows that the importance of peat to the Republic (though substantial) was probably exaggerated, and that of coal underestimated.

[119] Wintle, 'De economie van Zeeland', 109 and 124 note 28.

[120] Buis, *Historia forestis*.

[121] E.g., on the island of Schouwen, in the 1820s. De Kanter and Dresselhuis, *De provincie Zeeland*, 196.

Ardennes. But the flatness of the land had its advantages: with hydraulic ingenuity developed over centuries, the temperate climate, and the steady wind over the flat landscape that was perfect for windmills, the Dutch turned their bogs and sandflats into fertile fields. Thus the natural endowments were in fact superb for agriculture, which remained the principal sector of economic activity throughout the nineteenth century. From the earth and water sprang other raw materials: one of the most vibrant sectors of Dutch manufacturing has always been linked to agriculture, utilizing its products, from milk for butter and cheese, flax for linen and linseed, and madder for dyestuffs, to wheat for strawboard and beet for sugar. Indeed, it was Jan de Vries's assertion that the original ability in the sixteenth century of Dutch agriculture to shift from subsistence food production to those cash and industrial crops that was the basis of the prosperity of the Dutch Republic.[122]

The Dutch land area was accurately measured from 1833 with the completion of a comprehensive cadastral survey for land tax purposes. According to those estimates, the country consisted of 3.27m. ha. in 1833, a figure which rose to 3.30m. in 1877, and then fell to 3.25m. ha. in 1889, after which it remained constant. (The late shrinkage is actually an illusion, caused by a shift in the method of calculation between 1877 and 1889.) More telling for the purposes of agriculture are the figures for all farmed land, which amounted to 2.06m. ha. in 1833, and had risen to 2.36m. by 1899, representing a rise of no less than 14.5 per cent over sixty-six years.[123] Figures calculated and corrected by Van Zanden for arable and pasture land show a rise from 1.886m. ha. in about 1825 to 2.075m. in 1880 and 2.154m. ha. in about 1910; those data imply a 14.2 per cent increase over eighty-five years. The expansion in the land available was brought about by reclamation, partly from the sea and rivers, and partly from heaths and other unfarmed land. The most rapid rate of reclamation of farmland occurred before the mid-century, with 4,935 ha. being brought into cultivation each year in the 1830s, and 4,365 p.a. in the 1840s. After 1850 there was a decline in the trend, a decline which accelerated during the agricultural crisis down to just 1,092 ha. p.a. in the early 1890s, after which it began to rise slowly again in line with the fortunes of farming.[124]

Most of the drainage projects concerned lakes and bogs left over from peat diggings in the seventeenth century, rather than open sea, and took

---

[122] De Vries, *The Dutch rural economy*.
[123] *Jaarcijfers* (1900), 1 and 125.
[124] Van Zanden, *De economische ontwikkeling*, 86–7. See also Fockema Andreae, 'De land-aanwinning', 580–1; and *De Nederlandsche landbouw*, 228–48. There are some problems with defining 'uncultivated' land, especially before the mid-century: Van der Woud, *Het lege land*, 26.

place especially in the provinces of Noord- and Zuid-Holland. These massive projects, most of them launched by the interventionist government of Willem I, took place in the 1830s and 1840s; the greatest was the draining of the Haarlemmermeer in 1848–52, where Schiphol airport now stands. At the same time, the history of reclamation from the old enemy, the sea itself, also saw a renaissance in the nineteenth century. The Dutch had been building dikes around mudflats and sandbanks since the seventh century AD, and the bulk of reclamation was carried out between 1500 and 1725; however, between 1800 and 1850 that level of activity was achieved once more, carving out more than 600 ha. of seabed each year.[125] Such levels have never been reached again, even in the time of Cornelis Lely (1854–1929), the Minister for Public Works whose plan to transform the Zuiderzee into the IJsselmeer became law in 1918 and was completed after his death in 1932.

While the trend of reclamation projects follows the line of agricultural *conjoncture* after the mid-century, the massive activity before 1855 shows the impact of government policy in this area, launched in the teeth of a serious structural depression in agriculture in the 1830s and an extended crop-failure crisis in the 1840s. At the same time the enclosure of the common lands (*markgenootschappen*) in the east of the country experienced a *hausse* in these activities in the period 1820–60, also driven by government policy.[126] After the Enclosures Act (*Markenwet*) of 1886, there were further inland clearances in the east, spearheaded by the Netherlands Heath Company (*Nederlandsche Heide Maatschappij*), which was founded in 1888 and led a powerful campaign to turn heaths and other commons into productive farmland.[127]

These increases in land generally and in the internal reclamation of swamps and heaths represented a considerable move towards the optimization of resources. It was estimated that in 1795 only two thirds of the Republic's land was in use, so there was considerable room for improvement in a country where there is no mountainous terrain to deter agricultural exploitation.[128] It was partly a matter of technology: steam power was essential for many of the major drainage projects, and for maintaining water levels once the digging was finished. Furthermore, the new land needed fertilizers to keep it productive, which were not limitlessly available until the 1880s (see section 6.2 below). Population pressure was also a key, and there is no doubt that the increased agricultural resources represented by these figures meant a considerable release of population pressure, and that they were partly responsible for the fact that the

---

[125] A useful bar-chart appears at Bakker, *Major soils*, 20.
[126] Van Zanden, *De economische ontwikkeling*, 165.
[127] Brugmans, *Paardenkracht*, 296–7.   [128] Van Houtte, *An economic history*, 293.

Netherlands experienced relatively little emigration in the nineteenth century, despite crowded conditions. Most of the resulting land actually came into cultivation after the mid-century, when there was rising demand for agricultural products both at home and abroad. On the other hand, the increase in available land was nothing in comparison with the rise in population itself, especially after 1870.

Land was always at a premium in this, the most crowded country in the world.[129] The availability of the resource increased over the course of the century, mainly in the first half, and was utilized to the full in the agricultural boom of the third quarter of the century. The accruals tailed off as crisis struck in the 1880s, and began a recovery right at the end of the century. It is a case in which government policy as well as the market seems to have played a major role throughout.

The energy industries

If the natural availability of raw materials outside agriculture was modest, what of the actual production, especially in the all-important energy industries?

In the early nineteenth century, the few coal mines in southern Limburg served only the immediate vicinity, including German customers over the border; only two pits were of any significance: the Domaniale and the Neuprick. Foreign funds backed exploratory drilling after the mid-century, but no shafts were sunk. In the 1890s, with the economic upturn in Europe, there was increased interest in concessions, still all backed by foreign companies, one of which was awarded most of the contracts out to tender.[130] In 1899 a commission was set up to review the industry; the result was the Mines Act of 1901, which nationalized all the parts of the industry that were not yet irrevocably in private hands. Thus began the period of the *Nederlandse Staatsmijnen NV*, during which the majority of mining was carried out by a small number of large nationalized mines. They began production in 1907, and were well run. During the export ban enforced in the First World War, they began to be integrally linked to coking plants and specialized chemical industries.[131] Private interests ran a further group of smaller mines. The mining sector was never very significant outside a small area of Limburg, and because of the international crisis in the coal industry of the 1960s, caused by the switch to oil and gas, the whole operation was closed down in the 1970s, after little

---

[129] Excluding city-states. In 1987 there were 432 inhabitants for every km² (land only).
[130] Bos, 'Industrialization', 35–6. See also Lintsen, *et al.*, eds., *Geschiedenis van de techniek*, vol. IV, chapter 1.
[131] Brugmans, *Paardenkracht*, 350–3 and 479–80.

more than half a century of life, with funds generated by the natural gas bonanza.[132]

Production was modest, compared with the neighbours. At Kerkrade in the densest eastern part of this compact field, annual sales of coal did not exceed 40,000 tonnes until the 1890s;[133] the peak production years of the 1920s, when 1.4 million tonnes were produced, were puny compared to Belgium's annual output at the same time of 22 million.[134]

   Peat production, on the other hand, was substantial, and rose throughout the nineteenth century. Contemporary estimates tell us that 22 million tonnes were cut from the country's peat bogs in the year 1834, rising to 27m. in 1844 and 33m. in 1854.[135] A recent study of peat operations in the north and east of the country has generally confirmed the importance of peat to the economy in the nineteenth century. Measured in units called '*dagwerken*', of 10,000 turfs cut (which approximated to what a peat gang of six to eight specialized workers could produce in a day), annual production oscillated around 30,000 units in the seventeenth and eighteenth centuries. Early in the nineteenth century, production began to rise, reaching its peak in the half-century from 1875 to 1925, with output in the region of a million units a year, three times the earlier figure. Before 1850 there is little doubt that peat was the principal energy source in the Netherlands: the country's transport system of canals was occupied substantially with the distribution of peat (and coal).[136] The dominance of peat applied not only to households for their cooking and heating, but to many industries as well, such as brickmaking, brewing, baking and distilling. Throughout the nineteenth century coal made serious inroads into the rule of peat, but population growth allowed the peat business to prosper alongside coal, at least until the First World War. Thereafter it was in decline, and its role was at an end by 1950. In the middle of the nineteenth century, peat was a close second to coal in the share of Dutch energy consumption, measured in calorific value; after the 1870s, however, coal streaked ahead to become more than ten times as important, with a brief respite for peat during the Second World War. Peat prices remained fairly stable over the period, rising gently from about 50 to 70 cents per tonne over the nineteenth century.[137]

   Linked to coal, there was a gas industry in the Netherlands throughout much of the nineteenth century, supplying town gas mainly for lighting in urban areas. Town gas was produced by burning the impurities off coal in controlled conditions, leaving coke, gas and some by-products. Urban

[132] Messing, *Geschiedenis*.   [133] *Jaarcijfers* (1892), 94.
[134] Mitchell, *European historical statistics*, 184–94.
[135] De Bosch Kemper, 'Statistiek', 22–3.   [136] Filarski, *Kanalen*.
[137] Gerding, *Vier eeuwen turfwinning*, 11, 332–3, 338–40, 345, and *passim*.

gasworks were in evidence in the Netherlands from the mid-century onwards: the Amsterdamsche Pijp Gas Compagnie was the first in 1825, followed by a second in the capital in 1846. Leiden set up a gasworks for lighting the streets (instead of candles) in 1848, and others followed suit: for example, Vlissingen built one in 1861, which henceforth took the lion's share of local coal imports. By 1881 there were thirty-one gasworks in the country.[138] Gas effectively replaced oil (vegetable or animal) in street lighting; domestic interior lighting remained the province of the tallow and stearic candle.[139]

In addition, the legendary Dutch shipping and the world empire meant that the country had access to raw materials outside its boundaries which others did not always possess. Mineral oil is a case in point, even before the discovery of the European reserves, for by the last quarter of the nineteenth century, new products like oil, as well as tin and timber, began to be added to the more traditional Dutch East Indies plantation exports. The Royal Dutch Petroleum Company (*Koninklijke Nederlandsche Maatschappij tot Exploitatie van Petroleumbronnen in Nederlandsch-Indië*) was founded in 1890, and merged with the British competition into Royal Dutch Shell in 1907. It was shipping oil and derivatives around the world's oceans from 1892, and controlled three-quarters of production in the East and all the shipping of oil, building up an industry vital to Dutch domestic harbours and manufacturing. By the mid-1890s the Dutch industry could compete on the world market with American and Russian firms. Oil tankers were built and began to dominate the trade, becoming a familiar sight in the ports of the Netherlands.[140] The import of oil into the harbours of Amsterdam and Rotterdam began in the 1860s, and had reached 180,000 barrels p.a. by 1870. The million mark was passed in 1890; by 1900 it was 2.6 million and by 1905 3.3 million barrels.[141] So there was plenty of that commodity about; the only slight disadvantage was that it knocked the bottom out of the market for rapeseed and other vegetable oil, which had been quite important to the farmers on the sea clay at home.[142]

The generation of electric power really belongs to the twentieth century: the Netherlands produced 0.71 gigawatt hours in 1920 (as against Belgium's 1.2),[143] but it had only become a serious business during

[138] Brugmans, *Paardenkracht*, 211–12; and Kautz, *Der Hafen*, 21.
[139] Lintsen, *et al.*, eds., *Geschiedenis van de techniek*, vol. III, chapters 7 and 10, and vol. IV, chapter 12.
[140] Brugmans, *Paardenkracht*, 337–43 and 362–3; and Milward and Saul, *The development of the economies*, 200–1.
[141] Everwijn, *Beschrijving*, vol. II, p. 506. Barrels contained 150 kg of oil.
[142] As much was reported to the British Parliament in 1881: Jenkins, 'Report', cited in Sneller, 'Anderhalve eeuw', 84.
[143] Mitchell, *European historical statistics*, 290–1. See also Fischer, *Stroom opvaarts*.

World War I, by which time nearly all provinces had set up their own power stations and companies. From the 1880s there had been a few private personal generators, some installations supplying electricity to a city block, and some local power stations, often set up by an enterprising individual. The first publicly owned one was on the Kinderdijk in Rotterdam, and The Hague founded one in 1890.[144] The Dutch were not slow to use the new energy form, and it went hand in hand with the production of light bulbs and electrical appliances in which the Dutch specialized; electric power was especially important for small-scale industry. But it was not a substitute for the paucity of mineral resources.

Materials and economic development

The abiding question remains the effect of these circumstances with regard to materials, and especially fuel, on the development of the Dutch economy. The soil, wind and water certainly favoured Dutch agriculture and the resulting trade in its products. The mineral deposits used in manufacturing industry were less favourable, and it must be determined what the relative effect of that underendowment was, and whether it changed over time. In the nineteenth century the crucial materials input was coal, despite the importance of peat.

Using trade and taxation data, it has been estimated that the per-capita consumption of energy (calorific value) in the Netherlands increased eightfold in the course of the nineteenth century, caused by the calorific intensification of production, and made possible by the increase in the use of coal. The same data suggest that in 1807, peat accounted for 65 per cent of the country's energy requirements, with coal taking up the remaining 35 per cent (presumably timber and other fuels must have been all but negligible, while wind[145] is left out of the equation). By 1840 coal had risen to 41 per cent, and by 1860 to 58 per cent. By 1910 coal accounted for no less than 90 per cent of energy consumption in the Netherlands, while peat had shrunk to just 5 per cent, with oil creeping in at some 3 per cent.[146] We know that peat was increasingly available, and

[144] Brugmans, *Paardenkracht*, 349–50 and 474; Lintsen, *et al.*, eds., *Geschiedenis van de techniek*, vol. III, chapter 8.

[145] Some calculations were made on windmills in De Zeeuw, 'Peat', 4 and 19–21. His conclusion was that, even in the seventeenth century, wind accounted for less than 1 per cent of the energy generated by peat. The percentage was probably even smaller in the nineteenth century.

[146] Van Zanden, 'The Dutch economy', 273–7. The data were collected (though not published) by J. Teijl, who devised some of the early estimates of Dutch national income in the nineteenth century; there are clearly some problems with the figures, but the trend they suggest is unmistakeable.

at reasonably steady prices; that means that the critical variables are the availability and the affordability of coal.

Coal and economic development

The immense importance of coal to industrialization and European economic development in general, and of the Austrasian coal field in particular, is not disputed. This series of basins running in an arc from the Pas de Calais to the Ruhr is only rivalled in importance by the fields in northern England and in the north-eastern parts of the United States. Some industries need coal more than others: those associated with the Industrial Revolutions of Belgium and Britain, like metallurgy, machine-building, and textiles, are all heavy consumers. For these reasons, those regions which have plentiful supplies of industrial-grade coal have clustered their heavy industry around the coalmining areas, especially because of high transport costs due to the weight and bulk of coal.[147] For those countries which lack ample coal resources, like the Netherlands (but also France, Denmark, Spain and Italy, to name but a few), industry could not usually be sited at the pithead. To compete with coal-rich countries, they had to be able to import coal at reasonable prices, or achieve advantages in other factor inputs to compensate for their lack of coal. How important were these problems for the Netherlands?

Assuming that domestic production was negligible until the 1890s, the import surplus of coal gives us a good guide to consumption figures. The Dutch imported 1.2 million tonnes in 1850, 1.8m. in 1870, 3.6m. in 1890, and 6.3m. in 1910 (by which time they were beginning to produce some of their own on a commercial scale).[148] Again extrapolating from tax data, we know that in 1854 some 29 per cent of the imported coal was destined for gasworks, 18 per cent for sugar refineries, and just 9 per cent for the railways. The rest went on domestic fuel and other 'industry'.[149]

On the whole the Netherlands had a good transport system for bulk goods, via its myriad waterways, although the labour costs involved in transport were higher than elsewhere and therefore disadvantageous, certainly before the mid-century.[150] This inevitably meant that there was a significant differential in the price of coal between the Netherlands (especially the inland areas), and the areas of production, such as the English ports, or Essen in Germany. One set of data informs us that the price of coal in the 1840s on the docks in Amsterdam (not by any means

[147] See, for example, Wrigley, *Industrial growth*, 3–9.
[148] Mitchell, *European historical statistics*, 232–4.
[149] Ridder, *Een conjunctuur-analyse*, 140–1.
[150] See section 4.2, on nominal wages, and section 6.4, on the water transport system.

the most inaccessible place in the country) was about five times that of the same goods in England or Germany; in the 1850s it was still three times as high, and in the 1860s and 1870s twice the level.[151] According to Richard Griffiths' calculations, in 1855 a *mud* of coal (a sack, of about a hectolitre) cost 36 Dutch cents in Manchester, but four times that (*f*1.41) in Enschede, in the heart of Dutch cotton textile country; furthermore the quality of that available in Enschede (which came from Germany) was considerably inferior to that in Manchester. After the 1860s, the rapid expansion of mining in the Ruhr area and the building of links between the German and Dutch railway systems ensured a much more regular and cheap supply of good German coal, especially to the eastern and southern areas of the country. Belgian coal was also more expensive in the Netherlands, because of additional transport costs. On top of these disadvantages, there were at various times in the first half of the nineteenth century export duties on English coal, import duties on coal entering the Netherlands, national taxes, and local excises on the sale of coal in the Dutch municipalities. These were abolished in the 1840s, 1831, 1822 (to be reintroduced in 1833)[152] and 1863 respectively, but overall the situation was fraught with difficulty because of physical and fiscal barriers. This leaves to one side the undoubted imperfections in the operation of the market in general, and assumes that Dutch agents knew where to get coal and that foreign producers were willing and able to sell it. In the end, this highly complex situation meant that the principal industrial fuel cost a great deal more in the Netherlands than elsewhere until the 1860s at least, despite its increasing popularity.[153] Even in the 1880s and 1890s there were substantial differentials in the price of coal around the country, according to the proximity to sources of supply, whether from Limburg or abroad.[154] In something of a caricature, the English travel writer Samuel Laing reported in 1841 that the people in the Netherlands wore such heavy clothes and costumes because of the astronomical price of fuel, which drove them to wrap up warm:

The effect of the scarcity of fuel, or of the economy [price] of it, in the Dutch household, is visible in the usual costume of the working and middle classes. The proverbial multiplicity of the Dutchman's integuments of his nether man, and the tier above tier of petticoat which makes his bulky frow a first-rate under sail, are effects of the dearness of fuel in a raw, damp, cold clime.[155]

Laing was probably ignoring the availability of peat, but he certainly had a point when it came to coal.

---

[151] Lintsen, *et al.*, eds., *Geschiedenis van de techniek*, vol. IV, graph on p. 124.
[152] On the complex matter of tax on coal, see Engels, *De belastingen*, 407–8.
[153] Griffiths, *Industrial retardation*, 75–7; and Bos, 'Industrialization', 36–7.
[154] *Jaarcijfers* (1892), 52–3.   [155] Laing, *Notes*, 15.

Conclusion

The Netherlands clearly suffered from some disadvantages in the supply of mineral materials, especially coal. However, only certain industries or potential industries were affected by this disadvantage. According to French government calculations in the 1860s, only metallurgy and ceramics were really dependent on fuel in their factor mix (23 and 17 per cent of costs respectively), whereas chemicals, metal-working, food, textiles and leather all spent under 5 per cent of their costs on fuel. Other raw materials were much more important, with factor costs of between 23 and 76 per cent (76 in the food and leather industries).[156] The figures would have differed slightly for the Netherlands, but the point is clear: metallurgy would be difficult to sustain in the Netherlands, especially as it has virtually no ores, and indeed there was very little smelting in the Netherlands until the First World War, when the strategic importance of steel production forced the foundation of the Hoogovens works at IJmuiden, based entirely on imported materials, including fuel. Ceramics were concentrated in Limburg where the coal was located, or where peat could be substituted, as it could in brickmaking, for example in Groningen. Other industries were much less affected: the food industries, in which the Dutch came to specialize, had their raw materials on the doorstep, and only spent (according to the French calculations) 3 per cent of their costs on fuel. It was a case of some winners, and some losers.

A recent authoritative if challenging study, by Jan de Vries and Ad van der Woude, pronounced that coal shortages were not primarily responsible for a lack of industrialization in the Netherlands, in the sense of sustained modern economic growth after the early promise of the Republic; rather it was wage costs and overregulation which slowed things down.[157] For the economy as a whole that must be generally true; however, for certain key industries there *was* a shortage of fuel with a high calorific value, and the problem of its expense. In effect it meant that the new technologies of the industrial age, many of them based on steam, were not available to Dutch industry, and so it concentrated on other areas instead, for the most part quite profitably. There were exceptions where the costs of materials actually favoured certain 'modern' industrial developments, such as sugar refining where there was excellent access to raw materials, and the limited but successful marine engineering industry where other factor costs could compensate for fuel disadvantages.[158]

---

[156] Wrigley, *Industrial growth*, 53.
[157] De Vries and Van der Woude, *Nederland 1500–1815*, 832. Mokyr had advanced similar arguments: Mokyr, 'Industrialization and poverty', 440–4.
[158] Griffiths, 'Industrial retardation', 270.

In terms of materials, it is easy to see why the Dutch economy did not develop in the same way as that of its – on the face of it – comparable neighbour Belgium. The Netherlands was not well endowed with coal, whereas Belgium sat astride some of the richest seams in the world, running under the foothills of the Ardennes. The Dutch have virtually no iron ore; the Belgians, like the British, had enough to get them started, and plenty over the border in Luxembourg and Alsace-Lorraine. Of course the Dutch could not compete in coal-based industries, and would have been foolish to try. Only when international rail and water links were improved, and German mining had advanced to a certain level, both of which occurred after the mid-century, did that situation change. The decline in the cost of fuel was one of the major changes for the Dutch economy taking place between the first part of the nineteenth century and the second half,[159] but it cannot be maintained that the whole economy was therefore paralysed before that change took place.

4.5   The role of labour, capital and materials

A great deal of research has been conducted into the three main factors of production over the last generation, and we are now quite well informed as to the changing state of affairs. The labour force grew rapidly throughout the period in line with the population, except for a dip in the 1850s. There were no structural shortages in the labour supply, which was maintained by the domestic population and by various transferred forms of foreign labour. As far as we know, the quality of the labour force was relatively good, but it was expensive: until the 1860s nominal wages in the west of the country were higher than those in competing countries, with the exception of Britain (which was, after all, the market leader). This had been so for time out of mind, it only applied to the coastal provinces, and the margin was small, but there was definitely a disadvantage which needed to be made up by savings on other factor costs.

Capital was a different matter: there is no evidence that financial capital presented the slightest problems for any sector of the Dutch economy, or for any individual businesses except those which were inherently bad risks. The finance sector was highly efficient and very well funded; it was geared towards trade and shipping but there was also money available to manufacturing industry and indeed other sectors. Supply was not a problem, then; rather there was very little large-scale demand for capital before 1890, when new forms of industry began to exert pressure for funding (a pressure which was duly met). Meanwhile, recent research

---

[159] Van Zanden, 'The Dutch economy', 279–80.

indicates that capital stock – encompassing not only machines and factory buildings, but infrastructure and human capital as well – was the driving force of the economy after 1850.

As for materials, the Netherlands possessed virtually none outside the tiny southern tip of Limburg, with the exception of its soil and peat (and now gas). The effects of this clear disadvantage *vis-à-vis* her neighbours were palpable, but very selective. When fuel prices came down rapidly in the second half of the century, owing to better transport and the escalation of German coalmining, these problems were largely eliminated.

5 Economic influences: entrepreneurship, technology and government policy

5.1 Entrepreneurship

Alongside more general attention to land, labour and capital, in certain economic analyses entrepreneurship is treated as a full factor of production, its reward being profit. The entrepreneur exercises a co-ordinating function in the capitalist economy, and arguably had even more influence in the nineteenth century, before the functions of manager and financial backer became almost entirely divorced. But even when financial capital and managerial skill have been separated, it can be cogently argued that high-quality technical managers and outgoing investors, who are prepared to be adventurous on occasion without being rash, can be crucial to the success of an industry, a sector, or even a whole economy, especially in its developmental stages. An entrepreneur, or even better an entrepreneurial class, prepared to break with tradition where economic advantage is concerned, dedicated to the pursuit of profit, and unashamed of their profession of making money, could obviously be a qualitative asset to the factor-input constellation in any developing economic situation. The real question is very much just how important they were, and it is not an easy subject to assess systematically or quantitatively. Recent studies of the Dutch situation in the nineteenth and early twentieth centuries have tended to emphasize the steady and gradual improvement in the quality of entrepreneurship, rather than sudden leaps forward in managerial technique and capitalist risk-taking.[1]

The argument that there was a lack of entrepreneurs, or an absence of those with the right kind of qualities, has often been used to explain the slow growth of manufacturing industry in the nineteenth century. The attitudes of the capitalists were often blamed, on the grounds that they would not channel their considerable wealth away from trade and govern-

---

[1] See De Jong, 'Ondernemerschap', on the nineteenth century; and Bloemen, *Scientific management*, on the advent in the Netherlands of new (American) management methods in the early twentieth century.

ment bonds into manufacturing.[2] Conservative entrepreneurs were seen as a reason for the decline of the fortunes of the Republic in the later eighteenth century,[3] and a study of the Dutch tea trade in the first half of the century concluded that the careless and conservative Dutch had been outclassed by the aggressive entrepreneurship of their American rivals.[4] There were too few entrepreneurial captains of industry, it was said, and the Dutch even had to import their real entrepreneurs from abroad: the Englishman Thomas Ainsworth was centrally involved in setting up the Dutch cotton industry, and many of the mill bosses in the 1830s were Belgians who transferred northwards after the Revolution in order to secure their markets in the East Indies.[5]

The conservatism of the coupon-clippers is an easy target, but not an entirely satisfactory one. In the section above on the supply of financial capital (4.3), it became unequivocally clear that Dutch capitalists continued to make healthy sums of money throughout, and it is therefore hard to call their astuteness into question. Capital starvation has been ruled out as a serious explanation for Dutch economic performance in the nineteenth century. Moreover, it is a simple matter to demonstrate that there was indeed entrepreneurial talent aplenty to be found among the Dutch:[6] one only has to look at what they achieved in the East Indies, both under the aegis of the state in the first part of the century and after the 1860s in the private sector, to be assured that at least some of the Dutch knew how to put business opportunities together when they were there. Gerard M. Roentgen (1795–1852) with his Fijenoord shipyard in Rotterdam, Paul van Vlissingen (1797–1876) with his marine engineering works in Amsterdam, and Petrus Regout (1801–78) with his Maastricht glass and ceramics factories, are all examples of the classic nineteenth-century entrepreneur, bringing together management skills, technology and capital. Later on they were followed by the exploits of those who built up the famous Dutch multinationals and shipping companies. When the big opportunities arose, there were Dutchmen who could rise to the occasion. On a more modest level, most towns had groups of 'notables' constantly searching for new economic opportunities (and the chance to turn an honest profit at the same time). Many farmers were rationalizing their businesses as well, whether on the big model farms of the north and west, or on the smaller peasant holdings in the east,

---

[2] Examples of the traditional literature are found in Brugmans, *Welvaart*, chapters 2 and 9, where it is argued that there was no middle class or bourgeoisie in the Netherlands to take up the new challenges. In this vein see also Van den Eerenbeemt, *Ontwikkelingslijnen*, 91–7.

[3] Carter, *The Dutch Republic*, 132–3.   [4] Broeze, 'Atlantic rivalry'.

[5] See Griffiths, 'Eyewitnesses'; and Camijn, *Een eeuw*, 33–4.

[6] Van den Eerenbeemt, *Bedrijfskapitaal*, 6.

where some of the proprietors in the mid-nineteenth century have been styled 'genuine Schumpeterian entrepreneurs' in their attempts to specialize and bring their farms into line with the market.[7]

The arguments to do with the alleged psychological attributes of the stolid Dutch are minimally convincing; the research carried out on factor prices makes clear that, until the second half of the nineteenth century, the economic opportunities in manufacturing industry were partly limited and selective. Where niches occurred, they were effectively exploited by the Van Vlissingens and the Regouts, and by the Netherlands Trading Company (NHM) in the East Indies. Careful detailed studies of key industries show that, on the whole, Dutch entrepreneurs were good at what they did, and were rational in their pursuit of profit. The introduction of steam into madder mills in the 1860s was delayed, not because of any entrepreneurial conservatism, but simply because the factor costs made steam unviable at that stage.[8] In a study of the cotton printing and dyeing sector over nearly a century from 1835 to 1920, G. Verbong is able to show that Dutch entrepreneurs throughout the period were dynamic, intensely well informed about international developments in their field, and constantly modifying and adapting their complicated processes to take advantage of the latest developments. 'These men were not passive, or indifferent to change', writes Verbong in robust defence of this highly energetic group of industrialists.[9] When opportunities arose across industry later in the century, the Dutch were ready to take them, especially in industries based on new technology, where they suffered no traditional disadvantage. Meanwhile, the moneyed classes continued to increase their prosperity in all sectors.

There is, however, one aspect of the debate about the mentality of the Dutch which may make some economic sense, hard though it is to quantify. In its assumption that the entrepreneur was driven by purely rational economic forces, that debate misses many of the social, political and cultural aspects of industrialization. Indeed, the discussion about the Dutch mentality might be diverted to highlight the cultural difficulty the Dutch may have experienced in moving from one highly successful form of economic activity in the early Republic (it has been called merchant capitalism) to another in the later nineteenth century (called industrial capitalism).[10] The supply-side, factor-cost situation was obviously important early in the century, when transport had yet not solved certain fuel and materials problems, but we must be careful of imputing exclusively economic motives to business people in the past, any more than we

[7] Van Zanden, *De economische ontwikkeling*, 198–9.
[8] Schot, 'Het meekrapbedrijf', 93–4.   [9] Verbong, *Technische innovaties*, 289 and *passim*.
[10] Van Zanden, *The rise and decline*, 148–51.

should do so in the present. Entrepreneurs were not simply profit-and-loss calculators; their aspirations and decisions were driven by the culture in which they were embedded, and by their own idiosyncratic personalities within that culture, as well as by the cold reckonings of *Homo economicus*.[11]

5.2   Technology

In the Republic, entrepreneurial behaviour in general, and attitudes to technology in particular, were fundamentally conditioned by cultural factors unique in time and place;[12] the same was true of the nineteenth century. The received opinion has tended to be that the Netherlands was somewhat lacking in innovative technological genius at that crucial time. Partly this has been linked to a perceived general lack of entrepreneurial zeal, as we have noticed, and partly it has been seen to have to do with a lack of interest in technical matters. The Netherlands had a poor showing at the Great Exhibition at the Crystal Palace in London in 1851, which was thought to reflect the Dutch state of affairs with regard to industrial technology in general.[13] There were complaints in the 1850s about the 'deep-seated aversion to or timid fear of anything that could be referred to as new', and frustrated reformers thundered (in vain) that, 'Yea, there are many who identify the smoke of a steam engine with the horrendous fumes of the pit of damnation.'[14] The 'cancer' gnawing at the bowels of the economy 'was lack of skill and apathy' towards anything new, and towards any kind of technological advancement in particular.[15] This technological conservatism and lack of invention is alleged, then, to have been yet one more nail in the coffin of the abortive Dutch Industrial Revolution.

However, such judgements were made on the basis of very little thorough knowledge of the history of technology, and very limiting assumptions about the nature of technology itself, or its place in society and the economy. There were certainly indignant outbursts against ignorant and conservative artisans and peasants, but there is no evidence for any systematic or effective negative reaction to modern technology from any

---

[11] Cotton industry entrepreneurs were quite prepared to sustain losses over a long period in pursuit of a product they believed in, and their adventurousness with new processes was at least partly determined by their personalities: Verbong, *Technische innovaties*, 281–2, and *passim*.

[12] Davids, 'Shifts'.

[13] Lintsen, *et al.*, eds., *Geschiedenis van de techniek*, vol. VI, chapter 1.

[14] Koenen, *Voorlezingen*, 140.

[15] The quotation is from a former Minister of Justice, C. J. Pické, expostulating against conservative farmers, in *Verslag . . . Landbouw . . . Zeeland* (1874), 56.

group, whether social or religious.[16] And we now have the benefit of a major collaborative six-volume work on the history of technology in the Netherlands in the nineteenth century, from a team led by H. Lintsen,[17] which, as a culmination of the renewed interest in the subject since the 1970s, has done much to redress the situation and render a proper perspective to this important but often distorted aspect of economic and cultural history.

The problem lies in our conceptualization of technology, and it is a particularly Anglo-American problem, because of the pre-eminence, successively, of Britain and the USA in certain types of technology which have proved industrially and economically successful. The result has been to conceive of technology as something which is happily and accidentally discovered by some brilliant inventor and then applied to the industrial process as a gift from God, resulting in great savings and increased production and efficiency, and allowing the lucky innovators to undercut and out-produce all their rivals. Slowly the news leaks out, and rivals gradually manage to copy the new machine or technique, so the benefits of the technology, after giving great economic advantage to the initial innovators, are diffused gently to surrounding countries, as these eventually realize and understand the right way to produce the goods in question. The prime example in the nineteenth century is British cotton yarn and cloth, and in the twentieth century, any number of American consumer goods. 'Technology' is thus seen as a machine or method, which, once thought up and adapted to the production process, can be universally applied. In the late eighteenth and early nineteenth centuries, Britain underwent a process of Industrial Revolution which was partly based upon the application of a large number of new technologies especially suited to the industrial age; she became the 'workshop of the world', and was assured of a century and more of world domination before the rest of the European powers adopted similar methods and caught up with her.

It is no longer necessary, perhaps, to point out the many fallacies inherent in such an approach: it results in schemes to send combine-harvesters to help subsistence farmers in mountainous areas. Of course technology is important to economic development. Technology permitted the demographic transition in Europe, and is a key to the escape from subsistence agriculture. But it is of course only one key. Indeed, it has been persuasively argued that 'emphasis on technology, however, can impair historical understanding'.[18] It is almost completely useless on its own, in the sense of a device or machine. To be successful, a new machine

---

[16] See Van Lente, 'Ideology'.
[17] Lintsen, *et al.*, eds., *Geschiedenis van de techniek*.
[18] Goodman and Honeyman, *Gainful pursuits*, 170.

(like a Spinning Jenny, for example) needs a manufacturer, the materials to make it, a skilled operator, a mechanic to maintain it, the power to run it, the materials for it to process, several complementary technologies, and above all the market for what it produces, in terms of both its immediate product (cotton yarn) and its final market commodity (cotton cloth or finished garments and other items). All the other factors on both the supply and demand sides of the equation must be in place for the 'new technology' to have its effect; the Spinning Jenny was just what was needed in the late eighteenth century in Lancashire, but would be quite irrelevant to most other economic situations in the world, before or since. In fact, to define technology as a device or technique or formula is itself too narrow: to have any impact at all a device must be culturally accepted by management, the workforce and the market, and the cultural dimensions of technology are as important as its scientific or mechanical attributes. Technology is perhaps best thought of as 'ways of doing things': such ideas must be feasible and accepted by large numbers of people before they can have any impact on economic life, or indeed on life at all. Much if not most technology is actually a function of demand: a mill owner identifying a bottle-neck, and putting his mind to the problem, or late twentieth-century R&D departments specifically directed at production targets. In fact, much technology is gradual innovation, moving forward almost imperceptibly.[19]

In terms of economic development in the nineteenth century, it would therefore be unwise to look for replication of the British experience on the continent of Europe in order to identify economic or even industrial advancement. The concentration in large buildings of expensive capital stock ('factorization') was by no means characteristic of European industrialization: it occurred in cotton and worsteds, and in iron and steel; before 1914 it did not occur in many other industries, such as woollens, silk, linen, and many early consumer-durable industries, like watches, bicycles and cars. The sudden headlong adoption of a new technology was almost unheard of: gradual adaptation and modification were the rule. Very often, too, the craftsman or artisan continued to reign supreme in his workshop throughout the century, using his traditional skills and adopting parts of the new techniques as and when they were appropriate to his suppliers, labour force and markets. And in a single country there were often several different ways of making a single product, the new alongside the old, all of them viable according to local circumstance. The political and cultural constellation in different countries and regions also profoundly affected the dynamics of technology.

[19] Mokyr, *The lever*; Goodman and Honeyman, *Gainful pursuits*, especially chapter 4; Landes, *The unbound Prometheus*; and Mathias and Davis, eds., *Innovation*.

All this puts the analysis of technology in the industrial and economic growth of the Netherlands in a rather different light. It was a country with a small domestic market and a long tradition of interaction with foreign sources of supply and markets for its goods, whether agricultural or industrial. If a merchant-capitalist mentality persisted in the Netherlands, then in this case it meant a cultural internationalism on the part of entrepreneurs, who were quite happy to import new devices and techniques from abroad – there were never any import restrictions – from neighbours who had specialized earlier and had gained the advantage of economies of scale. Many captains of industry sent their sons abroad to learn their trade before taking their place in the business.[20] Patent laws existed until 1869, but then were repealed, and there was no protection of Dutch inventions until the law's reintroduction in 1912. According to one study, it seems likely that the absence of patent laws from 1869 to 1912 meant that industrial progress in the Netherlands was based less on domestic inventions and innovations than might otherwise have been the case, but there is no evidence that economic progress was slower in the later part of the century because of a lack of protection.[21] Effectively, the Netherlands had fairly free access by one means or another to British, German and Belgian technology, and did not originate a great deal of her own except in the marine, hydraulic and food-processing sectors. She tended to import much of her industrial technology in the nineteenth century, from Germany in the form of direct investment and specialists, and from Britain in the form of capital goods and skilled workers; however, prior to the mid-century these imports remained modest because of local circumstances like the factor-input mix.[22] The Netherlands was therefore, very largely, a 'diffusion country'; even much of the technology in the food-processing sector was imported and adapted to local conditions. This should be seen as a sign not necessarily of weakness (as Gerschenkron did, for example),[23] but of ingenuity, adaptability and international orientation. In the words of Verbong, 'The diffusion of technology cannot be represented as a simple process of imitation. Technological devices and systems needed to be adapted to local circumstances and requirements.'[24]

The Dutch education system produced modest numbers of engineers and technicians, especially to deal with the country's water defences, and

[20] Verbong, *Technische innovaties*, 286.   [21] Schiff, *Industrialization*, 51, 123 and *passim*.
[22] Bos, 'Techniek'; Bos, 'Industrialization', 51–2. See also De Groot and Schrover, eds., *Women workers*, 60–3.
[23] Gerschenkron, *Economic backwardness*, 9.
[24] Verbong, *Technische innovaties*, 286. See also Lintsen, *et al.*, eds., *Geschiedenis van de techniek*, vol. I, pp. 253–4, and vol. III, chapter 1; Van Zanden, ed., *The economic development*, x–xi.

after the reform of secondary education enacted in 1863 by J. R. Thorbecke, the number and quality increased. A textile college opened in Enschede in the 1890s. The state water-defences system accommodated extensive 'in-house' training for engineers, and the Polytechnic School at Delft (now the Technical University) was also founded in 1863. Engineers underwent a professionalization process, aided by central government, and their status in society rose.[25] Rather than generate a great number of original inventions, however, for most of the nineteenth century the Dutch followed their own developmental route, adapted specially to their own economic and cultural circumstances. As the century closed and the technical expertise of entrepreneurs increased, they integrated these new skills with the older ones of adaptation and modification of others' methods to Dutch circumstances.[26]

It is hardly necessary to *précis* here the six volumes of Lintsen *cum suis*; however, some examples partly drawn from their researches will amply illustrate the points made above. We shall examine steam power and heavy engineering, with an additional brief look at agriculture and cotton.

Steam power

The introduction of steam power was gradual, even in the UK. It was not so much the potential increase in power which was attractive about steam, but its locational flexibility: it was no longer necessary to site one's workshop alongside a fast-flowing stream (extremely rare in the Netherlands). On the other hand, however, one required fuel, and where there were large amounts readily available, as in the Midlands and the North of England, southern Belgium, and the Ruhrgebiet, steam became popular. Countries like the Netherlands and France did not share such advantages. Even in Belgium the new power source was confined principally to mining: in the iron foundries and metal-working industries, water power persisted well into the nineteenth century.[27]

In the Netherlands there was a steam pump sited in a polder as early as 1787, and in industry, an Amsterdam flour mill installed one in 1797.[28] When the trade blockades were lifted in 1814, more contact with England led to a widening application of steam to various branches of activity. The advantages of steam pumps for agriculture in controlling water levels in the polders were obvious, and from the 1820s they gradually began to

---

[25] Verbong, *Technische innovaties*, 287–9; and Lintsen, *et al.*, eds., *Geschiedenis van de techniek*, vol. V, especially chapters 4, 5 and 12.

[26] Lintsen, *et al.*, eds., *Geschiedenis van de techniek*, vol. II, chapter 8, pp. 235–7.

[27] Goodman and Honeyman, *Gainful pursuits*, 92–3, 190–5.

[28] Bruwier and Dhondt, 'The industrial revolution', 357.

Table II.5. *Steam engines in the Netherlands, 1850–1910, numbers and capacity.*

	1850	1860	1870	1880	1890	1900	1910
No. of machines in manufacturing and mining	286	819	–	2,737	3,925	–	–
Surface area of steam boilers, 1,000 m^2	–	–	70	80	140	220	340

Sources: Numbers: Business levy records, reported in Lintsen, *et al.*, eds., *Geschiedenis van de techniek*, vol. VI, pp. 269-70; capacity: Government statistics, reported in Bos, *Economic growth*, 13.

replace windmills. Steam was particularly valuable to agriculture on the clay soils for controlling the level of the water table, which was finally achieved around 1860. The draining of the huge Haarlemmermeer would not have been possible without steam.[29] In 1839 the first stretch of Dutch railway was opened between Amsterdam and Haarlem, with trains pulled by English locomotives; however, existing systems were persistent, and the rail network did not really come together until the 1860s. In industry, there were steam engines installed in cotton spinning and wool weaving in Eindhoven in 1820, in the wool industry in Tilburg in 1827, in a sugar refinery in Amsterdam in 1830, in a cotton-weaving mill in Haarlem in 1833, in a paper mill in the Zaan area in 1838, and in a diamond-cutting business in 1840.[30] However, these early incidents were more or less isolated: there were only seventy-two engines in the country in 1837, and most of those were for drainage purposes. Only towards the end of the century did things pick up, when the surface area of boilers reached 220,000 m^2 in 1900 (see Table II.5). A comparison with Belgium shows how far the Netherlands lagged behind: in 1850 there were 2,013 of the machines in Belgium, while the Dutch could muster only a puny total of 292.

However, these figures are highly misleading: until the 1850s, steam engines were used almost exclusively in mining, metallurgy and textiles. The Netherlands had no mines and few metals, whereas Belgium had a very great deal of both, and until the Belgian Revolution of 1830 the

[29] Van Zanden, *De economische ontwikkeling*, 237; Lintsen, *et al.*, eds., *Geschiedenis van de techniek*, vol. IV, chapter 6.
[30] Van der Pols, 'De introductie'.

country's cotton and woollens industries had been concentrated in Ghent and Verviers in the Belgian provinces; indeed they were some of the most successful centres of mechanized spinning and weaving in the world. In the 1830s and 1840s the Dutch authorities in the Netherlands Trading Company (NHM) were desperately trying to create and build up a modern northern Dutch textile industry, and did so mainly by employing hand-weaving behind heavy government protection from foreign competition. Only in the 1850s and 1860s did this situation alter, and were large factories and power looms introduced on a broad front. So if the steam engines in mining, metal and textiles are excluded from the 1850 figures, the Netherlands looks much more respectable, for 87 per cent of the horsepower in Belgian machines was to be found in those sectors in 1850. Even allowing for this adjustment, however, the Belgians still had four times as much steam power at the time of the mid-century.[31]

One area where one might expect the Netherlands to hold its own in steam was in shipping, especially compared to Belgium, whose merchant marine was small. The proportion of the world's shipping tonnage using steam power in 1870 is estimated to have been in the region of 12 per cent; by 1900 that had increased to 65 per cent, amounting to more than 63 million tonnes.[32] The Netherlands was not quick to follow these trends initially: whereas Britain had almost infinite supplies of excellent steamer coal and the iron industry to construct the new ships at low prices, the Netherlands was content to continue with wood and sail while gently introducing the new technology alongside the old. In many cases there was not competition but complementarity between the technologies: bulk non-perishable cargoes were well suited to sail, whereas perishables, valuables, and humans on long voyages were better off under steam.[33] Steel hulls and steam engines were particularly suited to ocean-going ships, and it was only after 1890 that the slow shift to steam really gathered momentum in the Netherlands, with the enormous expansion of its shipping activities in the East Indies, and in the world's oceans in general.[34] The proportion of the Dutch fleet under sail continued increasing until 1876/77; steam began to take off after 1880. In 1883 there was still twice as much under sail,[35] but by 1910 the Dutch percentage of steam-powered tonnage outstripped even that of the UK, and was well

[31] Lintsen, et al., eds., Geschiedenis van de techniek, vol. VI, chapters 3 and 7, especially pp. 52 and 62–3.
[32] Kenwood and Lougheed, The growth, 27–8; and Verhoog, De ontwikkeling, 82–5 and 95–7.
[33] Goodman and Honeyman, Gainful pursuits, 160–5.
[34] Wintle, 'Shipping'; and section 6.4 below, on shipping.
[35] Jaarcijfers (1883), 54.

ahead of other rivals like the US, France and Germany.[36] When expansion of imperial activities in the Far East demanded it, the Dutch were quick enough to shift definitively to the new technology; in the meantime, the new and the old co-existed and complemented each other.

The reputation of the Netherlands suffered for a long time because of its apparent tardiness in introducing steam technology (outside land drainage); it is now clear that this negative judgement rests on misinterpretation of crude statistics, and on a very blunt and unrefined conceptualization of technology.[37] In fact the Dutch employed modest amounts of steam in their industry to complement existing power technologies, and when the need arose with shipping they were capable of 'modernizing' very rapidly indeed.

The engineering industry

There is little doubt that technological development can be assisted by a strong domestic engineering industry, as it was in Britain and Belgium in the early part of the nineteenth century. In marine engineering the Dutch had a presence, because of their intensive trading in Europe and the world which they carried themselves in their own vessels. However, outside shipbuilding, the heavy engineering sector was very modest. Again, the near-absence of mining and metallurgy meant that on both the supply and demand side there was relatively little stimulus for machine building.

In marine engineering, the Belgian Secession removed the internal supply of steam engines and so stimulated early firms like the *Nederlandsche Stoomboot Maatschappij* (founded by G. M. Roentgen in 1823, which later became Wilton-Fijenoord) and the *Amsterdamsche Stoomboot Maatschappij* (P. van Vlissingen, 1825), both of which developed from shipbuilders into manufacturers of steam engines and other heavy machinery. There were a number of distinguished and successful Dutch marine engineers, such as Roentgen, Van Vlissingen, and B. J. Tideman (1834–83), who founded the shipyard 'De Schelde' in Vlissingen. In the face of daunting foreign competition, the Netherlands succeeded in establishing a significant engineering industry with substantial firms like the marine engineers already mentioned, and a small number of engineering works in Leiden, Delft and Deventer in the east of the country.[38] In textile machinery, British competition dominated the modest Dutch demands, but after 1850 there was a considerable increase in domestic demand, from drainage, shipping and industry. There were no import restrictions

[36] Burger and Smits, 'A benchmark', 145.
[37] Lintsen, *et al.*, eds., *Geschiedenis van de techniek*, vol. IV, chapter 4.
[38] Griffiths, *Industrial retardation*, 116–28.

on foreign machinery, and there was a continual import surplus, estimated at about ƒ1m. in 1860, rising to about ƒ3m. in 1890 and ƒ12m. in 1910.[39] Again, it was a case of the Dutch industry co-existing with foreign competition: the Dutch specialized in ships and some hydraulic machinery, while most industrial and agricultural plant was imported.[40]

Technology evaluated

The story of technological improvement is similar in other sectors. In agriculture, the technological achievements on the clay soils by the time of the French period were outstanding, and one of the showcases of Europe;[41] things were less advanced in the east, and the first half of the century saw little further progress in the west, but from the 1850s there were continual innovations and mechanizations, which developed into a general onrush after 1880.[42] In cotton, many of the technological advances pioneered in England and Belgium were implemented in the Netherlands about thirty years later, but from the 1840s and especially the 1850s onwards progress was very rapid. On close inspection, the technologies selected by the Dutch cotton entrepreneurs were quite rational in terms of market, scale of production, available skills and labour, and materials. This is not to deny that there were, at certain times and in certain places, 'clear arrears in skills' and 'deficient entrepreneurship'; rather this was part of the cultural environment into which any new technology would have to fit to be rendered viable. And the technological landscape was highly differentiated, even within the cotton industry: in the old textile towns of the coastal provinces the force of English competition was too strong, while in the eastern Twente region, the Dutch had a much better position and could maintain and modernize their spinning mills with much more success. While spinning in the east was rapidly mechanized, weaving was done by hand (with the flying shuttle) for much longer because of the presence of large numbers of weavers with the necessary skills. Printing, however, continued to be a hand-driven process for much longer. This differentiation persisted for good economic reasons in the region and in its markets, many of which were small and select. After 1850 the whole of the industry tended to factorize, driven partly by rising wages and the ease with which British machines could now be imported, transported and fuelled.[43] The verdict of a study on technology

---

[39] Bos, 'Long-term demographic development', 13.
[40] Lintsen, et al., eds., Geschiedenis van de techniek, vol. IV, chapter 2.
[41] See the plaudits of foreigners quoted in Wintle, 'Modest growth', 19.
[42] On agricultural technology, see Lintsen, et al., eds., Geschiedenis van de techniek, vol. I, chapter 2; and Van Zanden, De economische ontwikkeling.
[43] The literature on cotton is very extensive, but a good and stimulating summary is found in Lintsen, et al., eds., Geschiedenis van de techniek, vol. III, chapter 5.

in the cotton finishing industries could well be applied to the whole textile sector:

After a birth by Caesarean section . . . the industry was placed in an incubator. When this protection was removed, the new sector underwent a baptism of fire. But it succeeded in growing up to be a small but well developed branch of industry. By the turn of the century it had reached maturity and was in an excellent position to take on foreign competition.[44]

In summary, there was seldom a single way of doing things at any one time, but a variety of techniques employed, always dynamic and changing, but gradually rather than in a wholesale manner, with new technologies running in tandem with the older more traditional ones. The market was highly differentiated, and so was the technology. Foreign techniques were borrowed and adapted, but seldom slavishly; where they were appropriate to the production facilities in a given locality, they were adopted and adapted.[45] There were certain niche industries and sectors in which the Dutch excelled and in which their technology was very advanced in international terms (like food-processing and hydraulic engineering), but over the field as a whole the domestic market remained a small one and the Dutch were often ready to import and adapt. All in all, given the circumstances of supply and market, and understanding 'technology' to mean the culture and environment in which techniques and devices operate as well as the devices themselves, Dutch technology was alive, dynamic and resourceful throughout the period in question.[46]

5.3   Government policy

Finally in reviewing the supply-side aspects of the Dutch economy in the nineteenth century, there is the issue of government policy. In politics today, government policy can exert crucial influence on the demand side as well as on supply, but that was rare in the Netherlands before the twentieth century, and such attempts were almost certainly ineffective. More important in the nineteenth century were the supply-side issues of trade policy, government attitudes to agriculture and industry, the state's

---

[44] Verbong, *Technische innovaties*, 289.
[45] Another good Dutch example of this kind of piecemeal pragmatic technological advance is the chemical industry: see Lintsen, *et al.*, eds., *Geschiedenis van de techniek*, vol. IV, especially p. 270, which speaks of a 'unique Dutch model' which took parts of the prevailing German and English technologies, and combined them into something new, but suited to Dutch circumstances.
[46] That this assertion is still controversial is evidenced by the recent announcement of a new research project by two of the principal investigators in the national accounts project, Smits and Horlings, into why technology and technology diffusion were so *backward* in the nineteenth century: Smits, *et al.*, 'Sprekende cijfers!'

ability to run public finances without impoverishing the people or driving away its capitalists and entrepreneurs, and centralization.

However, it is important to avoid the pitfalls of anachronism. 'Economic policy' is really a concept of the twentieth century, and in the nineteenth it was little more than embryonic. There was a tradition of local economic regulation, especially concerning the guilds, and there is no doubt that in the Netherlands, as in the rest of Europe, there were countless opinions expressed about what was best for the economic health of the nation; however, the science of economics was in its infancy, and most of the views expressed tended to be based on group interests (for example, industrialist against landowner) or simply gut feeling. Very few of the contemporary pamphlets are logically convincing to anyone familiar with modern economics, yet that is the framework within which we often set the debate about 'economic policy' in the nineteenth century. More importantly still, the state had very few resources with which to implement any economic policies on which it might agree. It was not only a question of money: there were simply not the officials, committees, regulations, police, and all the rest of the apparatus of the modern state with which to enforce 'policy'. Such enactment mechanisms began to be built up at the end of the nineteenth century, and have been a special feature of the twentieth, but as the following sections will show, we should not overestimate the capacity of nineteenth-century governments to exercise very much economic policy at all.[47]

Despite the mismatch between the clamour of opinion expressed about the economy and the effectiveness with which governments were able to act in such matters, there was one area in which government had been active for centuries: that of trade policy. Primarily this was a question of revenue: tariffs, customs and excises were the traditional milch-cows of the state, and in these areas there actually existed an apparatus of officials who were able to make good many of the government's intentions. Furthermore, there was the often underplayed question of good house-keeping: if governments were less capable of proactively directing the economy than they claimed to be (something which has continued to afflict politicians up to and including our present day), they were certainly capable (as they still are) of wrecking an economy through endless ruinous wars, accounting mismanagement and sheer incompetence. Public finance was necessary to pay for the army, the state apparatus and the courts: in every age it is important that public funds are well managed,

---

[47] On the effectiveness of economic policy in the Netherlands (and Britain) through the ages, see Groenveld and Wintle, eds., *State and trade*, especially chapter 6 on the early nineteenth century. See also Van der Woud, *Het lege land*, 28–9.

and that the state does not incur debts which it cannot pay off or which cripple its own efforts or those of its citizens.

Public finances and the national debt

In general, the Dutch have enjoyed traditions of excellent public house-keeping since the seventeenth century. Interest rates have been kept low, and the currency has been extremely stable; taxation has traditionally been high, but government financial policy has been tight, or certainly not profligate.[48] However, there have been periodical variations in these traditional features. This is shown most clearly in the figures for the national debt. Expressed as a percentage of national income (NI), the fluctuations have been extreme, mainly owing to war. In the French period, and continuing through the period of union with and then separation from the Belgian provinces, the national debt was more than three times the value of NI. It then fell rapidly to about 60 per cent of NI in the 1860s, and continued to fall until the mid-1970s, when it was just 23 per cent. In the course of the decline there were the predictable temporary expansions of the debt for the World Wars, especially the Second. The burden of repayment has shown similar fluctuations, also explicable mainly in terms of war. It was high in the French period, and rose to more than 6 per cent of NI in the 1840s, before falling steadily to 1.2 per cent on the eve of World War I. (After fluctuations due to wars and depression, it returned to rates of under 2 per cent from 1955 to 1975, only to rocket again to 5.4 per cent in the 1990s.) Apart from putting today's public debt and expenditure problems in an illuminating historical perspective, these figures show the scale of the country's debt problems before the 1840s, which were caused by inherited debts to pay for Europe's wars in the seventeenth and eighteenth centuries, by the financial policies of King Willem I, and by the Belgian Secession of 1830 with its subsequent 'perseverance' or 'status quo' policy (*volhardingspolitiek*) in the northern Netherlands, which refused to recognize the new state and maintained a war footing along the border.[49] Public expenditure grew in absolute terms after the mid-century, but not as a percentage of NI until after the outbreak of World War I; indeed it fell until 1873.[50]

Despite Willem I's intense desire to intervene to help the economy, his attempts to do so were confounded by these huge levels of public debt; indeed some of his schemes were so expensive that they compounded the

---

[48] 't Hart, *et al.*, *A financial history*, 7–10.   [49] Van Popta, 'Staatsschuld'.
[50] 't Hart, *et al.*, *A financial history*, chapter 4, especially pp. 68–9; and Van der Voort, *Overheidsbeleid*, 67.

problem. The King's intervention in the economy by setting up funds and regulating a number of industries had some encouraging effects, but the resultant state-monopolistic tendencies, and the financial burdens brought on the state as a result, probably cancelled out most of the advantages.[51] He inherited an appalling situation.[52] In 1810 the national debt had risen to f1.2 billion, and although two thirds of it was repudiated by Napoleon when the Kingdom of Holland was annexed to France in that year, this *tiërcering* (reduction to one third) was rescinded after the defeat of the French Emperor, and the debt was back up to more than f1.8 billion in 1814. It continued at astronomical levels throughout Willem's reign, and stood at f2.1 billion in 1841 (including deferred debt), shortly after his abdication. There is no doubt that these levels of debt were indicative of the expense incurred by Willem's centralizing policies, of the government's money problems, and of the country's extraordinary financial resilience.[53]

Willem was therefore faced with a considerable problem. He wanted to use the state's resources – and his own – to help the economy, but revenues were limited (they consisted of excises on mass consumption items like bread, salt, etc., and some modest direct taxes on the rich), and were entirely consumed in servicing the debt. It was difficult to cut public expenditure – indeed, after the secession of Belgium, defence expenditure would rise sharply – and politically impossible to raise taxes. He therefore turned to extra-parliamentary sources of income, some of which were successful, and some of which were disastrous.

In 1822 a sinking fund, or *Amortisatie Syndicaat*, of fifty members was set up, to raise new loans on the unfailing capital market. Although these were ostensibly to help the debt situation, most of the money actually went to Willem's schemes for the economy. In a situation where parliament only scrutinized 'ordinary' expenditure (meaning most items apart from war) every ten years, the *Syndicaat* took over a number of national financial responsibilities besides the debt, paying out f14m. on infrastructural projects and f18m. in industrial subsidies in the 1820s. In 1830 the Belgian Secession, coupled with complaints about all this extra-parliamentary usage of public funds, resulted in the demise of the *Syndicaat*. Its replacement as Willem's financial legitimator was the Netherlands Trading Company (NHM), founded in 1824 to revive trade with the East Indies. The struggle against the debt continued in

---

[51] Griffiths, *Industrial retardation*, 43–55.
[52] On the financial situation in the French period, culminating in 'effectively a declaration of partial state bankruptcy', see Pfeil, 'Het Nederlandse bezuinigingsbeleid'.
[53] 't Hart, *et al.*, *A financial history*, 69; Van Zanden, 'The development of government finances'.

vain, and Willem's economic schemes continued to cost great sums, while the NHM was also footing the bill for the campaign against the Belgians, as well as for the initially expensive changes in the East Indies regime.

By the late 1830s, crisis point had been reached, and the final settlement with Belgium in 1839 required the unravelling of the secrecy behind the government's dealings. The man credited with saving the Dutch public finances and avoiding state bankruptcy was F. A. van Hall (1791–1866), an Amsterdam lawyer who was Minister of Finance from 1844 to 1847, and then Minister of Justice. That part of the debt which had been deferred (i.e. no interest was paid) was dealt with by converting it at very low rates to real debt. A large forced loan at low interest was exacted from the capital markets with threat of a wealth tax if it was not forthcoming, in order to reschedule the debt and pay off the government's bills to the NHM.[54] Van Hall's brilliance has perhaps been exaggerated, for the reduction in defence spending after 1839 and the increasing income from the Indies from the 1840s combined to make his technical solution to the debt problem actually work in practice.[55]

Nonetheless, it is remarkable how few problems the national debt caused after 1850, at least until the close of the century. The annual interest payments declined slightly from ƒ36m. to ƒ32m. over the half-century from 1848 to 1898, while the government's budget actually doubled over that period, thus reducing the percentage of revenue required for servicing the debt. No further manifestations of sinking funds and the like were forthcoming, for they were banned from public finances in the new constitution of 1848. Public expenditure on infrastructural projects continued (the railways, canals, roads and communications), but without the direct interference characteristic of many of Willem's schemes, which, however well intentioned, were often wasteful and led the state nearly to bankruptcy.[56]

The massive debt payments, which became more manageable but continued throughout the century, had another unplanned effect: in an age when taxation was not progressive (i.e. most revenue was raised by measures which bore equally on all citizens, irrespective of their ability to pay), the national debt was a very neat conduit of resources from the poor to the rich. The impoverished masses paid their excise taxes on everyday items like salt, soap and fuel, in order to make up the interest payments on the national debt which went straight into the pockets of the *rentiers* who

[54] Brugmans, *Paardenkracht*, 181–8; 't Hart, *et al.*, *A financial history*, 75–7.
[55] Van Zanden, 'The development of government finances', 70.
[56] Brugmans, *Paardenkracht*, 270–1 and 398–9; 't Hart, *et al.*, *A financial history*, 85–7; Horlings, *The economic development*, 295.

held the debt. The fact that profits from paper investments were not taxed until 1892 increased the efficiency of the mechanism, and the situation did not change substantially until the First World War, when direct taxation began to play a really important part in revenue collection.[57] As far as the macro-economy was concerned, this national debt mechanism meant two things: capital was concentrated in the hands of those best able to pass it on to the entrepreneur, but domestic demand was suffocated for most of the century. To be fair, this set of circumstances pertained in most countries, even if the debt was not proportionately as large as the Dutch one, and in any case the mechanism was hardly a conscious aim of government policy in the first place.

Currency and banking

Another area in which modern governments are expected to provide stability and support for economic enterprise is that of the currency. In this the Dutch government of the nineteenth century was successful, though it could claim little credit, especially early in the century. Until the mid-century the Netherlands operated a bimetallic currency (both gold and silver), though it leaned heavily towards gold. Despite serious mismanagement on occasion, Dutch money was remarkably stable against foreign currencies. In 1847 Van Hall decided to go over to silver alone, which was effective until the 1870s, when the rest of Europe moved to gold, and the Netherlands was forced to follow. Internally, these measures eventually eradicated local coinage, a step which was of considerable value in moving towards a single national market for the country.

Increasingly, these currency and issue matters were dealt with by *De Nederlandsche Bank* (DNB), founded by royal decree in 1814, with its charter renewed and remit expanded in 1838 and 1863. It was founded as a government circulation bank (also for the East Indies), but was very slow to take over operations in that area, so a variety of paper circulated, as it always had. However, by the 1840s DNB was important enough in circulation to be the instrument of the government in Van Hall's debt-cleansing operations, and in the overhaul of the currency in the late 1840s. 'From then on, both bank and currency enjoyed the confidence necessary for building up a sound financial system', especially when its geographic concentration on the Amsterdam area became less pronounced after the new patent of 1863.[58] In general, the government looked after money matters well enough, despite the enormous problems

[57] Carter, *The Dutch Republic*, 133. See section 5.3 below, on taxation policy.
[58] Quotation from 't Hart, *et al.*, *A financial history*, 97. See also Butter, *Academic economics*, 8–15; Brugmans, *Paardenkracht*, 169–72, 258–60 and 390–2; and Wijtvliet, *Expansie*.

present, and the commission of some errors, especially early in the century.

Taxation

A government can also affect the national economy by its taxation policy: excessive taxes on profits may well depress entrepreneurial zeal, and heavy indirect taxes on mass-consumption items may limit domestic demand, for example. Taxation techniques are now used universally by governments in the developed world in attempts to control the money supply or levels of demand in the economy; in the nineteenth century such concepts were rudimentary at best, and in any case relatively few citizens were in a position to pay direct taxes at all. Over the period 1850–90 only about 15 per cent of the population paid the householder's tax (*personele belasting*), only 10 per cent had a maid, and only 5 per cent had more than one maid.[59] In the Republic and in the twentieth century the Dutch were highly taxed; for much of the nineteenth century other nations like Britain and France were actually more heavily burdened, and the Dutch per-capita tax burden was less in the nineteenth than in the eighteenth century. From levels approaching ƒ20 p.a. in the eighteenth century, it fell to about ƒ15 from 1815 to 1840, and it did not regain the ƒ20 mark again until the 1870s and 1880s.[60] As a percentage of the national product, total tax income (including the burgeoning budgets of the local authorities) declined from over 10 per cent in the early 1850s to a low-point of 7.5 per cent in the early 1870s; it rose again to 10 per cent in the mid-1890s and then subsided once more until the First World War (just over 8 per cent).[61] In general, the increase in the tax burden was gradual throughout the nineteenth century, and did not really take off to pay for the embryonic welfare state until the time of World War I.[62] One might say that the nineteenth century was a unique period within the Dutch tradition of high taxation: defence cuts in the first half of the century, followed by economic growth in the second, allowed the tax burden to decline from some 12 per cent to 7 per cent of national income.[63] Successive governments, then, can hardly be accused of taxing the country out of any potential for economic growth.

The balance between direct and indirect taxation changed over the century, and moved slowly towards the system that we now know, by which most tax is collected according to ability to pay. Direct taxes on wealth (income tax, property taxes, taxes on capital and wealth) are now

[59] Van Dijk, *Wealth*, 23–4.   [60] 't Hart, *et al.*, *A financial history*, 68–9.
[61] Van der Voort, *Overheidsbeleid*, graph on p. 110.
[62] 'De opbrengst van de rijks . . . belastingen', 750.
[63] 't Hart, *et al.*, *A financial history*, 10.

predominant, as opposed to indirect taxes which hit most people more-or-less equally, in the form of consumption taxes or excises on everyday requirements such as food, clothes and fuel. But the shift towards direct taxation was neither rapid nor steep. In 1824, 62.3 per cent of central fiscal revenue came from indirect taxes and levies; the figure was 67 per cent in 1835, and 66 per cent in 1850. An amount equivalent to a fifth of central tax was also raised in local taxation in the years around the mid-century, and 72 per cent of that came from indirect taxes. From a ratio of about two thirds at the mid-century, the proportion of tax raised by indirect methods had fallen by 1910, but only to 54 per cent. It is possible to speak of a shift to direct taxation and to taxing wealth proportionately in the course of the century, but it was slow and late compared to other countries. There were no taxes imposed on the holding of stocks and other investment paper until the 1890s, which exempted most of the *rentier* class from a tax on much of their wealth, and the introduction of an income tax in 1892–3 was very late indeed, after the fending off of no less than seven bills to introduce one since 1848. Evidently the propertied classes were well represented in the Second Chamber, and knew how to defend their interests. In 1892 and 1893 the economist and Finance Minister Nicolaas Pierson (1839–1909) finally got income tax through parliament, half a century after Britain had done so, and even then the Dutch rates remained low until the Second World War.[64] Whatever our verdict on social justice, it cannot be said that the Dutch authorities taxed their capitalists and entrepreneurs out of existence in the nineteenth century.

The initial fundamental change to taxation came during the turbulent Batavian period in 1805 under the Minister for Finance Isaac Gogel (1765–1821). The significance of his reform was that it ushered in a national taxation system to replace the myriad local fiscal regimes which had obtained under the Republic. As it came into effect in the early nineteenth century, it was a powerful force for national unification (see the sub-section on centralization, below). In 1820 a committee was set up under Baron W. F. Roëll (1767–1835) to review taxation, and it came up with a new 'system', which then formed the basis of the 'System Act' (*Stelselwet*) of 1821, passed in the teeth of opposition from the Belgian provinces (for taxation was one of the bitterest points of issue between north and south). Its 'system' was intended to be one based on people paying according to their capacity to do so; in fact it contained many

---

[64] Schuttevaer and Detiger, *Anderhalve eeuw belastingen*, 29; 't Hart, *et al.*, *A financial history*, 84–90; Bos, 'Vermogensbezitters'. Two examples of popular calls for a tax on income to relieve excises are De Oude, *Neêrlands behoud* (1849); and Baart, *Een blik* (1867). On Pierson see Van Daal and Heertje, eds., *Economic thought*, chapter 5.

anomalies (most of them in favour of the *rentiers*), and was no more progressive than Gogel's scheme. For most of the century, the rich paid property taxes in the form of a household tax (*personele*), a land tax for those who owned land, and a business rate (*patentbelasting*, also paid by small businesses); as we have seen, these only amounted to about a third of revenue, the other two thirds coming from excises and levies. Local taxes (*opcenten*) could be added by municipal councils to the national ones. The effect of these excises on the price of labour has already been discussed in the section on wages above (4.2): the argument is that wages were particularly high in the west of the Netherlands partly because of high excises, which were needed to service the enormous debts held at national and municipal level, and to fund a generous poor-relief system. It may also have been the case that the domestic market was depressed because of a lack of purchasing power on the part of ordinary people caused by the high taxes; however, this has yet to be proved, and in any case would have to be weighed against the generally modest levels of tax compared to the eighteenth and twentieth centuries.[65]

The shift away from the preponderance of excises in the fiscal burden is one of the trumpeted achievements of the liberal administrations which dominated Dutch politics for forty years after 1848. Thorbecke expressed his belief that certain kinds of taxation were particularly onerous for the ordinary people of the country because they raised the cost of living, and he was referring to excises. The excise on milling grain was abolished in 1855, followed by those on coal and peat, and many others, with corresponding increases in the tax on spirits: *jenever* or Dutch gin was generally referred to as the 'milch-cow' for these reforms.[66] The local government laws of the early 1850s, and a subsequent act of 1865, removed the power of municipalities to levy excises. Apart from gin, the benefactors allowing this change (which it should be remembered was a gradual one) were the generally improved state of the national finances since the 1840s, increased receipts from the East Indies, and a general economic acceleration experienced in the whole of Europe in the third quarter of the century. The removal of most excises did, however, represent a liberalization of the economy, and perhaps a modest easing of the burden of the poorer people, who of course made up the vast majority of the population. The long-term effects of this policy, driven mainly by liberal ideology, are likely to have been favourable. The unificatory effects of the reforms,

---

[65] Knippenberg and De Pater, *De eenwording*, 142–3; 't Hart, *et al.*, *A financial history*, 82; Schuttevaer and Detiger, *Anderhalve eeuw belastingen*, 13–26; Engels, *De belastingen*; Griffiths, *Industrial retardation*, 47–55; Griffiths, 'The role of taxation', 264–5.

[66] On the details of these excise changes on household consumption items, see section 2.4 above, on the food supply.

bringing the country increasingly together as a national market with fewer internal barriers, were also beneficial.[67]

These taxation matters also need to be placed in the context of the preceding period. Under the Republic they had been dealt with largely by the towns; after 1798 there was a central government trying to impose an increasingly centralized tax regime, but with few of the instruments of policy and implementation which the towns had possessed in the eighteenth century. Only the reforms of Thorbecke after the mid-century provided the true legitimacy and equipment for national policy by regulating local government.[68] Centralization was a long drawn-out affair, as the sub-section below will reveal.

Laissez-faire *ideology*

The Netherlands had its own version of the international debate on the relative merits of government intervention and the *laissez-faire* tendency to let the entrepreneur have his head, and regulate as little as possible. It is folly to equate liberalism with *laissez-faire* and nothing else: it was those same liberals who, at the same time as they were demolishing much of Willem I's regulated economy, were busy increasing public expenditure, setting up national infrastructure projects, and making huge social provisions.[69] Nonetheless, around the mid-century there was a sea-change in government policy which shifted from a tendency to control and regulate the economy to one in which private enterprise was promoted and the number of impediments to economic initiative was reduced where possible. Only towards the end of the century did the pendulum swing back towards greater interference in the market, and in the twentieth century the Netherlands eventually became one of the most regulated economies in the capitalist world.

In this context, the description of Willem I's regime as 'mercantilist' refers to his keenness to interfere on the part of the government in order – as he thought – to maximize the chances of economic felicity for his subjects. 'Mercantilism' is an anachronism in the nineteenth century, and even when applied to the seventeenth century it is a much debated concept.[70] It certainly did not mean – necessarily – that governments acted in the interests of merchants; in general the latter favoured as little regulation as possible, although they were happy to accept an

---

[67] Brugmans, *Paardenkracht*, 223–6; 'De opbrengst van de rijks . . . belastingen', 750; Roovers, *De plaatselijke belastingen*, 73–8; Van Maarseveen, 'Gemeentelijke belastingen', 168; Horlings, *The economic development*, 303.

[68] See Davids, *et al.*, *De Nederlandse geschiedenis*, 14–19; and Davids and Lucassen, eds., *A miracle mirrored*, 442ff.

[69] See below, section 9.3.   [70] Groenveld and Wintle, eds., *State and trade*, chapter 3.

advantage over competition whenever they could obtain it without reprisals.

Willem certainly involved the government in the economy. As we have seen, he set up the *Amortisatie Syndicaat*, the NHM, the *Société Générale* and the *Fonds voor de Nationale Nijverheid*, all in order to use government resources to assist merchants and industrialists. He undertook massive public works, particularly in canals, and used differential tariffs, especially in colonial trade, to protect Dutch interests. He subsidized a protected new textile sector in the northern provinces, creating thousands of jobs in the process, and regulated industries to raise standards, from brewing to shipbuilding. In classic mercantilist vein, he attempted to prevent the emigration of technically useful individuals in 1814, restricted the export of capital in 1816 (the law had to be repealed in 1824), and in 1820 decreed that the armed forces, government agencies and even charities should use only Dutch products wherever possible. To deal with the problems of poverty and destitution, again he favoured state action, in opposition to many in the liberal and Calvinist Anti-Revolutionary camps, who believed that private or religious foundations should take responsibility. Willem was not dogmatic about his economic policy, and would be flexible where necessary. He was, one might say, a passionate believer in 'making things work' rather than letting things run their course, and he also believed in the power of the state to assist him to carry out his policies.

This brought him into periodic conflict with those who were more closely aligned with the Dutch merchants' interests, for until 1830 Willem had to consider the interest of the Belgian industrialists, who needed protection against British competition, as well as those of the northern traders. G. K. van Hogendorp (1762–1824) became a focus for the *laissez-faire* opposition to Willem's economic policy: he had been instrumental in designing the new constitutional arrangements in 1813–16, and from 1816 to 1825 he operated from the Second Chamber as something of a thorn in the side of the government on economic issues, opposing all forms of protection in his prolific publications. Liberal or *laissez-faire* arguments were thus very much present in the political arena in the Netherlands in the first half the century, despite the fact that the King favoured intervention; in any case, as a trading nation the Dutch had generally wanted to remove barriers to trade rather than throw up walls of tariffs and regulation.[71]

With the abdication of Willem in 1840, the interventionist urge ebbed, and the *laissez-faire* school came into its own. Led by Thorbecke, the

[71] Brugmans, *Paardenkracht*, 137–40, 150–5 and 175; Butter, *Academic economics*, 21–33; Boschloo, *De productiemaatschappij*, 63–77; and Zuidema, 'Economic thought'.

'doctrinaire' or first generation of liberals formally took over the reins of power in 1849, and were the guiding force in Dutch politics until the 1880s, when their influence was superseded by a new generation of more socially concerned liberals, by the rising confessional parties, and (a little later on) by the socialists. Three points need to be made about this generation of doctrinaire liberals. First, their reign coincided with the most successful economic period in the century, between 1850 and the mid-1870s: however much their policies contributed to that prosperity, they were fortunate in the extreme in benefiting from the upturn in all Western economies which took place in the third quarter of the nineteenth century. Second, the implementation of the economic programme of the liberals was not a truly radical break with the past, but more of a culmination of policy drift over several generations. There had been intense debates about free trade in the press and parliament for decades and more, and the government of Willem I had not been dogmatic in its protection and intervention, but rather pragmatic and practical. In many cases it was external pressure, from England, France and Prussia, rather than the agenda of the liberals at home, which actually carried the bills that 'liberated' the Dutch economy.[72] And third, at the same time as the liberals were repealing regulations and removing Willem's apparatus of economic intervention, they were also building up the economic and social power of the state by creating a national transport and communication infrastructure, social services and an education system.[73]

Nonetheless, something amounting to a 'liberation' took place between the 1840s and the 1870s. Tariffs were lowered, excises were cut, agriculture and industry were deregulated, and eventually even the colonies were thrown open to private enterprise. In 1854 the Dutch monopoly on trade with Japan was forcibly opened up, in the course of the 1850s all restrictions and differential duties were lifted from the fishing industry, government support for the cotton industry was withdrawn in 1849, and supervision of the wool industry was terminated in 1862. After 1846 state subsidies to industry were progressively wound down and abolished, and the increasing exposure to international competition through free trade must have focussed the mind of many an entrepreneur. In the 1870s even the mighty NHM ceased to be the government's economic instrument in colonial trade, and became simply another bank. It was quite a different style of 'economic policy' from that of Willem I.[74]

---

[72] Bläsing, 'Interne en externe oorzaken'.
[73] Kraemer, *The societal state*, 39–41; Brugmans, *Paardenkracht*, 227–45.
[74] Brugmans, *Paardenkracht*, 219–23; Van den Eerenbeemt, *Bedrijfskapitaal*, 6; Renooy, 'De Nederlandsche Handel-Maatschappij', 154–5.

Towards the end of the century, the mood of government policy on the economy changed once more, edging in the direction of the massive intervention and state involvement in the economy and social life which is so characteristic of the Netherlands today. The Dutch are renowned for their passion for planning everything, for universal regulation, and for state supervision of all activities outside the home and of many of those inside it as well.[75] There is some exaggeration in this caricature, but a great deal of truth as well, and the initial 'deliberalization' of the Dutch economy began to get under way towards the end of the nineteenth century. It has been argued that *verzuiling* or pillarization is essentially a matter of socio-economic control, and it began to typify Dutch society as the twentieth century dawned: the civil and moral offensives generated by the powerful religious pillars were successful in delivering a docile, sober workforce for much of the first half the twentieth century, which amounted to an 'entrepreneurial eldorado' for the Dutch.[76] The labour market had been largely free in the nineteenth century, but in the early twentieth century began to feel the hand of government control. After keeping poor relief at arm's length for decades, around the turn of the century a legislative programme began which slowly but surely put in place one of the most elaborate welfare states the world has ever seen. Perhaps the turning point was the Industrial Accidents Act of 1901, but since the 1880s there had been moves to regulate the free operation of the economy, from the confessional parties and of course from the socialists.[77] In the era of New Imperialism, especially after the 1890s, the Dutch government too would move towards state-assisted capitalism in the East Indies, and even in trade policy the protectionist lobby began to make itself heard after 1900.[78] We shall examine the effect on the economic fortunes of the various sectors exerted by these changes in government ideology over the course of the nineteenth century, beginning with trade, followed by industry, and then agriculture.

Government and trade

Trade was of great importance to the particular path taken by the Dutch economy in the nineteenth century, and therefore government policy

---

[75] See, for example, Faludi and Van der Valk, *Rule and order*.

[76] Van Zanden, *The economic history*, 4 and 11–14; see also Couwenberg, ed., *De Nederlandse natie*, 121–2; Peeters, *et al.*, eds., *Vijf eeuwen gezinsleven*, chapter 7.

[77] Van Zanden, *The economic history*, 72; Van der Voort, *Overheidsbeleid*, 205; on the socialization of the Dutch state, and the drawing together of society and the state at the end of the century, see section 11.1.

[78] Groenveld and Wintle, eds., *State and trade*, chapter 8; De Vries, 'De twintigste eeuw', 271.

towards it is of special interest. After the collapse of the Continental System and the lifting of the English blockade of Napoleonic Europe, which had together crucified Dutch sea-borne trade, the new government reintroduced protective tariff laws similar to those first imposed by a 1725 *Placaat* at a level of 10–20 per cent. The Belgian industrialists in the south were generally in favour; the merchants in the north were not. After the Secession, a major lowering of tariffs took place in 1831 (which meant that if Dutch industry was to be protected, other ways had to be found). During the 1820s and 1830s, the military patron and major trading partner Britain moved slowly towards freeing its trade, and the Dutch diplomats argued the points closely with their English counterparts. A commercial treaty was signed in 1837 between the two countries, and the British kept up continual pressure on the Dutch to free their trade from differential tariffs. Gradually the pressure took effect: in 1845 the liberal-influenced government introduced a new schedule which reduced 170 tariffs while raising only 60, and agreements between Belgium and Germany, plus mounting pressure from France, all forced the pace. In 1850 the Thorbeckian liberal government took a further step: the Finance Minister P. P. van Bosse (1809–79) brought in Shipping or Navigation Acts, which removed most of the differential on shipping except in the colonies. In 1862 Finance Minister G. H. Betz (1816–68) brought in another liberal tariff reform which reduced all tariffs to a purely fiscal level of no more than 5 per cent. By the 1870s all Dutch trade was entirely free, including that of the colonies, and the only duties levied were simply to raise money for services to trade, rather than to favour Dutch carriers against others. With very few adjustments, this was the system which pertained until the crisis of the 1930s.[79]

Transit trade, especially on the rivers, followed a similar pattern, but was something of a special case for this rivermouth nation. The Dutch had always profited from their position at the mouth of the Rhine and the Maas, but their traditional tactic of playing off one state against another in the hinterland saw its days numbered with the formation of the *Zollverein*, the German Customs Union, in 1834. Despite the continuing weakness of the Germanic federation, even in economic terms, there is no doubt that Germany-to-be was a rising force in the land, and when in 1843 a railway line was opened from Cologne in the German industrial heartland direct to the port of Antwerp in independent Belgium, the writing was on the wall for the Dutch domination of the river trade. The Congress of Vienna had designated the River Rhine as international waters, but the

[79] De Vries, *Geschiedenis van de handelspolitieke betrekkingen*, passim; Heringa, *Free trade*, 4–7; Van Tijn, 'De negentiende eeuw', 206; Wright, *Free trade*, 70–2; Brugmans, *Paardenkracht*, 140–2, 214–18, and 387–8.

Dutch took a very dim view of this limitation of their ancient method of making money, which at its most rapacious would be to treat transit trade (which consisted of goods passing through, not destined for the Dutch market at all) like ordinary trade, levying import duty on it as it came in, and export duty as it exited. In defiance they imposed duties on non-Dutch trade on the Rhine just before it reached the coast, and on all other rivers.[80] In 1831 the Mainz Convention obliged the Netherlands to accept internationally determined fixed rates on Rhine and Waal shipping, while treaties with Prussia in 1837 and with the whole of the *Zollverein* in 1839 further reduced Dutch domination. In 1851 a new treaty gave the Germans and Dutch reciprocal privileges, with a low standard duty for fiscal purposes only. All tolls, including those on the German Rhine, were abolished by the Rhine Navigation Treaty of Mannheim in 1868. By the 1860s the foreign policy of the Netherlands was largely being driven by economic considerations, as can be seen from the sale of the toll of the Scheldt River in 1863, a toll which had helped the Dutch to dominate the trade of the Belgian and northern French hinterland since the fall of Antwerp in 1585. These changes were slow, and doggedly negotiated by the Dutch, who were characterized by their practicality and pragmatism. And the benefits were considerable. The free trade on the rivers resulted in enormous earnings on the transit trade with Germany after the 1860s, when the new nation began to flex its industrial muscles, demanding ever more bulk raw materials and guaranteeing the meteoric rise of Rotterdam as a transit port. In the first half of the century, while the German neighbours' economy was still finding its feet, the Dutch learned the skills which would bring them success in the later nineteenth and twentieth centuries: those of the commission agent, the warehouseman, the shipper and the handler, rather than those of the trader on his own account. In the eighteenth century Amsterdam had dominated the Rhine trade, and after 1870 Rotterdam would do so again; in the interim, the Dutch adjusted in a practical manner to the new politics of economy and power, learned to operate as service providers under increasingly *laissez-faire* systems, and ended up making more money than ever before. They relinquished their monopoly, but by adroit and realistic negotiating suffered very little in the long run, and in this respect government trade policy must be deemed successful, as far as the river trade was concerned.[81]

The treaties negotiated by the Dutch government which concerned

---

[80] The Congress of Vienna had decreed that trade on the Rhine should be free of tolls '*jusqu'à la mer*', which the Dutch decided to interpret as being located at the river port of Krimpen-aan-de-Lek, where they slapped a hefty toll on foreign shipping.
[81] Brugmans, *Paardenkracht*, 120–4; Nusteling, *De Rijnvaart*; Smit, *Diplomatieke geschiedenis*, 202–3; Bläsing, *Das goldene Delta*.

seaward trade followed the prevailing economic thought of the day, moving from modestly protectionist to almost completely *laissez-faire* by the end of the century. Britain was the most important partner early in the century: the 1837 commercial treaty was, as we have seen, an important step towards the relaxing of trade restrictions with all partners. The basis of the treaty was that each granted the other 'most favoured nation' status, meaning that neither nation would award any other nation more favourable conditions than were awarded to the treaty partners. The 1849 Navigation Acts and the 1851 Treaty continued the trend of removing all protection in trade between the two countries, with the exception of colonial goods, which were finally freed in 1872. There was a treaty in 1840 with France effecting a modest lowering of duties and impediments, and after the Anglo-French Cobden Treaty of 1860, which ushered in free trade, the Dutch signed one with France in 1865 which removed some trade duties, though much of the protection of domestic industry remained. In 1842 an agreement was signed with the highly suspicious new neighbour Belgium; it was renegotiated in 1846 after disputes, and renewed in 1851 with very low levels of tariff. Further agreements in the 1860s reduced the barriers between the old northern and southern Netherlands even further. At the end of the century there was a tendency towards protection again; however, Britain and Germany remained true to their free trade principles as far as the Netherlands was concerned, and although France revoked its treaty in 1879 in order to protect its domestic market, it granted the Netherlands 'most favoured nation' status five years later in 1884, and Dutch trade with France prospered in the period up to the First World War.[82]

Finally on the policy of the Dutch government towards the commercial sector, there are the chartered trading companies. The enormous success of the Dutch East India Company (*Vereenigde Oost-Indische Compagnie*, VOC) and the West India Company (WIC) in the time of the Republic, followed by their ignominious decline and bankruptcy at the end of the eighteenth century, formed the backdrop. The most important of the nineteenth-century manifestations was obviously the NHM, running trade with the East Indies (see below), but there was also a Levant Company, which was revived by Willem I in 1814, and given a new charter in 1817; however, the problems provided by a combination of Ottoman officials and Algerian pirates caused the company to close quietly in 1826. The West India Company was reconstituted in 1828 (*West-Indische Maatschappij*), again as a personal initiative of the King, who also provided most of the capital, in order to run the trade with the

---

[82] Brugmans, *Paardenkracht*, 144–8, 245–8 and 388–9; and Bos, *Brits-Nederlandse handel.*

slave economies of the West Indies and South American colonies, to act as a centre for American trade in general, and even to foster an early scheme for the Panama Canal. Things did not go well, and when slaves were emancipated on Dutch plantations in 1862 (rather later than the English in 1833, and the French in 1848), the Company quietly folded the year afterwards. There was also an ill-starred chartered company for the trade in China tea, set up by the King in 1815 (*Nederlandsche Geoctroyeerde Maatschappij voor den Chinaschen Theehandel*). Willem put up half the capital, and it was given a monopoly on importing tea to the Netherlands, against the advice of the Chambers of Commerce in Amsterdam, Rotterdam and Dordrecht. It failed completely, and this 'débâcle' and 'unforgivable blunder' was closed down after only two years in 1817. These efforts were hardly successful, but King Willem I was certainly indefatigable in his efforts to support Dutch trade, and in his willingness to put his personal resources into it.[83]

By far the most important government-sponsored company was of course the Dutch Trading Company, the NHM. Earlier in this chapter we have seen the role played by the NHM in bankrolling the state, and in providing financial capital for the textile industry; we shall now examine its effect on trade, which was profound. The problem faced by Willem's government after 1815 was that the East Indies empire was losing money hand over fist. This was not a new problem, for the old VOC of the Republic had effectively been declared bankrupt in 1798 with the state taking over its massive debts; however, the French period had exacerbated the problem. The English and others, including the Americans, were now conducting much of the trade on the Dutch colonies and reeling in its profits, while the Dutch were left with the bills for the infrastructure, the state apparatus and the political costs (army, administration, etc.).

These things were explained to the King by a number of old Indies hands in the early years of his reign, and the foundation of the NHM in 1824 was a direct response to the problem. Again, the King put in his own cash (*f*4m. of the *f*37m. founding capital, which was subscribed twice over, thanks to the King's further guarantee of a dividend). It was not, strictly speaking, a revival of the VOC, for there was no monopoly on all trade; the NHM bought, shipped and sold in Europe the products of the East Indies government regime, and could use only Dutch vessels in the process. It also provided return freights mainly in the form of cheap textiles produced by Dutch domestic industry, as we have seen in the case of cotton cloth, in order to displace the hold established by the English on

---

[83] Brugmans, *Paardenkracht*, 150; Schmidt, *From Anatolia to Indonesia*; Reinsma, 'De West-Indische Maatschappij'; and Broeze, 'Laat mercantilist?', especially pp. 233–4.

trade with the East Indies. The NHM's control of the coffee and sugar crops (as well as spices, dyes, rice and other products) was highly profitable, and the distribution centres in the metropole also benefited. Amsterdam became the coffee capital of Europe, and indeed the subtitle of *Max Havelaar*, the great Dutch colonial novel of the nineteenth century, is *The coffee auctions of the Dutch Trading Company*.[84] There were inevitably some initial problems, and the NHM had to concentrate its activities on the East Indies, relinquishing the trade on America, the Mediterranean and China, but after 1825 the Dutch won back the Indies trade from the competition, and in this respect the policy was highly successful. The operations of the NHM were directly complementary to the Cultivation System on government plantations in the Indies, which after 1830 provided increasing net profits for the Dutch Treasury, and was immensely important for Dutch economic growth in general. The NHM's operations were very much under the wing of the government, and indeed in the early years, up to 1843, there were secret premiums of 12.5 per cent paid by the Treasury to the NHM on its exports of cotton cloth to the Indies. This amounted to protection, and indeed quasi-monopoly, and wits suggested that the initials NHM really stood for '*Niemand Handelt Meer*', or 'No-one Trades Anymore', because so many private firms were excluded. There was also the problem of the financial crisis of the state occasioned by the NHM's activities. It had not been easy for the new state to replace the complicated old system of the VOC, run by private merchants in the cities. Nevertheless, trade and its profits were back in Dutch hands, the cotton industry grew and prospered, and the Netherlands became a thriving centre for the distribution of colonial goods like coffee, sugar, indigo, spices and tin. A recent study concluded that the NHM was of enormous benefit to the Dutch economy, but that it hindered the shipping sector by sucking resources into the government monopoly: 'in the end colonial exploitation combined huge financial benefits with structural degradation'.[85]

Thus government policy ensured that the trade between the Netherlands and its colonies was almost entirely in Dutch hands between 1825 and the 1860s. Thereafter, because of the extension of *laissez-faire* policies to the colonies, protection was relaxed, and virtually abolished by 1870. The position of the Dutch merchants was therefore threatened. The English recaptured the Java sugar market almost immediately, the

[84] Multatuli, *Max Havelaar of de koffieveilingen*; an English translation (with a foreword by none other than D. H. Lawrence) was published as Multatuli, *Max Havelaar or the coffee auctions*.

[85] Horlings, *The economic development*, 194. See also Mansvelt, *Geschiedenis van de Nederlandsche Handel-Maatschappij*; and Brugmans, *Paardenkracht*, 108–17.

Germans threatened to move in on Sumatran tobacco, and 40 per cent of the trade in Java coffee, the jewel in the crown, had been lost to foreign competition by 1914. In 1910 the Netherlands received no more than a quarter of East Indies exports. However, because of the enormous expansion of trade and shipping, the value and volume of trade handled by the Dutch was greater than ever before, so although the Dutch had to share their profits, there was more than enough to go round. In retrospect, it was a classic case of dynamism having been restricted in the course of protecting a monopoly.[86]

Government and industry

A similar pattern is discernible in government policy with regard to manufacturing industry. The Batavian Republic appointed Johannes Goldberg (1763–1828) as the Agent (Minister) for the National Economy in 1798, and Willem I's administration was intensely involved with the control and regulation of manufacturing; that control was increasingly relaxed from the 1840s and especially from the 1850s and 1860s onwards. The result of the relaxation was an expansion of business, but it is arguable that the favourable conditions for that expansion had been formed – at least partly – under the protected conditions at the beginning of the century. The avowed aim of protection, after all, is usually to nurture a tender young plant threatened by overbearing competition from neighbouring giants, rather than to prop up decaying dinosaurs.

For example, Willem's government took control of the madder industry and retained its meticulous regulations until 1845, when the failure of the industry against French competition encouraged deregulation. The manufacture of clay pipes was regulated in 1818, and in 1824 the government imposed a set of rules about the installation of steam engines. Sugar-refining, shipbuilding, brewing and distilling were all the recipients of considerable attention in the 1830s and 1840s, in the form of subsidies and regulation; the first two did well in this hothouse, while the latter two languished. The NHM nurtured the cotton industry in the 1830s in order to provide competitive trade goods for the East Indies, and the foundations of the cotton industry in Twente were built in the process. Behind the broad back of NHM subsidies and monopoly, the Dutch textile industry on occasion was inefficient, was run as a charity where depressed Dutch paupers needed employment, was often slow to adopt new technology, and employed cumbersome marketing; nonetheless when protection was relaxed in the 1850s there was an industrial branch strong

---

[86] Blok, *et al.*, eds., *Algemene geschiedenis der Nederlanden*, vol. XIII, pp. 53, 274–6 and 284.

enough to withstand competition from established players in the European Industrial Revolution like Britain and Belgium. The fishing industry, including fish-processing, was minutely regulated, as it had been in the Republic in order to maintain standards, but failed to thrive at all. In the 1850s most of the regulation and control by subsidy was abandoned, particularly in the Fishing Act of 1857, and sea-fishing picked up again. After the 1870s there was very little interference by the government in industry, and no protection at all. There was some modest regulation of factories in the 1890s, heralding the start of a very comprehensive set of labour laws, but only the first signs of it were visible before the First World War.[87]

Government and agriculture

The pattern was also recognizable to an extent in agriculture. Again the Batavian Republic took the lead in 1800 by appointing Jan Kops (1765–1849) as its highly active Commissioner for Agriculture, and then until the 1840s the national government attempted to regulate and run the sector, before abandoning such interference in the liberal mood of the mid-century. Conventionally, the most potent instrument in the government arsenal for affecting the fortunes of agriculture was the corn law, which taxed cheap foreign grain on entry in order to allow domestic farmers to make a living. After the end of the Napoleonic Wars the international trade routes for grain opened once more, and Ukraine grain was again available through the Black Sea, resulting in a collapse of prices lasting into the early 1820s. As a result, most countries instituted corn laws in order to protect their peasants and farmers. King Willem was loath to follow this route, but by 1822 the plight of Dutch farmers was so dire that the government authorized a small tariff rise, followed by a tripling in 1825. The Belgian Revolution led to the reinstatement of the 1822 level, but the 1830s were disastrous years for grain farmers everywhere, not least in the Netherlands, and in 1835 a sliding-scale corn law was introduced, designed to protect Dutch farmers with high tariffs when prices were very low, but to lower the duties when prices were high enough to sustain domestic farmers in their livelihood. Richard Griffiths argued that the sliding scale was wrongly calibrated, and that the protection was therefore ineffective. In a carbon copy of the situation in England, the potato blight of 1845–46 provoked ministerial alarm at the

[87] Brugmans, *Paardenkracht*, 151–5, 220–2 and 311–12; Griffiths, *Industrial retardation*, 85–101 and 138–83; Sluijk, 'Meekrap', 32–3; Van de Voort, 'De Nederlandse Maatschappij', 210–11; Mansvelt, *Geschiedenis van de Nederlandsche Handel-Maatschappij*, vol. I, pp. 335ff.

prospect of hunger riots, and the free-trade lobby was successful in having the corn laws rescinded immediately. In 1847 a low import tax was substituted; in 1853 it was lowered further, and in 1877 entirely abolished. There were calls for agricultural protection from the late 1870s onwards when the international crisis struck again, but to no avail in the Netherlands until the First World War.[88]

Willem I put farming courses on the university curriculum for theology students, in the hope that a new generation of rural ministers would carry news of innovations and best practice into the villages. (Not surprisingly, most theology students had other things on their minds, and the scheme was dropped in 1840[89]). The government had agencies in each province, called the Agriculture Commissions (*Commissiën van Landbouw*), founded in 1805 by Jan Kops and re-established in 1814, which amassed data in Napoleonic style and attempted to spread good practice. They were abolished by Thorbecke in 1851 in favour of the private-sector agricultural societies which had grown up as rather late variants of the Enlightenment philosophical and scientific societies. Around the mid-century, deregulation and free trade led to expanding markets: English demand for Dutch agricultural products grew exponentially from the mid-1840s to the mid-1860s.[90]

By the 1880s, liberal policy towards agriculture was beginning to look like neglect or disinterest, for the Dutch government appeared to take few measures to counter the effects of the agricultural crisis which began in the late 1870s and lasted until the mid-1890s. Demands for protection fell on deaf ears, perhaps partly for the reason that Dutch farming in the 1870s was in pretty good shape.[91] On the face of it, this does not replicate the shift back to regulation and protection we have noticed in other sectors, which took place at the same time as the coming of mass politics, socialism, and the social effects of industrialization: Dutch economic liberalism seems to have lived on in agriculture after its time was cut short in industry and trade. Matters were in fact a little more complex. In the late part of the century, during the agricultural crisis, Dutch governments were not indifferent to the plight of farmers. Whereas in the 1840s the debate on corn laws had been about the price of bread for the masses, the officials of the 1880s were concerned about farming people themselves on a much greater scale, and sought to help in many ways without actually going down the road of full-scale protection, as did Germany and

[88] Brugmans, *Paardenkracht*, 142–3; Griffiths, *Industrial retardation*, 17–21; and Vermeulen, *Den Haag en de landbouw*.
[89] Huizinga, 'De invloed van het onderwijs', 236.
[90] Bouman, 'Landbouworganisaties'; Van Zanden, *De economische ontwikkeling*, 220–2; and Knibbe, *Agriculture*, 115.
[91] Koning, *The failure*, chapter 7.

France.[92] They used quality-control mechanisms to maintain standards, and encouraged improvements with education and co-operatives. A government testing station for fertilizers and seeds was set up in 1876 at Wageningen, and would later become the renowned Agricultural University. The government made it easier to commute certain tithes by means of an 1872 Act, and in 1886 there was similar legislation covering commons or 'marken'; tithes were finally abolished in 1907. Several other feudal left-overs were cleared out of the path of modern farming by legislation.[93] Even in the heyday of liberalism, government might be prepared to lend a hand: there was some protection for sugarbeet farmers in 1856 by means of a sugar excise,[94] and the government continued to help farming by providing more land drained from the sea, rivers and lakes, not least in the shape of the vast Haarlemmermeer polder in 1848–52. By 1906 government intervention was becoming more overt: there was a commission set up to look into the plight of the agricultural labourer (which albeit took until 1918 to result in a Farm Labourers Act, that made it much easier for them to buy their own land). By the twentieth century, agriculture had become virtually a trade-based activity, importing fertilizer and food for man and beast alike in vast bulk, and exporting the products of a highly intensive domestic processing industry. This made sense in peace time with few trade restrictions, but cut off from trade in World War I, and therefore from imports of basic foodstuffs, the government began seriously to lay its hand on agriculture once more, again, as in the 1840s, in order to feed the populace. In the crisis of the 1930s, under which comparable conditions prevailed, as the trade barriers were hastily erected around Europe and the world, the Dutch farming sector became probably the most regulated in the non-Communist world. Thus had the pendulum swung from interference in agriculture over to laissez-faire around 1850, and back to intervention as the century drew to a close, paving the way for the 'regulated society' of the twentieth century.[95]

Centralization

A significant aspect of government policy in most of the nascent European nation states was centralization. State and nation formation will be considered furthered in chapter 11, but here we need to examine its economic aspects and implications. In recent economic historiography

[92] Vermeulen, Den Haag en de landbouw, 97–9.
[93] Brugmans, Paardenkracht, 250–3 and 310–11; and Knibbe, Agriculture, 158. On tithes, see Wintle, '"Plagerijen"'.
[94] Blink, Geschiedenis van den boerenstand, vol. II, pp. 329–31.
[95] Sneller, 'Anderhalve eeuw', 107–17.

it has taken on considerable importance. A thorough geographical study of 'the unification of the Netherlands' has explained for the first time in detail how the process took place,[96] and since then economic historians have been inclined to lend more and more credence to the overriding impact of the political and infrastructural centralization of the country in explaining the dynamics of its economic fortunes.[97]

The modern Dutch state was formed in the period of the Revolt against Spain, but was a highly decentralized (though effective) federal structure. That structure was finally replaced in the French period when the Unitarist faction, with French support, established dominance over the old elites of the towns and provinces. The unitary state was strengthened by the constitutions of the restoration under the House of Orange in 1814 and 1815. The battle of principles over structure had been fought and won by 1815; the rest of the nineteenth century saw the working out of the details, sometimes energetically and sometimes imperceptibly, and the eventual carrying through of the logic of the unitary centralization to its full extent in all sectors. The Dutch state, then, has existed *vis-à-vis* other states since the sixteenth century, and has been officially unitary for the last two hundred years. The full implementation of that process, however, has taken a very long time.[98] Regional loyalties are still strong in the Netherlands today, and in the provinces and even in Amsterdam and Rotterdam, the national government is spoken of as 'Den Haag' (The Hague), as a sometimes remote and removed impersonal officialdom, rather in the way that the British today might refer to the European Union's administration as 'Brussels'.

The establishment of a centralized state in the Netherlands encountered particular problems because of the inherited highly devolved federalism of the Republic, in which the seven provinces had been sovereign, and where the towns were politically and financially semi-independent. In addition, there existed a strong tradition, especially in the north of the country, of orthodox Calvinism, and of Baptism (Mennonitism), both of which placed organizational emphasis on the congregation rather than the church: the local community was what mattered, rather than some overarching 'national' or international structure. These two elements added to the difficulties facing the centralizing regimes of the French period and of Willem I. In the words of Knippenberg and De Pater on the 'unification' of the Dutch since 1800, 'in the first half of the nineteenth century the Netherlands was a state, but its inhabitants did not yet make up one nation.'[99]

---

[96] Knippenberg and De Pater, *De eenwording.*
[97] Especially Horlings, *The economic development*; see below, at the end of this section.
[98] Knippenberg and De Pater, *De eenwording*, 207–8.
[99] Knippenberg and De Pater, *De eenwording*, 38.

Economic unification and centralization were essential to the process of political centralization. The west of the country had been served by an efficient transport system of waterways and horse-drawn barges under the Republic, and was well integrated in comparison with much of the rest of Europe (see section 6.4, on transport). Nonetheless, economic unity was restricted by the inadequacies of the transport system across the state as a whole, and by the institutional barriers between provinces and towns which were a continuing legacy from the federalized Republic: local duties, taxes, excises and even currencies, which prevented the establishment of an 'internal market'.[100] Regional differences in income per capita were very substantial in 1820, and only eroded slowly during the nineteenth century.[101] Generally speaking in Europe, it was not until modern economic growth set in that regional economic variations began to decline, and even then the improvements in economic efficiency on the larger scale could occur at the expense of regional economies: this has been characterized as the 'backwash' effect, or even as 'internal colonialism'.[102] Before the second half of the nineteenth century, there was little in the way of national economic integration in the Netherlands, whether in terms of new industry, urbanization, or trains and roads, and so the completion of the 'unification' and centralization of the Dutch state and nation continued to be somewhat hampered.

However, Dutch governments made considerable efforts to increase the efficiency of their grip on the affairs of the nation. There was resistance, of course, for local positions of power were being eroded, and many resented the intrusions of the state into the business of the village. Separate studies of rural life in remote areas of Zuid-Holland and of the Kempen in Noord-Brabant make clear first that in the course of the nineteenth century the state succeeded in establishing its authoritative presence even in the smallest hamlets, and second that the intrusion was often bitterly resented.[103] Polemical articles raged against the effects of the liberals' programme of 'suffocating and deadening centralization' around the mid-century (meaning the Provincial Act of 1850 and the Municipality Act of 1851), including the stifling of action and enterprise by petty regulation and mediocre bureaucrats.[104] There was undoubtedly an increasing central bureaucracy in the country, led by a new elite loyal to the national rather than the local level.[105] Much of the opposition came

[100] Knippenberg and De Pater, *De eenwording*, 94–7.
[101] Van Zanden, 'Economische groei', 54–5.
[102] Milward and Saul, *The development of the economies*, 535–6; Frank, *On capitalist under-development*, 73; Myrdal, *Economic theory*, chapter 3, pp. 23–38.
[103] See Verrips, *En boven de polder*, 18–19 and 226–8; and Barentsen, *Het oude Kempenland*, 307.
[104] E.g., 'Centralisatie en staatkundige vrijheid', especially pp. 425–31 and 437.
[105] Coopmans, 'Van beleid van politie', 588–91.

from local *prominenti* or *notabelen* whose autonomy in local affairs was suffering a process of attrition.[106] And indeed, the local particularism was still strong enough in 1849 for a zealous reforming centralist to rant in telling diction against 'the disastrous spirit of provincialism which still exists in many parts of our fatherland'.[107] Indeed, the Municipality Act gave considerable powers to local government (see below), and in the great cities a thriving local political culture continued after the mid-century.

Nonetheless, the centralization proceeded. A good example is that of the Polder Boards, or Water Control Boards, which were (and are) in charge of public works at local level, which in the Netherlands mainly refers to drainage and defence against sea and rivers. These Boards are one of the oldest forms of participatory democracy, for they originated in and still now continue to be associations of local property owners who band together to organize and fund works essential to the public safety and economic functioning of their locality. Once again it was the French who began the centralizing process: the disastrous floods of 1808 and the huge expense they entailed initially led Napoleon to favour abandoning many of the low-lying areas of his Dutch satellite; however, he was eventually persuaded of their worth, and in 1810–11 the government of his brother, King Louis Napoleon of Holland, set up a national network of committees to co-ordinate the work of the Polder Boards. With this the writing was on the wall for the autonomy of the local boards. King Willem I's government confirmed the French arrangements, and gradually the state took on more centralized power as the century progressed.[108] It was aided by the rising cost of maintenance and improvement of the water defences, which many areas simply could not meet without state assistance. The loss of independence that this centralization entailed, especially on the part of landowners who could cut a dash locally, but who counted for little at a national level, provoked some resistance to the centralization of the boards;[109] nonetheless, the process continued steadily.

The most important area in which power was transferred from the local to the central level was in the general government of the town or village. Before 1795, settlements with the status of a town (*stad*) were run by the local oligarchy of 'regent' families, and were autonomous in most matters, loosely knit together for purposes of defence into a provincial

---

[106] Van Miert, 'Verdeeldheid en binding', 675–6.
[107] A. Grevelink in *Tijdschrift ter bevordering van Nijverheid*, 13 (1849), 401.
[108] Dieleman, 'Inleiding', 28–9; Schama, *Patriots and liberators*, 560–1; De Bruin and Wilderom, *Tussen afsluitdam*, vol. I, p. 68; and Van der Woud, *Het lege land*, 50–2 and 72–6.
[109] For example, in that most watery of provinces, Zeeland, where the agricultural crisis of the late 1870s made the polder taxes unbearable, but where the influence of central government was much resented: Dieleman, *De Zeeuwsche Landbouw Maatschappij*, 49.

network, which was in turn federated to the national entity of the United Provinces or Republic. Rural areas were subject to widely varying regulations, but were controlled by a small number of '*heren*' or manorial lords, together with the landowners (who often partly coincided with the urban patriciate). The French period saw the first of a long series of reforms designed to bring uniformity and central control into the system, by regulating at national level the franchise for local elections, by hiving off the judicial function of local government into a separate Ministry of Justice, and by reducing local usage generally in favour of national uniformity. In 1824 and 1825 the government of Willem I introduced standard operational procedures for local government, one for towns and one for rural areas, and in the new Constitution of 1848 the influence of the manorial lords in rural areas was abolished. The 1851 Municipality Act (*Gemeentewet*) was a landmark in the subjection of local government to the authority of the state. The distinction between towns and rural districts was abolished, with all areas now being legally defined as municipalities (*gemeenten*), large or small. The municipality was to be autonomous, but was restricted by the supervision of the Crown, and by that of the provincial authorities in financial matters. Local government was welded into a national hierarchy of political authority, and subjected to regulation by the state; in the course of the next century the state was going to take more and more advantage of its right to interfere in local matters.

As was the case in most European countries, the Dutch central state expanded its competences at the expense of local control by unificatory policies in such areas as transport and infrastructure, taxation, poor relief, education and standardized language, currency, weights and measures, and military service. As one would expect, the French period witnessed a stream of centralizing measures. The apparatus available for carrying out the designs of the state was limited, and the time available to the regimes was too short for a thorough implementation, but a crucial start was made. Willem I largely adopted the unitarist state moulded by R. J. Schimmelpenninck (1761–1825) under French guidance in the years 1805–6.[110] The pattern is well illustrated by the example of the coinage: the state took over the monopoly of minting coin in 1806, but local (provincial) currency circulated widely until the 1840s. In the course of the nineteenth century the state apparatus increased and became more efficient, and a series of laws gradually expanded the state's control over monetary policy.[111]

The critical area, however, was finance: the control of the purse-

[110] Van den Eerenbeemt, 'Armoede', 485; and Schama, *Patriots and liberators*, 648.
[111] Brugmans, *Paardenkracht*, 167–8.

strings was always going to be the crux of authority in local government. Under the Gogel system, local government was permitted to raise funds by adding an additional percentage (*opcenten*) to national taxes and excises to fund its own operations; Willem I's government limited the mark-up to a maximum of 5 per cent on the direct taxes, and 50 per cent on the excises, though in 1831 these upper limits were abandoned. Some towns also used a poll tax.[112] This situation gave considerable freedom to local authorities to raise and spend revenue as they wished, and is reflected in the regional variance of the annual tax burden per capita, which in 1850 ranged from *f*7.90 in Noord-Holland to a mere *f*0.96 in Limburg.[113]

All this was changed by the prescriptions of the *Gemeentewet* in 1851. The Act stipulated that municipal finance should come in the first place from a mark-up on household and real-estate taxes levied by the state, then from poll taxes, and then from local excises, in that order; local taxation had to be approved by central government.[114] In 1865 the national government abolished all local excises, but compensated the municipalities by passing on to them 80 per cent of the national household tax levied in their area. This established the all-important principle of local government receiving most of its finance from the state. Further state subsidies for the local budgets became more and more necessary as central government legislated yet more expensive tasks to be carried out by local authorities, an early example being in education. In 1897 a new tax law replaced the 80 per cent convention with a fixed sum for each inhabitant.[115] By the end of the century, therefore, the process of fiscal centralization was more or less complete: the bulk of local government income came from central taxes, local government finance was subject to state approval, and much local government activity consisted of carrying out central government legislation.

These fiscal reforms were complemented by the gradual centralization of the financial system as a whole. As much was indicated in our consideration of the factor capital: a centralization process of government finance began in the French period, and was substantially advanced by the reforms of the 1840s and early 1850s. By the mid-century *De Nederlandsche Bank* was extending its operations outside Amsterdam and across the whole country, and the Amsterdam money market was a

---

[112] Griffiths, 'The role of taxation', 264–5; Roovers, *De plaatselijke belastingen,* 63–6.
[113] *Staatkundig en Staathuishoudkundig Jaarboekje* (1851), 220.
[114] Engels, *De belastingen,* 430–4.
[115] Brugmans, *Paardenkracht,* 402–3; Van Maarseveen, 'Gemeentelijke belastingen'; and Knippenberg and De Pater, *De eenwording,* 135–44, which provides an excellent summary of this financial centralization process. See also Van der Dussen, 'Financial relations'.

similarly unifying force. After the 1840s, 'Within twenty years a national financial system came into being', and both the public and private sectors continued to be a powerful force for nation formation in the Netherlands.[116] In addition, rather slow and painful progress was made towards more central control and supervision of the poor-relief system, with all its considerable financial implications,[117] and another area, public health, was gradually taken over by the state in the second half of the century.[118]

One of the more unusual but economically significant of the moves towards centralization and standardization was the whole issue of time across the country. According to the investigations of Knippenberg and De Pater, a single national time zone only came into existence by an Act of 1 May 1909. Local 'real' time was used until the 1830s, followed by a local 'mean' time, and then various time zones. The coming of the train and the telegraph showed the commercial impracticality of these differentials, and assisted the coming together of the nation and the economy in temporal terms in 1909.[119]

The economic effects of the 'coming together' of the Dutch nation were undoubtedly significant. There may have been some internal imperialism of the sort feared by certain development economists, and a draining of the profits of the periphery to feed the centre, especially from the agricultural provinces of Friesland and Zeeland; however, the effect was muted, especially in terms of industry (which often remained on the geographical periphery until the twentieth century).[120] Theoretically, the economic advantage of unification comes from the improvement and extension of the market mechanism from the local to the national (and international). Put crudely, the Dutch economy in 1815 was a series of micro-economies linked imperfectly, but by 1914 it had become a single entity, served well by all the aspects of the infrastructure. It allowed a much larger scale of exchange and trade within the national market, with the attendant economies of scale. To such advantages can be added the enhanced ability of such an improved economic unit to interact with other economies abroad. This neo-classical economic championing of the amelioration of the national internal market is a feature of the work of

---

[116] See 't Hart, et al., A financial history, chapter 4, and pp. 4, 109–12; quotation from p. 198. See also Jonker, Merchants, 271–2.
[117] Boschloo, De productiemaatschappij, 67–77. On poor relief, see section 10.3.
[118] Kooij, 'Gezondheidszorg', 113–14.
[119] Knippenberg and De Pater, De eenwording, 77–81.
[120] Knippenberg and De Pater, De eenwording, 132. For the fearful economists, see for example Myrdal, Economic theory, who talks of 'siphoning off the savings from the poorer regions to the richer and more progressive ones where the returns on capital are high and secure' (p. 28).

Edwin Horlings, whose book on the service sector concludes that the most important stimulus to the Dutch economy in the nineteenth century was in the form of infrastructural and institutional unification: 'Modern economic growth appears to have been conditional upon the physical and institutional integration of the Dutch economy.'[121] He places this integration at the mid-century, and not before: Willem's earlier efforts were apparently largely ineffective (though they prepared the ground) because of government financial difficulties and pervading political conservatism. In his conclusions Horlings places perhaps too much emphasis on this point, for it is clear that other factors (like the East Indies stimulus) have to be involved when explaining the modest performance of the economy before 1850, relative to growth rates thereafter; otherwise why did Willem's vigorous policies *not* work as well as he might have hoped, and why *was* it that 'the canal boom did little to integrate the Dutch infrastructure'?[122] In addition, perhaps overmuch attention is paid in such analysis to the national as opposed to international and local markets, which can be just as important. Nevertheless, the way in which first Knippenberg and De Pater, and then Horlings, have thrust to the forefront of our attention the significance of the economic and political integration of the country in the course of the century is an important addition to our understanding of the constellation of factors governing the economic performance of the Netherlands.

5.4   Conclusion: the role of organizational inputs

In the end, having examined the various aspects of government policy towards the economy in the nineteenth century, the question is whether their efforts helped or hindered the development of the economy, or indeed whether they had any effect at all. Looking at the aggregate growth rates discussed earlier, in section 3.1, the track record is generally good: the Dutch economy was successful throughout, with a probable step-up in performance around the mid-century, which it shared with most other European countries. Willem I's government consciously intervened to maximize the conditions for economic success wherever possible; it was not dogmatic in protectionism or regulation, but was certainly interventionist. That changed around the mid-century, when governments tended to retire from the economy and leave it to private enterprise, while at the same time diverting increasing amounts of the national resource to creating a favourable environment with the infrastructural, legal and diplomatic framework.

[121] Horlings, *The economic development*, 250 and chapter 7, *passim*. Quotation from p. 298.
[122] Horlings, *The economic development*, 296.

Despite all the ink spilled and regulations imposed and repealed, it remains very much at issue whether all this had very much effect at all on the nature of Dutch economic development, at least until the very end of the nineteenth century. Many of the government's efforts to influence the economy failed completely. Attempts at protection were confused and ineffective, while the tax regime was Byzantine and unsystematic.[123] Many of Willem's interventionist policies were 'wasteful' and led to near-bankruptcy; the government itself needed to be better organized in order to assist in economic growth.[124] The liberal regimes after the 1840s withdrew from much of the interference, but presided over a steady increase in public expenditure, and their attempts to regulate the currency were outflanked by events at every stage. In the twentieth century, counter-cyclical policy has demonstrably failed in the Netherlands as elsewhere and, in spite of tremendous economic success in the post-war period, Dutch government economic policy, especially towards trade, has generally failed.[125] The clearest example of the ineffectiveness of government economic policy is the regime of Willem I; despite a few happy outcomes, very few of the ideas expressed were ever successful, largely because of an almost total lack of state apparatus and policy instruments which might have enabled such ideas to be transferred into action.[126] The country certainly benefited enormously from the East Indies colonies, which poured money into government coffers from the 1840s to the 1860s, and then into private pockets. But most of the very limited success of conscious government economic policy for much of the nineteenth century was due to pragmatism, skilful negotiation, lack of dogmatism, adaptability and practicality: the best example is the dogged success of the Dutch in the river trade. It is almost as if the principled stand of politicians, on the economy at least, was largely irrelevant.

All this was to change in the twentieth century, with the growth of the welfare state and the mixed economy: we can see the stirrings of the new regime in the 1880s and 1890s, and its take-off around the time of the First World War. Government policy may often have been frustrated in the twentieth century, especially in international economic matters, but there is no denying that it has had an enormous impact on the economy. For most of the nineteenth century that was not the case, and it was therefore not the 1840s watershed between the interventionist regime of Willem I and the *laissez-faire* ones of the succeeding liberals which

[123] Heringa, *Free trade*; Schuttevaer and Detiger, *Anderhalve eeuw belastingen*.
[124] Horlings, *The economic development*, 295–6.
[125] 't Hart, *et al.*, *A financial history*, 159–63; Groenveld and Wintle, eds., *State and trade*, chapter 10; and Van Zanden, ed., *The economic development*, chapter 10.
[126] Groenveld and Wintle, eds., *State and trade*, chapter 6; Van Zanden, *De industrialisatie in Amsterdam*, 17–18.

changed the relationship between the government and the economy, but rather the transition from elite politics to mass politics, and the coming of socialism and social liberalism, at the end of the nineteenth century.

If government policy was on the whole generally benign in spite of itself, Dutch attitudes to enterprise and technology also did the economy no harm, and each of these three influencing factors on the supply side of the economy had beneficial effects at various times. Dutch entrepreneurs were very proficient, in that those with money tended to make more of it, and there are enough examples of highly successful businessmen, large and small, in all sectors, including manufacturing, to show that there was nothing generically wrong with the Dutch in this respect. As for technology, it is a mistake to follow a model derived from aspects of the Anglo-American experience in which machines are held to exert an autonomous, *deus ex machina* galvanizing effect on the economy: the Dutch skilfully adopted and adapted others' inventions as well as some of their own, using differential technologies and remaining very much aware of all the latest developments. The Dutch employment of new devices, methods and machinery was one not of wholesale takeover of whatever the British or the Belgians were doing (which would often have been entirely impractical), but rather a highly rational and precise response to current local circumstances in terms of supply, culture and market: in that respect Dutch entrepreneurs made the optimum use of the available technology in the circumstances.

6 Sectoral analysis

6.1 Introduction: the distribution of the labour force

We now come to the question of sectoral distribution within the Dutch economy. Regarding the workforce, it was noted in section 3.2 that the proportion engaged in manufacturing industry was modest in the nineteenth century, and in the section on the factor labour (4.2) that the growth of the labour supply was constant throughout the century, with the exception of the 1850s. Here we shall examine the sectoral distribution of the registered labour force, and how that distribution changed over time.

The occupational census figures, displayed in Table II.2 for 1807 and from 1849 right through to 1971, show the picture over time, though they take no account of the differential productivity of labour in the various sectors. (Figures for 'industrial' Belgium have been added to the table for purposes of comparison.) According to conventional development models, it is clear that the Netherlands trailed behind compared to its southern neighbour: at the mid-century, the Netherlands had just 19 per cent of its registered waged workforce in manufacturing as opposed to 32 per cent in Belgium, and by the eve of World War I the Netherlands still only managed 25 per cent in industry, compared to Belgium's 35 per cent. If extractive industry is added to manufacturing then she trailed even more, for there was very little extraction in the nineteenth century, with the exception of some peat-cutting. However, there were more building workers, proportionately, in the Netherlands than in Belgium. But where were the bulk of the workers in the Netherlands who were to be found, as it were, in the manufacturing sector in a classic Industrial Revolution-type country such as Belgium?

They were not to be found in agriculture. Belgium had a higher proportion of its workforce in agriculture than did the Netherlands. In 1849 43.8 per cent of the registered Dutch workforce were in agriculture, while the corresponding figure in Belgium was 51 per cent. By about 1890 Belgium's level had fallen to about a third in agriculture, level with

the Netherlands, and by 1910 Belgium had dropped below the Netherlands (respectively 23.9 and 28.3 per cent), but these were the lowest
levels in continental Europe: other countries had considerably higher
proportions of their workforces in the primary sector on the eve of the
First World War.[1] The point needs to be made that the Dutch had
achieved a 'modern' distribution of their workforce as early as the seventeenth century, with a large urbanized population having been 'released'
from the necessity of food production by a highly efficient agriculture. In
1650 almost a third were in 'industry' and less than half in farming.[2] In
other words, the 'advanced' employment structure of the UK in 1820 had
been achieved by the Dutch as early as 1700.[3]

In the course of the nineteenth century, the share of agriculture
amongst the workforce declined steeply, the share of industry grew slowly, and the share of the services expanded rapidly. The Dutch workforce
was increasingly concentrated in the tertiary sector, which by the end of
the nineteenth century was beginning to include significant numbers of
people from what is now often called the quaternary or government
sector. In a regional breakdown, the importance of the service sector is
even more salient. The provinces with the highest proportion of workers
in industry were Overijssel (cottons), Noord-Brabant (woollens, etc.),
and the two Hollands. The former pair, though, had very low percentages
in the services sector, and accordingly had low per-capita earnings, while
Noord- and Zuid-Holland had the highest. Indeed in national terms
today, the wealthiest countries are those with the largest service sectors.[4]

Occupational census figures do not take account of relative productivity; recent estimates of productivity are necessarily based on data originally collected for other purposes, but they confirm the impression that
the real epicentre of the Dutch economy was the service sector: 'Far more
than by a process of industrialization, the development of the economy
was characterized by the strong growth of production and employment in
the tertiary sector, which was of course dependent on the efficient and
highly internationally oriented primary and secondary sectors.'[5] Table
II.6 shows Van Zanden's estimates of changes in the production, employment and labour productivity of the three sectors between 1850 and
1910. Over those sixty years the data indicate that while production
doubled in agriculture, it quadrupled in industry and services. However,

[1] Milward and Saul, *The development of the economies,* 193.
[2] De Vries and Van der Woude, *Nederland 1500–1815,* chapter 11.
[3] Burger, 'Dutch patterns', 174–5.
[4] Griffiths, 'The creation of a Dutch national economy'. The estimates were 'pioneering',
    i.e. intelligent guesswork; regional income levels are based on retail turnover.
[5] Van Zanden, 'Economische groei', 67. Some more recent estimates of productivity in the
    various sectors are contained in Horlings and Smits, 'A comparison', 92ff.

Table II.6. *Estimates of the development of production, employment and labour productivity, 1850–1910.*

| Sector | Increase 1850–1910 | | | Sectoral distribution of increase in labour % | Relative productivity 1910 index |
	production %	employment %	labour productivity %		
Primary	112	30	60	14	70
Secondary	388	140	105	36	102
Tertiary	380	165	82	50	121
Total	282	90	101	100	100

Source: Van Zanden, 'Economische groei in Nederland', 66.

while the relative productivity of labour in manufacturing in 1910 was close to the national average (index 102; national average = 100) and in agriculture was low (70), in the services it was by far the highest of the sectors and stood at 121.

We shall return to the category of 'services' below. For now, it is clear that, compared to 'industrial' Belgium, the Dutch workforce was proportionately well represented in building, trade and transport, and other services: the tertiary sector generally. It is not intended here to go through the minutiae of each branch in each sector: in the last generation there have been so many detailed studies published that what is required now is an overview rather than more detail. Having gone into considerable depth in the accounts of factor inputs and other supply-side features of the economy, there will now follow relatively brief and partly descriptive sections on each of the three main economic sectors in the nineteenth century.

6.2   The primary sector

The primary sector in the Netherlands was overwhelmingly dominated by agriculture, and continued to be so until the discovery of natural gas in Groningen in the mid-twentieth century. There was a presence of mining, peat-cutting, fishing and forestry, but in employment terms all were tiny compared to agriculture. Mining and mineral extraction have been dealt with in section 4.4 above on raw materials; in employment terms only a little over 2,000 men were employed nation-wide in mining until after the 1860s, and although the total had risen to 23,000 by 1909, they still amounted to only 1 per cent of the working population (Table II.2), and most were from over the borders. Fishing took less than 1.5 per cent of the workforce, while agriculture provided the livelihood of 44 per cent at the mid-century, and well over a quarter (28.3 per cent) in 1909. Having already covered mining and peat-cutting (in section 4.4), we shall look here at the fishery sector, and then pass on to forestry and agriculture.

Fishing

The numbers of people earning their living from fishing in the Netherlands grew on average throughout the nineteenth century, especially after the 1860s. In 1807 there were more than 7,000 of them (0.82 per cent of the workforce), rising to 11,500 in 1849 (0.9 per cent). Thereafter the numbers rose more rapidly, presumably affected by the deregulation of the industry in 1857, to well over 20,000 by the end of the century: by 1889 the number involved in fishing (and hunting) had reached 16,650.[6]

Dutch fishing was dominated by the herring. Whaling and other long-distance catches had been undertaken in the Golden Age, but there was no deep-sea fishing to speak of in the nineteenth century, despite the efforts of Willem I to foster its revival. The sector was mainly concerned with catching herring in drift nets, into which the fish obligingly swam before being caught up, rather than trawling and other means, which had to wait for the twentieth century. Outside the herring season, the boats might turn their hand to flat fish and even round fish, but herring was king. The herring fishery had been one of the foundations of the Dutch economic miracle in the seventeenth century, and in order to maintain the quality of the product, which was salted and cured for export as well as for domestic consumption, a host of regulations was introduced, reminiscent of those governing a guild of artisans. Since then the business had been in gentle decline, and it had completely collapsed under the blockade of Napoleonic Europe. The herring 'busses' (*buizen*) used to number over 200, but by 1844 had slumped to 124, and by 1855 were down to just 79. The volume and value of catches had also fallen.[7] The general reason for this malaise in the first half of the century must have been that the European economy in general was experiencing a slow period after the end of the Napoleonic Wars up to the mid-century: the Kondratieff long wave was in downswing mode after 1815, and was only just bottoming out in the 1840s. There was also the problem of regulation. The rules of the *ancien régime* had been recodified in 1801, confirmed in 1814 and reinforced in 1818. The catch, the bringing-in and the curing were all subject to highly regulated monopolies, and the industry was supported with government subsidies at ƒ500 a boat, rising

---

[6] Horlings, *The economic development*, 333; *Jaarcijfers* (1900), 56–7; Table II.2.
[7] De Bosch Kemper, 'Statistiek', 23–4.

to ƒ750 in 1825. With each herring virtually hand-inspected several times, the Dutch fleet lost business to their Scottish rivals and others, while demand stagnated.[8]

After 1850 things began to improve. In the first place, the pace of the international economy picked up. Second, as we have seen under government policy, there was deregulation in the form of the Fisheries Act of 1857, which swept away even more than the investigating Commission had demanded: the ideologically motivated liberal Second Chamber seems to have wanted deregulation for the sake of it, even beyond what the experts and the industry requested. After 300 years of close regulation, the liberalization was a violent instrument: there was some disarray, and few of the fishermen were ready to change their ways very rapidly, especially if it involved replacing their highly expensive capital equipment in the form of their boats and nets. But demand was rising, and the numbers of employees did too, especially towards the end of the century.

Catches remained steady at 60,000 tons in the 1860s, but began to rise around 1870 to well over 100,000 tons. This was largely the result of a new technology in the shape of cotton nets machine-made in Scotland, which replaced the much heavier hemp ones, which had been manufactured in the Netherlands from home-grown material. The new nets allowed faster, sleeker ships called luggers (*loggers*) to replace the traditional, more cumbersome busses. The catches continued to increase rapidly, though slowed in the 1890s. The herring catch rose from 6.5m. kg in 1855 to no less than 65m. kg in 1896, a tenfold increase. Exports soared, mainly to Germany and to a lesser extent to Belgium and France (which had a high import tariff). Imports to the Netherlands were reduced to zero in the 1890s, while in 1860 some 20,000 barrels of Scots herring had been brought into the Netherlands. Steam was slow to progress in the North Sea herring fleet, for as we have seen the fish were gathered not by the movement of the boat, but by drawing in the nets; thus the steam capstan or winch was introduced on to a sailing lugger in 1876, while the first steam-powered engine to propel the boat itself was not fitted to a lugger until 1897. The internal combustion engine followed in 1901. By 1914 there were 155 steam trawlers in service: deep-sea boats which steamed under power to catch the fish, while luggers were coastal vessels which floated their nets freely. Marketing also improved: the port of IJmuiden was designated the national depot in 1899, and rapidly drew nearly all the catch, rising from less than a million guilders in 1900 to more than ƒ7m. in 1914, most of it by then coming from the steam trawlers. Growth continued throughout the war, although the losses to

---

[8] Van de Voort, 'De Nederlandse Maatschappij', 209–11; Brugmans, *Paardenkracht*, 152–4.

mines were chilling; by 1916 the Dutch fishing fleet reached the largest number of ships (to say nothing of tonnage) in its history: 150 trawlers and 900 luggers.[9]

In addition to sea fishing (*buitengats*), a large number of tiny vessels were employed, often on a part-time or seasonal basis, in the Zuiderzee and the river arms, especially of the River Scheldt where large numbers of anchovies and shellfish were to be had. French capital was injected into the oyster beds in Zeeland in about 1870, and by 1876 almost 3m. kg were being sent from the estuary near Kruiningen to neighbouring countries. In 1880, England alone consumed some 6 million fresh Dutch oysters. However, it was always a volatile and risky enterprise, with wildly fluctuating prices and harvests. In 1876 about 36.5m. oysters were sold, while the next year the total was down to less than 10m. By about 1890, around a million kg were being harvested each year, much of it still for export by train; indeed, the slow development of the Dutch railways linking her ports with the German markets may well have held back this form of enterprise. On the whole, however, fishing was a branch of economic endeavour steeped in tradition, which managed to modernize and even industrialize quite effectively in the second half of the century.[10]

Woodland

Wood as a crop is relatively unimportant in the Netherlands today, and has been for some centuries. In the west, the land has been much too intensively farmed since the sixteenth century to permit much woodland, except in very exposed areas on the dunes or in bogs before they were drained. In the east, there were originally large areas of hardwood, some of which was important as material and fuel to the industries of the Republic, but as the heaths were cleared the forests became much reduced in size. Wood had been important as a building material for ships and homes, but domestic supplies had long been replaced by imports from Scandinavia. The domestic forests were harvested for fuel, dependent on the ease of import of coal, and used for covering and strengthening dunes as sea defences in the west (including osiers). Oak bark was also used in the leather-curing industry. Forestry plantations of softwood firs and oak were laid out in the east, being interchanged as crops by their proprietors according to market conditions. Most of the Dutch woodlands were to be

---

[9] The best source for the fishing industry after 1850 is the series *Verslag van den Staat der Nederlandsche Zeevisscherijen*. Useful general accounts are found in Van Tijn, 'De negentiende eeuw'; Van de Voort, 'De Nederlandse Maatschappij'; and Boelmans Kranenburg, 'Visserij'. See also Pons, *De bakens verzet*.

[10] *Jaarcijfers* (1900), 124; *Verslag van den Staat der Nederlandsche Zeevisscherijen* (1880), 127–8.

found in the provinces of Overijssel and Gelderland. In 1833 there were some 900,000 ha. of uncultivated land in the country, of which less than one fifth was woodland; in 1888 the unfarmed area had fallen to 712,000 ha., and the woodland had risen in area and proportion to 227,000 ha., or nearly one third. By 1940, the uncultivated area had halved, while the wooded area had increased slightly to 258,000 ha., which represented 7.7 per cent of the total land area in the country (it had been about 5 per cent in the 1830s). This is a small share of land, and on a national scale forestry was of modest importance, which is hardly surprising in view of the lack of high country where it would be too hilly to plough or too exposed for crops.[11]

Agriculture

Regarding agriculture proper as opposed to other minor components of the primary sector, we have already seen in Table II.2 that in 1849 43.8 per cent of the workforce was in agriculture, and that the figure had fallen only to 32.9 in 1889 and to 28.3 in 1909.[12] Agriculture therefore was a major sector in the economy, responsible for the livelihoods of almost half the population at mid-century, if one includes the various dependent trades such as rural blacksmiths and other craftsmen orientated towards the farming economy. There follows a brief general account of this important sector over the course of the century.[13]

One issue which should be settled immediately is the efficiency of Dutch agriculture. In most economic models, the size of the primary sector is seen as an indication of backwardness, because it tends to be undercapitalized compared to other sectors and therefore less productive of labour. It is also assumed to be a less specialized economic activity. Quite apart from the fact that the Dutch sector was smaller than almost all its foreign counterparts around 1910, with the exceptions of Britain and Belgium, it cannot be regarded as the weaker partner to the same extent that it can in many countries. In the west, farming had by 1800 reached levels of sophistication which would not be surpassed in most parts of Europe for a century or more. There is a debate about the modernity of

---

[11] Slicher van Bath, *Bijdragen tot de agrarische geschiedenis*, 312–16; the standard work on the history of Dutch forests is Buis, *Historia forestis*, but it is largely concerned with the period before the nineteenth century.

[12] These figures include fishing.

[13] For more detail, see my earlier survey article on Dutch agriculture: Wintle, 'Modest growth'. See also Van Zanden, *De economische ontwikkeling*, revised and translated into English as Van Zanden, *The transformation of European agriculture*; Knibbe, *Agriculture*; and Bieleman, 'Dutch agriculture'. For more specialist works, a bibliographic guide to the historiography of Dutch agriculture appeared in 1991: Wintle, 'Agrarian history'.

farming in the east, but for the country as a whole throughout the century, and especially after the rigours of the 1880s crisis, the Dutch agricultural sector was highly productive, in no way comparable with a peasant-based low-productivity farming sector, such as was found, for instance, in much of southern Europe. In the twentieth century, it is true, Dutch farming employed proportionately more workers than in Belgium, but by then Dutch farming had become the efficient processing sector that we know now, highly intensive, working predominantly for the export market and to the most rigorous international standards. Van Zanden concludes that, up to 1870 at least, agriculture was a crucial force in the growth of the Dutch economy, and from 1850 onwards there was, in agriculture, a modern form of economic growth, based on rising productivity, rather than simply on increased factor inputs.[14]

The regional variations were based on soil differences. The map in Figure I.3 shows the four main soil types in the country: marine clays along the coasts, river clay lining the river systems in the centre of the country, sandy soils in the east and south, and a small area of loam at the southern tip of Limburg. Conveniently leaving the Limburg *Löss* to one side, the soils separate into fertile and infertile: the clay and the sand. After the introduction of cheap bulk artificial fertilizers, from the 1880s, this distinction gradually became eroded, but in the early nineteenth century, crop yields in the east were often only half of those in the west. The same east–west differential applied to labour productivity and to agricultural wages as well. The point to be taken is not that the east was backward compared to the rest of Europe, but that the western and northern clays were remarkably advanced. In the course of the century the sandy soils of the east and south became more integrated into the national and international market, partly assisted by government measures in organization and legislation, reducing the retardatory effects of the commons, tithes and the like.[15]

The general pattern of Dutch farming fortunes closely followed the long-term fifty-year Kondratieff cycle common to most of Europe; indeed the graph at Figure I.7 is an excellent example of that cycle, and is based on wheat prices at Arnhem, which are as good an indicator of agricultural fortunes as can be found. It was good to be a farmer in the 1860s and around 1900, but even in advanced agriculture like that of the Nether-lands, the 1830s and 1880s were disastrous structural depressions in most sectors of agriculture. In terms of output, farming hardly advanced before 1850, and if anything, aggregate domestic per-capita demand was

[14] Van Zanden, *De economische ontwikkeling*, chapter 12.
[15] Knippenberg and De Pater, *De eenwording*, 98–101; see above, in section 5.3, on government policy towards agriculture.

actually shrinking. Once the prices were back above normal after 1850, production rates increased: exports boosted demand, and rising labour productivity points to increased use of technology (and better weather). Agricultural prices were rising faster than consumer prices generally, but productivity did not stagnate in these golden years. After 1880 agriculture became much more efficient, increasing output to feed the industrializing urban masses at home, and abroad in Germany and Britain, while technological and organizational changes proceeded apace.[16]

In many ways those changes which accompanied the 1880s crisis and which were partly driven by it form the watershed of change in the century. It is not the case that nothing changed before the 1870s, for the third quarter of the century did see improvements across the board, but the last two decades were the time when the changes became universal and productivity really took off. Before the crisis, the ratio between grass and ploughed field was about 1.33:1 (1m. ha. pasture to 0.75m. ha. arable). However, in many areas, most of the cattle were kept primarily for their manure, so grass did not necessarily mean dairy or meat: in 1850 the actual ratio of dairy to arable was probably about 1:2.5. The grass produced butter and cheese; the arable produced grain, largely for the domestic market.[17] We have seen that the political structure did not favour farmers, especially before the Muncipality Act, and in effect until they received the vote in the last two decades of the century. Although there was a tradition of merchants purchasing country houses and titles,[18] compared to England and other neighbours there was no powerful landed gentry to counterbalance the trade lobby. The hydrological conditions in the Netherlands did mean that the various local polder boards were hooked up to a Department of Public Works, which gradually improved the situation in the course of the century, especially in the coastal and river areas. The enlightened bourgeoisie with an interest in farming formed societies and tried hard to spread the good word of new technology by circulating translations of foreign treatises on new methods, and a few model farms were set up with some success. However, the vast majority of farmers were not reached by these attempts. There was no primogeniture, so most Dutch farms were small, compared to England for example. New implements and machinery were therefore less attractive, and besides, there was the problem of who would maintain them. A Fowler's steam plough from England was used for the first time on a farm in Amersfoort in 1862, but the investment was simply too great for small

[16] Van Zanden, De economische ontwikkeling, 141 and 350–1; Knibbe, Agriculture, 124–34 and 218–20.
[17] De Jonge, De industrialisatie, 21.
[18] See Davids and Lucassen, eds., A miracle mirrored, 326–7.

plots. The largest farms were to be found on the heavy sea-clay soils, where expensive capital equipment (horses and heavy implements) was necessary to work the farm, so in these areas there was already a high degree of investment and capitalization, even with farms averaging well under 20 ha.[19] On the even smaller farms of the sandy soils, mechanical and technological improvements were very slow to penetrate before the 1870s. One indication of technological progress was the existence of fallow: there were 16,515 ha. of fallow in the country in the 1880s, which represented less than 1 per cent of the farmland available. The fallow area had dropped to 12,271 ha. by 1895, but the salient fact is the small area left redundant by 1880.[20] In a word, the state of farming was highly advanced in the Netherlands by 1800, and made only modest further progress before the late 1870s.

Towards the end of that decade, reports began to come in of falling prices, after several years of a plateau of the highest sustained prices ever paid for farm produce; this was to be the harbinger of the great agricultural crisis of the 1880s.[21] It was the impact of imported grain that caused the two-decade fall in agricultural prices: vast new areas were being integrated into the putative global market by railway lines across the continents and steamship routes across the world's oceans. The only sector in farming to be entirely unaffected was horticulture, with its fresh produce for the voracious urban markets at home and especially abroad, in Germany and Britain.[22] Contemporary estimates of the total cash value of the Dutch harvest of arable farming fell from a highpoint of well over 2 billion guilders in the 1870s to only ƒ1.3 billion in the mid-1890s.[23] As we have seen in section 5.3 on government policy, the frantic appeals to the authorities to introduce corn laws and other protective measures fell on deaf ears, for fear of retaliation and damage to trade; besides, cheap food was more than welcome in the other sectors.

The agriculture of Europe as a whole was stricken by the crisis of the 1880s, and the more capitalized and commercialized the farming, the

---

[19] In Zeeland, where some of the largest farms were to be found, together with Friesland and Groningen, the average size in 1910 was 15.5 ha., a figure which excludes the many smallholdings of less than 1 ha. By 1910 a degree of *morcellement* had set in, it is true, but earlier data are less reliable, and farms of more than 100 ha. had always been a rarity. Wintle, '"Dearly won"', 59–60. See also Priester, *Geschiedenis van de Zeeuwse landbouw*, 181ff.

[20] 0.83 per cent. Fallow figures are found at *Verslag van den Landbouw* (1887–89), 295 and (1894–95), 128; the estimate of total farming acreage is taken from Van Zanden, *De economische ontwikkeling*, 86.

[21] Wintle, 'Modest growth', 24–6.

[22] For prices, see Knibbe, *Agriculture*, 116–18 plus appendices.

[23] Values from 1851 to 1895 are found in *Verslag van den Landbouw* (1894–5), 129. See also Figure I.6.

worse it was hit. Britain and the Netherlands, as two of the most advanced farming nations, but with governments which refused to protect their farmers with tariffs, were especially affected. However, by 1900 prices were on the rise again, Dutch farming was prosperous, and enormous changes had taken place in the sector. There is a revisionist view of the crisis which highlights those sectors like market gardening where few ill-effects were felt, and sees the changes in the sector in the last two decades of the century simply as adjustments to a new market situation.[24] But changes there certainly were.

The government took note of the problem with a lengthy official enquiry into the crisis beginning in 1886, and its four substantial volumes recommended the following remedies: education, quality control, dairy factories and co-operatives.[25] All of these represented sound advice and were followed up. Productivity rises were achieved by intensification and specialization: there was a strong swing away from grains. On the sandy soils the move was to dairying and livestock rearing, especially pigs and poultry, and in the coastal areas there was, where possible, a swing to horticulture, much of it eventually under glass. The image of Dutch farming we know today was born at that time: flowers, bulbs and vegetables for export, and Frisian cows. Grains, seeds and madder were often replaced by sugarbeet. Co-operative organizations grew up, and in many ways represented perhaps the most important change of all. They began on the clay, with farmers clubbing together to resist exploitation by beet factories and other middlemen, and had become almost universal by 1890. They were initially at village level, for bulk purchase of feed, seed and fertilizer, all of which could be sample-tested for quality. Alongside these, there were co-operatives for marketing the farmers' products, for providing credit to each other, and in some cases for processing the products, especially in dairying and sugarbeet. The credit organizations were linked on denominational lines across the country (part of the pillarization process), and by 1898 a Raffeissen Bank in Utrecht and a Farmers' Credit Bank (*Boerenleenbank*) were national networks for providing farmers with operating capital. There were immediate financial advantages to be had from the co-operatives in the form of cheaper inputs and finance, but the most significant effect was probably socio-psychological. Life on the farm can be hard, but at least the peasant is his own master, and can maintain a proud independence and isolation. The co-operative movement reached nearly every peasant and farmer in the

---

[24] Reported and criticized in Koning, *The failure of agrarian capitalism*, e.g. p. 171: 'The revisionist view of the agricultural crisis is informed by a rather straightforward kind of neo-classical economic thinking.'

[25] *Uitkomsten van het onderzoek ... 1886.* The report is also an excellent source for historians.

country, and taught them to club together to solve their problems, to pool resources, to learn from each other, to organize, to mobilize, and generally to end their isolation. With antecedents in provinces such as Limburg, the *Nederlandsche Boerenbond*, a Roman Catholic farmers' union, was set up in 1896 to lobby for political action, and there was an agricultural labourers' trade union, the *Landarbeidersbond*, in 1900. The co-operatives boosted a social modernization process, where agriculture even in the most remote areas was finally brought into contact with the international market, and new technology was introduced to every field. By 1899 there were some 924 co-operatives registered in the country, 416 of them for dairying, and by 1913 there were no fewer than 1,177 agricultural purchasing associations, with 104,455 members.[26]

In general, the changes represented a massive intensification of agriculture in the face of competition from abroad. Agricultural entrepreneurship took a beating in the 1880s, but was ingenious and resilient in the end, adapting to new situations, adopting new technologies and innovative products and structures. The number of people working in agriculture continued to increase from the 1860s onwards right up to 1947, even though the percentage was declining slowly (Table II.2). Thus although many left the countryside for the towns and for destinations abroad as emigrants in the 1880s, the labour inputs into agriculture continually increased, as did the capital. It was a brave response to an acute problem.

The crisis was brought to an end by the rise in prices, determined by international forces beyond the control of the Dutch farmer, such as the working of the long-term cycle and the rise of industrial Germany with its enormous demand for food and raw materials. But Dutch agriculture had undergone a metamorphosis which, on balance, was to stand it in good stead for the next century. It was completely integrated into the international economy and had become a processing sector, importing cheap bulk materials and food for its animals and the domestic population, while exporting livestock and cash crops, especially horticultural ones, in return. The value added was considerable, and rose continually.[27] This commercial character of Dutch agriculture, however, left it entirely exposed to the effects of foreign tariffs, war and other impediments to trade, as would be amply demonstrated in the First World War, the 1930s Depression and World War II, all three of which saw the Dutch in danger of starving because they had abandoned the capacity to feed themselves in favour of growing much more lucrative crops for sale abroad, from which

[26] Hoogland, *Landbouwcoöperatie*, especially p. 73; and *Tijdschrift ter bevordering van Nijverheid*, nieuwe reeks, 4 (1900), 127. See also Bouman, 'Landbouworganisaties', 257–61; Sneller, 'Anderhalve eeuw', 90–107; and Knibbe, *Agriculture*, 149–57.

[27] Knibbe, *Agriculture*, 120.

they could pay for food imports. The result on all three occasions was full-scale takeover of the sector by the government, and a massive shift back to ploughed fields and grain cultivation.[28] Only in the second half of the twentieth century, and especially since the formation of the EEC in 1957 and the Common Agricultural Policy thereafter, has Dutch farming really reaped the benefits of its strategy, becoming (with the British) one of the most efficient farming sectors in the world.

As a contributor to the economy as a whole, agriculture accounted for 14 per cent of the increase in employment between 1850 and 1910 (Table II.6), and although its relative productivity was far behind that of the other two sectors, it was almost certainly a great deal higher than agriculture in most neighbouring countries. Agriculture was a net exporter throughout the century, which created a favourable trade balance allowing the import of capital goods; farming absorbed labour when other sectors were shedding before 1850, and supplied it when they were recruiting. The primary sector was prosperous enough to generate domestic demand for industry and the services after 1850, and through rents and taxes transferred much of its profits to the government and other branches of the economy. For much of the century it was the largest sector, and an essential one too; especially before 1870, after which the other sectors accelerated, agriculture was the main motor of a macro-economy which continued to perform well against its international rivals.[29]

6.3   The secondary sector

Manufacturing industry in the Republic had been based on trade, and to some extent it performed a processing function, rather than manufacturing in the sense of making a finished product from scratch. The Dutch imported raw or semi-finished materials, performed highly skilled and value-added-intensive processes on them, and re-exported them. When trade was booming, industry did well; workshops were concentrated in the commercial towns. As a result of these links with trade, the ascendancy of England in the eighteenth century, capped by the blockade of French Revolutionary and then Napoleonic Europe, resulted in a disastrous collapse of Dutch industry during the French period, from which the Netherlands emerged in 1815 to find that the British and others were now undercutting them systematically in most areas. The reports of Johannes Goldberg, Minister for the National Economy of the Batavian Republic, and later Director-General of Trade and the Colonies under

[28] On World War II, see Trienekens, *Tussen ons volk en de honger.*
[29] Van Zanden, *De economische ontwikkeling*, chapter 12.

King Willem I, on the state of manufacturing in 1800 and again in 1816, do not make for reassuring reading: the sector was deeply depressed, not to say in ruins.[30] Industrial recovery and growth was confined mainly to the southern Netherlands before 1830, where it was very successful, but that did little for the northern provinces' manufacturing.

After 1830, Willem's focus shifted to the north, and in the early 1830s the orders began rolling in from the colonies in the Far East, breathing life into the various branches of textiles, shipbuilding and those industries which processed colonial products, most notably sugar. The iron industry also grew rapidly, from almost nothing in the French period to a serious presence by 1850, with foundries and engineering shops, supplying the shipbuilding and sugar industries in particular. The role of the colonies and of government protection was an important one at this stage. In the 1830s and 1840s manufacturing continued to grow gently under the protective cloche, and when the liberals removed some of the insulation in the 1850s, and considerably more in the 1860s and 1870s, Dutch industry appeared to be strong enough to survive and even thrive. Steam was applied to manufacturing, and recent studies have stressed the benefits of an increasingly coherent national infrastructure from the 1850s onwards.[31] In addition to the trade-based and colonial industries, there were the traditional city-based manufactures of *jenever* (gin), vegetable oil, sawn timber, madder and the like, all on a small scale; there was also an advanced and mechanized paper industry in the Zaan area near Amsterdam.[32] Industries producing consumer goods all expanded faster than the rate of population increase, and so the generally golden years of the third quarter of the century smiled on Dutch industry as well.[33]

The turning of the long-wave Kondratieff cycle in the late 1870s also affected Dutch manufacturing industry, though not as heavily as it did agriculture. The decline in demand had reached crisis proportions by 1882, and industrial expansion was halted. The 1880s was a decade of restructuring, labour shedding and labour disputes (not unlike the 1980s). The 1890s saw an upturn, and by 1900 the heavy industry sector in the western harbour towns was leading the recovery, helped by competitive wage levels and cheap steel, now available from the German cartel. Machine-building for the shipping and rail sectors led the way, but many new industries sprang up or grew to maturity in this period, making motors, bicycles, cars, and of course the famous light bulbs at Philips.

[30] An abridged version of his 1800 reports was published sixty years later as Goldberg, 'Journaal der reize'; the 1816 report is located at ARA, Goldberg, no. 207.

[31] E.g. Van Zanden, 'Industrialization', 84–8; Horlings, *The economic development*, chapter 7. See also section 5.3, on centralization; and Van Zanden, 'Economische groei', 61–2.

[32] Ridder, *Een conjunctuur-analyse*, 133–7; and De Vries, *De Nederlandse papiernijverheid*.

[33] The exception, apparently, was the leather industry. Griffiths, *Achterlijk?*, 14–16.

The growth in the 1890s was not localized, but extended right around the country.[34]

Factorization was a feature of industry at the end of the century and in the run-up to the First World War, and it was the time when the future great multinational companies grew to strength and maturity, often after parlous beginnings in the 1870s and 1880s. A good example is formed by the firms of Jurgens and Van den Bergh, which were competitors in the margarine industry before forging an alliance in 1908, followed by a union to form the giant *Margarine Unie* of 1927, which two years later merged with the Lever company in England to become Unilever. Another is Royal Dutch Petroleum, or '*De Koninklijke*', which began in the 1880s on Sumatra, opened its first refinery in the Netherlands in 1902, and five years later also merged with a British partner, Shell, to become one of the leading oil multinationals of the century. Third, there was the Philips Eindhoven business, making incandescent lamps, founded in 1891 and by the time of the 1920s an industrial giant in Europe and America. AKZO, the chemicals, synthetics and pharmaceuticals conglomerate, began life in Arnhem as ENKA in 1911, making artificial fibres, and the steel multinational Hoogovens was begun as a blast furnace in 1918 in IJmuiden. At the turn of the century these firms were tiny, struggling or not even founded, but they were to become the flagships of Dutch industry in the twentieth century. They were all denoted by their location firmly in the 'second industrial revolution' of late nineteenth-century new technologies (oil, processed food, electricity, synthetics), and so could compete on an even footing with international rivals without having to break into a market already long dominated by others. Neither were they reliant on domestic raw materials or fuels: the Hoogovens steel works was founded to provide the Dutch with a steel production facility when international supplies of the essential material were cut off during the First World War. But it was sited at the other end of the country from the few coal and iron ore reserves which the Netherlands possessed, at IJmuiden, at the mouth of the industrial canal zone linking Amsterdam to the North Sea and the Atlantic (see Plate 2).[35] The First World War, in which the Netherlands was not a belligerent, provided a great stimulus to

---

[34] Van Zanden, 'Industrialization', 880–90; Knotter, *Economische transformatie*, chapters 6–10; De Jonge, 'The role of the outer provinces', 219–20. There is a comprehensive survey of Dutch manufacturing on the eve of the First World War in Everwijn, *Beschrijving*.

[35] See Wilson, *The history of Unilever*; Schrover, *Het vette, het zoete*; Heerding, *Het ontstaan van de Nederlandse gloeilampen industrie*; Gerretson, *The history of the Royal Dutch*; De Vries, *Hoogovens IJmuiden*. There is no standard work on the history of AKZO, but a useful summary of the early history of all these firms appears in English at Van Zanden, *The economic history*, 29–35.

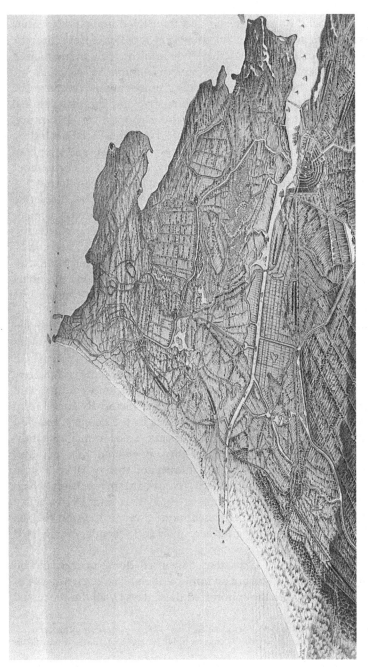

Plate 2 The North Sea Canal, lithograph, 1876, Amsterdam. A 3–D map, showing the recently drained Harlemmermeer, the growing rail network, the North Holland Canal (running from Amsterdam north to Den Helder), and the North Sea Canal (west to Ijmuiden).

Dutch industry, and during the war and the period immediately afterwards, production and productivity grew very rapidly, representing the watershed which changed the Netherlands into the truly industrialized economy it has been for most of the twentieth century.[36]

Two features can be selected for special comment in this summary: the importance of agriculture to much of industry, and the international orientation of Dutch manufacturing. In the early part of the century, much of the stimulus to Dutch industry came from the Dutch East Indies, in the form of demand for its textiles through the NHM, and supply of many of its raw materials (sugar, tobacco, dyestuffs, etc.). Throughout the century, agricultural industry found a buoyant market abroad, especially in England, which could consume all the butter and cheese the Dutch could produce. The industrial boom of the 1890s saw a major expansion of industrial exports of potato flour, glass, paper, strawboard, cigars, chocolate, dairy products, pottery, sugar, textiles and metal goods. The Dutch output went to European markets, but also further afield, especially to the East Indies, to which exports such as cottons and metal goods rose by a quarter in the 1890s, and by 150 per cent in the first decade of the twentieth century.[37]

Agriculture had always been important to parts of Dutch industry: the industrial cash crops on the fertile sea clays provided the raw materials of flax, madder, hemp, hops, chicory, potatoes, straw and suchlike which were then processed into industrial products, to say nothing of the dairy and wool industries. These continued in the nineteenth century, and were an important core activity in the secondary sector. By about 1900 there were nearly 4,000 flax-processing plants in the country and 584 co-operative factories making butter and cheese (apart from all the individual farms). In 1899 there were sixty-three powdered-milk factories, supplying 80 per cent of the English market for that product. Potato flour (like cornflour) and strawboard (cardboard made from wheat straw) production saw rapid growth in the 1860s and 1870s, while sugarbeet with its attendant factories became a major item on the sea clays after the 1860s, producing refined sugar and secondary cattle feed products.[38]

The foodstuffs industries, whether they used domestic agricultural produce or not, were and still are an important and characteristic part of the Dutch economy, perhaps epitomized these days by all the processed

---

[36] De Jong and Albers, 'Industriële groei'; Van Zanden, *The economic history*, chapter 6.
[37] Bos, *Brits-Nederlandse handel,* especially chapter 6; De Jonge, 'De industriele ontwikkeling', 86–9.
[38] Minderhoud, 'De landbouwindustrie', 409–24; Milward and Saul, *The development of the economies,* 189–92; Bieleman, *Geschiedenis van de landbouw,* 260 and 266–7.

meat and other products of Unilever which fill our supermarket shelves. The milling of flour and the baking of bread underwent an industrialization process in the nineteenth century, moving into great factories and adopting new technology; butter, margarine ('artificial butter'), beer and sugar were subjected to similar changes involving mechanization, factorization and a substantial increase in production.[39] Not all such increases in the foodstuffs industry were accompanied by factorization – for example, small private slaughterhouses modernized, proliferated and greatly increased their output for domestic and foreign markets without moving into large factories before the 1890s[40] – but perhaps the best example of a Dutch foodstuff industry modernizing, mechanizing, factorizing and expanding was sugar.

Behind the protection of colonial imports, government subsidies and a premium on exports, there was mechanization and expansion in the sugar industry between 1830 and 1855. Amsterdam became Europe's chief sugar town, with cane coming from Surinam and the Dutch Antilles as well as from Java, and beet from domestic agriculture. Exports of refined sugar rose from 28m. kg in 1834 to 93m. kg in 1871, much of it going to Britain and the countries of the Mediterranean. This is a good example of an industry nursed back to health period behind protective tariffs after the Napoleonic blight, but which then grew to be a world competitor, diversifying its sources of supply and its markets, adopting and adapting new technology, and expanding all the while.[41]

Thus while manufacturing industry was not an obvious or characteristic strength as it was in Britain or Belgium, it survived a difficult period in the first half of the century to achieve major production increases in the second, and levels of productivity somewhere between the primary and the tertiary sectors, at about the average level for the economy as a whole, by 1910 (Table II.6). It provided employment for almost a third of the workforce at that time (including the building trade; Table II.2), and a similar share of the national income.[42] In the sections above on banking, technology and entrepreneurship, manufacturing industry was entirely vindicated of any charges of backwardness. This was, then, a healthy, resourceful and dynamic sector of the economy, participating in the generally successful economic life of the country as a whole.

---

[39] Lintsen, et al., eds., Geschiedenis van de techniek, vol. I, chapters 3–7.
[40] See Koolmees, Symbolen.
[41] Lintsen, et al., eds., Geschiedenis van de techniek, vol. I, chapter 4; Milward and Saul, The development of the economies, 189–90; Griffiths, Industrial retardation, 88–92; Van Zanden, The rise and decline, 151–4.
[42] Van Zanden, 'Economische groei', 57.

6.4   The tertiary sector

The dynamics of a sector

As for services, Milward and Saul pointed out as long ago as 1977 that they formed the critical sector in the Dutch economy, being responsible for an estimated 57 per cent of national income by 1913, with only Norway (at 51.5 per cent) coming anywhere near that figure among international competitors.[43] The data on the sectoral distribution of the workforce in Table II.2 show that services were a major employer, overtaking the primary sector in the third quarter of the century, and always much more important in labour terms than manufacturing. Adding together the categories in Table II.2 for trade and finance, transport and other services, 30.6 per cent of the working population were engaged in the service sector in 1807, rising to 33.7 per cent in 1859, and 37.9 per cent in 1909. Before the First World War these figures were far higher than in other European countries, including the UK. The Dutch percentage continues to be exceptionally high: by 1971, services provided 51.4 per cent of employment, and by 1989 it was up to 70 per cent, a figure only equalled by the USA and Canada in the OECD group of nations.[44] It is clear that this was a very important sector for the Dutch economy in more ways than one.

It is not generally the case that services have been highly productive of labour, especially in the nineteenth century: armies of waiters, cleaners and domestic servants do not the benefit the macro-economy in the way that skilled metalworkers in a factory do. On the other hand, the labour of brokers, bankers and agents can be very highly productive, as can that nowadays of management consultants and computer programmers, all of whom we would also place in the service sector. It is apparently a question of definitions: of what exactly did the service sector consist, and did it change over time as it grew? We shall need a more detailed breakdown of the sector in the nineteenth century. And the question is important, for we have already seen in Table II.6 that the relative productivity of the Dutch service sector in 1910 (121 per cent) was very much higher than that of manufacturing (102) or of agriculture (70 per cent). Clearly, much of the answer to the conundrum of the Dutch economy in the nineteenth century lies herein: if the service sector was both relatively large and

---

[43] Milward and Saul, *The development of the economies*, 194; they were using Kuznets's figures.
[44] Table II.2; Smits, 'The size and structure', Table B on p. 94; and for 1989, *Netherlands*, OECD 1989/90. Naturally there are some problems with the changing definitions of certain occupations over time.

relatively productive, then it explains why the Dutch did so well without a particularly pronounced secondary sector. In order to come to a conclusion, we need to examine the size and dynamics of the various subdivisions of this residual sector, the only uncontested definition of which is one that excludes raw material production and manufacturing industry. Fortunately, there are two recent studies available, one of the first and the other of the second half of the century, by E. Horlings and J. P. Smits respectively, which give us some of the material not previously available in order to answer our questions.[45]

Smits has broken down the large occupational categories in the Dutch service sector into more detail, and has then tried to relate the changes and shifts to accelerations in the economy as a whole. Four sub-groups are adopted: distributive services (trade, transport, storage, communications), producer services (finance, services to business), social services (government, education, health, social, etc.), and personal services (catering, servants, consumer services like hairdressing, etc.). To enable analysis using these categories, Table II.7 provides a detailed breakdown of the occupational census data for the service sector from 1807, right through to 1909.[46]

The first thing that becomes clear is that the service sector does not consist simply of a host of relatively unproductive domestic servants (the UK and the US, for instance, had proportionately many more of them).[47] Producer services were very small in employment terms (still under 1 per cent of the service sector in 1909), and can be grouped together with distributive services for purposes of analysis in the nineteenth century. Table II.7 shows that the basic pattern of change in the Dutch service sector in the nineteenth century was *away from* personal services, moving through distributive and producer services, into social (or government) services by the time of the early twentieth century. Where the Dutch were internationally exceptional in the nineteenth century was in the size of their trade and transport sector, which was very large – more than 11 per cent of employment in 1901, compared to Germany's 5 per cent. It had long been so: trade and transport accounted for some 16 per cent of the workforce as early as 1650 (higher than the level reached in the first three

---

[45] Horlings, *The economic development*, a dissertation on the period 1800–50; and Smits, 'The size and structure', an article on 1850–1914. Both are associated with the national accounts project led by J. L. van Zanden, and both are in English. (Smits' work is more fully explored in his subsequent dissertation: Smits, *Economische groei*.) These works go a long way towards answering the call in Milward and Saul, *The development of the economies*, 537, for serious research into the Dutch service sector.

[46] The 1807 data are calculated from Horlings, *The economic development*, 33; the other years are taken from Smits, 'The size and structure', Table A on p. 94.

[47] Smits, 'The size and structure', 87.

Table II.7. *Share of occupational groups in the service industries on the basis of occupational census, 1807–1909 (in %).*

	1807	1849	1859	1889	1899	1909
Trade	23.2	22.0	19.9	24.3	23.3	22.4
Transport, storage, communication	14.7	14.6	16.1	20.6	17.6	20.7
Banking	0.4	0.1	0.1	0.3	0.3	0.4
Insurance	0.4	0.1	0.1	0.2	0.4	0.5
Civil Service	3.5	3.7	3.9	4.3	4.1	3.5
Military	8.9	10.3	6.1	3.7	3.0	2.3
Education	2.2	2.2	2.1	4.2	4.7	4.8
Medical and social services	1.4	1.1	1.2	1.1	1.7	2.1
Administration personnel	–	0.5	0.6	2.9	3.9	5.4
Art, science, and entertainment	–	0.8	0.8	0.7	0.9	0.9
Lawyers and solicitors	–	0.2	0.2	0.1	0.1	0.1
Domestic services	38.2	37.4	42.7	27.9	29.6	25.6
Catering	5.4	3.5	2.6	3.2	3.9	3.5
Religion	1.0	1.5	1.7	2.1	1.5	1.2
Cleaning	–	–	–	2.5	3.3	2.9
Hairdressers	–	0.6	0.6	0.7	0.8	0.9
Photographers	–	–	0.0	0.1	0.1	0.1
Chemists	–	0.6	0.5	0.3	0.4	0.4
Other services	1.1	0.8	0.8	1.0	0.5	2.9

Sources: Smits, 'The size and structure of the Dutch service sector', 94; and Horlings, *The economic development of the Dutch service sector*, 333.

quarters of the nineteenth century).[48] These shifts away from the preponderance of relatively unproductive domestic servants towards a predominance of highly productive trade, transport and finance personnel were rapid and large enough for Smits to term them 'drastic structural alterations' between 1850 and 1890, slowing down somewhat thereafter. It was the distribution sector of services which was the key at that time (in the twentieth century it was overtaken by the 'social' sector), and this can be attributed in the Dutch case to the importance of the colonies and international trade in general to the economy, but also to a highly specialized domestic agricultural economy, which required inter-regional transport and commercial exchange.[49]

The position of the service sector as a whole in the Dutch economy was

[48] De Vries and Van der Woude, *Nederland 1500–1815*, chapter 11.
[49] Smits, 'The size and structure', 87–93.

quite distinctive. Measured over the whole century against a constructed 'European average' (which tends to reflect the North-West European industrializing core countries), and employing the latest estimates of GNP,[50] the service sector transpires to have been unusually large in the Netherlands, at least until 1890, in terms of its contribution to GNP as well as its share of the labour force. (Industry was high too, compared with the neighbours, whereas agriculture was low.) The importance of trade in the economy, expressed in terms of exports as a proportion of GNP, was extremely high throughout the century: 19 per cent in 1850 (15 in Europe), 58 per cent in 1870 (20 in Europe), and 55 per cent in 1910 (27 in Europe).

The international trade and services part of the sector began the century under an appalling cloud, in the shape of the Continental System and the British blockade;[51] thereafter there was a recovery up to the mid-century, especially in the trade and transport sectors. Value added for the sector as a whole stagnated from 1807 to 1815, and then grew steadily to double itself by 1850. Distributive and producer services led the growth; catering actually declined and domestic servants hardly increased at all, probably because of the slight de-urbanization taking place in the first half of the century.[52] However, it was after 1850 that things were really to take off, especially in terms of employment. In Horlings' words, 'The period 1807–1850 was the dark age of tertiary employment ... After 1850 the service sector was the driving force behind the growth of Dutch labour.'[53] Much of the early growth in services was government induced: Willem's policies, centred on commerce with the Indies, 'resulted in astounding rates of growth' of value added in the affected branches of the services.[54] After 1850 demand increased in all parts of the tertiary sector: urbanization and rising incomes required more personal services (servants, etc.), trade and transport boomed both at home and abroad as the country became more economically unified and the barriers to international trade came down, and later on social services began to proliferate.[55] In the period 1850–1910, the tertiary sector increased its workforce by 165 per cent (half the total labour increase) and its production by 380 per cent (Table II.6).[56] According to some recent estimates, by 1910 the Dutch service sector was phenomenally efficient and

---

[50] Burger, 'Dutch patterns', 167–8. The Dutch data are provisional, and the European figures come with the usual caveats.
[51] A certain amount of the East Indies shipping survived unscathed: Eyck van Heslinga, *Van compagnie naar koopvaardij*.
[52] Buyst, *et al.*, 'National accounts', 74; Horlings, *The economic development*, 100 and 460.
[53] Horlings, *The economic development*, 247–8.
[54] Horlings, *The economic development*, 300.   [55] Smits, 'The size and structure', 90–1.
[56] See also figures which to a large extent confirm Van Zanden's, at Smits, 'The size and structure', Table 1 on p. 89.

productive compared to the equivalent sectors in its European neighbours (only the United States had even better rates). There is little
doubt, then, despite lingering uncertainties about some of the data, that
the tertiary sector was an immensely important part of the national
economic progress of the Netherlands throughout the century, and especially so after 1850.

In the rest of this section the emphasis will fall on providing a brief but
more flesh-and-blood portrait of this crucial sector, to fill out the skeletal
picture afforded by the more abstract and conceptual material which is
presented by the recent work on the national accounts project and by
international comparisons. It is undoubtedly so that services were important: of what did they actually consist, and what were the major
developments in their main branches? Various parts of the service sector
are treated in other sections of this book; here the focus will fall on trade,
transport and communications, and financial services.

Trade

The occupational data in Table II.2 group trade and finance together, but
the numbers involved in finance were tiny, representing less than 1 per
cent of the whole service sector even by 1909 (Table II.7). Therefore we
may take the trade and finance figures as being a good indicator of the
commerce sector, including both international and internal trade, as well
as retail. The percentages of the labour force in trade hovered around 6 or
7 until the last quarter of the century, when they rose to 10, and to 12 by
1909. In terms of absolute numbers, the trade sector increased its personnel more than fourfold in the century between 1807 and 1909 (63,000 to
269,000), considerably outstripping the growth of the labour force as a
whole, which increased by just two and a half times in the same period.
The share of trade in the service sector remained constant at just under a
quarter of tertiary labour (Tables II.2 and II.7). Generally, the Dutch
traded far more per head of population than any other nation in Europe:
in 1911, the value of imports and exports per capita in the Netherlands
was the equivalent of 2,157 gold francs, which was twice the level of
Belgium and three times that of the UK, two of her closest rivals.[57]

Imports and exports were an unmitigated disaster until 1813: it is
estimated that the Dutch lost 60 per cent of their market share in exports
in the French period.[58] However, a recovery began in 1814 – probably
aided by the survival of some of the East Indies shipping[59] – which

[57] Milward and Saul, *The development of the economies*, 540. Switzerland lay in third place,
between Belgium and the UK.
[58] Buyst and Mokyr, 'Dutch manufacturing'.
[59] Eyck van Heslinga, *Van compagnie naar koopvaardij*.

continued indefinitely for imports. Exports were another matter. There was a very serious decline in exports right up to the early 1830s, at a time when imports were rising: the Netherlands was not producing enough, and faced punitive protection abroad, especially against its agricultural products. Dutch merchants were being excluded from their previously lucrative markets and sources of supply, and were less and less necessary as middlemen. The answer devised by Willem I's government, which was immensely successful in solving the problem as defined by the trade figures, was to introduce a new colonial regime, based on protected trade in colonial agricultural products and domestic industrial ones. The launch of the NHM (1824) and the Cultivation System (*Cultuurstelsel*, 1830) resulted in a revival of Dutch exports from about 1830, which joined imports in a steep rise (with a slow-down in the early 1840s) continuing beyond the mid-century. Trade on the whole was quite buoyant after the Indies intervention, but – Horlings makes the point – the success was concentrated in a few branches and, being based on exploiting the East Indies, it was not very closely related to the domestic economy. Only a small amount of home production was exported, and the benefits were regionally very concentrated, especially in the provinces of Noord- and Zuid-Holland.[60] This had also been the case, of course, in the time of the Republic, and in this sense colonial trade in the first half of the nineteenth century may have been grappling with the challenges of transition. Van Zanden has advanced the theory that the trade-based growth of the period 1825–55 was rooted in a return behind protection to an early-modern form of merchant capitalism, based on the Java–Amsterdam axis. The price the Dutch paid for their colonial products through the Cultivation System was considerably less than the reproduction costs of domestic labour (the resources needed for the labour to reproduce itself demographically). This was possible because of the location of production in an area of cheap labour like the East Indies, and by fixing prices well below the market value, even in the Indies.[61] It was certainly an effective ruse in view of the exports problem, but may well have retarded private initiative by its monopolistic regime. Whatever the case, by 1850 the trade levels of the Kingdom of the Netherlands had exceeded those of the great Dutch Republic at the height of its Golden Age. In terms of the value of imports and exports, the peak years of the seventeenth century had probably never produced more than *f*400m., while by 1850 the average exceeded that comfortably.[62]

[60] Horlings, *The economic development*, 119 and Appendix III. The figures are sophisticated, and very much better than anything previously available, but are still based at least partly on estimates of their various components, and may be subject to some revision.

[61] Van Zanden, *The rise and decline*, especially chapter 8.

[62] Van Zanden, 'Economische groei', 63.

Table II.8. *Dutch external trade, imports and exports, excluding transit trade, in millions of guilders (current prices), 1850–1920.*

	Imports	Exports	Total	Index of total (1910 = 100)
1850	188	137	325	6
1860	316	251	567	10
1870	507	399	906	15
1880	840	630	1,470	25
1890	1,300	1,088	2,388	40
1900	1,968	1,695	3,663	62
1910	3,265	2,632	5,897	100
1920	3,345	1,722	5,067	86

Source: Mitchell, *European historical statistics*, 300–5.

In the second half of the century the domination of trade by the colonial sector was relaxed, and prosperity became much more diffuse. Far more of the domestic economy was involved, as the internal infrastructure reduced the isolation of many parts of the country. The value of trade continued to soar. The combined value of imports and exports (excluding transit trade, in current prices) is shown in Table II.8 for the period 1850–1920: there was continuous and exponential growth up to 1910. Even bearing in mind the deficiencies of the data and the lack of a deflator, this represented an impressive eighteenfold rise.[63]

The part played by the Indies trade continued to be important in this post-1850 expansion. Between the mid-century and the First World War, the annual value of exports to the East Indies rose from ƒ7.9m. to ƒ113.7m., and of imports from ƒ45.2m. to ƒ129m.[64] The continuing reservation of the Indies trade for the NHM until the 1870s meant that the numbers of beneficiaries were restricted while activity increased, but private enterprise was let in on the bonanza after 1870. Exports from the East Indies of its seven principal products nearly doubled in the 1870s and 1880s, increasing from 254m. kg in 1870 to 449m. kg in 1890, and then between 1890 and 1910 they almost quadrupled, up to 1,457m. kg.[65] After struggling to establish itself in the period of free trade, the export trade from the Netherlands supplying the East Indies took off after 1890, increasing by 25 per cent by 1900, and by another 150 per cent by

[63] The equivalent rise for Belgium was a fifteenfold one, from 501m. to 7,672m. francs. Mitchell, *European historical statistics*, 297–309.
[64] Broek, *Economic development*, 106.
[65] Blok, *et al.*, eds., *Algemene geschiedenis der Nederlanden*, vol. XIII, p. 284.

1910, by which time new products like oil and tin were being added to the total.[66]

Meanwhile the river trade with the hinterland expanded enormously as well. We have seen (in section 5.3) how the government's negotiators handled the series of talks and treaties which charted the loosening of the Dutch stranglehold on the Rhine trade with Germany, and in retrospect it is clear that they organized their tactical retreat very creditably, with the Dutch not only salvaging something but diversifying into new areas of trade and shipping to feed the increasingly ravenous German industrial leviathan. In 1871–75 there were 264,000 tonnes of the main bulk products of grains, ores and petroleum shipped up the Rhine each year; by the eve of the First World War (1911–14) it had risen to 15.5m. tonnes annually, which represented almost a 6,000 per cent increase in forty years.[67]

In essence, the whole of Dutch commerce was responding to a series of changes, and on the whole it came through the ordeal very well. The sector faced three major fresh challenges in the new century: shifting centres of economic gravity within Europe, the rise and further rise of free trade, and the shrinking of the world market. Each of these was fraught with difficulties, but in all three the Dutch eventually won through with flying colours. The Netherlands (and Belgium) owe much of their prosperity through the ages to their position at the crossroads of Northern Europe: at the mouth of the major rivers of the continental mass, opposite the estuaries and ports of eastern England, while at the same time well placed on the route between the Baltic and the Mediterranean. That economic-geographic position is still the fundament of their success as trading nations. However, the Dutch lost their Braudelian market centrality in the course of eighteenth century. As first the UK and then Belgium, northern France and parts of Germany began to industrialize around her, this boom in heavy industry left the Netherlands to one side. There is a sense in which the Dutch no longer sat aside the trade routes which mattered; one author has called the Dutch shift one 'from centre to periphery'.[68] They were still at the mouth of the Rhine and the other major rivers, it is true, but, as we have seen in looking at government policy, there was immense pressure on the Dutch to retreat from their favoured position. Here again, the geo-political and economic situation was changing. The rising economic strength of the German states, symbolized in the building of the Iron Rhine railway between Antwerp and

---

[66] Milward and Saul, *The development of the economies*, 200–1.
[67] Blok, *et al.*, eds., *Algemene geschiedenis der Nederlanden*, vol. XIII, pp. 53–6 and 274–6 (customs figures at Lobith); Nusteling, *De Rijnvaart*; and De Vries, 'De problematiek'.
[68] Bos, 'Van periferie'.

Cologne in 1843, caused a 'qualitative internal economic contraction' on the part of the Dutch, and drove them to give up their privileges on the Rhine trade. Transit trade, where they were agents rather than in control, took over from the staple trade.[69] There was still the trade in agricultural produce to the urban markets of England, but demand was growing so fast there that the Dutch could not meet it all, and other players came into the trade, notably the Danes.[70] Despite all these challenges, the Dutch restructured their trade, and, assisted by the rise of the German industrial machine, regained a central position in European trade towards the end of the century.

The second main challenge was the rise of free trade, which we have examined extensively (in section 5.3) under government economic policy. There was once again an adroit adaptation, this time to quite hostile protectionist surroundings in the early nineteenth century: a contemporary in 1829 called it an 'encirclement'.[71] Then came the liberalization of trade on river, sea and land around the mid-century, eventually extending even to colonial goods, which meant the relinquishing of the staple idea for ever. Again, the Dutch retreated from their privileged position won in the time of the Republic, but did so with skill and pragmatism, and increased their trade all the while.

Finally, there was the process of what is now called 'globalization'. The electronic media have recently made an important contribution to this continuing process, but the world market has been forming and improving since the Middle Ages. The enormous nineteenth-century advances in transport and communication meant that the middleman function of the Dutch merchant had been eclipsed by 1850 except in protected colonial products, especially that of the merchants 'of the second hand': those sorters, processors and distributors. Now improved information and standardization meant that many forms of business could be done without an intermediate 'expert': samples would be sent and bills could be paid with the benefit of stable exchange rates, helped by the gold standard.[72] The day of the great independent merchant prince was giving way to that of the travelling salesman with his suitcase full of standard samples and order forms.

The three main sectors of Dutch commerce, the river trade, the seaward trade and the colonial trade, rose to these challenges in the course of the nineteenth century. The river traders adapted, and moved into work as commission agents, running entrepôt warehouses for transit

---

[69] Bläsing, 'Interne en externe oorzaken', 328; and Nusteling, *De Rijnvaart*, chapters 2–5.
[70] Bos, *Brits-Nederlandse handel*, chapter 6.
[71] The senior official Bakker Korff, quoted in Bläsing, 'Interne en externe oorzaken', 327.
[72] Bos, 'Van periferie', 89–90.

trade which was not going through immediately, and servicing the burgeoning trade in bulk goods bound for Germany. In the seaward trade, the staple in all goods but colonial products had long since dissipated, and after the 1870s even the tropical products were unprotected. The middleman as independent trader was bypassed, and the grain trade with the Baltic was no longer the 'mother trade' (*moedernegotie*) it had been in the Republic, with Ukrainian grain going straight to the traditional Mediterranean markets from the Black Sea port of Odessa, instead of northwards to the Baltic and then through the Sound in Dutch bottoms. After the 1870s, grain was available to anyone who wanted it direct from North America, India and elsewhere at rock-bottom prices. Again, adaptation was necessary, and the Dutch were adroit. They took advantage of rising levels of world trade, and increased their own, as we have seen. Servicing the massive German trade became a major sector in its own right.

The pace of change was less hectic in the colonial world: the mighty state mercantilism of the NHM and the Cultivation System resurrected the partial staple trade in colonial goods, turning Amsterdam into a hub of commerce once more for a few select colonial products. Multatuli's character of Drystubble (*Droogstoppel*) in *Max Havelaar*, the odious first-person narrator with his sanctimonious hypocrisy as he cheerfully exploits the rotten system, is an archetypal staple merchant 'of the second hand'. He buys coffee at the auctions of the NHM, and then functions as a specialist dealer with product-specific expertise. Multatuli was writing that novel in the 1850s, by which time there would have been no coffee staple, had it not been for the powerful effects of the Dutch government's monopolistic colonial policy.[73] But after 1870, as we have seen, the monopoly was abolished under liberal pressure, and the foreign competition came straight in. Again the Dutch adapted, and took a smaller slice of a larger cake, as the volume of trade between the Indies and the Netherlands continued to grow, especially exports.[74]

In summary on foreign trade, the determining factors were dictated by forces outside the control of the Dutch: England and France moving towards free trade, the German states slowly coming together and growing in economic strength, and the colonies being prised open by private enterprise and foreign competition. Dutch politicians and traders alike were slow to change, but they were nonetheless highly astute in extracting a great deal of business from what may often have seemed a depressing situation, especially in the first half of the century. Free trade theories had been hotly debated since the early eighteenth century, but steps towards it

[73] See section 5.3 above on government policy, and section 7.2 below on colonial demand.
[74] Broek, *Economic development*, 106; see above for the figures themselves.

were taken in the most pragmatic manner, as were the wranglings with the Germans on the river trade. The Dutch adapted adeptly.[75]

Internal and retail trade   Measured in terms of value added at constant prices, domestic trade rose from some ƒ20m. in 1815 to almost ƒ60m. in 1850. Its growth rates outstripped other services branches in the first half of the century, with the exception of transport. Retail trade was dependent on real incomes, which did not begin to rise significantly until the second half of the century (section 7.4), and internal trade was also reliant on the transport infrastructure, which indeed grew before 1850, but which really only began to come together thereafter.[76]

In 1850/51 there were more people employed in the nation's 61,000 shops than there were in its factories; the omission of many working women from the census data probably disguises an even higher figure.[77] By 1890/91 the numbers of shops had risen to more than 106,000. There were consumer co-operatives founded from the 1870s onwards, which competed with independent retailers, and the practice of payment in vouchers to be spent in company stores was widespread until restricted by a law of 1907 on labour contracts. In 1887, the High Street grocery chain Albert Heijn was founded, as were several department stores in the last two decades of the century.[78] In the larger towns such stores could do thriving business, but most shops were very small indeed, and their numbers increased only slightly ahead of rates of population growth. Most shops had very low levels of turnover, especially in the east of the country, reflecting the poverty in which most people continued to live for most of the nineteenth century, despite the success of the economy as a whole and the prosperity of the middle and upper classes. The growth rates in trade we have observed did not mean for most of the Dutch populace that there was very much respite in their daily grind, certainly before the 1860s and 1870s.[79]

Transport

In Jan de Vries's study of internal passenger shipping,[80] he contended that the *trekschuiten* or horse-drawn tow-barge services between the Dutch towns formed an integrated system or infrastructure, which held the country together and actually lent it its modernity. Because the barges ran

[75] These points are the general burden of Bläsing, 'Interne en externe oorzaken'; De Vries, 'De problematiek'; and Bläsing, *Das goldene Delta*.
[76] Horlings, *The economic development*, 220–1.
[77] See Schrover, '"De affaire"', 59.   [78] Miellet, *Honderd jaar*.
[79] Blok, *et al.*, eds., *Algemene geschiedenis der Nederlanden*, vol. XII, pp. 75–6; and vol. XIII, p. 280. See section 2.5 above on diet, and section 7.4 below on the standard of living.
[80] De Vries, 'Barges and capitalism'.

on time, and were reliable and went everywhere, they encouraged the development of a modern mentality based on modern concepts of time, with businessmen and indeed customers making modern rationalist decisions in this integrated, connected society. De Vries's data ran right through to 1839, and despite some decline at the end, the overriding impression was of a superb, seamless system, transporting people about like clockwork, which was so efficient that it even delayed the introduction of railways to the Netherlands.

In fact things were rather different, and the impression left by De Vries needs some considerable adjustment. There were other shipping services, of course, but the barges themselves carried virtually no freight, were excruciatingly slow, and were confined to the west of the country. In 1815 sea shipping had been virtually annihilated, roads were unspeakable, and communications were extremely slow. Even in the west, a journey could be quite unpredictable: alongside the barges there were diligences which were often quite impossible to tie down to time or place, especially in winter or at high water. The postal service was patchy and very expensive, and the time zones were not even regional, but entirely local. Travel other than between the larger cities was a dangerous business, fraught with difficulty and completely unreliable. There were pockets of reasonable transport, like the *trekschuiten* themselves, or occasionally the diligences, but a *system* of transport, or infrastructure, was not a feature of the early nineteenth century in the Netherlands, any more than it was elsewhere.[81]

A century later, however, things had altered. There had of course been many changes: new technologies of steam and electricity had been applied, massive investment had taken place, and communications had leapt forward. But the most important change was qualitative rather than simply an extension of what was there before. It was possible to talk of an infrastructure, in the sense of a system of communications and transport which linked the various parts of the country, and linked the country with the surrounding world in Europe and further afield. Perhaps the most characteristic feature of the Dutch economy in the twentieth century has been the government's determination to reduce all barriers, internal and external, physical and fiscal, to commerce with the countries around her. Here we shall examine the transport and communications links as they took shape and matured in the nineteenth century.

Waterways What the Netherlands has always possessed is a great deal of water, along which boats could sail, could be hauled or (later on) could steam. The great rivers needed maintaining, and indeed canalizing; early

---

[81] See Van der Woud, *Het lege land, passim*; and Groote, *Kapitaalvorming*, 66.

in the century only the west was well served. The focal points of the canals and rivers were the two harbours of Amsterdam and Rotterdam, but they required constant attention to their access both to the sea and to their up-river connections. Amsterdam's links with the Rhine were attended to with the Cologne Waterway (*Keulse Vaart*) in 1824 and the Zederik Canal in 1826, and steam tugs began operating on the route in the 1830s. The capital's access to the sea, however, remained highly problematic, and the route to the North Sea through the Zuiderzee via Den Helder was a difficult one (see Plate 2). In 1824 Amsterdam received a new link to the sea, called the Noord-Holland Canal, cut due north through the tapering triangle of the northern part of (*Kop van*) Noord-Holland to the port of Den Helder itself. The route was extremely long, with several locks and many bridges, and so was far from ideal, but at least it allowed Amsterdam to remain open as a port. It was, however, obsolete almost as soon as it was built (ships still limped through the Zuiderzee), and the modern approach to Amsterdam, from due west and the port of IJmuiden on the coastal dunes, had to wait until the hydraulic technology was available for cutting through those dunes and straight across the province horizontally, radically shortening the approach to the capital and breathing new life into the port. This North Sea Canal was one of the infrastructural projects undertaken during the tenure of the liberals, from the mid-1860s onwards, and was finished in 1876.

Rotterdam had similar problems. Its access to the sea at the beginning of the century threaded through the various islands and mudbanks in the Maas estuary and was tortuous to say the least, doubling back on itself several times.[82] By cutting a canal through the island of Voorne in 1830 things were much improved, but the real breakthrough had to wait until the 1870s (as with Amsterdam), when steam technology was sufficiently advanced to undertake the work involved in cutting a new route straight through the Hook of Holland westwards to the North Sea in 1871. The resulting New Waterway (*Nieuwe Waterweg*) is still the route by which one approaches Rotterdam harbour from the sea, although most of the bulk cargoes now stop in the Europort half way up the canal. From the 1870s there was rapid development south of the river, and the Maas harbour was on its way to taking over the lead from Antwerp and becoming the biggest port anywhere. Other harbour towns in the Netherlands received new canals and harbours in the course of the century, and maintenance was a constant preoccupation, as it remains today.

The definitive version of most of these developments took place in the third quarter of the century, under the wing of the liberals: a Canals Act of 1863 regulated the state funding of the sea access to both Amsterdam and

[82] Van Oostveen, *De economische ontwikkeling*, 36.

Rotterdam. Healthy state finance was important to such massive public works, and the availability of technology was also important in the timing. This is somewhat remarkable, in the light of King Willem's efforts to help the infrastructure, especially in canal-building. He certainly ploughed money into his projects in the 1820s, and realized some 800 km of waterways as a result, like the Zuidwillemsvaart, at a huge 123 km, between Maastricht and Den Bosch (though many of the waterways were in the southern, Belgian part of the country, as was part of the Zuidwillemsvaart). He spent as high a proportion of national income on them as was expended on the Delta Project after the 1953 floods, 130 years later. His policies were highly unpopular with parliament, and helped cause the near-bankruptcy of the state. Despite his keenness to intervene as canal-builder, infrastructural benefactor and general economic facilitator, the transport system remained flawed, though his labours did function as essential groundwork for the progress made after the mid-century.[83]

Shipping   The ships which provided services in the harbours, on the canals and rivers, and at sea were an important part of the growing national infrastructure, along with all the facilities which went with the shipping, such as wharves, locks, sluices, pilots, warehousing and the like. The merchant fleet had been virtually eliminated under the Continental System, so Willem I set about building a new one. There were direct premiums on shipbuilding until 1829, and his NHM granted comfortable contracts to Dutch shipwrights from the 1820s to 1868; this protection resulted in rather small ships to make maximum use of the subsidies, and some rather inefficient use of the shipping concentrated in the colonial sector, but there was certainly a good supply: from zero to 2,500 vessels between 1815 and 1860. Some recent attempts to calculate output in maritime shipping, expressed in capacity-ton-km, show a rise from 3,000 of these units in 1816 to more than 19,000 in 1850, while value added (for all merchant shipping) rose almost exactly in proportion, from just under ƒ3m. in 1816 to ƒ18.3m. in 1850. In the second half of the century the Dutch share of East Indies shipping was falling, but the expansion of the trade meant that absolute growth continued in the 1850s and 1860s in all maritime sectors except the Mediterranean, where English competition was too much. The river trade grew apace: in the 1850s there was a 16 per cent increase in registered tonnage, and there was a 36 per cent increase between 1860/61 and 1878/79.[84]

---

[83] Van der Woud, *Het lege land*, 95–140; Brugmans, *Paardenkracht*, 128–9 and 229–30; Horlings, *The economic development*, 301; Filarski, *Kanalen*; Van Dijk, *The three seaports*; Baetens, *et al.*, eds., *Maritieme geschiedenis*, 53–88.
[84] Brugmans, *Paardenkracht*, 89–91; Horlings, *The economic development*, 215 and 403–4; De Jonge, *De industrialisatie*, 132–9, 146 and 155–6.

Table II.9.   *Dutch mercantile marine,*
1870–1913 (× 1,000 net tons)

	Total	Sail	Steam
1870	390	370	20
1880	328	264	64
1890	256	127	129
1900	347	79	268
1913	688	40	647

Source: Milward and Saul, *The development of the economies of continental Europe,* 199.

After 1870 there was a huge expansion in world shipping: it is es-timated that levels rose by 160 per cent in twenty years. At this time (1870–90) Dutch shipping lagged behind a little, with only a 120 per cent increase, occasioned by the steep decline in the sail-powered fleet (see Table II.9). Meanwhile the steam tonnage increased, and from 1890 up to 1910 Dutch activities accelerated rapidly, increasing by 240 per cent in twenty years while the world at large could only manage half that rate.[85] When it came, the shift to steam was swift: in 1880, as much as 80 per cent of Dutch merchant tonnage (92 per cent of ships) was under sail, but by 1898, only 29 per cent had still not yet switched to steam (still 80 per cent of vessels). By the end of the century, the Dutch had a rapidly advancing merchant fleet, spearheaded by large, newly built steam-ships.[86]

Alongside the booming river-freight business, much of the growth in Dutch shipping in the second half of the nineteenth century had to do with the expansion and proliferation of intercontinental Dutch shipping lines. Around the mid-century there already existed in the Netherlands a number of major shipping lines, some of which had already moved into steam, and which were focussed on the continent of Europe. By the 1920s the Dutch, alongside other capitalist nations with imperialist ambitions, had built up a genuinely global shipping network, based on the large motorized vessel and geographically focussed on their colonies in the Indonesian archipelago. The Silver-Java-Pacific Line circumnavigated the globe, the Java-New York Line served all the harbours of the eastern American seaboard from Halifax to the Gulf of Mexico. The Pacific was criss-crossed with regular Dutch lines, and the inter-island traffic in the

[85] De Jonge, 'De industriele ontwikkeling', 83–5.
[86] *Statistiek van de scheepvaart over het jaar 1898,* 1; Baetens, *et al.,* eds., *Maritieme gesch-iedenis,* 158ff; Table II.9.

Dutch East Indies itself was controlled by the officially sponsored Royal Packet Company (KPM). Most of the maritime nations of Western Europe, and America and Japan as well, achieved something along these lines; the remarkable feature in the Dutch case was that the Netherlands was so small and had so few mineral resources (the same was also true of Denmark and Norway). This enormous expansion of transport systems across the world's oceans either side of the turn of the twentieth century was a crucial stage in the creation of a truly global capitalist economy. The niche carved out for themselves by the Dutch, founded on the East Indies colonies, and maintained in the face of menacing competition, was essential to the development of the Dutch domestic economy, based as it was substantially on the service sector.[87]

In summary, Dutch shipping was a pivotal sector, whether on the rivers, in Europe or on the world's oceans. Some early 'guestimates' suggest that shipping contributed only between 3 and 4 per cent of Dutch national income in 1913,[88] so in itself it was not a large sector, but its facilitating and enabling role for the rest of the economy was crucial. More recent estimates assure us of the advanced nature of Dutch maritime transport. The Netherlands' sea shipping had the highest productivity levels of all its international competitors (including the US) in 1910: for instance, the value added per worker was 20 per cent higher in the Netherlands than in the UK.[89]

Roads and railways In the nineteenth century, the roads in the Netherlands were not the strong point they are today. There were very few decent roads at the beginning of the century; the east and north had virtually none at all. In the coastal and river areas there were so many canals and ditches that freight transport, for example of agricultural produce, was always possible, but the tens and even hundreds of wagonloads of farmyard manure which were deposited on the farms had to be moved from farm to field on 'roads' which were unserviceable for several months a year.

Before 1850, the only good highways were the national trunk roads, linking the provincial capitals. Some funds were available for provincial roads, joining the major market towns, and from 1860 to 1880 (again under the liberals), small roads were eligible for subsidy and many were built. As the sugarbeet crop on the sea clays expanded to fill the vacuum

[87] For a full account, see Wintle, 'Shipping'; and Baetens, *et al.*, eds., *Maritieme geschiedenis*, 158–256.
[88] De Jonge, 'De industriele ontwikkeling', 85, 89–90.
[89] Burger and Smits, 'A benchmark'. The data are impressively gathered, though the methodological problems abound. The general point is nonetheless clear, on the high relative productivity of Dutch producer and distributive services.

left by outmoded madder, local farm roads became an economic necessity. They were usually the only ones that were free: most roads carried a
toll throughout the century, and the tolls were high. The advent of the
railway, and then the tramline (in rural as well as urban areas) allowed
people to forsake the roads, and that they did until bicycles became
widespread. The current Dutch road-users' association, the ANWB, was
founded in 1883 as a cycling club (General Netherlands Cyclists Union,
or *Algemeene Nederlandsche Wielrijders Bond*), and the application of air-
filled tyres in the 1890s made the infernal machines comfortable and
faster. In the twentieth century they became a means of transport for the
proletariat, and enabled more labour mobility and the integration of the
village with the economic and social allure of the towns. By 1899 there
was one bicycle for every fifty-three Dutch people, and the ratio was
dropping rapidly. The new roads built in the nineteenth century were,
predictably, concentrated in the west: elsewhere, for instance in Limburg,
the roads played a very minor economic role, and things were not much
better in the north and east. The Dutch ran just 4,000 motor vehicles in
1913, and it was only in the 1930s that the number exceeded 100,000:
only with the arrival of the motor car *en masse* did the road network really
come into its own.[90]

The earliest Dutch railway was constructed between Amsterdam and
Haarlem in 1839, which was something of a vanguard position, for the
first in the world – the Stockton and Darlington line – had opened just
fourteen years before. The new attraction was a great novelty; however, it
had little or no economic importance, was not extended, and carried
virtually no freight. There was very little large-scale building until the
1860s (again under the liberals), and not much freight carried until after
1870. A Railway Act of 1860 marked the state's takeover from a number
of private firms, and by 1890 the main network had been built. What
impact did the coming of the railway have on the Dutch economy, and
what were the reasons for and consequences of the slow start?

Let us first examine the timing of railway construction, based on the
figures in Table II.10, which also has the Belgian data for comparison.
After the early start (17 km), only 335 km were built before 1860, by
which time Belgium had laid more than 1,700 km of track. Belgium was
the earliest and most intense railway nation on the continent, but is of
comparable size. After the 1860 Act, Dutch track took off, and the totals
rose steeply until 1890, and continued rising rapidly until 1920. A peak of

---

[90] Van der Woud, *Het lege land*, 142–69; Griffiths, *Industrial retardation*, 69–71; Knippenberg and De Pater, *De eenwording*, 46–7; Luurs, 'De aanleg'; Lewe, '*Invoer*'; Mitchell,
European historical statistics, 350. On bicycles, see also Goodman and Honeyman, *Gainful
pursuits*, 148–51; Brugmans, *Paardenkracht*, 371–2.

Table II.10 *Length of rail track open in the Netherlands and Belgium, 1840–1939, in kilometres.*

	The Netherlands	Belgium
1840	17	334
1860	335	1,729
1880	1,841	4,112
1900	2,771	4,562
1920	3,606	4,938
1939	3,314	5,140

Sources: Jaarcijfers (1895), 182 and (1901), 218; and Mitchell, *European historical statistics*, 315–19.

more than 3,600 km was reached in the 1930s, after which gentle decline set in. Belgium, on the other, saw rapid growth right from the start in the 1830s, and by 1900 the basic network was finished, which at its height was some 40 per cent larger than the Dutch one. In 1911 the Dutch had laid 5.45 km. for every 10,000 inhabitants, which put them in thirteenth place out of nineteen European nations. It must be remembered that the UK, Belgium and Germany towered above all other countries in rail matters: in 1911, those three nations each sent about 10,000 tons of freight for every inhabitant, whereas the Dutch were in a quite respectable second group with only 2,630 tons; most countries in Europe sent less than 2,000 tons per inhabitant.[91]

Traditionally the late start has been explained in terms of the conservatism of the old staple merchants and the watermen, but there is only anecdotal evidence for this. In a country like Belgium the railways were used intensively to transport industrial labour around the country (the *pendelaars*), whereas the Netherlands may have had less need in this respect. Then there are the physical conditions in which the track had to be laid. Most of the country is very low-lying and more or less a morass: the Amsterdam–Rotterdam line required no less than ninety-eight bridges. However, the physical geography of the Netherlands must be kept in perspective: there were no hills, no mountains, no ravines, no tunnelling. In some ways it must have been one the easiest parts of Europe in which to lay track. There was inadequate legislation to enable compulsory purchase orders, and so attempts to lay railways were often delayed and even completely frustrated, but that problem was more or

[91] Milward and Saul, *The development of the economies,* 541. The Dutch figures are for 1909; most of the other countries are for 1911.

less solved with the Expropriation Act of 1850. There may also have been problems with the financing of the railways: it appeared to be difficult to get Dutch investors to put money in for a 4 per cent return when they could get double that and more for railway adventures abroad, for instance in America or Russia.[92]

The matter of capital provision for the Dutch railways is an interesting one, for it covers the debates explored earlier in chapter 4 to do with entrepreneurial mentality and capital starvation. As with all the other case studies we have examined, the Dutch can be resoundingly exonerated of any charges of unbusinesslike conduct. Detailed studies have shown that although the railway firms were always searching for capital, the lack of it never slowed them down. The entrepreneurs found much of their funding abroad, and were ingenious in raising the very large amounts they needed. The Dutch investors clearly wanted a speculative tinge to their railway investments: they could get 4 per cent in Treasury stock. Laying the track was speculative, and the Dutch investors were ready to fund it; running an existing railway was not, and the domestic investors tended to take their capital elsewhere.[93]

Equally importantly, the state had stood aloof until 1860, when central government stepped in to sponsor the creation of a proper network in the country. It provided massive investment after 1860 – about two thirds of the total – and much of it came from the profits of the East Indies Cultivation System. This addition of central control and co-ordination together with heavy funding in the 1860s and 1870s (f24m. in track alone, as opposed to less than f4m. in the 1840s and 1850s) resulted in the completion of the main network by 1890. Direct public control was relinquished in 1890 with the Railway Agreements (*Spoorwegovereenkomsten*). In order to increase efficiency but prevent monopoly, the system was divided between two companies, the HSM (*Hollandsche IJzeren Spoorweg Maatschappij*) and the SS (*Maatschappij tot Exploitatie van Staatsspoorwegen*). After 1900 there was a further burst of investment, but this time largely by local authorities to improve services for their regions. In 1937 the various companies were merged into the NS (*NV Nederlandsche Spoorwegen*, which still provides the national service today), with heavy state support. Compared internationally, investment in the Dutch network was poor until 1860, and then stood up well with all competitors other than the UK and Belgium. Given the state of the rest of the infrastructure, coal prices, demand, and economic opportunities at home and abroad, the behaviour of both entrepreneurs and investors was

[92] Van der Woud, *Het lege land*, 170ff.; Brugmans, *Paardenkracht*, 101–2; Griffiths, *Industrial retardation*, 71–4. See also Veenendaal, *De ijzeren weg*.
[93] Van den Broecke, *Financiën*.

credit-worthy, and 'it can be argued that resource allocation was rational'.[94]

By the 1890s, then, the Dutch had a railway network which increased the economic integration of the kingdom in itself, but, more importantly, linked it with its neighbours. The dominant one was Germany, and the rail links were the complement to the waterways which already existed. Freight on the Dutch railways rose from 4m. to 9.6m. tonnes annually between 1880 and 1900, and then to 16.7m. tonnes by 1920.[95] The economy of the Netherlands was becoming increasingly entwined with that of Germany as the century drew to a close. This was to be the shape of things to come for the Dutch, and rail played a key role in the further embedding of the Netherlands in the North European economy.

Other transport and communications   Other forms of transport also grew in the long nineteenth century. Trams made their entry in the 1870s, and there was major investment in this local form of railway in the years 1880–83. Many were horse-drawn at this stage, but they improved local and regional infrastructure, especially for the sugarbeet areas. In the 1890s whole regional networks grew up, many of them run on steam, and after 1900 the cities and towns began to invest in urban networks of the electric trams whose successors we still know today. There is little doubt that these improvements were of assistance to the integration of the labour market. Growth in the length of track was steep until nearly 3,000 km was reached in the 1930s (the same zenith period as the railways), after which decline was equally sharp.[96]

Dutch air transport grew out of World War I, and the need to communicate more rapidly with the colonies. In 1919 Royal Dutch Airlines (*Koninklijke Luchtvaart Maatschappij*, KLM) was formed, with the major shipping companies as founding shareholders, launching daily flights from the Netherlands to London in the next year. Government interest increased until it took a majority share in 1927. In 1924 the first experimental flight was made all the way from the Netherlands to Batavia in the East Indies, and by 1930 there was a regular service, which began by taking ten days each way, later coming down to five and a half. The Indies developed their own branch, called the Royal Netherlands East Indies Airline (*Koninklijke Nederlandsch-Indische Luchtvaart Maatschappij*, KNILM), which grew rapidly both in its passenger and its freight operations, flying from Batavia to such locations as Hong Kong, China and

---

[94] Groote, *et al.*, 'Dutch rail- and tramways', 54 and *passim*.
[95] Mitchell, *European historical statistics*, 330.
[96] Brugmans, *Paardenkracht*, 371; Knippenberg and De Pater, *De eenwording*, 48–50; Groote, *et al.*, 'Dutch rail- and tramways', 48.

Japan, and Sydney. There was also an experiment with airships, which foundered on Nazi refusal to export the technology in the 1930s. The Dutch were quick to see the potential for transport and communications of airplane technology, and, significantly, the government took the lead from an early stage.[97]

The communications network of a modern state is a powerful force for integration and modernization; it also serves the business community well in allowing rapid transactions and exchange of information. It can act as a transport service for some parts of the tertiary sector which deal in information and intellectual property rather than conventional commodities, and it can put whole economic classes, like middlemen, almost entirely out of business. We shall consider briefly the press, postal services and electronic communications media.

Edwin Horlings has managed to construct a series for the value of production in the communications sector in the first half of the century, which hardly changed at all, hovering between 1 million and 1.5 million guilders at current prices.[98] The Netherlands had long been known as the bookshop (and publishing house) of the world, and the number of bookshops in the country rose from 582 in 1810 to 861 in 1849, and then to 1,561 in 1907. The number of published titles rose from virtually nothing at the end of the French period to 141 in 1848, and then to 3,918 in 1910.[99] This circulation of reading material, most of it in the Dutch language, was important for an increasing sense of national integration, and the works included the dissemination of important economic information such as agricultural treatises. However, the daily press had a greater impact on the transmission of information (and political gossip). The Dutch were a literate people, for commercial and religious reasons.[100] Most of the press was local until the mid-century, much of it heavily censored or the mouthpiece of local government, along with various lively but scurrilous radical broadsheets and a host of almanacs and suchlike. The liberal *Algemeen Handelsblad* was the first national daily, from 1830 onwards. The technology of printing improved, and the effectiveness and therefore the popularity of advertising enhanced the financing; however, the breakthrough came (as it did in most countries) with the abolition in 1869 of Stamp Duty on newsprint (the *dagbladzegel*).

---

[97] See Wintle, 'Shipping'. See also Brugmans, *Paardenkracht*, 486–7; Blok, *et al.*, eds., *Algemene geschiedenis der Nederlanden*, vol. XIV, p. 114; Ten Brink, *De geschiedenis van het postvervoer*, 74–81; Brugmans, *Tachtig jaar varen*, 156–60; Dierikx, 'De positie van Nederlands-Indië'.

[98] Horlings, *The economic development*, 432.

[99] Lintsen, *et al.*, eds., *Geschiedenis van de techniek*, vol. II, p. 187.

[100] Davids and Lucassen, eds., *A miracle mirrored*, chapter 8, pp. 229–83; and section 10.2 below.

In 1850 there were ninety-two registered daily and weekly newspapers; by 1894 the total had risen to 760. The numbers of newspapers despatched by post rose from 5,107 in 1860 to 42,494 in 1883. The printed word was becoming more popular.[101]

The postal service itself was an important form of communication. Ever since the ancient cleft stick, delivery of written messages had been available at a price to the elite, and in the French period all the local private services were brought together with a distance-related tariff of 10–35 cents. The 1850 Post Office Act reinforced the state monopoly and reformed the system, bringing the rate down to 5–15 cents. In 1871 a standard tariff of 5 cents was introduced. The number of letters and cards sent rose from 5 million in 1850 to 120m. in 1900, and then to 346m. in 1930, with the number of post offices swelling accordingly.[102]

Finally, there was electronic communication. The Dutch passed a Telegraph Act in 1852, governing both official and commercial traffic, introducing a state monopoly (*Rijkstelegraaf*), and gradually achieving a national network linked to countries abroad. By 1867 there were some ninety offices in the country, and the number of telegrams sent inland rose from 247,000 in 1857 to 4.6 million in 1897. The telephone, transmitting speech itself, made its debut in the Netherlands in 1877, and from the late 1880s onwards local exchanges were set up in Amsterdam, Haarlem and other cities as private initiatives. In 1897 the state took over the links between the exchanges, and from 1913 began to take over the exchanges themselves. Clearly the authorities had decided that electronic communication was at least partly a national responsibility, as the waterways, roads and railways had been. Radio telegraphy began around the turn of the century, which was important for maritime operations, and nearly all seagoing ships carried a radio receiver by 1914. Broadcast media, however, only became numerically significant in the 1920s, though cinemas began attracting audiences before the First World War, and from an early date were assisting communication with newsreels.[103]

For the Netherlands, communication with its colonies was in some ways as important as that amongst its domestic population and with its near neighbours. The first direct postal service between the Netherlands and the East Indies was awarded to the 'Nederland' shipping line in 1871; there had been a Royal Packet service to the West Indies in the 1830s, which had closed down until a Mail Service started up again in 1884. In

---

[101] Hemels, *Op de bres*, 643; Knippenberg and De Pater, *De eenwording*, 66–70.
[102] Knippenberg and De Pater, *De eenwording*, 63–6.
[103] Lintsen, *et al.*, eds., *Geschiedenis van de techniek*, vol. IV, pp. 289–98; Knippenberg and De Pater, *De eenwording*, 60–2 and 74–7; Brugmans, *Paardenkracht*, 371–4; De Wit, *Telefonie*.

the meantime, there were British and French services, and various indirect routes, which could be employed for the mail, and which were
improving all the time. The principal development in postal services was
the coming of air transport, and its application to the inter-continental
services. Air transport was also bound up with electronic communications: radio was first used in the East in 1896, the various private telephone companies on Java were taken over by the government in 1898,
and by the early 1930s there were almost 2,500 licensed radio receivers
on Java.[104]

The coming together of the infrastructure   By the end of the nineteenth
century there was indeed, it can be argued, an infrastructure in place.
Infrastructures are infinitely improvable, and the Dutch government has
laboured hard throughout the twentieth century to extend, modernize
and fine-tune whenever possible. However, the critical mass seems to
have been achieved in the last decade or two of the nineteenth century. It
was then that the main railway network was finished, that the shipping
services had thoroughly embraced steam power and were growing at
twice world rates, and that roads and communications seemed to have
settled into a coherent system. There had been earlier partial development throughout the second half of the century, especially in waterways,
and even some in the first half. Before 1850 the integration of the Dutch
economy, despite the efforts of Willem I, was minimal;[105] there was
increasing investment in physical capital after 1850, and the investment
in the infrastructure peaked in the 1870s and 1880s. It rose again after
1900 with increased spending on public utilities and telecommunica-
tions. Many factors allowed the state to lead this integration of the
transport network after 1850: the reformed national finances, the income
from the East Indies, free trade, the eruption of German production and
markets, and an increasingly integrated global market, to which the
Dutch were contributing with their shipping and trade routes. In the
mid-1890s, by the time of the world's recovery from the Kondratieff
downturn of the 1880s, the Netherlands' transport infrastructure had
achieved a significant level of maturity.[106]

The economic significance of the transport sector and of the timing of
its development is not to be underestimated. There is even an argument
articulated which posits the Dutch transport sector as a sort of Rostovian
leading sector, with forward and backward linkages to other sectors,
providing the catalyst to development throughout the economy, because

[104] Ten Brink, *De geschiedenis van het postvervoer*, 63–8; Furnivall, *Netherlands India*, 331–2.
[105] Horlings, *The economic development*, 265.
[106] Clemens, *et al.*, 'The contribution', 182–3; Groote, *Kapitaalvorming*, especially p. 60.

it allowed the Netherlands to ride up on the back of the German economy through the Rhine trade, and then to take full advantage of the
world trade boom after 1890 up to World War I.[107] The image is taken
from Industrial Revolution historiography, which (as we have repeatedly
seen) is quite inapplicable to the Netherlands, and is best left aside.
However, the timing is correct, and recent scholarship has endorsed the
conclusions of a previous generation of historians searching for the date
of the acceleration of the Dutch economy. Looking in detail at capital
investment in the transport sector, Peter Groote finds that his data
'support the main tenets of the old vision of the macro-economic development of the Netherlands in the nineteenth century'.[108] From the point
of view of capital formation in transport, the groundwork was laid from
the 1860s onwards, and came to fruition in the 1890s. This small sector,
employing 4.5 per cent of the workforce in 1807 and 8 per cent in 1920
(Table II.2), was certainly one of the keys to the economy, enabling the
rest to realize its potential.

Other services

Having covered the distributive groups in the service sector (trade and
transport) in some detail because of their centrality to the extent and
nature of Dutch economic performance, we can deal relatively briefly
with the rest. It includes the producer services (banking, insurance,
professions), social services (government, education, religion, health)
and personal services (domestics, catering, etc.).

Finance   The numbers involved in finance as a profession (banking and
insurance in Table II.7) were very small: just 0.4 per cent of the tertiary
sector in 1807, and only 0.9 per cent in 1909. Clearly, others made their
living in this sector, not least the *rentier* class of investors, and many of the
lawyers and solicitors. However, the numbers remain tiny. Banking has
already been covered in the section on the factor capital: accumulation,
investor mentality and the mechanisms of finance for business require no
further comments here (see section 4.3). However, we shall devote some
attention to insurance, and to the expansion of retail banking of various
sorts, as well as to the overall contribution of finance to the economy.

Very little banking took place at all outside the trading cities of the west
in the first half of the nineteenth century. There were cashiers for the
merchants, and merchant banks and investment banks, but none of this

---

[107] Milward and Saul, *The development of the economies*, 195–7; and Bos, 'Van periferie',
86–90.
[108] Groote, *Kapitaalvorming*, 73.

concerned the man or woman in the street. Starting in Amsterdam and radiating outwards, there began to be a proliferation of banking activities as the century went on: credit associations for small businesses from the 1850s, loan banks (*voorschotbanken*) linked to life insurance, savings banks, mortgage banks, municipal and private pawn shops (*banken van leening*) and, after 1870, colonial banks, savings offices (*spaarkassen*), small loan banks (*hulpbanken*), Post Office savings banks (the *Rijkspostspaarbank*) and various forms of co-operative banks.[109] From the official statistics on these banks we can see that the municipal pawn banks more or less replaced the private ones: there were twenty-five of the former and eighteen of the latter left in 1890. The savings banks witnessed the most spectacular growth, to 273 offices in 1880, then falling back slightly to 254 in 1900. Over the same period the number of account holders rose from 54,000 to 829,000, and the deposits increased seventeenfold to nearly ƒ39m. (In addition there were 122 *hulpbanken* and *spaarkassen* by 1900.) This must have been an early form of modern consumer banking, which was to develop further with the Post Office savings banks when introduced in 1883. By 1900 they had amassed their own clientele, numbering 829,131.[110] In 1900 the total deposits of savings and loans banks amounted to ƒ165m., and by 1920 (the First World War had only a momentary impact) the figure had reached ƒ730m.[111] These were substantial sums and large numbers of savers, but they also represent increasing numbers of people earning their livings as clerks in these retail and consumer banks up and down the country.

As for insurance, the Republic had been the home of an advanced insurance industry, and in the nineteenth century many of the activities expanded. Much was based on private enterprise, with the government playing a relatively minor role until the 1923 Insurance Services Act (although Willem I's government took a predictable interest in the 1830s, especially in pension funds).[112] Marine insurance had been an essential feature of the Netherlands economy for centuries, and there were life insurance companies working the Dutch market, though not always with great success: many of the widows' insurance funds failed towards the end of the eighteenth century.[113] Industrial and agricultural insurance was much later to start, with some initial attempts to set up business from

[109] 't Hart, *et al.*, *A financial history*, 118; Klein, 'Het bankwezen', 139–42.
[110] *Jaarcijfers* (1895), 66ff.
[111] *Statistisch Zakboek* (1924), 37. The figures are for the *Rijkspostspaarbank*, private savings and loans banks, and *Boerenleenbanken*. See also Van Gerwen and Van Leeuwen, eds., *Studies over zekerheidsarrangementen*, 450–65.
[112] See Van Gerwen and Van Leeuwen, eds., *Studies over zekerheidsarrangementen*, especially pp. 17 and 251–75; and Van Genabeek, *Met vereerende kracht*.
[113] Riley, 'That your widows may be rich'; see also Gales and Van Gerwen, *Sporen van leven*.

the 1820s on, but most of the growth coming after 1850. Insurance against fire, the weather and cattle sickness began to crop up, though the kind of house-and-contents insurance we know now was rare. By 1900 agricultural insurance was widespread.[114] There were also established mutual insurance societies for illness and funerals, which remained stable in number but which saw their membership grow rapidly: between 1827 and 1879 the number of societies rose sedately from 348 to 367, while the members shot up from 69,000 to 636,000.[115] Many of the mutual societies were local, and had grown out of the work of the guilds (abolished in 1798, but still exercising an effect until the 1820s), whose work in insurance was eventually taken over by the trade unions.[116] By the end of the century, social insurance was beginning to come under the aegis of the state, with its growing welfare commitments.[117] Again, the administrative staffs in insurance were increasing as well, and becoming professionalized, as they were in the financial sector generally.

Much of the insurance business was connected with investments in the Indies by the end of the century. Income from capital has been dealt with above (section 4.3), but the colonial sector deserves a mention here. It is estimated that there was f750m. in Dutch funds invested in the colony around 1900, which had risen to f1.4 billion by 1914 and again to f4 billion by 1930. This was earning some f250m. per annum in the 1920s for the Dutch economy, while income from investments in the colonies was bringing possibly as much as 8 per cent of national income by 1938.[118] This colonial sector of the finance and financial services sector was extremely important to the Dutch economy, especially from about 1890 to 1939. We shall return to it in section 7.2 on the colonies.

Social and personal services   Table II.7 shows large numbers of domestic servants in the Dutch economy, but their share in the workforce declined after 1859, from 42.7 per cent of the service sector to 27.9 per cent in 1889. This radical decline made the Dutch much less servant-intensive than their competitors, which rendered their tertiary sector as a whole much more efficient and labour-productive, by allowing the relative expansion of the distributive services (trade and transport).[119] Other

---

[114] Brugmans, *Paardenkracht*, 175–7; *Verslag van den Landbouw* (1903), 122–3.
[115] Van der Valk, 'Zieken- en begrafenisfondsen', 194. Some of these activities might well be classified under the social services part of the tertiary sector.
[116] Bos, '*Uyt liefde*'; and Van Genabeek, *Met vereerende kracht*.
[117] See Van Leeuwen, 'Armenzorg'; Van Gerwen and Van Leeuwen, eds., *Studies over zekerheidsarrangementen*, 520–69 and 570–604; see also section 10.3 below.
[118] Lindblad, 'The economic relationship', 113–17; Verstegen, 'National wealth'.
[119] Meanwhile absolute numbers rose, especially of German maidservants, after 1918: Henkes, *Heimat*.

categories in the personal services group (hairdressers, chemists, etc.) were very small. In the social services, which is more or less what we would now call the quaternary or government sector plus health, the armed forces still played a significant role at 10.3 per cent of the services in 1849; however, they had dwindled to a mere 2.3 per cent by 1909. Education was increasing towards the end of the century, with 4.7 per cent of service employment by 1899, as a result of increasing attendance at all levels but especially in secondary schools, and of the need to do everything several times over because of the pillarized system, with separate schools for each ideological community. Administrative personnel and civil servants were also growing in number.

The role of the tertiary sector

In recent years the service sector has received some of the attention from economic historians it deserves, and it has become quite clear that it provides the principal explanation (in sectoral terms) for the generally healthy macro-economic performance which the country turned in. This was true nationally, but also in the provinces, for instance in Leeuwarden, the capital of Friesland, where it has been shown that it was the growth of the service sector, rather than manufacturing, which could 'initiate and accompany modernization'.[120] As a result of concentration and growth in highly productive areas of the services, such as trade, transport and (though much smaller) finance, the Dutch were able to hold their own with and indeed outperform many of their neighbours whose economies were characterized by classic Industrial Revolutions. The armies of unproductive servants and cleaners were proportionately smaller than in other European countries, and the relative productivity of the Dutch transport and trade sectors was very high indeed; organizational and technological changes enhanced their earning power. Estimates based on the year 1910 put the United States way ahead of the field, but within Europe the Dutch led the UK in comparative services productivity by a nose, while France and Germany came way down the scale.[121] Table II.6 shows that, within the Netherlands, services had attained a relative productivity far in excess not only of agriculture, but of manufacturing as well (70:102:121). The fortunes of the sector were heavily dependent on the internal infrastructure (transport and communications) and the

---

[120] Van der Woude, *Leeuwarden*, 366 and *passim*.
[121] Burger and Smits, 'A benchmark', 152–4. Using national weightings with the UK as 100, the services productivity of the US scored 124, the Netherlands 106, Germany 91 and France 84. For the productivity of the economy as a whole, the scores were, respectively, 100, 144, 95, 88, 79.

integration of the national economy,[122] and on external development (Germany, the UK and the colonies), through trade on an increasingly open economy.

6.5   Conclusion

It is clear from the sectoral analysis in this chapter that the service sector was quite the most important one for the Dutch economy. While the share of the workforce in manufacturing grew modestly over the nineteenth century and that in agriculture declined, the tertiary sector streaked ahead and was by far the largest at the end of the century. Within services, trade and transport provide the key: these were the 'enablers' for the rest of the economy, allowing it to specialize and achieve competitive advantages. In retrospect it was the service sector that was mainly responsible for the comparatively excellent performance of the country as a whole in the nineteenth century, which gives an indication of how misplaced the endless disputes about the development of Dutch manufacturing have been.

Not that there was anything very much wrong with the rest of the economy. In the primary sector, farming was very advanced indeed even by the beginning of the nineteenth century, and in the golden years of the third quarter of the century it was probably the largest engine of economic growth in the country. In manufacturing, the first half of the century was difficult in some branches, especially if they were unconnected with the favoured colonial sector, but there was real expansion after 1850, and the position of Dutch industry *vis-à-vis* technology, entrepreneurship and capital showed no obvious flaws. It was simply that the services – especially trade and transport – overshadowed everything else.

The accounts of the various branches and sectors indicate that, viewed over the whole century, in many (though not all) parts of the economy it was the 1850s which signalled a new departure. In common with much of Europe, the first half of the century was a difficult time for the Dutch economy, and it was government policy in the colonies which provided the only really innovative developments, in trade, shipping and selected manufactures. After 1850 it was a different story. Fishing modernized, agriculture came into its own, and manufacturing expanded across the whole field. Trade made a good recovery in the first half of the century from the disaster of the French period, characterized by an ability to adapt to changing circumstances beyond Dutch control. Then a boom set in which lasted for the rest of the century. As for transport and

---

[122] As concluded by Horlings, *The economic development*, chapter 7; see above, section 5.3, on centralization.

communications, the energetic policies of Willem I did not pay off until
the 1850s and 1860s, when rising levels of activity and investment eventually culminated in a genuinely coherent internal and external infrastructure by the end of the century, in time to ride the world boom up to
the outbreak of the First World War. Again, all sectors participated fully
and honourably, but it was the service sector, and especially trade and
transport, which carried the day.

7 Features of demand

7.1 Introduction

Much of the examination of the economy in the preceding chapters has concentrated on the supply side. Production is easier to research than consumption, there were more data on production collected by contemporaries, and until the post-war years most economic policy focussed on the supply side. The characteristics of an economy are easier to pick out in terms of production: what makes it distinctive, unusual, interesting. But very little can happen in the economy without demand for the goods and services produced, and if we are looking for growth trends and particularly for the timing of growth spurts, then for the dynamics of economic growth and development, demand is probably more important than supply. Fortunately some of the work done in recent years on the Dutch economy has begun to redress the historiographical imbalance.

In the course of the analysis we have already noted the importance of foreign demand to certain sectors in the Dutch economy. Three areas predominate. The urban markets of industrialized England could consume almost any amount of food that the Dutch could produce, especially fresh horticultural products and dairy goods. Demand was particularly strong from the mid-1840s to the mid-1860s (a critical time for the Dutch economy) and from the 1890s. Then there was the German giant next door, industrializing rapidly from the 1850s, with a massive demand for raw materials of all sorts except perhaps coal. And finally there were the colonies, and more particularly the East Indies. We have observed that the East Indies policies followed by the Dutch government managed to generate a demand for Dutch trade goods which was essential to the cotton industry, and of great assistance to shipbuilding, marine engineering, and machine building. We shall further examine the colonial case below, but it should be borne in mind that as trade was increasingly freed after 1850, the characteristically open Dutch economy became more and more dependent on the dynamics of foreign demand.

The vast majority of Dutch production, however, was consumed at home, and domestic or internal demand is one of the key indicators in the country's economic development. The prodigious demographic development of the Netherlands meant that demand was almost always on the increase. We have noted that this was particularly important for the tertiary sector after 1850; urbanization generated demand for personal and other services, while transport further united the country, and pillarization demanded separate services for each ideological community. Therefore we shall examine the complex relationship between demographic and economic growth in the Netherlands. On the other hand, because of the regressive taxation system, growth in mass demand generally remained modest until the end of the century despite population growth (as it did everywhere in Europe), and before 1850 per-capita demand for agricultural products may even have stagnated. The final part of this chapter will therefore look at per-capita domestic demand, concentrating on consumption and the standard of living.

Of the three issues considered below, only the final section on domestic per-capita demand is exclusively to do with the demand side of the economy. As we have seen, the colonial empire had a major role to play on the supply side, and population growth was at least as important for its supply of the factor labour as for its generation of more demand, as the account below will indicate. However, for the purposes of analysis it is convenient to treat these three subjects here together under the heading of demand, while noting their simultaneous importance to the economy in other ways.

7.2   The colonies as an economic stimulus

It is already clear from earlier sections which have dealt with the colonies that the possession and exploitation of a colonial empire formed an essential part of the economy;[1] what is now required is to draw matters together and assess their collective significance. In doing so it will be necessary to explain the workings of the Cultivation System in the East Indies, a regime for which the Dutch were renowned, admired and vilified, and which brought very large sums into the government's coffers at a critical time in the middle of the nineteenth century.

In the seventeenth century and for much of the eighteenth, the Dutch had administered a seaborne empire on an enormous scale, in succession to the early Iberian ones, and before the British took over as the leading colonial power. Between them, the East and West India Companies ran

[1] As a 'trigger' for economic growth around the mid-century (section 3.3); capital investment in the Indies (4.3); the WIC and the NHM (5.3); colonial demand for Dutch manufactures (6.3); and the importance for Dutch trade and shipping (6.4).

operations in West Africa and the Cape Colony, up the east side of Africa
and round the coast of the Arabian peninsula, all the way around the
Indian subcontinent, Ceylon, and in much of South East Asia including
all of present-day Indonesia, Taiwan (Formosa), Canton and other ports
in China, Nagasaki, the New York region, the Caribbean islands, all the
Guyanas, and Brazil. By the end of the eighteenth century this was all
vastly overstretched, and during the French period the Dutch lost them
all to the British, with the exception of a toehold on Java. In the peace
settlements of Vienna after the Napoleonic Wars, the Dutch gave up
many of their colonies to the senior victors (mainly Britain) in return for
the expansion of their kingdom in Europe to include what had been the
Austrian Netherlands, or present-day Belgium and Luxembourg. Thus
Britain gained the former Dutch possessions in Ceylon, South Africa,
India and much of Guyana (Demerara, Essequibo and Berbice; Surinam
was returned to the Dutch). The jewel in the crown, the East Indies,
reverted to Dutch control, although, as we have seen, it was anything but
an economic asset in the years after 1815, with a top-heavy administration and enjoying few of the benefits of its own trade (section 5.3). Thus
after the Congress of Vienna (and a further Anglo-Dutch Treaty of
1824), the Dutch had the islands of Java and Madura in the East Indies
more or less comprehensively under their control, and a titular claim to
the rest of the Indonesian archipelago, although other powers had claims
as well, like the English on northern Sumatra and on Borneo. In the West
Indies they had the islands of Curaçao, Aruba and Bonaire near the
Venezuelan coast, and St Maarten, St Eustatius and Saba in the archipelago east of Puerto Rico. On the South American mainland the Dutch held
the sugar colony of Surinam, with its capital of Paramaribo at the mouth
of the Surinam River. Beyond that, the Dutch flag flew at a number of
'factories' or trading posts around the world, notably on the island of
Deshima in Nagasaki harbour, where until the 1850s and the dramatic
intervention of the Americans the Dutch were the only contact between
the Japanese and the West. They also had a presence in Canton, and on
the West Africa coast in modern-day Ghana, centred on the old slaving
port of St George del Mina. South Africa was of no further special
economic importance to the Dutch (though cultural and especially religious links continued), and the West African ports were exchanged with
the British for the latter's claims to parts of Sumatra, by the Treaty of
Sumatra in 1872.

We have noted the rise and fall of the new West India Company, from
1828 to 1863. Macro-economically speaking, it was not a major under-
taking, nor was it particularly profitable. The trade in slaves had been
outlawed (though Dutch plantations continued to be worked by slaves

until the 1860s), and it was the trade in tropical agricultural products such as sugar, cotton and cacao which was the essence of the colonial economy as far as the mother country was concerned. The Netherlands exported some cotton manufactures and other trade goods to the plantations, but the market was not large. At the mid-century, some 5 per cent of the value of Dutch imports came from the Antilles and Surinam: not insignificant, but not enough to shift the pace of the domestic economy. On the whole, investments in the West Indies were not very satisfactory. There was a compensation bill which had to be met by the Dutch government in 1862 for the emancipation of the 33,621 slaves in Surinam, at ƒ300 a head, totalling almost ƒ10m. (another ƒ2m. was paid out for the Antilles); nearly all the slaves left the plantations, and had to be replaced by indentured labour from China, India and the East Indies. However, the receipts from the East Indies regime were still rolling in at the time, so the colonial cash was simply being recycled.[2]

The meat of the colonial empire was of course the East Indies. This huge group of islands covers some 2 million km², or about four times the size of Germany, spread over an area the size of Europe; Multatuli immortalized it as 'a girdle of emerald, flung around the equator'.[3] It included Java, Madura, Bali, Sumatra, most of Borneo, Celebes, the Moluccas and half of New Guinea, with a myriad of smaller islands. The old Company, the VOC, had folded by the end of the eighteenth century, and passed on its possessions and ƒ120m. in debts to the Dutch state on 1 January 1800. The phases in the colony's fortunes in the nineteenth century have already emerged: loss-making from 1816 to about 1830; the Cultivation System and great profits for the Dutch from c. 1830 to c. 1870; and after 1870, privatization and continuing profitability, largely in the form of interest on investment capital. After the ending of the state monopoly, the colony underwent an apparently classic imperialist phase in the Leninist/Hobsonian sense, by forcibly extending its military and administrative powers to far-flung parts of the empire in the East over which it had previously held only titular authority: the Achin War (*Atjeh Oorlog*), of 1873–1914, to enforce Dutch rule on northern Sumatra, is only the largest of many examples. This assertion of authority has become known as the Forward Movement, and laid down the administrative structure of (capitalist) law and order, which in turn permitted the investors to follow in its wake, exporting their 'surplus capital' in search of

---

[2] '*Vestzak – broekzak*', or 'waistcoat pocket – trouser pocket', as the Dutch say. See Brugmans, *Paardenkracht*, 248–50; Renkema, *Het Curaçaose plantagebedrijf*; Reinsma, 'De West-Indische Maatschappij'; Colenbrander, *Koloniale geschiedenis*, vol. II, pp. 30–5; and section 4.3 above on the destination of capital.
[3] Furnivall, *Netherlands India*, 1.

the investment opportunities which had dried up in the domestic economy. This attempt 'to enhance Indonesia's productive capacity' was
highly successful: exports from the colony doubled between 1870 and
1900, while imports quadrupled. In the twentieth century further resources were opened up: Sumatran rubber, Achin oil, Billiton tin, Riau
bauxite and Borneo oil.[4] This bout of imperialism spawned its own
reaction back in the Netherlands, known as the Ethical Policy, from
about 1900 onwards, which manifested all manner of guilt feelings and
evangelistic piety (see Plate 4): it was legislated by the confessional
government of 1901 led by the neo-Calvinist Abraham Kuyper (1837–
1920, Plate 5). In the Leninist, anti-imperialist view, the Ethical Policy
served the function of providing the basic welfare systems to enable the
'natives' to become a reliable westernized workforce and embryonic
consumers in a white man's capitalism.[5] After the Forward Movement
and Ethical Policy, there was a drift through nationalist, socialist and
Islamicist dissidence towards eventual independence in December 1949,
assisted by the catalyst of the Japanese occupation of the islands in the
Second World War. Of these succeeding stages in the colonial regime of
the nineteenth and early twentieth centuries, we shall examine here the
second one, that of the Cultivation System.

The *Cultuurstelsel* (literally 'Culture System', but less confusing translated as 'Cultivation System') was introduced in 1830 by Johannes van
den Bosch (1780–1844), who was Governor-General of the East Indies
from 1828 to 1833, and subsequently Minister for the Colonies (1834–
39). It was essentially a way of taxing the East Indies population in kind,
at an extremely high basic rate of about 20 per cent: those who had land
turned a fifth of it over to government crops, and those who did not gave
up about a fifth of their labour to work the government's fields. The
harvest of cash crops – coffee, sugar, spices, dyes, tobacco and even rice –
was the property of the government, and was shipped by the NHM back
to the Netherlands, where it was traded on to domestic and international
markets. After payments of interest, salaries and the like, the profits of the
operation were handed over annually from the treasury of the Dutch East
Indies colonial administration to that of the Netherlands itself. This was
the so-called '*batig slot*' or favourable balance, the net profit or bottom
line, which was simply transferred from the colony to the metropole
without further ado, much in the way that the Spanish silver fleet used to

---

[4] Hall, *A history* (1981), 624 and 834. On the Forward Movement, see Kamerling, ed.,
   Indonesië, 19–20; Van Goor, *De Nederlandse koloniën*, 256–64.
[5] On the Ethical Policy, see Hall, *A history* (1981), 795–6; Kamerling, ed., *Indonesië*, 20–2;
   Van Goor, *De Nederlandse koloniën*, 269–76. For an anti-imperialist account, see Zainu-
   ddin, *Indonesia*, 19–25; and Breman, *Taming the coolie beast*. On this period in the Indies,
   see also Langeveld, *Hendrikus Colijn*.

J A V A;

OR,

HOW TO MANAGE A COLONY,

SHOWING

A PRACTICAL SOLUTION OF THE QUESTIONS
NOW AFFECTING BRITISH INDIA.

BY

J. W. B. MONEY,

BARRISTER-AT-LAW.

IN TWO VOLUMES.

VOL. I.

LONDON:

HURST AND BLACKETT, PUBLISHERS,

SUCCESSORS TO HENRY COLBURN,

13, GREAT MARLBOROUGH STREET.

1861.

The right of Translation is reserved.

Plate 3 Title page of J. W. B. Money's *How to manage a colony* (1861). The Dutch were perceived by the British, the Belgians and many others to have solved the problem of how to make colonies pay.

Plate 4 Colonial guilt. Cartoon by Albert Hahn, November 1904. Prime Minister Abraham Kuyper (left) and his confessional cabinet colleagues, haunted by the spirit of the East Indies, launch the Ethical Policy.

Plate 5 'Dr A. Kuyper at his desk.' Religious, political and journalistic leader of the orthodox Calvinists, and Prime Minister in 1901, Kuyper wrote prodigious amounts: the list of his published work runs to three large volumes (Rullmann, *Kuyper–bibliografie*).

lug home the loot from the central American colonies in the seventeenth century. From a functional point of view the system was quite brilliant: it provided huge net revenues for the Dutch government, it made the 'natives' pay tax usually without killing them, it provided full freights for the ships of the NHM, and it revitalized the staple market at home in colonial goods. It spread prosperity around it in the home economy like a successful alchemist. The system began on Java in the 1830s, and was extended to other areas in a piecemeal fashion until the late 1860s, when private enterprise was allowed into cultivation by the liberals' reforms (the Agrarian and Sugar Acts of 1870), and the NHM monopoly on distribution was undermined by free trade legislation. It lasted in pockets – especially in coffee – until the twentieth century, but its back was broken by 1870. As the novel *Max Havelaar* points out, the effects on the indigenous population were very burdensome, not so much on account of the system itself, but because, being based on coercion, the opportunities for corruption and abuse were rife, and could be exploited by the Dutch and native administrators and officials alike. As late as 1865 there were only 175 Dutch civilian officials administering the system on the huge and densely populated island of Java, while the day-to-day supervision and collection was delegated to the local elite of the 'regent' class, whose 100,000 agents were vulnerable to all kinds of pressures, temptations and corruption. In some of the more prosperous parts of the colony, the system worked reasonably well for decades; in others, its effects were catastrophic, as with the rice famines of Eastern Java in the 1840s.[6] However, our main concern here is with the benefits (or otherwise) derived from the regime by the Dutch economy.

The 'colonial benefits' started flowing into the Dutch treasury in 1832, and registered a modest ƒ761,500 in that year. Five years on, in 1837, the figure was almost ƒ20m., and by 1857 it was no less than ƒ41.7m., representing more than 40 per cent of total government revenue. In general the transfers made up about 19 per cent of public revenue in the 1830s and 1840s, and no less than 32 per cent in the 1850s. At times in the 1850s it was well over 50 per cent; after the early 1860s the percentage declined steeply to virtually zero in 1875. Some ƒ800m. or more was transferred in total.[7]

Now some of this revenue was transferred back to the Indies in one form or another, but the majority went straight into Dutch pockets, so to speak, as clear profit. In addition, some huge private fortunes were made from the system, for example by the sugar contractors who processed the crop before export to the Netherlands. The most famous example is that of I. D. Fransen van de Putte (1822–1902), who in 1849 was a local administrator on Java struggling on ƒ4,200 a year, but by 1859 had become a millionaire on the back of sugar contracts, and who went on to be a reforming Minister for the Colonies in 1863.[8] The revenues allowed the public finance miracle for which Minister van Hall received the credit in the 1840s, and permitted the government to undertake all kinds of infrastructural projects in the 1850s and 1860s which were crucial for the economic development of the country, such as the canals for Amsterdam and Rotterdam, and the railway network. It is not logical to assume that these investments would not have been made without the colonial levy, but it certainly made things very much simpler. All those connected with the NHM did well, whether they were shareholders, employees, industrial suppliers (textiles and ships) or merchants distributing the colonial produce around Europe.

[6] On the *Cultuurstelsel* generally, see Kamerling, ed., *Indonesië*, 17–19; Hall, *A history* (1981), 590ff.; Fasseur, *Kultuurstelsel*; Van Goor, *De Nederlandse koloniën*, 220–30.
[7] De Bosch Kemper, *Inkomsten en uitgaven*, 12. The '*baten*' include interest on the East Indies national debt. See also Van der Voort, *Overheidsbeleid*, 213–14; Fasseur, *Kultuurstelsel*; and Horlings, *The economic development*, graph on p. 172.
[8] Baudet and Fasseur, 'Koloniale bedrijvigheid', 323–4.

The question is not whether the colonies were beneficial (which they certainly were), but whether they were crucial. There is a long tradition of opinion to the effect that without its colonies the Dutch would have been economically insignificant: this small nation with its lack of minerals and absence of belching blast-furnaces could only compete on the international stage by virtue of its empire, and could only manage to keep up with its neighbours in economic development by dint of the help received from its colonies, first through the state, and later through private enterprise. Clearly this is all tied up with the Dutch inferiority complex about not having 'enjoyed' the same kind of Industrial Revolution which characterized the admired England and the despised Belgium, and later the loved/ hated Germany. It has already become very clear that the Dutch did not suffer at all from not following the path to the satanic mills. Nonetheless, the idea of inverted colonial dependency (that of the metropole on the periphery) has some powerful adherents. The whole attitude is summed up in the phrase, 'the Netherlands and the rank of Denmark', taken from the financier and diarist Ernst Heldring (1871–1954). It implies that without its colonies the Dutch would be reduced to the level of 'a Denmark', robbed of any influence in the world and counting for nothing at all; only through their colonies, then, do the Dutch achieve greatness, both economically and politically.[9] The Governor-General and later Minister for the Colonies J. C. Baud (1789–1859) coined the phrase that the Indies were 'the cork upon which the Netherlands floats',[10] and the liberal politician C. T. van Deventer (1857–1915) was convinced the Dutch owed the Indies a 'debt of honour'. The Dutch economy, he reasoned, was entirely dependent on the colony: 'without prosperity in the East Indies, neither trade, shipping, nor agriculture which supplies products to the European market, can flourish in the long run'.[11] The Papal Internuntius at The Hague Angelo Bianchi (1817–97) agreed, and had reported to the Vatican Secretary of State Antonelli in 1869 that 'the colonial question is not only interesting for the Netherlands, but vital'.[12] The post-colonial anti-imperialist lobby are certainly of the opinion that the Dutch rode on the backs of the Indonesians.[13] But what was the actual extent of that dependence?

In terms of national accounts, generally accepted figures show that, by

[9] See Baudet, 'Nederland en de rang van Denemarken'.
[10] Baudet, 'The economic interest', 235–9.
[11] From his *Rechtvaardige koloniale politiek* (Amsterdam, 1901), translated and cited in Baudet, 'The economic interest', 246.
[12] ASV, Segreteria di Stato, 1869, Rub. 270, p. 43: Bianchi to Antonelli, despatch 73, dated 30 Sept. 1869.
[13] See for example Frank, *On capitalist underdevelopment*; on the East Indies case, see Caldwell, *Indonesia*; Zainu-ddin, *Indonesia*.

1938, no less than 13.7 per cent of the entire Dutch national income was derived from the East Indies connection. Jan Tinbergen calculated that 8.4 per cent was contributed directly, in dividends, salaries and the like, with a further 5.3 per cent from indirect or multiplier effects.[14] Some estimates put it up to 15 or even 16.5 per cent of national income.[15] The figures before 1938 are a little shaky still, but if anything they are likely to have been even higher in the 1920s, and perhaps around 5 per cent of national income in 1913. These are very substantial shares of the total economy – anything up to a seventh in the late 1930s, and perhaps more in the 1920s.[16]

However, this must be kept in proportion. The trade between the East Indies and the Netherlands was not actually all that significant after 1870, when the NHM relinquished its monopoly. Using East Indies statistics in order to circumvent the effects of the transit trade on the Dutch figures, it has been shown that only one thirtieth of the value of Dutch exports was destined for the Indies in 1903: certain sectors were heavily dependent on the colonial market, like textiles and machinery, but the share of these sectors in the total Dutch export package was tiny. Meanwhile, the Dutch share of Indies imports declined from a once substantial position: 'The Netherlands grew less important as a supplier of foreign imports in colonial Indonesia, whereas the colony remained *insignificant* as a market outlet for Dutch exports at large . . . Colonial Indonesia expanded fast, but not to the benefit of trade with the Dutch.'[17]

In investments and invisibles, however, we have seen that colonial business was truly significant: that is where the bulk of the 14 per cent of national income lay in 1938. But again, let us not exaggerate: the Netherlands placed 40 per cent of its very considerable foreign investments in its colonies, and almost all of that in the East Indies. However, the equivalent figure for the UK – another nation with huge investments abroad – was even higher, at 50 per cent, and France also had 30 per cent of her foreign investments in her own colonies.[18] So for a colonial power with an advanced financial infrastructure – which is an accurate description of the Netherlands at the start of the twentieth century – this was not an *over*-dependence, but more of a sensibly protected investment.

Let us look further at the qualitative side of the matter, alongside the quantitative. There is little doubt that the colonial connection gave the Dutch some important leverage when it came to trade negotiations with

[14] Reported in Baudet, 'The economic interest', 237–41.
[15] Respectively Derksen, 'Long-term changes', 30–1; and Derksen and Tinbergen, 'Berekeningen over de economische beteekenis'.
[16] Van Zanden, *The economic history*, 21–5.
[17] Lindblad, 'The economic relationship', 112–13 (emphasis added).
[18] Baudet, 'Nederland en de rang van Denemarken', 439.

larger powers, and afforded them some diplomatic seniority, not least because they had retained their empire for so very long. If that is what was meant by not sinking to 'the rank of Denmark', then Heldring had a point. The Cultivation System in particular was an almost universal model amongst putative imperialists in the nineteenth century: the melodrama villain, King Leopold II of Belgium, admired it greatly, and his grotesque and tragic failure to implement a version of it in the Congo was due mainly to the fact that he did not understand its workings. But he was not the only one: the French, the Germans, the Spanish and the British were full of admiration, and envy as well.[19] The title of the Englishman J. W. B. Money's didactic study of 1861 says it all: *Java; or, how to manage a colony: showing a practical solution of the questions now affecting British India* (see Plate 3).[20]

On the other hand, there were some disadvantages to the colonial millstone as well. The guilt feelings of this most moral of nations when it comes to public life have been inconvenient and expensive (see Plate 4): the Ethical Policy was a failure but cost the Dutch dear, and their uncertain feelings about the colonial past have continued since decolonization in a way unrivalled in any other nation, reflected in their very high overseas aid payments lasting to this day. Also on the debit side are the start-up costs of the Cultivation System in the 1830s, which nearly brought the Dutch state to its financial knees under Willem I, before the 'favourable balances' started rolling in. The colonies provided very little in the way of a permanent emigration destination for this very crowded country (though many soldiers and temporary migrants made their way to the East and back again); on the other hand there were plenty of other destinations (like the US) for those who wanted to go. And then there was the monopolism of the Cultivation System and the NHM regime. Some personal fortunes were made, but the exclusion until the 1860s of private enterprise from much business in the Indies and nearly all of the trade with the Netherlands had certain structural disadvantages, as we have observed in the section on government policy (5.3). Furthermore, the Java War of 1825–30 and the Achin War of 1873–1914 (to name but two conflagrations) cost the country dear in cash and reputation. Indeed, there is a general debate amongst colonial historians about the overall profitability of empire: the figures on national income quoted above make the case for the Dutch instance quite cogently, but it should not be forgotten that the beneficiaries of colonialism, although very numerous, tended to be confined to certain sectors, as we saw in the trade figures after 1870.

[19] *Papers of the Dutch-Indonesian historical conference*, 4–16: paper by H. L. Wesseling, 'The impact of Dutch colonialism on European imperialism'.
[20] Money, *Java*.

A generation ago, Peter Klein expressed the view that post-1850 economic growth was stimulated by others' industrialization and by the profits of the East Indies.[21] More recently, Van Zanden has established that the colonies were essential in providing demand for the Dutch economy, especially in the first half of the century, when domestic demand was stagnating.[22] The textile industry, and later the machine-building sector, relied heavily on the colonial market. But in the end the effect of the colonies was probably more qualitatively important than for its sheer bulk; other imperialist nations were doing very similar things after the 1870s. But in the 1840s and 1850s, when the government had been struggling with debt problems, the Cultivation System and the NHM regime ushered in a breathing space which untied some of the knots binding the efforts of entrepreneurs and government alike; the impetus to the infrastructure and certain industries at home, and the huge increase in shipping and trade, were surely crucial developments at a critical moment. Horlings has summarized the NHM regime in the phrase, 'colonial exploitation combined huge financial benefits with structural degradation'.[23] The structural degradation in shipping and trade recovered rapidly towards the end of the century; in the meantime, the 'huge financial benefits' were precisely the right prescription at the critical juncture.

7.3   Population growth and economic growth

The Dutch population doubled in the nineteenth century and doubled again in the first half of the twentieth (Table I.1); these were much higher rates of increase than in most neighbouring countries. There is a debate about whether industrialization across Europe created its own labour force by allowing population increase, or was actually the inevitable outcome of an expanding population. This chicken-and-egg argument needs to be applied at this juncture to the Netherlands in the nineteenth century in so far as domestic demand is concerned; what effect did the prodigious increase in the Dutch population have on the home economy?

The Dutch population started to expand at an accelerated rate in the 1870s, and an older generation of economic historians, such as I. J. Brugmans, were in no doubt that the acceleration was generated by economic expansion from the 1860s onwards (what Brugmans called the Dutch 'industrial revolution').[24] This was firmly denied by a succeeding generation of analysts, like J. A. de Jonge, who explained the growth of the population from the 1870s in terms of better diet because of the reduction

---

[21] Klein, 'Het bankwezen', 242.
[22] Van Zanden, 'Economische groei', 63; and Van Zanden, *The rise and decline*, chapter 8.
[23] Horlings, *The economic development*, 194.
[24] Brugmans, 'Nederlands overgang', 78; Brugmans, *Paardenkracht*, 201.

in excise taxes on essential food items rather than industrialization, which he placed in the 1890s.[25] It is certainly demonstrable that there were links between economic indicators like the price of cereals and rates for marriage or birth.[26] The economy could also affect fertility in a less direct way: a study by Engelen and Hillebrand of the town of Breda takes E. W. Hofstee's concept of a mentality formed by industrialization (or the lack of it), which can then influence marriage and fertility patterns, in this case delaying and slowing the decline in fertility which was occurring at the beginning of the twentieth century in neighbouring countries.[27]

On the other side of the picture, it can also be argued that population affected economic fortunes as well. Growth in the labour supply must have resulted, and the fact that the Dutch population in the age-groups 20–24 and 30–34 grew by 50 per cent in the course of the 1830s and 1840s was obviously significant for the factor labour;[28] on the other hand the percentage of the population aged from twenty to forty-four years rose only one percentage point in those years, from 35.3 to 36.3, which means that the youngest and oldest parts of the population – less important for the labour force – were increasing at similar rates.[29] De Jonge argued the importance of population growth for both the demand and the supply sides of the economy, increasingly after the mid-century as the population accelerated, growing by some 17 per cent between 1850 and 1870, 26 per cent from 1870 to 1890, and by 30 per cent between 1890 and 1910.[30] The expanding, moralized labour force produced by Dutch pillarization has been identified as a major factor in Dutch economic prosperity after 1880,[31] and a recent study has called population growth in the twentieth century 'fundamental' for economic growth.[32]

The not altogether satisfying answer to the conundrum must of course be that the interaction between the economy and the level of population was reciprocal in its effects.[33] Population growth can be a powerful stimulus to the economy, but it must – like most other single factors – be accompanied by a favourable constellation of other inputs and markets to be effective; otherwise it can be detrimental. In De Jonge's opinion, it was probably an accelerating or contributing cause of economic growth,

[25] De Jonge, De industrialisatie, 261–2.
[26] Noted by contemporaries, for example Evers, Bijdrage tot de bevolkingsleer, graph 1; and by modern historians: Hofstee, De demografische ontwikkeling, 228.
[27] Engelen and Hillebrand, 'Vruchtbaarheid'.
[28] Lee, ed., European demography, 23.
[29] Bos, 'Long-term demographic development', 2; see also Van der Woude, 'Bevolking en gezin', 25.
[30] De Jonge, 'De industriele ontwikkeling', 92–3; De Jonge, De industrialisatie, 268–73.
[31] Van Zanden and Griffiths, Economische geschiedenis, 12–15.
[32] Van Ark and De Jong, 'Accounting', 226.
[33] Baudet and Van der Meulen, eds., Kernproblemen, 135–6.

rather than an original one in the Netherlands.[34] Nevertheless, Dutch population growth was about 40 per cent higher than that of North-West Europe in the second half of the century, and 70 per cent more in the first half of the twentieth:[35] that must have counted for something. There was no mass emigration, which meant that the economy was capable of supporting the increase, and indeed per-capita income rose healthily. Where technology and other factors were available to supply this implied increase in demand, Dutch industry did well, and a good example is the cotton-weaving sector, which rose to the challenge; many other industries were not in a position to benefit from the increased demand until the last decade of the century.[36]

In the final analysis, the increase in the population was actually part and parcel of the economic advance of the country, both drawing on it and helping to generate it. As the death rates fell rapidly after 1870 and growth accelerated, especially after the 1890s, the augmented demand must have become increasingly significant, especially as the shift to direct taxes took effect towards the end of the century. At the very least, the relatively rapid population expansion actually conceals a certain amount of the economic growth which was taking place: in absolute terms the expansion of the Dutch economy, especially in the early twentieth century, was considerably greater than that of her neighbours and rivals. The exceptional demographic growth made the per-capita GNP growth rates look merely healthy.

7.4 Domestic per-capita demand

Introduction: the standard of living

The predominance of indirect taxation for much of the century meant that, despite the prodigious population growth, mass demand never became the mass consumer demand which now characterizes modern Western economies. It was nonetheless crucial to the Dutch economy, and although work is still very much in progress in this area of research, it is important to assemble the evidence presently available about levels of aggregate domestic demand, which takes us straight into the debates about the standard of living, and about real wages. Domestic mass demand could only rise, let alone become consumer demand, when real incomes were increasing, or when more people were rising above the poverty line, for whatever reason; what were the dynamics of the

[34] De Jonge, 'De industriele ontwikkeling', 91–3.
[35] Petersen, *Planned migration*, 16.
[36] De Jonge, *De industrialisatie*, 267–8.

standard of living of Dutch people over the course of the nineteenth century?

The 'standard of living debate' has continued for several decades, and is concerned with whether the material condition of ordinary people in Europe improved significantly between 1750 and 1900 along with the massive rises in GNP and national income, and if it did, when and by how much?[37] The material welfare of the mass of the Dutch people can be estimated in a number of ways, and we shall review them here: certain forms of tax-yield data can be a proxy for consumption; the percentage of conscripts rejected because of perceived physical deficiencies can indicate levels of physical and therefore material well-being; the changing number of people claiming poverty benefits can indicate the extent of adequate income levels; real wages may be able to tell us about spending power; and estimates of consumption of certain goods – whether aggregate figures or individual household budgets – should inform us of the ability of the populace to generate demand at certain times.

Tax estimates

The government published data on its revenues, including those from the taxes on wealth and consumption. For example, the franchise depended on payment of direct taxes, and work has been carried out to estimate prosperity levels on the basis of how many people were achieving the taxation threshold between 1850 and 1917. Increasing numbers of voters do indicate rising levels of prosperity, especially in the twenty years after 1897, but the expansion of the wealthy middle classes cannot be equated with the fortunes of the masses.[38] Similarly, the householders' tax (*personele belasting*) took account of the rent value of dwellings, the number of doors and windows, the number of hearths, and the value of furniture; from the 1840s onwards the figures are regularly available.[39] However, we have noted that only about a sixth of citizens paid direct taxes at all over the period 1850–90 (section 5.3). Some work has been done on tax receipts in Amsterdam from 1815 to 1870 on consumption items like meat, alcoholic drink and wheat (luxury) bread, which indicates a general decline in per-capita consumption of these items until 1855, and a rise

---

[37] For a survey of the methodological problems, an inventory of European research, and a review of the standard of living debate, see Scholliers, ed., *Real wages*, especially chapters 1 and 4. On the British debate, see Taylor, ed., *The standard of living*.

[38] De Vries, 'Het censuskiesrecht'. A comparable study was carried out for the 1840s, looking at regional disparities: Blok and De Meere, 'Welstand, ongelijkheid in welstand en censuskiesrecht'.

[39] See, for example, *Jaarcijfers* (1892), 48, with data covering the years 1846–92.

thereafter.[40] Indirect taxes are therefore of some help as a source for mass demand, but we need more corroborating evidence.

The dimensions of cannon-fodder

In the search for an indicator for the material prosperity of the mass of the people, some scholars have tried to use the well-preserved archival data on the numbers of armed forces conscripts rejected each year because of their failure in a medical examination to measure up to the minimum height specified.[41] There is evidently a relationship between the price of foodstuffs, for example rye, and the number rejected from the military, and (perhaps surprisingly) the lag appears to be only a year or two between a rise in food prices and a rise in the number of rejections.[42] The methodological problems with this technique and source are legion,[43] and in many ways it remains a game of estimates; however, some work on the province of Drenthe on this 'biological standard of living' has delivered some interesting and plausible results.[44] Rejections there on grounds of physical inadequacy were high until 1844, then declined to a relatively low level and remained there until the early 1870s, whereupon they rose rapidly again. If rejection was linked inversely to the standard of living, then people did badly until the 1840s, enjoyed prosperity until the 1870s, and then suffered again for the rest of the century, which would suggest high levels of demand from the late 1840s to the early 1870s; this coincided roughly with the liberal tenure of power, the expansion of the infrastructure, deregulation and privatization, and free trade. The implied decline in demand at the end of the century could be seen as a result of the 1880s crisis in agriculture and industry. Certainly, placing the 1850s and 1860s at the centre of an extended period of relative prosperity fits with most of the analyses of the economy we have encountered to date, especially in farming (Figure I.6). One would certainly have expected an upturn again at the end of the century, which these data do not support; however, it seems that mass domestic demand may well have

---

[40] Knotter and Muskee, 'Conjunctuur en levensstandaard'; they also concluded that this indicator of the standard of living was in inverse proportion to the international trade cycle.

[41] See section 2.1 above, where conscript rejection data are used to provide an indication of changing levels of general health over the nineteenth century.

[42] See a contemporary graph covering the years 1833–60, reproduced at Lintsen, et al., eds., Geschiedenis van de techniek, vol. II, p. 31.

[43] See for example Brinkman, et al., 'The representativeness'; and Brinkman, et al., 'Lichaamslengte'; both deal with the methodology of linking conscript height to national income. De Beer, 'De levensstandaard', links conscript rejection with the standard of living, but conclusions are only tentative.

[44] Groote and Tassenaar, 'Infrastructurele vernieuwing'.

been a driving force behind the economic resurgence of the middle decades of the century.

Levels of poor relief

A similar picture emerges from the data available on poverty and poor relief, although comparable methodological problems abound, and there is some contradiction between the various detailed studies. Statistics were published throughout the century on the number of those on temporary and permanent poor relief;[45] all the various categories and agencies of relief complicate the picture immensely, but in principle some conclusions are possible, on the assumption that high levels of structural poor relief indicate large numbers of people below the poverty line, which in turn indicates depressed domestic demand. However, that assumption itself holds some anomalies; the level of charity depended at least as much on the generosity of the donors as on the extent of the need to which they were attending. Some poor-relief agencies cost very little – in Den Bosch endowments footed virtually the whole bill from 1750 to 1900[46] – so the relationship between the cost of poor relief and actual poverty is also dubious. And did poor relief cause economic growth or obstruct it, or was it merely a function of that growth, whether positive or negative?[47] The questions are legion. Nevertheless, Horlings has collected national figures for numbers of people on permanent or long-term poor relief from 1815 to 1901 (the temporarily poor he consigns to seasonal fluctuations);[48] the numbers per thousand population grew rapidly from about forty in the 1820s to about sixty per thousand in the 1840s. The figure then dropped from 1855 to 1875 (coinciding with the golden years of agriculture), and stayed low until the 1890s, when it became even lower. This would suggest that domestic demand declined until 1855, rose rapidly until 1875, stagnated for twenty years, and then rose once more at the end of the century: again, very much in line with our expectations, based on the fortunes of agriculture as reflected in grain prices (Figure I.6). It is certainly not an indication that high grain prices meant depressed domestic demand, for good prices at market in agriculture seem rather to have meant prosperity for the vast majority of the population.

Horlings' masterly marshalling of the data is more or less in line with earlier partial studies. There were alarming reports of increases in vagrancy

---

[45] E.g., in *Statistisch Jaarbooekje* and *Jaarcijfers*.
[46] De Kruif, 'De prijs van de armenzorg', 48–9 and *passim*.
[47] Nusteling, *Welvaart*, 175; De Meere, *Economische ontwikkeling*, 42–3.
[48] Horlings, *The economic development*, 225.

and begging up to the 1850s,[49] the expenditure on poor relief rose substantially from 1818 to 1848, and the housebound poor rose from 5.4 per cent of the population in 1830 to 7.1 per cent in 1849.[50] On the other hand, figures for those on permanent relief in Leiden had been higher in the preceding period from 1750 to 1813 (10 per cent as opposed to 8.3 per cent over the period 1814–54), and anyway it is doubtful whether the poor could have lived off the handouts they received, suggesting that they had other forms of income.[51] Evidence from Alkmaar seems to confirm our expectation of a decline in numbers of those in the poverty trap right at the end of the century, after a temporary rise for the 1880s depression.[52] Poverty statistics evidently were affected by a large number of variables, some of them contradictory, but it seems clear that the poverty 'problem' increased until the mid-1840s, and declined after the 1850s, with a temporary delay during the 1880s depression. If the relationship is a clear one, that would suggest stagnating domestic demand until the mid-century, rising consumption in the 1850s, 1860s and early 1870s, a slow-down to 1895 or so, and a resumption of growth thereafter. It is a familiar pattern.

Real wages

Most of the work on the standard of living has concerned real wages, in the belief that an accurately deflated wage series will tell us about disposable income, and therefore about mass demand. The dynamics of nominal wages were discussed in the section on the factor labour (4.2); information on consumer prices then needs to be applied to deflate the nominal levels to a real index. Consumer prices stayed fairly constant with a slight upward drift between 1824 and 1850, and then rose rapidly from 1850 to the late 1870s; after that they declined until about 1900, and only at the time of World War I did they achieve anything like the levels of the 1870s once again.[53]

Combining the series for nominal wages and consumer prices in order to arrive at real wages, a number of local projects covering different periods have been undertaken; once again it is Edwin Horlings who has produced a single series and a graph for the century 1800–1910 (produced here as Figure II.4), and it conforms largely to the expectations of earlier scholarship and the more recent detailed studies.[54] Real wages stagnated or even declined slightly until about 1850, with short-term

---

[49] Blink, *Geschiedenis van den boerenstand*, 551.
[50] De Meere, *Economische ontwikkeling*, 45 and 52.
[51] Pot, *Arm Leiden*.   [52] Van Loo, *Armelui*.   [53] Maddison, *Dynamic forces*, 295–8.
[54] Horlings, *The economic development*, graph on p. 224, which uses data collected by Paping and Vermaas.

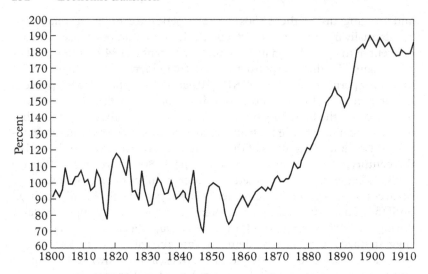

Figure II.4. The development of real wages in the Netherlands, 1800–1913 (index, 1850 = 100).

Source: Horlings, *Economic development of the Dutch service sector*, 224 (using data assembled by Paping and Vermaas).

fluctuations based on variations in consumer prices which could sometimes be quite violent. From the 1850s onwards, they rose rapidly and constantly until the late 1890s, with a short hiccough in the late 1880s. After 1900 they stagnated again.

This generalized national picture simplifies the local one, but Van Zanden has demonstrated that most regional differences in wages in 1820 were cancelled out by cost of living differences;[55] in other words, real wages were similar across the country. They had declined for most of the eighteenth century,[56] and stagnated or fell in Overijssel up to the 1840s.[57] In Kampen and Alkmaar real wages declined between 1790s and the 1830s.[58] A series for skilled craftsmen in Amsterdam shows a rise to the 1820s, and then a fall to the 1840s, after which an increasingly steep rise was sustained beyond the end of the century.[59] A study of Groningen shows real wages declining in the last quarter of the eighteenth century, and then slowly increasing up to 1860, all the time subject to quite radical fluctuations in the short term.[60] A number of studies have combined

[55] Van Zanden, 'Regionale verschillen', 272.
[56] De Vries and Van der Woude, *Nederland 1500–1815*, 711.
[57] Slicher van Bath, *Een samenleving*, 605–8.
[58] Van Zanden, *The rise and decline*, 136.   [59] Kok, *Langs verboden wegen*, 89.
[60] Paping, '*Voor een handvol stuivers*', graph on p. 204.

working men's budget books with series for prices and wages; such budgets were published periodically by contemporaries,[61] and can tell us about changes in consumption patterns. The studies indicate a considerable rise in real incomes after 1850 up to the First World War, although periods of relative stagnation may have occurred after 1895 and in the 1920s.[62] From the evidence of real wages, then, the indication is that there was no demand stimulus to speak of from the home market in the years before 1850, but that thereafter there was a secular rise continuing into the twentieth century, with occasional short slow-downs in the 1880s and perhaps in the 1890s. In combination with external stimuli, the home demand seems to have been working hard for the Dutch economy from the mid-century onwards.

Per-capita demand evaluated

The evidence is not conclusive, and despite the work of recent years there remains much that we do not fully understand about the history of the standard of living in the Netherlands. One recent attempt to combine a number of different indicators suggests that there was considerable variance in the standard of living across the country in 1850, with the east actually faring rather better than the west.[63] But generally speaking, the indications of recent scholarship are in line with our expectations derived from the work of an earlier generation of historians. Given the variations to be expected between different regions and social groups, from the French period to the 1850s the standard of living was marginally reduced, and perhaps on occasion quite steeply. Real wages stagnated, poverty increased and consumption per capita probably declined slightly, including that of food items.[64] Taxation was repressive of demand, by putting a great emphasis on indirect taxes on consumption; this was to change with the taxation policy of the liberal governments after the mid-century. An attempt to combine a number of partial indicators of private consumer expenditure into a single index showed very little growth before 1850, followed by some movement up to 1865, and then rapid growth.[65] After the mid-century things indeed began to improve, with demand in the golden years of the 1860s and early 1870s not adversely affected by rising agricultural prices: consumption continued to rise as real wages rose too (nominal wages were rising faster than prices). There is a suggestion that

[61] E.g., a set pertaining to 1854: Van Vlissingen, 'Huishoudelijke budjets', 229–34.
[62] Baudet and Van der Meulen, eds., *Consumer behaviour*, 80; Scholliers, ed., *Real wages*, chapter 8.
[63] Noordegraaf and Van Zanden, 'Early modern economic growth', 416–21.
[64] Van Zanden, 'Industrialization', 85; Horlings, *The economic development*, 248–51; and section 2.5 above on food consumption.
[65] Horlings and Smits, 'Private consumer expenditure', 19–20.

real wages and therefore the standard of living marked time from 1896 to the First World War and again in the 1920s, but this research is not yet confirmed by other studies – indeed it is contested by most of them, which posit a rise in mass demand in the 1890s – and needs to be treated with caution for the moment.[66]

7.5   Conclusion

Bringing together what we know about the demand side of the Dutch economy in the nineteenth century, aggregate home demand was of little assistance before the mid-century, and government policy did little to stimulate it, concentrating more on the production side. However, the government was eventually highly successful in generating demand through its colonial policy, which began to have a favourable effect on the Dutch economy from the mid-1830s, albeit at some cost in terms of start-up investment and monopolism. Governor-General Baud, the man on the spot at the time, would seem to have been correct in his dictum that the Indies had kept the Netherlands afloat (in demand terms). In the 1840s English demand for Dutch farm produce burgeoned, and the Indies continued to consume Dutch exports and especially services for more or less the rest of the century. German demand began to kick in after the 1850s, and more crucially so did domestic mass demand, as the liberals changed the taxation system. After the mid-century the demand side of the economy truly began to fire on all cylinders: the home population was increasing all the time and really accelerated after 1870, with a further redoubling of the expansion after 1890. Domestic per-capita consumption reached a high plateau in the 1860s and 1870s, while foreign demand from industrializing neighbours and the colonies continued apace. Any faltering of per-capita home demand which may have taken place in the 1880s and 1890s was more than compensated for by the accelerating rise in population and the international boom of the last decade of the century which led up to the First World War.[67] All in all, the various strands of domestic and foreign demand seem to have served the Dutch economy well after a shaky start in the 1820s and 1830s.

[66] Scholliers, ed., *Real wages*, chapter 8, especially pp. 210–23.
[67] De Jonge, 'The role of the outer provinces', 218.

8   Economic transition: conclusion

8.1   Summary of findings on the economy

In Part II we have approached the Dutch economy in the nineteenth century from a number of different angles. It is now time to draw the strands of these separate approaches together, first in a summary, and then in the form of some conclusions. The macro-economic performance of the area which is now the Kingdom of the Netherlands can be very favourably compared to its neighbours over the period of the nineteenth century. To some extent the Dutch were victims of their own success in the early modern period. In the province of Holland they had attained levels of GDP per capita in the second half of the seventeenth century which were on a par with those reached by England in 1820.[1] A modest decline probably then took place, accelerating towards the end of the eighteenth century and especially during the French period, but the Dutch were still in the leading group of nations in the early nineteenth century, perhaps behind Britain, but level with or ahead of everyone else in Europe. From 1800 onwards we have the results of the project on the reconstruction of the national accounts, which generally confirm the balance of previous estimates: that growth was modest before 1850, but in line with the other leading economies of Europe. After 1850 the economic growth rates of the leading group of industrializing nations in North-West Europe took off, and the Dutch kept pace with them. Growth was marked in the period from 1850 to the late 1870s, after which it levelled out until the mid-1890s, in line with the long-term international business cycle. From 1895 it took off again in an increasingly steep line up to the First World War, during which the Dutch continued to enjoy substantial macro-economic prosperity while their neighbours were locked in mortal combat.[2]

Shifting the attention to the internal structures of the Dutch economy,

---

[1] Van Zanden, 'Een debat', 90.
[2] Buyst, et al., 'National accounts', graph on p. 63; Smits, Horlings and Van Zanden, 'Sprekende cijfers!'.

the analysis of economic inputs and organizational influences revealed that they were all plentiful and qualitatively sound, but that there were some characteristics of the Dutch situation which were unusual. Labour was abundant, educated and (except in the western provinces in the first half of the century) cheap. (A previous generation of economic historians would have phrased that differently, to the effect that wages were prohibitively high in most of the country for most of the century.) In the urbanized west the high level of nominal wages until the 1860s needed to be compensated for by other more competitive factor costs, such as capital. In any case, then as now, very often the productivity of labour was as important as its nominal price, and the labour market in Europe was anything but transparent or perfect. The Dutch capital market was very sophisticated and highly active; it did not supply large amounts to new domestic manufacturing because there was relatively little demand from that sector until the 1890s (as De Jonge had told us long ago). As far as factor costs go, finance was not a problem for the Dutch economy in any sector; capital stock grew and improved throughout the century, especially after 1850. When it comes to materials, the Dutch did have an unusual and potentially disadvantageous situation *vis-à-vis* Britain, Belgium, Germany and parts of France: it had virtually no natural resources other than its soil (including peat), wind and water. Ore-based industries were bound to be limited, and businesses founded on cheap coal were unlikely to thrive in the Netherlands until fuel prices came down, which they did after 1850 with the improvement of the internal and international infrastructure. But the economic activities affected by these two negative conditions were few, and not surprisingly the Dutch were less than quick to invest in such areas until the factor-cost problems had been counteracted. Meanwhile labour and capital were plentiful, and the economy as a whole continued to grow, indeed grow swiftly from the 1850s onwards.

The behaviour of the people active in the Dutch economy (as opposed to the more impersonal 'resource' situation) has excited debate in the past between those who blamed the 'psychological' characteristics of the Dutch and those who pointed the finger at 'economic circumstances' (factor inputs) in the search for a scapegoat to saddle with the ignominy of non-industrialization. However, on closer inspection the slate is clean. Dutch entrepreneurs behaved sensibly and skilfully, and the technological aspects of the economy were sound, with the Dutch often proving highly adept at adopting and adapting others' devices to their own circumstances. As for government, Willem I nearly bankrupted the state but achieved two crucial things: he launched a massive infrastructural programme based on waterways which was to bear fruit after his abdication, and he presided over the inauguration of a colonial policy, involving the

Cultivation System, the NHM and domestic industry, which was probably the most important single boost to the economy in the critical period of the 1830s and 1840s, and which helped lead towards the drive to sustained growth after 1850. Thereafter the liberal governments of the middle decades of the century continued the infrastructural policies (with considerably more immediate success) and added to them a great edifice of education, health and environmental policies, while dismantling much outdated regulation.

The sectoral analysis of the Dutch economy, in chapter 6, while being more descriptive than the preceding chapters, was in many ways more revealing about the unusual characteristics of the subject in hand. The fastest-growing sector was clearly the tertiary one, and by 1910 it dominated in the economy in terms of employment, production and productivity to an extent for which most other European economies would have to wait until the second half of the twentieth century. Agriculture was very advanced by 1815, especially in the coastal areas, and after a generally difficult first half of the century (a structural crisis in the 1830s, followed by harvest failures in the 1840s), the third quarter of the century was a period of rising prices, yields and prosperity; again this was shared with the farming sector in neighbouring countries. Manufacturing struggled against British and Belgian competition in certain sectors for the first half of the century, while textiles were shielded and nourished behind a protective barrier thrown up by the government's colonial policy. After the mid-century, and especially after the 1860s, industry was strong enough to compete without protection, and went on to boom in certain sectors towards the end of the century as relative wage levels and fuel prices came down, especially in new-technology industries in which there was no mountain of long-standing competition to climb. In all three sectors the watershed period seems to have been the 1850s, once again in common with the rest of Europe: the whole economy, led by services and especially by trade and transport, enjoyed an acceleration in growth after 1850, with a slow-down in the 1880s and a return to rapid growth in the 1890s and early 1900s.

Finally, our attention turned to demand issues, which have been relatively underresearched in the Netherlands (and elsewhere). Government policy played a role here; its taxation policies suppressed mass domestic demand until the last decades of the century (again in common with its neighbours), but the colonial policy of the 1830s generated essential demand for Dutch industry at a critical moment. English and German demand for Dutch farming products was important, especially after the 1840s, and increasingly so at the end of the century. The massive rise in the home population helped to cushion temporary falls in per-capita demand in the crisis period of the 1880s. The Dutch economy was well integrated into the international market, especially through its contact with its industrial neighbours and through its own colonial connection; the combination of foreign and domestic markets would seem to have worked well for the Dutch economy after the 1830s. The critical boosts apparently came from the colonies in the 1830s and 1840s, from England in the 1840s, and from Germany and from home demand from after 1850, as real wages rose rapidly from the 1850s to the 1890s.[3] The rise in the various sources of demand accelerated at the end of the century, with increasing rates of population growth at home and with an international boom which was to lead into the First World War. Demand seems not to have been a problem for the Dutch economy after the 1830s.

8.2   Characteristics

In terms of the long-term performance of the Dutch economy as indicated by its GDP per capita or equivalents, a number of conclusions emerge from the data examined here. First, we are far better informed now than we ever have been; we are now in a much better position to compare the Dutch experience with that of its competitors, although in many of these reconstructed series (in the Netherlands as elsewhere) there are still cavernous assumptions made to cover lacunae.

Second, it is extraordinary how much of the earlier work of economic historians has been confirmed in its general contours by more recent research. The traditional view of a supreme seventeenth century, replaced by economic coasting for much of the eighteenth century, declining steeply from about 1780 to 1815, recovering painfully until 1850, and entering sustained economic growth thereafter, has all been largely vindicated. Almost forty years ago I. J. Brugmans dated what *he* called an Industrial Revolution in the 1860s, which slowed down in the 1880s and resumed thereafter; some time later J. A. de Jonge dated modern industrial growth from the 1890s; Griffiths and De Meere found evidence of the beginnings of modern economic growth prior to the mid-century: all these historians have more or less been proved right.[4] What has changed, rather, is the attitudes and questions with which economic historians have come to their research. Until very recently most historians were essentially looking for an explanation for why the Netherlands failed in the

---

[3] Horlings and Smits, 'Private consumer expenditure', 23 and *passim*.
[4] In a provisional report on the results of the Utrecht University national accounts projects, Brugmans was entirely rehabilitated, and the others largely so – with some reservations about De Jonge and the 1890s: Burger, 'Dutch patterns', 165–6. On the basis of the same data, however, Buyst, *et al.*, 'National accounts', vindicates De Jonge as well (p. 63).

nineteenth century, why it did not 'industrialize', why it did not perform like Britain and Belgium, why it did not invent the Spinning Jenny or the Bessemer convertor, why its heavy industry did not develop until the last decade of the century, why it was 'retarded', and the like. The modesty of Dutch economic historiography amounted almost to an inferiority complex, and for no good reason: it is clear from the evidence presented in chapter 3 that the Dutch performance in the nineteenth century was among the best in the world. What historians are now beginning to ask is how the Dutch achieved these creditable results if they did *not* follow the Industrial Revolution model of Britain and Belgium.[5]

Third, it has become clear that in nearly all aspects the Netherlands was fully locked into the international long-term business cycle for the whole of the nineteenth century. Considerable attention has been lavished in the past on showing how the country was at various times out of step with international short-term business cycles, which was taken to be an indication of an absence of economic modernity;[6] however it is clear that, in the long term, the fortunes of almost all areas of business in the Netherlands were exactly in tune with the general rise and fall of international prosperity. There were structural depressions in the 1830s and 1880s, and two-decade *hausses* starting in the 1850s and the 1890s. In this sense the Dutch experience no longer appears exceptional, and indeed becomes mainstream: it was simply a part – with some of its own idiosyncrasies – of the North-West European developed core of nations. When her neighbours did well so did she; when they struggled, the Dutch did too. Once again, in per-capita terms the Netherlands was one of the leaders of the leading group, and very much party to the mainstream European experience, despite her lack of minerals and heavy industry.

Because of the embeddedness of the Dutch economy in its international surroundings, there are few surprises when it comes to the timing of economic growth in the nineteenth century. The unusual feature of the Dutch economy was its possession of colonies and the policies followed there from the 1830s onwards; it is likely that colonial policy prepared the ground in the Netherlands for the higher level of sustained per-capita growth which took place from the 1850s onwards. The 'liberalization' of the economy around the mid-century may also have been important, but was by no means unique to the Netherlands.

---

[5] This is very much the conclusion reached by the spokesman for the Utrecht national accounts project: Burger, 'Dutch patterns', 174–5. However, another version of the results of the project reverts to the old regrets that the Dutch 'came off extremely badly' in comparison with their neighbours: Smits, Horlings and Van Zanden, 'Sprekende cijfers!' The tradition is apparently a hard one to shake off.

[6] Classic examples are Ridder, *Een conjunctuur-analyse*; and Brugmans, 'Economic fluctuations'.

In the course of analysis we were led to question some of the approaches taken to the issue of economic growth in the past: two cases in point are government policy and attitudes to technology. Economic historians are often guilty of anachronism: they seek to place a statistical grid on the past which the data simply cannot and never will support, and they seek to analyse the developing economies of the past in terms of complex economic models based on late twentieth-century post-industrial societies (indeed this book itself is in some degree guilty of the same offence). They expect governments in the past to have been capable of exerting the same kind of influence that they can wield today, which is of course absurd: they had virtually no apparatus for doing so beyond the partial control of tariffs and some taxes. Much of the Dutch state's 'economic policy' was ineffective or counter-productive, especially under Willem I; grand visions often went wrong, and shrewd practical negotiation of the detail of commercial treaties was on the whole of much more service to the economy. On the other hand, the restructuring of the polity and economy of the Dutch state in the first half of the nineteenth century was in itself a major achievement, albeit sometimes a costly and wasteful one. The 'liberalization' of the economy around the mid-century probably cleared out some cobwebs, and most importantly began to shift some of the burden of taxation away from excises. Thorbecke's reason for doing so was moral, for he thought it unfair that the poor should pay the most taxes (which of course it was). However, an economic issue which probably did not occur to him was just as weighty: with their disposable income reduced to zero by a regressive taxation policy, the vast majority of the Dutch people were hardly in a position to generate mass domestic demand. Further tax changes in the second half of the century, and the beginnings of a welfare state towards 1900 (see below, section 10.3), were of some real economic importance in this respect, as we can see from figures for levels of consumption. So governments may have helped here, but it was hardly a grand strategy. The major exception to the failure of governments consciously to affect the economic fortunes of the country in any important way was of course the East Indies policy. The protection of the textile and related industries, the stimulus to shipbuilding and marine engineering, the fostering of the trade and shipping sectors, and the use of the filthy lucre to smooth the path of excise reduction and crucial infrastructural projects were all critical at the mid-century, the moment of acceleration in the country's economic growth. Thereafter private enterprise got its hands on the empire, and the financial sector in particular continued to profit from it. If one of the meanings of 'imperialism' was the state in service of business abroad, then the Dutch were early masters of the game. This aspect of government policy was perhaps the most important palliative in the difficult transition from the mercantile traditions of the Republic to the modern financial and industrial economy of the late nineteenth century.[7]

If government policy was on occasion successful, the enduring message is nonetheless that the Dutch were skilled adjusters. The maverick colonial policy was in many ways untypical; much more characteristic was the level-headed and dogged negotiation of treaties and agreements, and adjusting to changing international geo-political circumstance. The same was true of entrepreneurs, and of their attitudes to technology. There were some imposing captains of industry who cut an international dash, and there were a few Dutch inventions, but most of economic life was more concerned with the adaptation of new ideas, sources of supply and markets, wherever they came from, at home or abroad, to fit the changing local environment. The search for the industrial equivalents of merchant princes, for a Dutch replica of the Belgian Cockerills or any number of great English industrialists, has often led to disappointment: such figures did exist, like Regout and Van Vlissingen, but most Dutch entrepreneurship and technological advance was much more a question of gradual improvements according to local circumstance. What is more, this was in tune with the bulk of European experience, rather than the more swashbuckling exploits of certain individuals in British and Belgian heavy industry, who appear in retrospect to have been something of an exception on the European stage.[8] And the results of such steady adjustment and fine tuning were thoroughly satisfactory in macro-economic terms, especially after the mid-century.

8.3   Retardation?

The term 'industrial retardation' is usually applied to the British economy towards the end of the nineteenth century when its European rivals appeared to be catching up to some extent; that is to say it refers to a mature industrialized economy which is experiencing a relative slowdown. However, in the Dutch case the expression derives from the debate about why the Netherlands did not 'industrialize' at all in the nineteenth century, and why it did not undergo an Industrial Revolution.[9] The analysis of the economy here has largely outflanked the Dutch historiographical debate on industrialization and its retardation: the economy was

---

[7] A transition point tentatively dated to the first half of the nineteenth century, in Van Zanden, 'The Dutch economy', 279–80. See also Davids and Lucassen, eds., *A miracle mirrored*.

[8] See Goodman and Honeyman, *Gainful pursuits*, chapter 4; and section 5.2 above.

[9] See the title, for example, of Griffiths, *Industrial retardation*.

thoroughly successful in macro-economic terms, and it was led by an unrivalled tertiary sector which was responsible for its being perhaps the most modern economy in Europe (the USA may well have been a competitor in that respect). But if only to tie up loose ends, it is fitting to return briefly to the question of why the Dutch economy, despite doing very well overall, did not actually move into manufacturing industry in the same way that some of its neighbours did.

In very brief confirmation or dismissal of the traditional arguments, the first point to be made is that the other sectors in the economy besides manufacturing were very healthy, and thus were not driving labour or capital into factories. Second, there was Belgium. King Willem I, as monarch of the combined Low Countries from 1815 to 1830, had envisaged a division of labour between north and south, with the south making the goods to be exported around the world by the north. As a result, his considerable efforts in interventionist economic policy had favoured heavy industry in the south, perhaps at the expense of that sector in the north. Those efforts had then been lost to the Dutch in 1830 with the Belgian Revolution, and Dutch government finance had been hamstrung for a decade until the settlement in 1839, with the maintenance of an armed peace and high military expenditure along the border. This argument is not of central importance, but deserves to be articulated. Theories attributing Dutch industrial 'retardation' to the psychological characteristics of capitalists, entrepreneurs or workers have been comprehensively dismissed here. The reserves of labour, capital, entrepreneurship and technology show no structural weaknesses whatsoever.

To be taken much more seriously are reasons for modesty in manufacturing which have to do with factor costs, namely the price of labour in certain regions, and the price of fuel. Until after the mid-century, the west of the country suffered from marginally high nominal wages (as did successful Britain) and seriously expensive coal; these facts may well have slowed down factorization and mechanization in those industries which required high coal inputs and those which had to compete with other sectors – trade, transport and the more advanced forms of agriculture – for labour. However, these differentials were eroded by 1860.

Finally, historians have traditionally brought in the absence of a strong proto-industrial sector, and the powerful influence of external, international economic factors, to explain the modicum of manufacturing. Regarding the first, the Belgian historian J. A. van Houtte remarked that proto-industry, a potential precondition for industrialization, was much better represented in Belgium than in the Netherlands because the strong central monarchy in medieval Flanders had prevented the urban guilds in what later became Belgium from stamping out rural competition; in the north, where central authority was weak and power resided in the towns, the guilds were free to exert their monopoly.[10] There was indeed only a modest Z-good sector in the Netherlands in the nineteenth century, most of it concentrated in the east, but the main reason for this was probably the high productivity of labour in agriculture in all but those regions.[11] A recent study of two villages in Twente, characterized by a degree of proto-industrialization from the 1830s to the 1860s, concluded that the dual economy of weaving and small-scale agriculture was a survival strategy against poverty resulting from an overdependence on either farming or manufacturing.[12] In most areas, however, Dutch agriculture was simply too effective to require proto-industry as a second string, and in this sense one could say once more that the Dutch were the victims of their own earlier success.

That leaves us with the question of the international perspective, particularly interesting because it concerns demand as well as supply. There are two parts to the argument. With regard to the long-term economic geography of Europe, the Netherlands had held a central and pivotal position in the seventeenth century, but had lost that centrality some time in the eighteenth century, and remained peripheral to mainstream European economic development until the second half of the nineteenth century, especially to that of industry-led Britain and Belgium.[13] With the formation of the *Zollverein* in 1834, Germany began its economic unification and later its political coming together, and the Netherlands was able to use its river trade and its increasingly coherent transport system to rise on the crest of the German economic awakening, the most powerful economic force on the continent of Europe. At the same time, while Britain, Belgium, northern France and then Germany were industrializing in classical mode, the Netherlands found herself and her infrastructure once more at the epicentre of economic activity, and took full advantage of it. Not only could she profit from the almost limitless urban markets in these countries for quality agricultural produce, but she could now import fuel, raw materials and semi-finished goods more or less as she wished, simply by skimming it off the burgeoning transit trade, which allowed her domestic manufacturing sector to develop. By the end of the century, with her transport system nurtured by

[10] Van Houtte, 'Economic development', 109–10.
[11] Van Zanden, *The rise and decline*, chapter 6.
[12] Hendrickx, '*In order not to fall into poverty*'.
[13] R. Bos is generally credited with the articulation of this set of ideas, in his doctoral thesis, *Brits-Nederlandse handel*, and in a seminal essay, Bos, 'Van periferie naar centrum'; see also Bos, 'Remarks upon long-term economic fluctuations', 41. However, others were moving towards a similar position at the same time, for instance De Vries, 'De problematiek'; Nusteling, *De Rijnvaart*; and Bläsing, *Das goldene Delta*.

the efforts of the government and central elite to bring the nation together in terms of standardization and infrastructure, she was participating fully in the economic boom which was to lead up to the First World War. These arguments which attempt to show why Dutch heavy industry did not develop until the 1890s are helpful in that they oblige us to locate the Dutch in their North European context, and in that they place emphasis on the infrastructure – for the Dutch strength in transport and trade was crucial to her success. However, in the sense that they suggest that Dutch manufacturing and therefore economic growth was crippled until the last decade of the century, they are not helpful at all.

The other strand of the international context of the Dutch economy, although it has little to do with industrial retardation, is the colonial connection. Driven by a determined government policy from the 1830s on, by the 1850s the clear profits from the East Indies were providing half of government revenue in the mother country. In the 1860s the prevailing climate of economic liberalism insisted on the privatization of this lucrative state monopoly, and the East Indies was turned over to private capital investment and exploitation on a vast scale, aided and abetted by the state and the churches. There have been some attempts to deny that the Dutch became involved in the New Imperialism at the end of the nineteenth century, on the grounds that they made no new conquests beyond the lands of which they already had titular control,[14] but in a financial-economic sense they were full participants, and by the early twentieth century perhaps as much as 15 per cent of the Dutch national income was derived from her East Indies colonies.

8.4   Typologies of industrialization

Joel Mokyr, at the end of his extended cliometric study of the Netherlands and Belgium, during the course of which he had been at pains to talk up the manufacturing industry of Belgium and regret its absence in the Netherlands, fell to musing, 'Might one, therefore, not conclude that the fact that the Dutch did not industrialize was perhaps not all that unfortunate from their point of view? Was it Belgium's destiny to suffer the disamenities and pains of industrialization while the Dutch were rich enough to be able to dispense with modern industry?'[15] It was a rhetorical question, which Mokyr chose not to answer directly. What is clear from the preceding chapters on the economy is that while maintaining only a modest manufacturing sector, the Dutch suffered no disadvantage in general, aggregate economic terms, and have not done so in the twentieth

[14] See M. Kuitenbrower's essay in Groenveld and Wintle, eds., *State and trade*, chapter 8.
[15] Mokyr, *Industrialization*, 259.

century either. Indeed, one could argue that Belgium and Britain, with their archetypically nineteenth-century industrial base, have increasingly been dogged in the twentieth century by the law of diminishing returns, whereas the major initiatives in Dutch industry took place in the 1890s, the 1920s and the 1950s, with new technologies which have not yet begun to suffer from the British or Belgian disease. At any rate in the nineteenth century, Dutch economic growth was spread evenly over the sectors. Economists and economic historians have long pointed to the importance of agriculture to industrialization,[16] and we have noted the significant contribution of agriculture to Dutch economic growth. Dutch growth was also spread across the decades, taking place gradually over time,[17] a point emphasized by Crafts for Europe as a whole.[18]

The analysis here has emphasized that the Netherlands was very much a part of the advanced economic core of North-West Europe, and that its prosperity was intimately related to the economic fortunes of its neighbours and indeed the emerging global market. What, then, does the Dutch experience show us about economic change and development in general, and about the nature of industrialization in particular? In a narrow economic sense, industrialization can be defined as the shift of the dynamic focus of an economy from the primary to the secondary sector: secondarization, or de-agrarianization. In a historical sense, however, that definition does not go far enough. That shift towards the secondary sector was important because of the generally higher productivity of labour in the secondary than in the primary sector. But there are many other aspects to the increased levels of income and production which make up modern economic growth, and, as we have seen, by no means all of them are exclusive to manufacturing. Primarily it is a question of a more efficient use of existing and newly acquired economic resources. This involves an economic intensification – of either capital or labour or both – rather than simply an enlargement of factor inputs. It involves economic specialization, and the trade that goes with it. It involves the development and application to the production process of technology in the widest sense, including new management techniques and work practices, and it involves increasing engagement in enlarging market mechanisms. It requires human capital as well as investment in plant and infrastructure. And it involves the transformation of society from the pre-industrial to the industrial, which has endless social, political and cultural ramifications, including gender relations, labour relations, political

---

[16] E.g., Maitra, *The mainspring*, 14; De Jonge, 'The role of the outer provinces', 218; Milward and Saul, *The development of the economies*, 528–32.

[17] Bos, 'Economic growth', 14; Bos, *Brits-Nederlandse handel*, 67.

[18] Crafts, 'GNP in Europe', 397–8.

structures, cultural identities and social movements, all of which are the concern of Part III of this book. If we accept the concept of industrialization as having this wider raft of meanings, then to limit it to the growth of manufacturing industry becomes almost a nonsense. In short, industrialization is too important to be treated exclusively as a concern of manufacturing industry.

This much is thoroughly reflected in the search for typologies of industrialization, and paths to it. Models of industrialization have been constructed, and most of them rapidly discarded. In an article of 1986 Patrick O'Brien ran through the contenders, from technology diffusion, proto-industrialization, Rostow, Gerschenkron, Hoffmann, the role of banking, the role of government, tariff protection and entrepreneurship.[19] O'Brien had some respect for Gerschenkron for furnishing a kind of negative yardstick, and indeed some of the more interesting work in the Netherlands has been conducted with the Gerschenkron model as a framework, although the 'great spurt' has remained elusive.[20] O'Brien's final word is an entreaty to develop the data sources, so that we can compare directly such things as factor endowments, scale, demographic structures and comparative advantages.[21]

In a separate exercise, Adelman and Morris conducted an extensive statistical search for the critical variables leading to industrialization in the period 1850–1914. They took twenty-five countries, and employed thirty-five variables. Their conclusion was that institutional influences were important, and by this was meant such things as land-tenure systems, political regimes and market institutions.[22] Few would disagree, and the attention paid in this book to demographic matters (Part I) and to social and political institutions (Part III) falls in with such an insistence on the importance of socio-cultural and political factors when considering the economy. Adelman and Morris lay their emphasis not on factor endowments, or proto-industry, or trade connections, but on more cultural factors. Milward and Saul's model, back in the 1970s, was one which proposed downgrading the role of manufacturing industry within European economic growth and emphasizing the position of agriculture,[23] while Goodman and Honeyman have more recently refused to accept any model of industrialization which reserves an exclusive central place for manufacturing, technology, deskilling or factorization; this is a rejection of the British-led model, and it has the explicit blessing of

[19] O'Brien, 'Do we have a typology?' See also O'Brien, *The industrial revolution*, Introduction, especially pp. xxv–xxxii.
[20] E.g., Klein, 'Het bankwezen'; and Griffiths, *Achterlijk?*
[21] O'Brien, 'Do we have a typology?', 330–3.
[22] Adelman and Morris, 'Patterns of industrialization'.
[23] Milward and Saul, *The development of the economies*, 522–37.

Crafts' statistical work.[24] Once more, the relative unimportance of an overdeveloped manufacturing sector to economic growth and prosperity is amply supported by the Dutch experience.

That experience can be remarkably illuminating. A politically light-weight small nation, which has been in the top economic league for four centuries, and has kept up with the frantic growth of the likes of Britain and Germany in the nineteenth and early twentieth centuries, but which had no more than a modest industrial sector, must tell us something about the nature of 'industrialization', and the paths to it. The main object lessons are four. Balanced growth was experienced between all the sectors. Second, in terms of timing there was an important acceleration of growth in the 1850s, and again in the 1890s, but growth was a continuous process right throughout the century, with no caesurae separating periods which bore no relationship to each other. Third, the agricultural sector was a major contributor to modern economic growth in itself. And finally, the service sector was probably the main motor of growth in the period of so-called 'industrialization'.

[24] Goodman and Honeyman, *Gainful pursuits*; Crafts, 'GNP in Europe', 397–8.

Part III

Social transition: state, society, individual and nation

Introduction

Revolutionary changes have occurred in social relations over the last two centuries, not least in the Netherlands. Collective society in the form of the state has become immensely powerful, reaching into every crevice of personal life, dictating what is acceptable behaviour in the home between parents and children, and in the workplace between employer and labour force. We have seen in Part II the state adopting a greater role in the economy throughout the nineteenth century, and will see here that it did so in social matters as well. Little of this social intervention was in place in 1800, and it was almost exclusively at local level; much of the writing was on the wall by 1914, as a function of central government. At the same time, while the state was expanding its influence over the lives of individuals, the latter were not entirely passive in the matter. Whereas only a tiny elite took part in political life at the start of the nineteenth century, nearly all the adult nation did so by 1919, and not only by voting: most people were by then 'organized' in one form or another. Voluntary participation in bodies with a public function grew with revolutionary rapidity in the nineteenth century, especially in its second half. In 1815 there was very little identification with national groups except through the army and certain of the churches; by the First World War there were the advanced beginnings of a Dutch civil society, and a Dutch nation to boot.

The matrix of relationships between the individual and society in the Netherlands is the general framework which has been adopted for the final part of this book, on social transition in the nineteenth century. It is a loose and flexible framework, rather than a tight theoretical structure, and intentionally so. It permits and encourages a series of different theoretical approaches to be taken up without the need for any single one to dominate; for example, models of consociationalism and of the nation state will be used in the Dutch context for the nineteenth century, but without any attempt to impose a single overarching paradigm. Second, it allows us to arrange the enormous production of recent decades in Dutch social and political history. Much social-history writing is theoretically driven and rightly so, but the subject matter is so diverse – both empirically and theoretically – that it is simply unencompassable in a single rigid theoretical context. Finally, the framework of the relationship between society and the individual allows us to give full attention to what is traditionally held to be the distinguishing feature of modern Dutch society: *verzuiling*, or vertical pluralism, whereby the country was divided into four or more ideological pillars, or separate socio-political worlds. *Verzuiling* served the function of providing relative political stability in a country which was deeply divided in ideological as well as socio-economic terms. It dominated the Dutch political system up to the 1960s; its foundations were laid in the nineteenth century, and we shall study them here. In many ways *verzuiling* was the method the Dutch devised, or stumbled upon, for conducting relations between the burgeoning new nation and the evolving welfare state on the one hand, and its individual citizens and traditional social groupings on the other. It is for these reasons that we shall organize the material of the following four chapters around the theme or within the flexible framework of the interaction between individual and society.

Chapter 9 will deal with matters of formal authority and representation in the Dutch state. We have registered (in section 5.3) the process of political and economic centralization which took place in the nineteenth century; how did citizens respond to this, and interact with the increasingly intrusive state? We shall examine the process of democratization, and the role played by political liberalism and toleration in this process; and the concept of *verzuiling* will be fully explored. Chapter 10 will concentrate on the services which the emerging modern state began to provide for its citizens, and the costs and restrictions involved. State-sponsored education was the major socio-political battlefield in the Netherlands (and in many other European countries) in the second half of the nineteenth century, and we shall examine the role of education in the evolving relations between the people and the state: both sides had high expectations. Social services will also come under scrutiny. Chapter 11 turns to the topic of the nation. The importance afforded in the chapters on the economy to the 'coming together' of the Netherlands, especially from 1850 onwards, points us towards an examination of the way in which the Dutch evolved from a people with primary allegiance to locality, to one which played a full part in the New Imperialism at the end of the nineteenth century as a small but fully fledged member of the club of nation states. Finally, in chapter 12, we shall examine a number of social groups in the Netherlands, and their changing function as intermediaries between state and individual. Region, gender, religion, politics, ideology, labour market position, class, family: all these will be part of a survey of how Dutch people and their leaders dealt with the problems and indeed the advantages and social goods resulting from the demographic, economic and social changes we have encountered in this book.

9 Authority and representation: the citizen and the state

9.1 Introduction

Nowadays the Dutch are famous or even notorious for the particular kind of relationship they have evolved between themselves and their public bodies. They have an almost universal reputation for their 'liberal' regime or 'liberal state', with 'liberal' used here in the sense of tolerant, permissive, generous, humane, non-repressive. Is there any evidence in the nineteenth century of such 'liberalism' and tolerance? What was the Dutch official attitude to non-standard forms of behaviour and under-privileged groups?[1]

In seeking out this historical process of defining the relationships between state, interest group and individual, three principal areas will be investigated in this chapter: the growth of democratic political institutions; the role of the liberals in that process; and finally the famed Dutch tolerance. Where did this 'tolerance' originate, and how did it develop? How was it manifested (if at all) in Dutch political and social institutions as they developed in the nineteenth century? This is a large subject area, and here we shall take certain specific aspects of it. We shall focus in turn on traditions of religious and political freedom interspersed with examples of intolerance, and finally and most importantly on that particularly Dutch brand of political tolerance, *verzuiling*.

9.2 Democratization

The Dutch were not in the vanguard of the evolution of the institutions of parliamentary democracy, in comparison to other European nations. In particular, the suffrage was expanded only very gradually in the nineteenth century.[2] The percentage of the population enfranchised in the Netherlands in 1850 (*after* the great constitutional reform of 1848) was 2.5, which was indeed ahead of Eastern and Central Europe (0 per cent)

---

[1] Parts of this chapter draw on Wintle, 'The liberal state'.
[2] Van Holthoon, ed., *De Nederlandse samenleving*, 318–21.

and Belgium (1.8 per cent), but behind the UK (4 per cent) and Scandinavia (6–15 per cent), and very much behind France (20 per cent), Switzerland (22 per cent) and Greece (23 per cent). Twenty years later in 1870 only 2.9 per cent of the Dutch population could vote, which meant it had been overtaken by Austria, Hungary, Portugal and Serbia; in 1910, 14 per cent of the Dutch had been enfranchised, which was ahead of Germany, Portugal, Italy and Hungary, but behind every other country in Europe, whether West, East or Central. The Netherlands was the only country in which the 'Revolution' of 1848 actually *decreased* the electorate (from 3 per cent in indirect elections to 2.5 per cent in direct elections). R. J. Goldstein commented that the much vaunted liberal reforms of the second half of the last century were basically conservative, and thus 'allowed the major parties to ignore social issues and the yawning gulf between rich and poor'.[3]

However, this should not obscure the fact that progress was made. At one level, the United Provinces of the *ancien régime* Dutch Republic functioned as an oligarchy trying to fend off claims of absolute authority from the House of Orange. At another, the locus of power was in the towns, which enjoyed a high degree of autonomy, and where local interest groups, often represented by the guilds, ran local affairs and social relations in a great organic, corporative structure, which was to die out at the hand of the centralization measures effected in the first half of the nineteenth century.[4] The son of *stadhouder* Willem V was installed as King Willem I in 1815, with very extensive powers enabling him to rule as an enlightened despot when he chose to (which was most of the time). However, a century later, in 1919, the country had changed into a full-blown parliamentary democracy, with universal male and female suffrage, and with sovereignty firmly planted in the Second Chamber (lower house) of Parliament. As a percentage of the male adult population, the electorate grew excruciatingly slowly during the great liberal decades of the 1850s, 1860s and 1870s, from 11 per cent in 1853 to just 12.3 per cent in 1880; however, by 1890 it stood at 26.8 per cent, by 1900 at 49 per cent, and in 1917 there was total male adult franchise. (Female franchise followed in 1919.) In 1853 there were something over 80,000 voters; that total had increased tenfold to over 800,000 in 1910 (and another tenfold to nearly 9 million in 1972).[5]

A parliament existed in 1815, but it could exert very little influence on

---

[3] Goldstein, *Political repression*, 187, 195, 210, 241.
[4] See Prak, *Republikeinse veelheid*, for a study of the transition in the town of Den Bosch in this period.
[5] Lipschits, *De protestants-christelijke stroming*, 13. The percentage figures relate to the male population of twenty-three years and over in the period 1853–1890, and for 1900 and 1910, of twenty-five years and older.

the king owing to the convention (enshrined in the 1815 Constitution) that expenditure on all but extraordinary items (such as war) was voted on a decennial basis: the monarch only had to face his paymasters once a decade, and so parliament's control over the purse-strings was effectively neutralized. The king could rule almost entirely by Royal Decree, and Ministers were his personal servants without responsibility to parliament. Willem I indulged his autocratic character reasonably freely until the late 1830s, when there occurred simultaneously a threat of concerted parliamentary action over the budget, a scandal concerning the King's second marriage to a Belgian Catholic, and a need for a new constitution to accommodate the final loss of the Belgian provinces in 1839. These factors together provoked a constitutional revision, and with it the King's abdication in favour of his allegedly more constitutionally minded son, Willem II. The 1840 changes introduced a limited form of ministerial responsibility, biennial budgets for all government expenditure, and – crucially – the regulation of franchise arrangements by parliament rather than by the localities.

This paved the way for the major constitutional reform of 1848, which although almost bloodless in the Netherlands (there were some lively disturbances in Amsterdam, but King Willem II seems to have given in to the threat of political violence abroad rather than at home) was nevertheless a revolution real and proper. The number of direct voters may have declined, but two things were established which laid out the road to full parliamentary democracy: the seat of power was rooted henceforth in the Second Chamber, and its members were to be directly elected on a national basis, with no electoral colleges acting as a buffer between the voters and their representatives. As well as establishing these two principles, the franchise was henceforth to be decided by the amount of direct taxation paid. The First Chamber was also to be elected, but indirectly, by the members of the Provincial Estates or assemblies, and its members had to be very rich to qualify for nomination. Parliament received the right to question the government and to amend its bills, and was given control over important areas of public business, such as the colonies, public works and local affairs, which had previously been under the sceptre of either the king or local government.[6] Thus 1848 was not only a democratizing measure, but a centralizing one as well, and indeed was rapidly followed by two laws on local government, the Provincial Act (*Provinciale Wet*) of 1850, and the Municipality Act (*Gemeentewet*) of 1851, which, while granting some important local competences, rigidly

[6] Van Raalte, *The Parliament*, 2–6.

cemented political power in the hands of the new, directly elected national government.[7]

With the primacy of the Second Chamber established, it was thereafter only a matter of time before the franchise was inexorably expanded with a descending threshold,[8] and before the Second Chamber relegated every other political forum to a subsidiary position. Indeed, the monarchy was one of the first to be downgraded to a formal constitutional role; this was helped by the fact that Willem III, who ascended the throne in 1849, the year of the first election under the new constitution, and who remained on it for forty-one years until 1890, was a difficult figure with no great popularity or acumen. Ministerial responsibility was theoretically conceded in 1848; ministers were to be responsible to parliament rather than to the king, but Willem III was reluctant to accept the change. It was only after extensive public rows, which culminated in the unequivocal rejection by the voters of his governments in the Luxembourg question in 1866–68, that he finally accepted the inevitable, and resigned himself to spending more time on his hunting estates.[9]

So 1848 was a watershed. Even the criteria for general taxation changed so that indirect taxes could gradually make way for more equitable and 'democratic' taxes on income and wealth.[10] The electorate may have grown only slowly, but the whole concept of the legitimacy of power switched from an aristocratic-monarchical one to a liberal-democratic one. In this sense it represented the beginning of the final and irrevocable end of the *ancien régime*.[11]

The next major constitutional revision after 1848 came in 1887; suffrage was no longer determined by a tax threshold, but in terms of 'general fitness', to be defined more precisely in further legislation. Meanwhile, it was made marginally easier to stand for the First Chamber, and the number of seats in the Second Chamber was expanded to one hundred. After extensive debate, a new Franchise Act was passed in 1896 at the instigation of the liberal Samuel van Houten, in which 'general fitness' to vote was expressed in terms of 'having a stake', however small; by this means the *petite bourgeoisie* was enfranchised (or rather its males aged twenty-five and over were). Finally, in 1917, partly as a reward to the working classes and their representatives in return for their contribution to national unity in the First World War (a testing time, despite Dutch neutrality), universal manhood suffrage was granted, followed by female

[7] See above, on centralization, in section 5.3.
[8] De Vries, 'Het censuskiesrecht', 179–81.   [9] Kossmann, *The Low Countries*, 287–8.
[10] Schuttevaer and Detiger, *Anderhalve eeuw belastingen*, 28. See section 5.3 above.
[11] Stuurman, *Wacht op onze daden*, 170.

suffrage in 1919. The middle classes received their reward in the form of a free choice of state-subsidized education. At the same time, compulsory voting and proportional representation were introduced for elections to the Second Chamber, the latter in a quite distinctive and pure form which has been a characteristic of the Dutch electoral system ever since. Eligibility for the First Chamber was made the same as that for the Second.

With these reforms, the formal aspects of democratization in the Netherlands were complete, bar the shouting. Some adjustments followed: elections to the First Chamber were subjected to proportional representation in 1922, government ministers were barred from being Members of Parliament and the monarch was relieved of the right to declare war in 1938, and the Second Chamber was expanded to 150 members in 1953.[12] The voting age came down to twenty-three again in 1946, to twenty-one in 1967 and to eighteen in 1972. After 1919 it was a matter for the gradual adjustment of political culture to the letter of the law. The period between 1848 and 1917 had seen the evolution of the Netherlands from a regime exclusively dominated by the king and the political elite to a full constitutional democracy, where the elite was no doubt still firmly in the saddle, but where it had to sell its leadership directly to the people at regular elections. The Dutch were not leaders of this kind of democratization in Western Europe, but they were part of the general movement, and in their proportional representation and female suffrage provisions they were arguably ahead of their time.

9.3   Liberalism

In this transformation from *ancien régime* to modern democracy, a major role was played in the Netherlands, as elsewhere, by liberalism. Dutch liberalism was generally secular, compared for example to England, where it was linked with religious dissent. In Roman Catholic countries like France, Italy and Belgium, liberalism could be and often was fiercely anti-clerical; Dutch liberals were less often so. Dutch liberal political culture was legally minded, secular and intellectual, harbouring no special relationship with any particular religious denomination.[13]

The greatest figure in Dutch liberalism, and probably the most important statesman of the nineteenth century, was Johan Rudolf Thorbecke. He is often referred to as the founder of the modern Dutch state; he was

[12] Van Raalte, *The Parliament*, 6–7.
[13] Stuurman, *Wacht op onze daden*, 324–34. Stuurman points out that Dutch liberals, in so far as they were religious, tended to favour the progressive sects, like the Remonstrants, whereas English liberalism was tied closely to Methodism. See also Wintle, *Pillars*, 7; and Kruijt, 'Mentaliteitsverschillen', 74.

the principal author of the 1848 Constitution, and led three of the great reforming liberal ministries in 1849–53, 1862–66 and 1871–72. For Thorbecke and his followers, the state was by no means unimportant: it conditioned and made possible individual freedom.[14] This 'doctrinaire' phase in Dutch liberalism did not outlast Thorbecke, who died in 1872; the state was an even more important instrument for his liberal successors. The coming generation, led by Samuel van Houten, has been dubbed the 'Scientific Liberals', and stood for rationalism and social reform, rejecting any ideas of pure *laissez-faire* as socially irresponsible. They in turn were challenged towards the end of the century by the Social Liberals, who showed evidence of the influence of socialism, and of German *Kathedersozialismus* or intellectual 'historical' liberalism.[15] The Social Liberals were led in the Netherlands by M. W. F. Treub (1858–1931), and their philosophy represented a final rejection of the original liberal 'self-help' message, in the guilty knowledge that much of the population of *fin-de-siècle* Netherlands simply did not have the means to help themselves.[16]

To what extent was the contribution by the Dutch liberals to the changing relations between the state and the individual unusual, or central to the process as a whole? In terms of legislation, our neo-liberal age tends to remember the liberal ministries of the third quarter of the nineteenth century as 'rolling back the frontiers of the state', and indulging in an orgy of deregulation. In the 1850s and 1860s, the Dutch liberals certainly dismantled a fair amount of King Willem I's edifice of state regulation of the economy, but the same liberal era saw the launch of the modern state, with education, communications, transport (railways, canals, shipping and roads), banking and medicine all being the target of comprehensive legislation for general provision of services on behalf of the state.[17] The Dutch liberals also exercised an important reforming influence in areas away from the debate about *laissez-faire*. In terms of simple humanity and civilization, we can point to their abolition of most of the infamous Cultivation System in the East Indies, of the death penalty, of restrictions on the freedom of the press, of assembly and of religion, and their final defeat of royal pretensions against constitutionalism.

However, the liberal era in the Netherlands was followed around the

---

[14] Te Velde, *Gemeenschapszin*, 21–3.

[15] *Kathedersozialismus* is translatable as 'lectern' or 'armchair socialism', which conveys that it comes from non-activist academics; it was one of the forms of 'historical' liberalism which criticized pure *laissez-faire* liberalism. See Boschloo, *De productiemaatschappij*, 236.

[16] Stuurman, *Wacht op onze daden*, 175, 222–3, 305–17; Dudink, *Deugdzaam liberalisme*, chapter 8.

[17] Kraemer, *The societal state*, 38–42; and section 5.3 above.

turn of the century by something so profoundly different, in the form of confessionally dominated pluralism (*verzuiling*), that we should not exaggerate the Dutch liberals' role in creating the modern Dutch permissive and generous (liberal) state: the discontinuity with what succeeded them was simply too great.[18] Other factors were evidently involved. However, nineteenth-century liberalism made a major contribution to a modern state system, with its insistence on a legally based constitutionalism, individual freedoms and state provision of essential services, perhaps more so than in other countries because of the need in the Netherlands to replace the old city-based system of the Republic. The strong influence of Social Liberalism in the twilight years of the century, perhaps together with the catharsis generated by liberalism's dismantling of the colonial state, was particularly important.[19]

9.4   Tolerance and *verzuiling*

Many Dutch people are liberal-minded – quite possibly more so than elsewhere – but many are certainly not: the unusual feature is the liberal nature of the state, of public office, rather than of the people as individuals. Nonetheless, the United Provinces had been (comparatively) a haven of tolerance in the seventeenth century, and the Dutch state today is generally held to be exceptionally liberal and tolerant compared to most other regimes.[20] What happened in between, and what is the explanation for this long history of 'tolerance'?

First there is the pragmatism argument: the Dutch were not really in a position to enforce intolerance any more than they did in the Republic, and so they made a virtue of necessity.[21] But beyond that, there are other aspects of the characteristic development of tolerance in the Netherlands, in its sense of a willingness to co-exist alongside other groups with very different attitudes, beliefs and behaviour. One is the tradition of tolerance and freedom in the Dutch nation from the time of the Republic at least, but which – significantly – was periodically interrupted, especially in the nineteenth century, by some rather intolerant and authoritarian incidents. Second, there is the difficult but fundamental issue of vertical pluralism or *verzuiling*: what was the role played by this emerging Dutch form of political culture in the changing relationship between individual and society?

There is a tradition of liberty in the Netherlands which stems from the

---

[18] Stuurman, *Wacht op onze daden*, 363–7.
[19] Cf. Dudink, *Deugdzaam liberalisme*, chapter 4 and *passim*.
[20] Wintle, 'The liberal state', 126–7.
[21] Essay on 'Tolerantie toen en nu' in Kossmann, *Politieke theorie en geschiedenis*.

Republic, which has its intellectual antecedents in Erasmian Humanism, and which is substantially concerned with freedom of religious expression. It was continued in liberal political rhetoric in the nineteenth century, and in the important presence in the Netherlands of the international peace movement around 1900 and thereafter.[22] One nuanced manifestation of this tradition, and a sensitive indicator of the relationship between government and people, is the history of the country's policing policy.

The Dutch police regime was on occasion politically driven, but after 1851 was overtly occupied with democratic accountability, and was generally motivated by a concern to present authority as liberal, democratic and fair. D. C. Bayley has argued in his studies of the history of Europe's police that all police forces are virtually by definition politically formed; C. Fijnaut has confirmed and documented a similar thesis, with particular emphasis on the Netherlands. The gradual formation of a police force, maintains Fijnaut, is essentially the nationalization of the apparatus of political repression.[23] The government ethos of King Willem I was statist in tone; there were members of his government circle who openly preached a Hegelian doctrine of expanding the apparatus and the power of the state.[24] Policing tended to reflect such government positions in the first half of the century. However, the liberal ministries after 1848 ushered in a new era, and Thorbecke announced that 'we wish a police force that is seen as little as possible and about which as little as possible is said'.[25] Policing may have been a nationalized form of political repression, but in the Netherlands Thorbecke wished it to be seen to be responsible; compared to most other nations it probably was. After the liberal intervention there was certainly an obsession with the legitimacy of police authority, which even hampered the efficient workings of the police on occasion. Nonetheless the principle was seen to be more important than the practicality, and by and large (with certain exceptions) the attitude was maintained by the confessional governments at the end of the nineteenth century and the beginning of the twentieth.[26]

However, this tradition of liberty has operated more as a background motif than as a constant reality, and it knew important limitations. In fact, the tolerance of the Dutch Republic had been a curate's egg, where all non-Calvinist groups suffered passive discrimination right up to 1796, and several were actively disadvantaged, especially in the east. Dutch

[22] Van de Giessen, *De opkomst*; Wintle, 'The liberal state', 120–2.
[23] E.g., Bayley, 'The police'; Fijnaut, *Opdat de macht*.
[24] Ribberink, 'Van Ghert', 332–3.
[25] Cited in Punch, ed., *Control in the police organization*, 14.
[26] For a full account, see Wintle, 'Policing the liberal state'.

history contains plenty of religious and other bigotry and intolerance; enough to show the Dutch how unpleasant life could be if they could not 'live apart together'. The religious wars of the sixteenth century, the feuding between orthodox and moderate Calvinists in the seventeenth century, the political factionism of the eighteenth century: all these were object lessons to the Dutch. In the nineteenth century, King Willem I was classically Erastian in religious matters, and Napoleonic in his enthusiasm for the coercive power of the state.[27] Later governments viewed the early socialist movement as potentially criminal, and in the decade of the 1880s used all the power of the state to shadow its adherents at home and abroad, to deny them meeting venues, government contracts and employment.[28]

In the twentieth century, proof that the Dutch could be illiberal in the most sinister way is provided by the long-running episode of the 'antisocial families'. These were groups of people first identified in 1914 because of the refusal on the part of landlords to rent them living accommodation, but the definition was rapidly expanded to include many kinds of 'social deviants' like alcoholics, child neglecters, criminals, sometimes the mentally deficient, and those guilty of 'immorality'. These people were rounded up, isolated, and placed in segregated districts (and later in separate settlements), where inspectors and other officials attempted to teach them how to live in a civilized society. At the height of this regime no less than 3 or 4 per cent of the population were involved, and the emphasis had shifted from a mild form of eugenics to a mighty civilization offensive, determined to inculcate in these 'deviants' the social and civic values of the bourgeois majority, right down to putting vases of flowers on the table.[29]

These suffocating bourgeois civilization offensives of the late nineteenth and early twentieth century add a revealing dimension to the tradition of liberty – indeed almost a negative image of social programming. Alcohol consumption plummeted as we have seen, as did illegitimate births, infant mortality and suicide rates.[30] The picture emerges of a safe, clean, respectable, hard-working, religious and highly moral society, which had its roots in developments in the later part of the nineteenth century. In the twentieth century the Dutch gained a reputation as 'the

[27] Wintle, *Pillars*, 12–15. See also Tamse and Witte, eds., *Staats- en natievorming*, 76–97.
[28] Charité, *De Sociaal-Democratische Bond*, 40–53.
[29] Dercksen and Verplancke, *Geschiedenis, passim*; on the definitions of 'anti-social' in terms of those with soiled linen, dirty and ill-equipped kitchens, and no plants or flowers, see p. 92. Not surprisingly, the more open thinking of the 1960s rejected all this behavioural prescription, and in 1971 the whole programme was abandoned.
[30] Van Zanden and Griffiths, *Economische geschiedenis*, 11–13; section 2.5 above.

moral nation'; the reasons for that seem to have centred around the effectiveness of the teaching of the churches, and the high levels of general prosperity and welfare provision, reducing risk and marginalization.[31] So while there was an important tradition of freedom of expression and religion, and a genuine concern with the legitimation of public office, it went hand in hand with occasional repression and coercion, and a high degree of self-regulation. This puts 'toleration' in a rather different light.

The other set of circumstances to do with the peculiarly Dutch development of tolerance has to do with vertical pluralism, or *verzuiling* (literally, pillarization).[32] Political scientists have had a special interest since the 1960s in observing the political culture and system of the Netherlands, and what has fascinated them is how such an apparently harmonious stability in the early twentieth century could have been achieved in a nation so obviously divided along denominational and ideological lines. The divergent Dutch seemed to have found a way of 'living apart together', which, if not the envy of the world, was felt to be a splendid object lesson for nations which manifestly could not live with themselves. (Sometime during the 1960s, the stability faltered and crumbled, and the mirror image of *verzuiling* occurred, which was in turn made an object of the social-science observing industry: depillarization, or *ontzuiling*.)

The literature on *verzuiling* is vast, and the academic commentators are very numerous (including several from abroad).[33] The concept was widely and publicly identified by Dutch socialist academics in the 1950s who were heartily sick of the compartmentalization of Dutch society into Catholic, Calvinist, socialist and liberal pillars, and wished to clear it all away;[34] in the international academic circuit the situation was brought to light by Arend Lijphart, in *The politics of accommodation*, first published in 1968. (A second edition, which included the concept of depillarization or *ontzuiling*, was published in 1975.[35]) In Lijphart's view, Dutch society in the early twentieth century was characterized primarily by vertical divisions based on religion or a secular ideology, rather than by horizontal divisions based on socio-economic status or class. Thus there was a Roman Catholic bloc, an orthodox Calvinist bloc, a socialist bloc, and a fourth neutral or liberal 'pillar'. Only the elite of each bloc came into contact with the world outside the pillar, which formed the second characteristic of the system: there was an overarching superstructure of

[31] Kok, *Langs verboden wegen*, especially chapter 8; and Kok, 'The moral nation'. See also section 12.4 below.
[32] The following section on *verzuiling* draws on material in Wintle, 'Pillarisation'.
[33] A list, in English, is provided in Bax, *Modernization*. See also Pennings, 'Verzuiling'.
[34] E.g., Kruijt, 'Sociologische beschouwingen'.
[35] Lijphart, *The politics of accommodation*.

government apparatus, made up of the political elites of each pillar, whose business it was to run the country through a succession of well-oiled compromises, in order that the rank and file of the pillars' followings would be able to live in virtually hermetically sealed isolation. The object was that Catholics could exist within an almost exclusively Catholic world, and indeed they attained a reputation in this period for being 'more Catholic than the Pope'. Dutch socialists, meanwhile, could lead a socialist life 'from the cradle to the grave'. Dutch orthodox Calvinists could exist in their own world, being born in a Calvinist maternity ward, attending a Calvinist nursery, primary and secondary school, a Calvinist college or university, joining Calvinist clubs, probably working for a Calvinist employer and joining a Calvinist trade union, voting for the Calvinist parties, listening to Calvinist radio, reading a Calvinist newspaper, entering a Calvinist retirement home and eventually being laid to rest in a Calvinist graveyard. Only the fourth pillar, the neutral or liberal one, was less internalized: it tended to be the place where those who could not be accommodated in the Calvinist, Catholic and socialist pillars ended up, and in that sense might even be referred to as a pile rather than as a pillar. Watching over all this was a benevolent and impartial government apparatus, in the widest sense, which performed the perhaps unpleasant but necessary task of regulating the very limited interaction between the pillars, making sure everything was shared out fairly, and running the central corporatist bureaucracy where the pillars were all represented according to the strict PR rules by which everything was done in Dutch society after 1917. In this model form, it was a very cosy and well-run system.

Lijphart's work has come under endless criticism in the last thirty years, but it still dominates the debate and is cited by every commentator who ventures into the field. Several have complained that the model did not adequately represent empirical reality.[36] Lijphart's analysis was an extension and systematization of the view of many Dutch commentators, for whom the emblem of the system was a classical portico, where the four ideological pillars of society both support and are held apart by a common pediment or roof, which represents the government and corporatist apparatus.[37] Later on, scholars refined and added to Lijphart's model, and in particular furnished it with some more historical respectability by emphasizing the typically Dutch aspects of this form of consociationalism.[38] The rationale behind the system was that the Dutch could not live

[36] E.g., Middendorp, *Ideology*, 266–7.
[37] E.g., Schöffer, 'Verzuiling'; and Goudsblom, *Dutch society*, 124.
[38] Summarized and continued by Bax, *Modernization*, 109–10 and 139; Bax admires Daalder's analysis.

together in an open society, because of their yawning chasms of ideological difference, which went back to the Reformation and beyond; therefore this contrived and artificial system had been devised in order to solve the impasse. What is more, it worked: the Dutch democracy was one of the most stable in the world up to the mid-1960s, allowing stupendous economic growth.[39]

This mechanistic analysis seemed a shade contrived for some scholars, especially those who took an implicitly Marxist approach. *Verzuiling* came about, they argued, not because the Dutch people could not live with themselves, but because the contending elites in Dutch society were successful in marshalling their support in that particular way.[40] For Siep Stuurman, for example, *verzuiling* was a device to maintain the status of the leaders of the confessional pillars against the forces of modernization and secularization, and as such it effectively delayed the emancipation of the working classes and of women in the Netherlands.[41] *Verzuiling* has therefore been represented as a form of social control, either in order to keep the warring ideological factions apart, or in order to keep the lower orders docile.

Some of the leading commentators have recently begun to express doubts about the explanatory power of the concept of *verzuiling*.[42] Part of the problem rests in a confusion of terminology: pillarization, consociation and corporatism are often discussed in the same context. All three are related, but not identical, and should not be used interchangeably with *verzuiling*.[43] Strictly defined, 'pillarization' refers to the organizations and institutions which proliferated around vertical or ideological groups from the later nineteenth century onwards: in politics, education, religion, welfare, leisure, and many other spheres. Then there is consociationalism (as systematized by Lijphart), where political stability is achieved in situations where groups of roughly equal status are pitted against each other ideologically, by means of proportional influence being allocated to all groups, according to a well-defined set of rules, rather than dominance for one group in a majoritarian, first-past-the-post system.

And then there is corporatism. It consists of interest groups making deals with government to take over certain parts of the state's activities, and participating in negotiation structures to devise and execute government policy. Unlike many countries with a strong corporatist tradition, the Dutch enshrined much of theirs firmly in legislation, more so than in

[39] Van Zanden and Griffiths, *Economische geschiedenis*, 15–16.
[40] Gladdish, *Governing from the centre*, 28.   [41] Stuurman, *Verzuiling*.
[42] See for example, Blom, 'Pillarisation'; De Rooij, 'Zes studies'; and Toonen, 'On the administrative condition of politics'.
[43] See Hemerijk, 'The historical fragility'.

Belgium for example. This corporatist tradition complemented *verzuiling*, and provided machinery for its working. In common with many of the centre-dominated democracies of Western Europe, the Netherlands was heavily influenced by a corporatist ethic from the early decades of the twentieth century up to the 1960s, and in many sectors the spirit (if not always the letter) of corporatism is still prevalent.[44] Economic and social planning and policy were both designed and executed from the 1920s onwards by committees of tripartite representation, involving delegates from the unions, the employers and independent experts. This kind of round-table approach to problem-solving was an essential part of the Dutch social and political fabric for much of the twentieth century, and was taking form towards the end of the nineteenth. It encouraged a state of mind inclined towards co-existence, or in other words towards (albeit rather negative) tolerance. This dovetailed in perfectly with a long tradition in Dutch politics on which many have remarked, and which E. H. Bax has articulated under the heading of 'living apart together'. He points to the geographical pluralism of the Republic, where each province was sovereign, making for a political culture based on compromise;[45] the strong local particularism present in congregationalist Calvinism may have caused great conflict over the centuries, but it also led to a realization that people were always going to be different, and that the only way to get along with one's neighbours, locational or denominational, was to be 'tolerant'. It was indeed the confessional parties growing up at the end of the nineteenth century which taught the dominant liberal groups the concept of pluralism, or *political* tolerance.[46] These maturing parties went on in the twentieth century to develop their skills in political 'accommodation' to a degree famous in the Netherlands.[47] Thus it is important to distinguish between these various concepts of pillarization, consociation and corporatism. All of them are close to *verzuiling* in the Dutch situation, but they are not identical, and need separating for purposes of analytical clarity.

In the end, *verzuiling* can mean one of two things. First it is simply the word in Dutch for the political-science model of consociationalism; alternatively it can signify the *specifically Dutch* form of that consociationalism or vertical pluralism, combined with pillarization and corporatism, which grew up towards the end of the nineteenth century and then served as the Dutch political culture for much of the twentieth.[48] The Dutch variant

---

[44] The most comprehensive works on Dutch corporatism are Verhallen, *et al.*, eds., *Corporatisme*; and Akkermans and Nobelen, eds., *Corporatisme en verzorgingsstaat*. See also Blok, *et al.*, eds., *Algemene geschiedenis der Nederlanden*, vol. XIV, pp. 236–42 for the pre-war period; and Gladdish, *Governing from the centre*, 138–40, on corporatism from 1945 to 1970.   [45] Bax, *Modernization*, 73–82.   [46] Fogarty, *Christian democracy*, 152.
[47] Lijphart, *The politics of accommodation* (1975), 103–21.
[48] Ellemers, 'Pillarization', admirably identified the difference between the model and the Dutch specificity.

was 'dynamically conservative', and was an institutionalized form of the age-old Dutch tolerance. It could not be installed as the dominant political culture until the coming of universal suffrage, for it was based upon the proportional equality of the pillars. It was partly the result of the preceding nineteenth-century emancipation of most of the groups involved. It was also fundamental in the process of nation-formation (see chapter 11), and in the generation of the modern Dutch liberal state we know today.[49] The ideological pillars expanded into the apparatus of the modernizing state, and in dividing up the cake they developed a way of 'doing business' which eventually became legislated into a host of written and unwritten rules, and defined Dutch political culture. Dutch historians and political scientists are right to question the explanatory power of *verzuiling*, and we should certainly not permit it to block out other important factors and agents in modern Dutch society. On the other hand, in the revision of what has perhaps been something of an obsession with *verzuiling* amongst Dutch scholars, there is considerable reason to counsel against over-reaction.

In all but a few of the most recent commentaries, *verzuiling* is held to be the most characteristic aspect of the Netherlands in the modern period. From the discussion above it is clear that, whatever the theoretical approach taken, *verzuiling* in the Netherlands represented some artificial and temporary state, occasioned either by self-inflicted isolation or by manipulative elites; Kossmann insists that it was a system generated by conflict, not by peaceful pluralism,[50] and that it was a necessary measure to 'calm the Dutch state of mind'.[51] Developing the idea of social control, Berting emphasized the way *verzuiling* could be and was used to control and regulate all new developments in society like education, the media, social services and everything else to do with mass politics.[52] We have seen that Dutch 'tolerance' has often been rather negative: it is certainly better than intolerance, and avoids much open hatred, but it was born of a necessity to live alongside people whose ideas one thinks are wrong, rather than of genuine, generous, spontaneous freedom. Dutch tolerance is damage limitation – the avoidance of unpleasantness and conflict; everyone must have his or her say, and the government and state apparatus will ensure that this is guaranteed with impartiality, according to the rules of proportional representation. All views will be registered, heard and filed away in their proper place. The safest way to deal with new threats to stability is to recognize them, incorporate them into the existing

---

[49] As I have argued elsewhere, in Wintle, 'The liberal state'.
[50] Kossmann, *De Lage Landen*, 436–7.
[51] ' . . . de Nederlandse mentaliteit dankzij de verzuiling tot rust was gebracht.' Kossmann, *De Lage Landen*, vol. II, p. 231.
[52] In Couwenberg, ed., *De Nederlandse natie*, 121.

pecking order, and give them a (proportional) voice. Everything is tolerated, everything has its right to influence the organic state.

There are echoes here of the Dutch Republican traditions of pragmatic
tolerance and of 'living apart together'; there are clear echoes of the
legalistic liberalism of Thorbecke, with his insistence that each individual
or group be permitted to add its voice. There are echoes of all the
traditions outlined in this chapter. But in surveying the history of this
kind of Dutch tolerance, as the sociologist J. A. A. van Doorn has
remarked, the most obvious and monumental manifestation was of
course *verzuiling*, for it was traditional tolerance legislated into a comprehensive system and adapted for mass politics: tensions could thus be
politically controlled, and it had the effect of a truce or cease-fire, if not of
a lasting peace.[53]

9.5   Conclusion

In this chapter we have covered the main political aspects of the changes
in the relations between the state and the individual in the nineteenth
century, in so far as they relate to authority and representation. The
Netherlands became a political democracy during the period in question,
changing from a near-autocracy in 1815 to a full parliamentary democracy in 1919 with universal suffrage. This brought most adults into direct
participation in the workings of the state. The liberals, in their various
guises, played a considerable role in these changes, emancipating the
individual with their economic and political reforms. But it was not a
simple Thorbeckian legend, and certainly bore very little relation to a
laissez-faire fairy tale. At the same time that the citizen was becoming
empowered, the state was burgeoning in the services it provided and in
the control it exercised over the people. Towards the end of the century,
the stirrings of *verzuiling* grew into a political system which was to
dominate the country for at least half a century. This form of inter-group
relationship, forming a buffer between the individual and the state, and
indeed increasingly taking over parts of the state's function, is best seen as
the culmination of the Dutch tradition of tolerance. That tolerance was
on the whole negative: it was grudging and used in self-defence, but it
enabled each group to survive and indeed to enjoy the fruits of emancipation. We shall follow the fortunes of these groups more closely in chapter
12; meanwhile, in chapter 10, the means employed to lock the Dutch into
this participatory structure will be examined: the growing state provision
of education and welfare services.

[53] Van Doorn, 'Schets van de Nederlandse politieke traditie', 38–40.

10 Education and welfare: empowerment and protection

10.1 Introduction

In this chapter we focus on those two stalwarts of the modern democratic European welfare state: education and social services. The theme of our approach will be, as in all the chapters in this part of the book, the changing relationship between the individual and society, the citizen and the state. Education was provided in increasing breadth and depth throughout the nineteenth century, but it was also the vehicle for a degree of national integration, and for the formation of ideological interest groups (or pillars) across the nation, like the orthodox Calvinists and the Roman Catholics. The embryonic welfare state, on the other hand, was a developing prototype of the situation current today, where one of the prime characteristics of the state is that it should provide services and protection for all, especially those who cannot do so fully for themselves.

10.2 Education

Education was a vehicle through which the state sought to expand its competences and reform the country, while at the same time it was a tool with which individuals and groups sought to defend their own way of life or ideology. Education was one of the great issues of the second half of the nineteenth century, especially for those with an overtly religious point of view. Nowhere was this more so than in the Netherlands, where the *Schoolkwestie* or Education Question was quite as important as the Social Question as a political divider.[1]

This importance was afforded to education across Europe for several reasons, all of them powerful. Industrialization in its broadest sense was ushering in a much more socially mobile society, and education was one of the more important criteria for ascent within it: the middle classes could hardly get enough of it, in the relatively meritocratic brave new world of the nineteenth century. Second, education is one of the

[1] Some of the following material on education draws on Wintle, 'Natievorming'.

conduits in society through which ideology is handed down. To perpe-
trate their creed, ideological groups needed to be able to exert some
control over their children's education. Conversely, education was the
place to launch fundamental change in society, for it was a battleground
for the minds of the young. Regimes with ideas of using the power of the
state to reform the population would naturally look to education to
implement their plans. The government's onslaught against Roman
Catholic education in the 1820s in the south of the country was indicative of a determination to remove the protective barriers sheltering some
parts of the population against the reforming power of the state.[2] Education was a perfect vehicle for centralization, for top-down nation-building by the state, and therefore a natural arena for reaction against such
initiatives, given the importance of education's ideological content to
confessional groups.

Furthermore, it was a matter of resources: the government's financial
commitment to state-funded education mushroomed as the century
went on. On primary education alone expenditure increased eightfold
from ƒ2.26m. in 1860 to ƒ17.64m. in 1900.[3] Total national expenditure
on education – by both private and public bodies – rose rapidly in the
second half of the century from 0.3 to 2.5 per cent of a rising national
product, especially in the 1870s. This was accounted for largely by
increasing participation in primary education, but secondary education
also began to attract resources from the state: within two years of the
Secondary Education Act in 1863, it was costing the country more than
its higher education programmes.[4] And as we have seen in chapter 4,
education was economically important: human capital was one of the
driving forces behind Dutch economic growth throughout the century,
and especially after 1850. Literate culture itself is a key element in
modernization.[5] Education was evidently extremely important, from a
number of angles.

In examining education in the nineteenth century, two particular
themes will occupy us here. One is to do with the expanding instruction
of the populace, for the most part at primary level but also in other
forms. This can be measured by such indicators as statistics on literacy;
it is to do with participation, modernization, the skills of the labour force
and economic advantage. The other theme is much more political, and
has to do with ideology, and the self-determination of certain groups in
the population: the key matter here was the religious content of the
education on offer.

[2] Wintle, *Pillars*, 62–3.   [3] *Jaarcijfers* (1895), 32 and (1901), 46.
[4] Van der Voort, *Overheidsbeleid*, 93–4 and 204.
[5] De Jonge, 'De industriele ontwikkeling', 91–2; Boonstra, *De waarde*, especially chapter 3.

Participation, literacy and skills

The French-influenced Batavian Republic brought in a number of important education measures, culminating in the 1806 Education Act, introduced by A. van den Ende (1768–1846), which formed the foundation of educational legislation for the rest of the century. In accordance with many of the laws of the period, it took the main responsibility for primary education out of the hands of voluntary, charitable and religious bodies, and made it the business of the state. There were some Latin and French Schools, and Athenaea and Gymnasia, but these forms of secondary education were very few and reserved for the sons of the political elite, as they had been under the *ancien régime*. In the general provision of primary education little changed after the 1806 reform until J. L. L. van der Brugghen (1804–63) brought in improved standards in his 1857 Act, together with an additional curriculum for those who might go on from primary to some form of secondary education. It may be something of a cliché, but it is as well to note the contribution of Calvinism to Dutch primary education, for the early nineteenth-century *Réveil* or Reawakening movement, which was strong in the Netherlands,[6] renewed Dutch interest in education as a means to fight the dangers inherent in mankind's fallen state. The importance attached in Calvinism to the members of a congregation actually reading and understanding the Bible was also important for literacy.[7] There were civil societies too, like the *Maatschappij tot Nut van 't Algemeen* (Society for the General Good), which were keen promoters of education in the early nineteenth century.

The 1806 Act did not introduce mandatory schooling for all children: it was left to the discretion of the parents, and school attendance only became universally legally required in 1901. However, a number of provinces, especially in the north, had regulations in place which effectively made primary school compulsory, and by 1900 the regional differences had in any case become very much eroded. In 1826 it is estimated that some 62 per cent of boys and 47 per cent of girls attended school in the Netherlands; by 1888 the figures had risen to 73 and 65 per cent respectively. By 1900 there was more than 90 per cent attendance.[8]

The results of this increase in participation were to be seen in the figures for literacy. There had long been relatively high standards of literacy in the Republic, and in the period 1813–19, 75 per cent of grooms and 60 per cent of brides were able to sign their names in the marriage

[6] On the *Réveil*, see Kluit, *Het Protestantse Réveil*; and Wintle, *Pillars*, 21–4.
[7] See Kruithof, *Zonde en deugd*.
[8] Knippenberg and De Pater, *De eenwording*, 136–9; Van der Voort, *Overheidsbeleid*, 98.

register, with such data concealing large regional variations.[9] As a result of
the national laws passed in the French period, together with the efforts of
the learned societies, the teachers, and particularly the Schools Inspectorate, by the mid-century considerable improvement had been registered.[10]
By 1890, 95 and 90 per cent of male and female newly weds respectively
were able to sign their names.[11] The records of military conscription
throw additional light on the subject: perhaps an education was unneces-
sary for cannon-fodder, but while 18.2 per cent of military conscripts in
1865 were illiterate, by 1895 only 5.4 per cent were obliged to sign with a
cross or mark instead of a written signature.[12] Modern quantitative studies have confirmed this picture: in 1800 the Netherlands was one of the
best-educated countries of Europe as defined by literacy, along with
Prussia, Scotland, Iceland and the Scandinavian countries. By mid-
century only about a quarter of the Dutch were illiterate, while more like a
half of Belgians were (more so in Flanders).[13] By the last quarter of the
nineteenth century the Dutch were still in the group of the most literate
peoples of Europe, along with the British, the French and the Belgians,
led by the Prussians.[14] Clearly there was a convergence between economic growth and literacy, whatever the direction of causation: in the
Netherlands, a relatively well-educated people had maintained and improved their literacy skills in the course of the century, representing a
considerable advance in human capital, and no doubt in terms of modernization and even of personal quality of life.

As for the skills represented, the primary schools dispensed reading,
writing, simple arithmetic, and some history and geography. In the secondary sector, the breakthrough came with legislation from Thorbecke's
liberal government in 1863, with a Secondary Education Act which set up
fifty Higher Burgher Schools (*hogere burgerscholen*), designed to produce
administrators and managers in business of all kinds. They taught such
new subjects as modern languages and science, and by the end of the
century had produced perhaps 10,000 graduates. Technical skills were
also improved in the second half of the century, with some 18,000
attending some kind of technical school in 1900, compared with 4,000 in
1860.[15] A good example is agricultural education, which had the potential
to enhance what was still the largest sector of the economy in employment
terms at the mid-century. There was an agricultural college founded in
Groningen in 1840, and the universities began free winter courses on

[9] Knippenberg and De Pater, *De eenwording*, 174–6. On literacy in the Republic, see Davids
and Lucassen, eds., *A miracle mirrored*, 229–83.
[10] De Bree, *Het platteland*, 52–74, 105–9 and 132.   [11] Boonstra, *De waarde*, 5.
[12] *Jaarcijfers* (1895), 33.   [13] Van der Woude, 'De alfabetisering', 256–72.
[14] Boonstra, *De waarde*, 21–2.   [15] Kossmann, *The Low Countries*, 414.

agricultural technology. In 1876 the National Agricultural College (*Rijks-landbouwschool*) was set up in Wageningen, and national agricultural and horticultural winter schools were founded in 1893 and 1896 respectively.[16] The universities remained reserved for the privileged elite, and functioned as nurseries for the pulpit and the bar. Leiden, Utrecht and Groningen had their statutes confirmed by Royal Decree of 1815, but their use of Latin strengthened their isolation from the rest of the country. There were two additional universities founded in Amsterdam in the 1870s: an Athenaeum was upgraded to the Municipal University in 1877 (now the University of Amsterdam), and the orthodox Calvinist Free University (initially very small) was set up there in 1878 by Abraham Kuyper and others to train suitably orthodox ministers for Reformed congregations. Other higher-education institutions had to wait until well into the twentieth century.[17]

The religious content of primary education

We have noted the importance of Van den Ende's Education Act of 1806, in transferring the main responsibility for primary education from the private sector to the state and from local to central government. As for its religious content, it was intended to be generally Christian but denominationally neutral; it was to be a school with the Bible, but one where Dutch children of all faiths could meet on equal ground. It is easy to see the nation-building elements of the 1806 Act. But although it was an important keystone in primary education, few religious groups were happy with it. Public money could go only to state schools, and the inspectorate was heavily biased in favour of Protestant teachers and indeed Protestant Bibles, which did not go down well with the Catholics (who were in a large majority from 1815 to 1830). Neither were orthodox Calvinists impressed: Christianity in these schools was not much more than a general code of ethics, with little or no doctrinal content. Increasing disquiet resulted in a commission of enquiry launched by Willem II, after the 1840 constitutional revision which had to follow the Belgian Secession had failed to address the issue. However, the resulting royal decree of 1842, permitting voluntary religious instruction after school hours for those who wanted it, again failed to satisfy any of the parties.[18]

[16] Koenen, *De Nederlandsche boerenstand*, 121–3; Sneller, 'Anderhalve eeuw', 107; Huizinga, 'De invloed van het onderwijs', 236–9.
[17] Verberne, *Geschiedenis van Nederland*, vol. VII, pp. 223–4.
[18] Knappert, *Geschiedenis der hervormde kerk*, vol. II, pp. 296–8; Verberne, *Geschiedenis van Nederland*, vol. VII, pp. 231–2 and 333–8; Rasker, *De Nederlandse Hervormde Kerk*, 94; Homan, 'Catholic emancipation', 202.

State-dominated education was clearly unsatisfactory for the confessional groups, but there was little agreement about which steps should be taken to address the situation. This was amply borne out in the controversy surrounding the 1857 Education Act, known as the *Schoolwetje*, which was necessary because of undertakings in the 1848 constitution to deal with the whole issue of education, undertakings which had not been fulfilled by Thorbecke's ministry before its fall in 1853. This measure was taken through parliament by the Calvinist Van der Brugghen, and indeed in its early stages the Bill proposed state subsidies for confessional schools in the private sector. This was not to the liking of the orthodox Calvinists such as G. Groen van Prinsterer (1801–76), who at that stage favoured state schools with a Calvinist ethic. An amendment, however, killed off the subsidies, and as a result once more no-one was satisfied: the liberals were unhappy, there was no funding for confessional schools, and Groen the Calvinist resigned his seat in Parliament. The state school was still 'neutral Christian', educational standards were improved somewhat, and although it became easier to found private confessional schools, there was no public funding for them.[19]

The next major law in respect of primary education was in 1878, the work of J. Kappeyne van de Copello (1822–95). It was largely a liberal restatement of the 1857 Act, but thereby denying any progress at all to the confessionals in more than twenty years. The controversy was immense, and the Bill was passed despite enormous confessional outrage and fury. Confessional schools had to do without subsidies, then, until 1889, when the first confessional government in the Netherlands, led by Baron A. Mackay (1838–1909), passed an Act which provided some government funding for teachers' salaries in all schools, whether state or private, as long as they complied with certain minimum standards of quality and size. Abraham Kuyper's ministry of 1901 to 1905 increased the subsidies to confessional education at all levels. It was only in 1917 that a satisfactory resolution was achieved, with the pacification settlement whereby each pupil carried with him or her an equal grant at all levels, regardless of creed. For well over fifty years, then, the education controversy had dominated domestic Dutch politics (as it had done in many other European countries), and in 1913 it was left to P. W. A. Cort van der Linden (1846–1935) to remark, when launching his conciliation initiative which was to lead to the 1917 'pacification' of the *Schoolkwestie*, 'The political battle over the schools issue is a wedge, so to speak, driven into our national life and splitting our nation into two nations.'[20]

---

[19] Schmal, *Tweeërlei staatsbeschouwing*, 141–2 and *passim*; Kossmann, *The Low Countries*, 292; Wintle, *Pillars*, 63–5.

[20] Cited in Lijphart, *The politics of accommodation* (1975), 110. See also Kossmann, *De Lage Landen*, 211.

Education: agent of radicalization and integration

In their study of the 'unification' of the Netherlands, Knippenberg and De Pater single out education policy in particular as a vehicle employed by centralizing governments concerned to stimulate what Ernest Gellner would have called a 'universal high culture'.[21] Obviously this did not pass without a reaction on the part of many who were inclined to resent the incursion of the state, and especially from those religious groups who felt their integrity threatened. In the 1820s the government's 'unificatory' education policy in the southern provinces was so deeply resented that it became one of the prime causes of the collapse of the United Kingdom of the Netherlands in 1830. In Kossmann's words, education policy 'utterly failed as a means of forming a new unitary nation'.[22] In the liberal heyday after the mid-century, the curriculum itself in the state schools was steered in a liberal and secular direction, for example with the introduction of natural history in 1863; this evoked great protest from certain confessional groups, who feared the encroachments of the Darwinian 'monkey business' into their children's education.[23] Increasingly antiliberal pronouncements from Rome had led Catholics to take a more openly hostile line against the state schools, culminating in an episcopal exhortation in July 1868 that Catholics should avoid sending their children to such establishments. In 1860, Groen and some supporters set up the Society for Christian National Education (*Vereeniging voor Christelijk Nationaal Onderwijs*), and in 1872 the Anti-Education Law League (*Anti-Schoolwet Verbond*) was founded by Jacob Voorhoeve (1811–81). The Calvinist Anti-Revolutionary parliamentary grouping,[24] now led by Abraham Kuyper, joined with the League to fight the 1874 elections, and went on to found together the Anti-Revolutionary Party, the country's first modern political party. We have seen that Kappeyne's Education Bill of 1878 evoked great opposition: of the near half-million petition signatories, about a third were Catholic. There is no doubt, then, that the state's attempts to impose uniformity and centralization through education legislation, both under Willem I and then later under the liberals, contributed directly to the raising of political awareness amongst great new swathes of the population, and in particular those with a confessional interest – of whatever denomination – in education.[25]

---

[21] Knippenberg and De Pater, *De eenwording*, 135–9; Gellner, *Nations and nationalism*, 35 and 89; see also Mijnhardt, 'Natievorming', 549; and Kossmann, *De Lage Landen*, 258.

[22] Kossmann, *The Low Countries*, 129.   [23] Hegeman, 'Darwin', 306.

[24] Called 'anti-revolutionary' because of its opposition to the principles of the French Revolution, its leading light had been Groen, and its philosophy – which was by no means a programme – was encapsulated in Groen van Prinsterer, *Ongeloof en revolutie*.

[25] Knappert, *Geschiedenis der hervordme kerk*, vol. II, p. 298; Lipschits, *De protestants-christelijke stroming*, 26–7; Van der Kroef, 'Abraham Kuyper', 331.

It can be argued that the education issue, which was principally about central control of education and its religious content, not only made certain groups of the population politically aware, but also radicalized them into action much faster than would otherwise have been the case. The historian Boogman believed that Groen used the education issue to break the Anti-Revolutionaries away from their links with the political conservatives in parliament – a direction continued by Kuyper. The failure of the petition movement against the Kappeyne law of 1878 drove many orthodox Calvinists into the politically active camp, with the realization that the only way of ending the discrimination against them was to organize politically and thereby achieve power; to lie low and adopt a humble attitude was simply not enough. Similarly, Roman Catholic outrage at the passing of Kappeyne's bill in 1878 was probably the most important factor in hauling them over the line from loose association with the liberals and conservatives to a close working alliance with the Anti-Revolutionaries in the 1880s.[26]

There is little doubt, then, that the *Schoolkwestie* performed the function of political awakener and radicalizer, even to the point of upsetting the rule of the traditional liberal local elites.[27] The control of the religious content of primary education was one of the most potent forces in the divorce of the northern and southern Netherlands in 1830, and continued to be a catalyst for political emancipation throughout the century. Government attempts to unite the country and build the nation through the medium of education were ultimately successful; however, the issue empowered many ordinary Dutch people for the first time, and many of them from the orthodox Calvinist and Roman Catholics groups used the empowerment to defend themselves from what they saw as the intrusive power of the state, in a way which eventually contributed crucially to the Dutch political culture of the twentieth century known as *verzuiling*. In this way education was a powerful influence on the changing relations between individual and society. In addition, the increase in school attendance and literacy was linked with important economic changes, in which the Dutch, without having a really leading technical education sector like Germany or Denmark, remained at the cutting edge of both economic development and literacy.

---

[26] Boogman and Tamse, eds., *Emancipatie*, 145–7; Hendriks, *De emancipatie*, 110–16; Thurlings, 'The case of Dutch Catholicism', 122.

[27] Of several examples of local studies illustrating this point, see Wintle, 'Natievorming', 20–1.

10.3   The state in service: the evolution of social legislation[28]

One of the defining features of the modern Dutch liberal state is its welfare provisions: alongside those in some Scandinavian countries, they are known to be the most generous in the world.[29] But in his account of the development of Western welfare states, A. de Swaan also pointed to the rather slow start of the Dutch version: his section is called 'a long fuse and a great bang'.[30] Kossmann reckoned that by 1914 the Netherlands was no longer backward in social legislation,[31] but a recent historian of Dutch poor relief, L. van der Valk, concludes that by 1940, there was church charity aplenty in the Netherlands, alongside limited social insurance for employees, but there was no state assistance to those who did not pay premiums, and as such the system was not very far down the road towards the modern welfare state.[32] The Dutch now have – despite swingeing cuts in the last two decades – a state which exists primarily to care for its citizens; what was the situation with regard to social services in the nineteenth century?

Poor relief [33]

In looking at the origins of any modern welfare state, one of the clearest trails to pick up is that of the poor-relief system. The Dutch Republic was noted for its provisions for the poor; some of the measures were punitive, and some were charitable, but the problem was certainly addressed. This has usually been attributed to the bourgeois wealth of the Republic, where the burghers had a great deal to lose from a poorly policed society. In the nineteenth century, the poor-relief system continued to function as 'central' strategy of social control by the middle and upper classes.[34] From the French Revolutionary era onwards, the classic debate was vigorously pursued about whether the state should take responsibility for the poor, or whether it should be left to private agencies, meaning the

---

[28] For the following, see section 2.6 above, on working conditions, and Wintle, 'The liberal state', 124–6. In the discussion on the welfare state, where much of the major legislation took place after the First World War and indeed after the Second, the treatment will be carried chronologically farther forward than in most of the other chapters of this book.

[29] In 1990, transfer payments and subsidies amounted to some 30 per cent of GDP, compared to an average of around 20 per cent in other OECD countries. *Netherlands*, OECD 1991/1992, 57.

[30] De Swaan, *In care of the state*, 210.   [31] Kossmann, *The Low Countries*, 500.

[32] Van der Valk, 'Poor Law', 114–16. See also Postma, 'Sociale zekerheid'.

[33] On the debate about government policy and poverty, see section 5.3; and on expenditure on poor relief, section 7.4. Mutual insurance societies were also important: see section 6.4 above, on other services.

[34] See Van Leeuwen, *Bijstand in Amsterdam*; and Van Leeuwen, 'Armenzorg'.

churches. The constitutions of 1798 and 1800 gave the state absolute centralized control; those of 1813 and 1815, which shaped the regime of the interventionist and statist Willem I, gave the state the role of overseer, although the work of the churches was also seen as essential. Paupers were declared, in an Act of 1818, to be the responsibility of the muncipality where they had been based for the previous four years; however, there were endless wrangles between the partially dispossessed churches and the new municipal poor boards.[35] The constitution of 1848 contained little on poor relief, but Thorbecke's Poor Law Bill of 1851 was a highly centralizing measure strengthening the role of the state. However, his ministry fell for other reasons before the Bill could be passed, and the Act of 1854 was a very different animal, leaving the state (through the municipalities of the paupers' *birth*) the role only of a safety net, to clear up those who fell through the hands of the church poor-relief boards. This was a classic *laissez-faire* measure, but not necessarily typical of Dutch liberalism as represented by Thorbecke. In 1870 the Act was amended to transfer civil responsibility for paupers from the place of birth to the place of most recent residence; these were seen as essentially police measures against the poor, rather than as attempts to address the problem of poverty itself.[36] In practice at local level this often led to some very complicated relationships between the various church poor-boards and the municipal one, all yoked together in often awkward disharmony.[37]

The role of the churches was maintained in the next major Poor Law, of 1912, the product of a confessional government, which still viewed poor relief as charity provision by the churches in the first place; a structural approach to the causes of poverty and an active role on the part of the state to combat them were not part of the package. The 1912 Act stayed in force until 1963, when it was replaced by the General Income Support Act (*Algemene Bijstandswet*), which formed one of the main planks in the modern Dutch welfare state platform. So between 1854 and 1963, the state's role was subservient to handouts from private charity.[38]

However, there were mitigating factors. First, work creation programmes in the Netherlands had always impressed visitors, from the time of the Republic onwards, and later there were workhouses (*armenfabrieken*) under Willem I in the 1820s and 1830s, usually producing low-grade textiles for the closed colonial market. After the 1854 Act there was work creation for an estimated 13,500 people, and it continued in some

[35] Smit, 'De armenwet', 218–23; Berger, *Van armenzorg*, 46–54.
[36] Berger, *Van armenzorg*, 64–74; see also Douwes, *Armenkerk*, 61–5.
[37] E.g., Wintle, *Zeeland and the churches*, 182.
[38] Van der Valk, 'Poor Law', 100–3. See also Postma, 'Sociale zekerheid', 198–200; and De Groot and Schrover, eds., *Women workers*, 14–18.

degree for the rest of the century.[39] Second, these issues were continually the subject of very wide ranging public debate, both in parliament, and especially in countless pamphlets in which seemingly every thinking man (very few women) expressed their considered views.[40] The point to be taken is that although for a century the Dutch poor-relief system was charity based, this was a product of political circumstance where the confessional interest managed to prevail over very strong political feeling from the other side. The failure of Thorbecke's 1851 Bill is a prime example of this kind of fortuity. The increasing strength after the mid-century of the confessionals in Dutch politics must explain the persistence of the *caritas* ideal, and it should also be borne in mind that the provisions of the churches, although charity based, were often pretty comprehensive. The confessional governments prior to the First World War were bent on setting up a real welfare system, but were equally determined to do so on a pillarized basis, so that each church or other organization could provide for its own. Dutch legislation, then, may have been slow (as Van der Valk complains) to adopt the state-assistance characteristics of the modern welfare state, but that does not mean that the issues were not constantly discussed, or that provisions were by any means miserly.

Labour laws and industrial arbitration

Comprehensive labour laws were similarly late to get off the ground in the Netherlands: the 1874 Child Labour Act was the first, and it was largely ineffective. Some of the worst offences against personal health, in the field of working conditions, had been substantially eradicated by 1914 (section 2.6). Nonetheless, in 1900, the Labour Inspectorate reported the presence of the following eye-opening notice nailed above the entrance to a straw-cardboard factory: 'The workers are warned not to speak with their wives about the factory. Men whose wives are found talking about the factory will be immediately sacked, and will not be reinstated.'[41]

In 1897 the Social Liberals took office, and began to prepare the foundations for the modern Dutch welfare state. Their major achievement was an Industrial Accidents Act (*Ongevallenwet*, with elements of workmen's compensation) of 1901, which had to be implemented in the teeth of uproarious entrepreneurial opposition.[42] In 1897 Chambers of

---

[39] Berger, *Van armenzorg*, 222–6.
[40] These debates have been studied by a number of authors, for example De Vrankrijker, *Een groeiende gedachte*; Butter, *Academic economics*; and Van der Valk, 'Poor Law'.
[41] 'Ervaringen onzer arbeidsinspectie', 14.
[42] Van der Valk, 'Poor Law', 105–8; De Swaan, *In care of the state*, 212.

Labour (*Kamers van Arbeid*) had been formed in an attempt to regulate matters of social legislation and insurance. They were not a great success, and were modified into Labour Boards by the confessional government in 1913, to be finally abolished by the Labour Disputes Act of 1923. In spite of their limited success, they were essential as a prototype of the state-sponsored negotiating apparatus which was to grow into a great corporatist machine between the wars and in the post-war period. The confessional government before the First World War introduced a welter of legislation setting up a Christian social policy; many of the bills were scotched, but again the issue was constantly in discussion, and the infrastructure continued to grow. Numerous 'councils' were set up in the early twentieth century, the most famous of them being the High Council of Labour (*Hoge Raad van Arbeid*) in 1919, in which there was tripartite representation of labour, the employers and government-appointed independent experts. These councils were advisory bodies, but increasingly were recruited to assist with the execution of policy, and were given a public-law and statutory task to fulfil. It was the beginning of the mighty Dutch corporatist state.[43]

Corporatism was launched by the Social Liberals in the 1890s, and taken up by the Protestants in the decade before the First World War, by the Catholics in the 1920s and by the Socialists in the 1930s; by the time of the Second World War there was a general consensus (which included even most of the entrepreneurial interest) that the country should be run in that consultative consensual way. Its structures based on proportional representation of all parties served to feed in the views of all the disparate groups to the planning process, and increasingly also to distribute in an even-handed manner the social goods provided by the burgeoning state – the welfare state. It was an operational technique akin to the Dutch variety of tolerance: it limited conflict and made life possible.

Public expenditure

Nowadays the Netherlands leads the world in the share of its national income channelled through the state in one form or another.[44] This huge government superstructure did not come about without a debate over its merits, and there was incessant discussion about the proper level of public expenditure for much of the nineteenth century.

King Willem I had ambitious and controversial infrastructural plans

---

[43] See for example Valkhoff, 'Vermaatschapelijking', 273–8; and Verhallen, *et al.*, eds., *Corporatisme*. On the Labour Chambers and Boards, see Kossmann, *The Low Countries*, 499–501. On the growth of employment-based insurance, see Postma, 'Sociale zekerheid', 204–6.

[44] In 1981 it stood at 67 per cent. 'Ruffles', 17.

which forced up public expenditure (section 5.3). However, from 1850 onwards government expenditure still rose, despite the reputation of the liberals for 'small government'. As a percentage of the rapidly rising national income, government spending did not increase until after the outbreak of World War I; indeed it fell until 1873.[45] The increasing 'osmosis' of society and the state, resulting in the present 'societal state', with its huge public sector and welfare provisions, can be dated from the liberal constitution of 1848.[46] This 'socialization' of the Dutch state continued apace in the twentieth century, with the dialogue between the public and private sector becoming more and more intimate, and the two-way communication of advice, consultation, investment and regulation increasing all the time.[47] Sometimes the growth in the machinery of the state has been rapid, and at times in the twentieth century it has been less so; the secular trend has been inexorably ascending.[48] Still, before World War I Dutch government expenditure as a percentage of GDP was low (8.2 per cent in 1913) compared to other countries (though by 1960 it was a leader in the field, with 36.1 per cent).[49]

The beginnings of a welfare state

In simplified schematic terms, the build-up of the early Dutch welfare state was as follows.[50] After a decade of debate on the Social Question (the social consequences of industrialization) into which socialists, Protestants and Catholics all had positive input, ironically it was the Liberals who passed the landmark Industrial Accidents Act in 1901. Calvinist Christian Democrat plans for a comprehensive set of social reforms, provided by the Minister of Agriculture, Trade and Industry A. S. Talma (1864–1916), consisted of Acts on old-age and invalidity pensions and health insurance, but after their passage in 1913 their implementation was interrupted by the First World War. Only the old-age pensions were actually set up (in 1919), and comprehensive regulation of the other concerns of the future welfare state had to wait until the ravages of the 1930s and the Second World War had shown the hopeless imperfections and numerous casualties of the free market when assisted only by a safety net of charity. A similar trajectory was shared by health-related benefits, which were addressed by a General Health Service Act (*Ziektewet*) passed by Talma in 1913, but not implemented until 1930 because of disagree-

---

[45] Klein, 'Het bankwezen', 137; Klein is partially contradicted by a more recent study: Van der Voort, *Overheidsbeleid*, especially p. 67.
[46] Kraemer, *The societal state*.   [47] Valkhoff, 'Vermaatschapelijking', 276–7.
[48] Van Holthoon, ed., *De Nederlandse samenleving*, 283–304.
[49] A. Maddison's figures, quoted by Bax, *Modernization*, 151.
[50] A factual account is provided in Van Holthoon, ed., *De Nederlandse samenleving*, 187–202. On the role of trade unions, see also Van Leeuwen, 'Trade unions'.

ment about whether it should be administered by a central state apparatus or by private (religious) organizations. The 1930 compromise put it in the hands of separate boards for each industry. Thereafter the Dutch fell into line with other North European democracies. During the Second World War the government in exile in London held discussions about post-war welfare plans, and in 1945 and 1946 Britain's Beveridge plans were taken over and adjusted to the Dutch situation by a committee chaired by A. A. van Rhijn. From then on the structure grew to become what it is now.

Clearly there were elements of social control in the evolution of these provisions, as there undoubtedly are in the present high-level welfare state. Social policy is in itself partly designed to reduce tension, and the effect of the support rather than the rejection of potentially marginal groups is to integrate them into society, rather than to alienate them.[51] The present Dutch welfare state is at least in part a product of the desire to minimize conflict and to live together in a civil society. In the Republic, visitors were impressed with the level of provision for the poor and other socially disadvantaged groups. This is often interpreted purely in terms of social control; Simon Schama posits that there was a 'feel-good' factor involved as well, for charity justified wealth in the Dutch mind of the Republic.[52] In the nineteenth century, and especially in the twentieth, the 'control' has been directed at even-handed conflict-minimization without the benefit of any particular group in mind. In this sense the welfare state has been similar in its development to that of the democratic system, and of tolerance.

10.4   Conclusion

In this unfolding saga of the relations between the individual, interest groups and the state, the commitment of the state to provide services made the critical leap at the time of the 1848 liberal constitution, while the implementation took a century to complete. Not for nothing, then, is Thorbecke called the father of the modern Dutch state. Public expenditure was rising from the mid-century onwards, despite our preconceptions about liberalism in government, which was replaced towards the end of the century by confessional administrations ready and willing to oversee the co-ordination of what was to become a welfare state, with the government in partnership with private-sector providers. Ideologically and financially, then, the Dutch were committed early to the idea of the state in service.

[51] Couwenberg, ed., *De Nederlandse natie*, 113.
[52] Schama, *The embarrassment of riches*, 576–7.

11   Loyal subjects: state formation and nation formation

11.1   Internal colonization: the osmosis of state and nation

Nationalism and national identity are once more at the top of our agenda, while state formation has been there for some time.[1] State building is to do with structures in international and national law, constitutions, and infrastructure; the second, nation building, is more to do with culture and consciousness, with sentiment and perception. Nation and state are not the same, but in the course of the nineteenth century the two grew towards each other, and as the state expanded the citizen began to identify more with the state through the nation; 'nationalism' can therefore be seen as the desire to achieve confluence between state and nation.[2] Once the structure of the state is externally determined, attempts are made to realise the new structure internally as well as externally. Especially in a country with such strong traditions of local particularism as the Netherlands, there were considerable reactions against the imposition of a centralized state unity, and successive governments found it necessary to penetrate society by reforms in government, law, finance, infrastructure and defence. In order to make these reforms which intruded upon local positions acceptable and permanent, in the words of Coen Tamse and Els Witte, governments pursued 'a nation-building policy through education, use of a national language, an Erastian church policy, control of the press, army recruitment, and patronage'.[3] The Patriot Movement of the late eighteenth century, and especially the Batavian Republic of 1795–1806, made vigorous attempts in this direction. The governments of Willem I continued, but failed signally in their task, being rewarded with the Belgian Revolution, reminding us that neither state nor empire is likely to be imposed permanently if there is no *successful* campaign of persuasion that the imposed values are acceptable and bear some rela-

---

[1] The following draws on Wintle, 'Natievorming'; and Wintle, ed., *Culture and identity*.
[2] Knippenberg and De Pater, *De eenwording*, 14; Leerssen and Van Montfrans, eds., *Borders and territories*, 3.
[3] Tamse and Witte, *Staats- en natievorming*, 16–17. My translation.

tionship to reality. External circumstance continued to be important to the further definition of the state: examples are the Belgian Revolution and its attendant Ten-Day military campaign, the threat inherent in Franco-Prussian rivalry after the mid-century, the pretensions of the Vatican under Pio Nono and, most obviously, the challenge thrown down to the Dutch state by the New Imperialism at the end of the century. All these things continued to confirm the Dutch state and stimulate the Dutch nation from outside, and we shall examine some of them more closely in section 11.2.

The progress of nation formation, on the other hand, was more subtle: a largely internal and cultural process, on the road to a common perception of the Dutch nation more or less in tune with the Dutch state. By the 1890s, the Dutch were fully behind the state in its entanglements in the imperialist imbroglio, their Orangist sentiments were almost universal, and they conformed fully to Gellner's typology of 'integral' nationalist feeling, coinciding with the phase of full-scale industrialization.[4] Throughout the century there were central attempts to impose what Gellner calls a 'universal high culture', assisted by an army of willing civilizers anxious to create a uniform language and spelling, an improved and standardized education, and generally shared concepts of cultural behaviour.[5] In the years 1813–15, for example, the restoration government set about inspiring the Dutch people by presenting 'the fatherland as a moral community of pious and righteous citizens', with a series of national prayer and thanksgiving days.[6] These 'civilization offensives' took place as early as the second half of the eighteenth century, continued throughout the nineteenth century, and reached a deafening crescendo in what must have been a suffocating bourgeois offensive in the early part of the twentieth century. At the same time, however, and inextricably linked to the top-down initiatives, local movements towards national identity and consciousness took place, with more and more previously uninvolved ordinary people taking part in the celebration of the nation, and moving towards a definition of their own community, class or ideology group in terms of the national past, present, and future. There was a celebration of the nation's history of great cultural achievements, manifested in such events as founding a national art gallery in the Huis ten Bosch in The Hague in 1800, and the Rijksmuseum itself a few years later (the present building by P. J. H. Cuypers (1827–1921) in Amsterdam, constructed in the 1870s and 1880s, is also a powerful icon of national sentiment). In

---

[4] Gellner, *Nations and nationalism*.
[5] Gellner, *Nations and nationalism*, 35–39; and Knippenberg and De Pater, *De eenwording*, chapter 6.
[6] Van Rooden, *Religieuze regimes*, 103.

similar vein were the erection of statues of William of Orange, a celebration of the cult of the national artist Rembrandt, and the admission to respectability of the philosopher Spinoza. This kind of 'cultural nationalism' extended to the celebration of Dutch music and poetry, a certain sentimentality over folklore and costume, the development of a national architecture, and the commemoration of past religious achievements, not confined to those of the Calvinists.[7]

We have, therefore, one distinction between state formation and nation formation, and another between the top-down and bottom-up aspects of the latter.[8] This framework allows us to place a number of developments in the history of the country in the context of nation and state building, and to locate developments in the framework of the nation-building process as a whole. Important strands in that framework are constitutional definitions of the state of the Netherlands by both internal and external authorities, the centralization or unification of the Dutch state carried out after the imposition of a generalized unitary constitutional order at the beginning of the nineteenth century, and the introduction of a national political system, with gradually increasing participation on a uniform basis across the country (see section 9.2). Taxation also played an essential role, as we have seen in section 5.3. Meanwhile a cultural acceptance of this unity was reinforced by changes in education, metrology and currency, while keen proselytizers spread the bourgeois message through the civil society and charity networks, led by the Society for the General Good (the '*Nut*').

It is important to recognize that there were many different forms of Dutch national feeling in the nineteenth century, and therefore several different forms of national identity.[9] Very few people harboured national feelings in the sense of identifying with the Dutch nation *as a whole*. There was evidently no single nationalism, and indeed nationalism is always multi-faceted. Feelings of loyalty and identity are often infinitely varied about the same nation. The identity of an individual is always multi-layered and complex, involving identification with and allegiance to any number of institutions which can and often do conflict with each other, such as gender, family, class, territory, religion and race. And so with collective identity.[10] If we look at the nature of public pronouncements of national feeling on the part of the active religious groups in the second half of the nineteenth century, then they are so separate and so different that it is almost a wonder that the Netherlands did not become

---

[7] 'Civil initiatives to monumentalize an assertedly illustrious past'. Bank, *Het roemrijk vaderland, passim*; quotation from p. 9.
[8] Van Sas, 'De mythe Nederland', 9.   [9] Van Sas, 'Varieties of Dutchness'.
[10] Smith, *National identity*, 4–7.

a late twentieth-century Belgium, increasingly and irrevocably split into vertical groups, with the only true nationalist in the country, in the sense of being genuinely identified with the country as whole, being the king. J. A. Bornewasser, in examining the nationalistic feelings of Dutch Catholics around 1845, declared that they never enjoyed a *national* religious movement at all in the nineteenth century.[11] The Great-Protestant Netherlands movement was nationalist and Orangist, but fiercely anti-Catholic, as was shown in the April Movement of 1853, which evoked passions strong enough to bring down the government of the day. In turn, Kuyper's nationalist rhetoric was deeply coloured with orthodox Calvinist particularism and indeed was self-consciously so: it held little appeal for anyone who did not share his religious beliefs.[12] Dutch polemicists and publicists had no hesitation in singling out a particular group as being the 'essence' or 'backbone' of the nation.[13] In the transition from the local particularism of the elite in the Republic, to the mass national identity of the twentieth century, the most remarkable development was not the common ideology, but the *integration* of a number of particularist and party-based national identities into an all-embracing national feeling and awareness. Religious groups from all the various shades of orthodox Protestantism (Calvinist and otherwise), Catholics and Old Catholics, Jews and (come to that) free-thinkers, discovered their nation-wide identity and formed institutions and pressure groups to strengthen their group identities and their places in the nation and in the national traditions. Other non-religious groups followed the same route, for example socialists, women and (later in the twentieth century) immigrants, all seeking and locating their position within the framework of the national identity.

National feeling was hardly invented in the nineteenth century: many of its roots lay in the eighteenth,[14] and there is no doubt that, despite the Dutch Republic of the *ancien régime* being a very disparate political entity, with 'regional culture' generally having a much stronger character than any national equivalent, at elite level there existed a national Dutch consciousness. Orangist and anti-Orangist pamphlets could command wide-ranging support in the eighteenth century, but what subsequently occurred during the nineteenth century was that these generally elite-based national feelings were worked out, enlarged, embroidered, multiplied, and above all extended to a much wider public than was politically

---

[11] Bornewasser, 'In 1845 een Nederlandse Ronge?', 223 and 238.
[12] Van Koppen, *De Geuzen*, especially pp. 233–4; see also Schutte, *Het Calvinistisch Nederland*.
[13] Te Velde, 'The debate', 89.
[14] Mijnhardt, 'Natievorming', especially p. 553; see also Van Sas, 'Varieties of Dutchness', 10.

active or aware during the French period or Republic.[15] To a degree, then, the subject under consideration here, taking place in the nineteenth century, was the fuller implementation of something which already existed at elite level. As in so many other aspects of history, the nineteenth century was one of gradual democratization, consisting of an extension of political activity to the majority of people, rather than being exclusive to a narrow elite in the metropole.[16] It is this process of extension of national awareness and national identity – and by no means a single, uniform awareness or identity – that we shall observe through an account of the route taken by certain religious groups towards a national self-awareness.

Government policy in religion-related matters had alienated many in a range of denominations; first the reactions were against the Erastian policies of Willem I and his government in the mainstream Calvinist church (the *Nederlandsche Hervormde Kerk*), the intolerance shown to orthodox Calvinist secessionists, and the persecution of Catholics because of their refusal to allow the state into their schools. Then, in the second half of the century, many Calvinists were infuriated by the liberal state's insistence on the separation of church and state, and as we have observed (in section 10.2), by its refusal to propagate the true faith through state-sponsored Christian education. Many others, especially Catholics, were also alienated by the liberal tendency to deny public money to religious schools. Religion was certainly under threat, with many of its traditional functions being usurped by the state, and by professional bodies of medics, academics, social workers and politicians; the reply on the part of the orthodox Calvinists and Roman Catholics to this threat was to organize themselves politically and defend their turf with vigour.[17] Van Miert has pointed out that, in the *Nederlandsche Hervormde Kerk* at least, a number of changes in church order in the early and mid-century, like the *Algemeene Reglement* of 1816, and especially the changes in 1867 to procedures for elections to the parish council or *kerkeraad*, allowed lower-middle-class Calvinists increasing influence in church affairs at local level. In the Catholic Church that increase of participation by relative newcomers to the politics of religion came about as a result of the erosion of the power of traditional local elites at the hands of the new episcopal hierarchy installed in 1853.[18] In addition the improvements in communication networks, especially the cheap daily newspaper, very much assisted the organization and mobilization at

[15] This extension of national feeling from elite to mass level in the nineteenth century is one of the themes of Hobsbawm, *Nations and nationalism*.

[16] See Knippenberg and De Pater, *De eenwording*, 34–8.

[17] For a case-study of this process in the province of Zeeland, see Wintle, *Zeeland and the churches*, 104–32, and especially p. 214.

[18] Van Miert, 'Verdeeldheid en binding', especially pp. 673–6.

national level of these new participants, as one of the most powerful manipulators of public opinion of the day, Abraham Kuyper, readily admitted. He reckoned the cheap daily to be more important than the invention of printing itself, and identified the crucial function as being the creation of a sense of unity ('*gemeenschap*') in the lives of individuals. The press could give, he declared, a lead and 'direction to public opinion', though he was quick to add that he, as an editor, would never dream of attempting such a thing (Plate 5).[19] With the help of such technological developments in the media, then, the issues of religion and education gave rise to a host of new political impulses in the country amongst a wider constituency than had previously been interested in national politics over a sustained period.

As this activity on the part of religious groups gained pace, they began to develop a nation-wide identity or self-consciousness, perhaps for the first time. Peter van Rooden is at pains to point out that the *volksdelen* or ideological divisions of the Dutch nation (the Catholics, the orthodox Calvinists, the socialists and the liberals, all to become 'pillars' in due course) were actually constructed in the course of the nineteenth century, rather than having existed for time immemorial.[20] The best-documented case is that of Kuyper's orthodox Calvinists or *Gereformeerden*, moulded by the master-manipulator from a disparate collection of disgruntled and marginalized local groups into a national force with an identity, self-consciousness and sense of mission, both national and international, which could take part in government in 1888 and dominate it from 1901 onwards. Kuyper certainly drew on earlier images from the Calvinist identity which had pertained during the Republic, but remodelled them extensively according to the needs of the late nineteenth century.[21] His 'vision of the Dutch nation' was a particular one which centred on the Calvinist values and virtues. Kuyper constructed it and publicized it through his newspaper *De Standaard*, and it was immensely important for the emancipation of his orthodox Calvinist followers. However, his nationalism was nothing like the patriotic nationalism of, for example, the liberals.[22] Kuyper sometimes differentiated between the Dutch people (*volk*), by which he meant *his* people, and the Dutch nation, by which he meant all the Dutch, but he generally confused the two, and conflated *the* nation into *his* Calvinist nation or people, which had a Calvinist mission in the world, for example in South Africa, and in the Ethical Policy in the

[19] Kuyper, 'De rede', 179–81.
[20] Van Rooden, 'Studies naar locale verzuiling', 439–52.
[21] Brunt, 'Over gereformeerden', 55; Schutte, *Het Calvinistisch Nederland*, 20–2; see also Schutte, 'Nederland: een Calvinistisch natie?'
[22] Kuiper, *Zelfbeeld*, 243–6.

East Indies.[23] This highly manufactured national identity of the followers of Kuyper was quintessentially Calvinist, but in no way could it be described as a modern nationalism for the whole of the Dutch nation: it was the national identity of a specific part of the nation.[24]

It was of course not only the Calvinists who were busy constructing their own particular Dutch national identity; the Catholics did so as well. The Catholic revival or emancipation in the Netherlands from 1795 onwards allowed and indeed made necessary a whole process of identity construction and metamorphosis which would transform them, as the orthodox Calvinists were being transformed, from a marginalized and discriminated group to a powerful part of the nation, partaking in authority and government at every level in almost every part of the country. The restoration of the episcopal hierarchy in 1853 was of critical importance in legitimating a whole range of Catholic activities. P. Raedts has written on 'the process of forming an identity by means of reconstructing the Middle Ages', by which he means the reinterpretation by Dutch Catholics, like J. A. Alberdink Thijm (1820–89) and others, of the heroic Catholic period in early Dutch history, as opposed to the relatively repressed one since the Reformation.[25] There were an estimated ten Catholic churches built every year after the 1853 restoration,[26] and Thijm and his brother-in-law the architect P. J. H. Cuypers developed the neo-gothic style as an emblem of the Catholic revival.[27] Catholics also created a national identity for themselves in all sorts of other ways, in their rituals and ceremonials, and in their attitudes to current political and social problems, such as the position of the Holy See around the turbulent year of 1870, and in respect of the great Social Question addressed in the 1891 encyclical *Rerum Novarum*.[28] But these national identities, whether Catholic or Calvinist, were specifically Catholic or Calvinist, and not universally Dutch. We are dealing not with a single, shared national identity, but with a number of quite separate identities, tailor-made for the needs of the groups for which they were developed.

The same could be said of local nationalism, or rather of the participation of various regional populations in the cultural exercise of nationalism. Van Miert sees the general nationalism of the early part of the nineteenth century as being linked mainly to the traditional elite, which was made up, especially at local level, of liberals in the widest sense of the word.[29] The power position of these local liberal elites was challenged by

[23] Van Koppen, *De Geuzen*, 232–3.   [24] Kossmann, 'Some questions', 12.
[25] Raedts, 'Katholieken op zoek'.   [26] Van Leeuwen, *Honderd jaar Nederland*, 257.
[27] Van der Woud, 'Ondergang en wederopstanding van de neogotiek', 738.
[28] See for example Wintle, 'Something for everyone'.
[29] Van Miert, 'Verdeeldheid en binding', 685–7. Kossmann would agree with him: Kossmann, 'Some questions', 12.

the rise of confessional groups, and they responded by banging their own nationalist drum, and also by building more of a national identity at local level by celebrating national festivals, but with an increasingly local 'spin' to them, involving a wider and deeper section of the local population than ever before.[30] On the other hand, in the long run the state-building and nation-building processes were highly damaging to localism and regional variety in the Netherlands, as in most other countries. The Republic was home to a very strong tradition of local loyalties, especially to the towns, but also to regions or provinces. The Dutch *doyens* of the national integration process, Knippenberg and De Pater, refer to this erosion of regional differences in language, literacy, folk culture, demographic traits, political attitudes and religious behaviour as nothing less than a 'cultural revolution', with all the connotations of wanton destruction that those words have carried since the 1960s.[31] A study of Groningen has documented the inroads made by bourgeois cultural offensives against local folk festivals and practices in the nineteenth century.[32] In its negative sense, Gellner portrayed the triumph of 'the nation' in the following words:

It is the establishment of an anonymous, impersonal society with mutually sub-stitutable atomized individuals, held together above all by a shared [universal high] culture of this kind, in place of a previous complex structure of local groups, sustained by folk cultures reproduced locally and idiosyncratically by the micro-groups themselves.[33]

Finally, there is an intimate connection between nation formation and *verzuiling* in the Netherlands. With the exception of the liberals, who were on the defensive, the various other groups evolving their own national identity were involved in some form of emancipation struggle. Their nation-building efforts were much to do with creating a location for themselves within the framework of the nation at large; it was a search for legitimation, for a just and recognized place for themselves as an active, important, but unique part of the Dutch nation, past, present and future.[34] Not only was there pluralism of national identity, but there was convergence, fostered by the culture of 'living apart together' in the nation. Each group demanded a mutual respect as a *part* of the nation, or

---

[30] Van Miert, 'Nationalisme'; and Van Miert, 'Confessionelen en de natie'. See also De Jong, 'Dracht en eendracht', which shows how traditional (local) dress was used in the nineteenth century to promote *national* feelings.

[31] Knippenberg and De Pater, *De eenwording*, chapter 6; quotation from p. 191.

[32] Sleebe, *In termen van fatsoen*, especially chapter 6. See also, on Friesland, Jensma, *Het rode tasje*.

[33] Gellner, *Nations and nationalism*, 57.

[34] Van Sas, 'De mythe Nederland', 18; Van Miert, 'Nationalisme', 62.

volksdeel.[35] National identity assisted the process of *verzuiling* by providing a common concept, even if the content of the concept differed considerably from group to group. The whole process of *verzuiling* came about in order to locate new participants in political and other power in the national framework; when that adjustment had taken place, *verzuiling* fell away. National identity played its part in that locating process. *Verzuiling* and the evolution of Dutch national identity were mutually complementary, and indeed part of the same process.

11.2   The nation abroad

After the state had been forged mainly by external forces and was enshrined in the constitutions of 1813–15 and 1840, we have seen the government labouring to increase the internal coherence of the new unitary creation, and various agencies concerned to promote the concept of the Dutch nation within it; thus the two concepts of nation and state drew closer and closer together in the course of the century. One manifestation of this development was the behaviour in foreign affairs of the young kingdom.

The formation of any human identity, individual or collective, is made up of a number of complex internal processes, but it is also heavily dependent upon the location and selection of a collection of opposites or 'others', against which the identity can be set. Some of these were internal – the persecuted orthodox Calvinist Seceders in the 1830s, Catholics during the No-Popery riots of the early 1850s, the 'gypsies' especially after 1868,[36] and so on. But outside its borders the process of nation formation in the Netherlands also sought its 'others'. This was a complicated matter, and the subtle differences which the Dutch imagined they noticed between themselves and the Germans or the English (let alone the Belgians) were all part of the construction of Dutch identity in the nineteenth century. In addition, colonial activities were evidently crucial, and the literary output generated by the East Indies experience was some of the finest of the century, as witnessed by the work of Multatuli and Louis Couperus, to take just two examples. Such writers, together with officers in the colonial army, officials in the Indies civil service, missionaries, academics, teachers and many others all played their part in the Dutch version of the construction of an 'Orientalism', in the way that Edward Said has shown took place through French and English writings at this time.[37] The Dutch position *vis-à-vis* South Africa and the West

[35] Te Velde, 'The debate', 90.   [36] On 'gypsies' see section 12.5 below.
[37] Said, *Orientalism*. On this process amongst the Dutch, see Gouda, *Dutch culture overseas*, especially chapters 3 and 4.

Indies was also highly significant for the construction of a perception of the Netherlands' place in the world – and indeed for its manifestation. At the same time as these basically Eurocentric activities were taking place, there was nation building going on closer to home, in diplomatic relations with the Netherlands' neighbours. From this great range of national assertion in one form or another, we shall select but a small number of examples: the experience of foreign domination in the French period, the reaction to the Belgian Revolution, exchanges with the Vatican around 1870, diplomatic relations with Great Britain concerning the colonies, Dutch feelings regarding South Africa, and Dutch imperialistic aspirations in the East Indies archipelago.

Dutch national feelings were understandably stimulated by such external events as occupation by the French (and during World War II by the Germans). In February 1795 the Dutch Republic had capitulated before the military might of revolutionary France, and for eighteen years the Dutch administrations were to one extent or another influenced by Paris. In June 1806 Louis Napoleon, brother of the French Emperor, was installed as the King of Holland, and took as his royal palace that emblem of Dutch civic virtue and independence, Van Campen's magnificent Town Hall on the Dam in Amsterdam. Such symbolic acts were not enough, however, for Napoleon annexed the Netherlands to France in July 1810. From that point until late in 1813 the Dutch were governed directly from Paris, were conscripted into the *Grande Armée*, and had their seaward trade entirely suspended and their national debt (the interest on which was the lifeblood of the Dutch elite) reduced to one third (the *tiërcering* of 1811). These were not good days for national pride, and during and after the period of French domination there were manifestations of anti-French feeling which nurtured the sense of Dutchness left over from the federal state of the Republic before 1795. It was sullen resentment rather than open revolt, and the elite were prepared to fawn on the new rulers when it looked as if the invaders were going to be in place for the foreseeable future.[38] But nonetheless, during the French period a 'collective self-perception' of the Dutch as a single people or nation emerged quite clearly.[39] When the French finally left, the skill of G. K. van Hogendorp in uniting the country behind the son of the last *stadhouder* Willem V, as King Willem I, was much aided by the surge of

[38] Kossmann, *The Low Countries*, 82–100; Van Sas, 'Varieties of Dutchness', 11; and Bank, *Het roemrijk vaderland*, 50. On the resentment in one of the front-line provinces: Heeringa, 'Zeeland'.

[39] Kossmann, cited in Frijhoff, 'Identiteit', 631. See also, on the French period, Mijnhardt, 'Natievorming', 546–7.

nostalgic and sentimental national feeling on the part of the Dutch people.

The Belgian Revolution was a similar external stimulus to Dutch nationhood. After a reasonable start in 1815, the United Kingdom of the Netherlands, created by the European powers to act as a northern containment zone against any possible French resurgence, began to experience deeply divisive tremors in the later 1820s, involving the economy, religion, education and politics. In an echo of the July Revolution in Paris, in August 1830 there were riots in Brussels which escalated, and by 10 November Belgian independence had been proclaimed. After a London conference sponsored by the powers, King Willem, who was faced with the loss of more than half his kingdom, into which he had sunk much of his personal fortune, and for which he had paid in 1815 by relinquishing many of the Dutch colonies, was prepared to accept a settlement; however, the Belgians rejected it because it required shouldering enormous debts which they considered to be Dutch, and giving up most of Luxembourg.[40] In early August, after a further stand-off, the Dutch army invaded Belgium and engaged in the Ten-Day Campaign, inflicting defeats on the enemy forces in Flanders. Many a heroic painting portrayed the smart officers and phlegmatic soldiery of the north, and to have won one's spurs in the campaign was *de rigeur* for social advancement for some time afterwards; it was one of the defining moments of Dutch national identity.[41] Unfortunately for the Dutch, after ten days of triumph over the almost non-existent Belgian army, the French moved a force northwards into Belgium to put a stop to the mayhem, and the Dutch were obliged to beat a hasty retreat. There followed eight years of the 'status quo' policy (*volhardingspolitiek*), in which Willem and his senior ministers led by Baron H. J. van Doorn van Westcapelle (1786–1853) (Internal Affairs) flatly refused to recognize the new state. The Netherlands was vilified and humiliated by the powers, who blasted them out of the Antwerp citadel, blockaded the Dutch ports, and laid an embargo on Dutch ships. In 1839 Willem, exhausted and embittered, finally caved in, agreed to the original terms of 1831, and abdicated in disgust. Apart from the heady heroism of the brief but glorious campaign of headlong cavalry charges across the Belgian heathlands, the whole affair had been thoroughly humiliating, and was probably the most important external boost to Dutch national feeling between the exploits of the invading dictators, Napoleon and Hitler. Bitter resentment against all things Belgian persisted throughout the 1830s, 1840s and 1850s,

[40] The Dutch kings were also grand dukes of Luxembourg from 1815 to 1890.
[41] Kossmann, *Een tuchteloos probleem*, 68–9.

especially in the border areas where much of the hardship of the nine-year state of alert was borne, where cross-border financial traffic was viewed as international economic terrorism, and where foreign (Belgian) workers could be lynched during labour disputes.[42]

Another manifestation of national assertion abroad might be detected amongst the liberals' behaviour with regard to the Roman Question in the late 1860s. It was a time of high conservatism in the Vatican, with Pius IX and Cardinal Antonelli ruling the Papal States and indeed the Catholic Church worldwide with consummate reactionism. In 1864 the Bull *Quanta Cura* and its appended *Syllabus Errorum* condemned all vestiges of liberalism, and in 1869–70 the Pope used the Vatican Council to force through some of his more provocative Ultramontane doctrines, such as papal infallibility. Against this the liberals and Gallicans in the Catholic Church railed and fumed across Europe and the world (though in the Netherlands they were relatively docile), and the Italian nationalists vowed to liberate the Papal States from this archaic regime. In September 1870 Rome fell to the Piedmontese monarchy, Pius fled, and the temporal power of the Pope outside the confines of the tiny Vatican City came to an end. Up to this point the Dutch state had played little part; Dutch Catholics dutifully collected subscriptions, and raised petitions in support of the beleaguered Holy Father. In December the liberals defeated a motion from a Catholic Member of Parliament to take steps to restore the temporal power, and in the debates on the 1871 budget, radical liberals insisted that the money supporting the diplomatic representation of the Netherlands at the Vatican be withdrawn, on the grounds that it would conflict with the principle of separation of church and state to send a diplomatic representative to the leader of a church which had no territory or temporal power. The funds were withdrawn, and so was the Dutch delegation despite the uproarious opposition of loyal Dutch Catholics, who produced outraged petitions and pamphlets in abundance.[43] These events symbolized the final end of the already disintegrating alliance between liberals and Catholics in Dutch politics, which had lasted since before the mid-century. They can also be construed as an example of Dutch liberal national feeling, as it located its domestic 'other' in the Ultramontane Catholic leadership in Church and parliament. The same political elite was not averse to casting its weight about internationally, if

---

[42] Examples abound from Zeeuws-Vlaanderen, on the northern shores of Antwerp's River Scheldt: Wintle, *Zeeland and the churches*, 146–8 and 150–1; and Van Damme and Van Neste, 'Oost-Zeeuws-Vlaanderen'.

[43] Suttorp, 'Nederland en het Vaticaan', 9–14; and Goulmy, *Nederland naar het Vaticaan*, 7–8. From the Vatican side, both the revenues from the collections and the dismay at the political developments can be followed in ASV, Segreteria di Stato, Anno 1872, Rub. 165, Fasc. 5.

there was little to lose. This was an issue which could do the Dutch little economic harm; they had recognized the new Italy in 1861, for trade reasons. Now, in being one of the first nations formally to jettison the arch-conservative papacy, they were striking a pose on the diplomatic stage, asserting the liberal and moral high ground, and flying the flag for nationalism at the same time.

By the 1880s the Dutch were approaching the critical stage of economic development and imperialism which Gellner identified as evoking or even requiring a new kind of nationalism, and their relations with Southern Africa provided a suitable external vehicle for it. They had lost the Cape Colony to the English during the Napoleonic period, and had little further contact with the Afrikaners, many of whom could trace some of their ancestors to Dutch immigrants. Suddenly, at the end of the 1870s, Dutch public feeling erupted, especially among the neo-Calvinists led by Abraham Kuyper. The occasion was the annexation of the Boer Republic of the Transvaal by the mighty British Empire in 1877, followed by disturbances, negotiations and war between the plucky men of the *Veld* and the overbearing world power across the North Sea. The Dutch – those who were interested – certainly knew which side they were on. Emotive language in the vein of 'our kinsmen' and 'our Transvaal brothers' made clear the identification of the Dutch with the South African farmers, who also spoke a Germanic tongue close to Dutch. (The sentiment was by no means reciprocated: the Dutch were often unpopular in the Transvaal.) The motivation for the support was clear: here were co-religionists and close linguistic cousins of common ancestry, standing up to the power of the greatest empire on earth; the Dutch saw their past and their present and their future in that struggle, and applauded the underdog loudly. There were those who thought that South Africa might be a lucrative market for the Dutch, but much more importantly it was a form of 'Dutch cultural imperialism which enlarged the Netherlands' self-esteem and importance'.[44] The Transvaal action was an extension of Dutch culture (from the Dutch point of view), and the incidents around 1880 provided an opportunity for cultural assertion which was readily seized, especially by the growing neo-Calvinist movement in its search for a national identity. Suddenly Calvinism had a new role in the world. The support continued, and flared up again at the end of the century, at the time of the Anglo-Boer War. Again led by Kuyper's Anti-Revolutionary movement of neo-Calvinists, the Dutch avidly supported the Transvaal and the Orange Free State in their heroic struggle against the behemoth that was the British Empire. The assertions of brotherhood, kinship,

[44] Schutte, *Nederland en de Afrikaners*, 40–1 and 205–7; quotation from p. 205.

co-religion and nationhood were all repeated.[45] The Dutch government was embarrassed and fearful of an open breach with England, and declined to invite the Boer Republics to the Peace Conference in The Hague in 1899 (neither was the Vatican included on the guest list).[46] However, popular feeling knew its mind, and when the King-Emperor Edward VII visited the Dutch port of Vlissingen (Flushing) in the royal yacht in February 1901, the crowds had the temerity to sing the Transvaal national anthem in the presence of His Imperial Majesty. Lord Howard, the British Ambassador to The Hague, explained in his confidential telegram to the Foreign Secretary in London that 'the offenders . . . seemed to belong to the working class', and that 'The Netherlands government is alone to blame', for 'the precautions they took to prevent the same proved wholly inadequate'.[47]

These assertions of Dutch culture and the Dutch nation were often directed at Great Britain, for the simple reason that – in competition with Germany – it was the nearest and most important great power, and perhaps the most obvious 'other' in the formation of Dutch national feeling. The Anglo-Dutch relationship was basically an amicable one, but one which the English sometimes found tiresome and with which the Dutch had great problems during the nineteenth century. It was clear from the start that the British were the protectors of the Dutch, both in Europe, against threats from France or Germany, and in the world, against hostile colonial powers. The British wanted to contain the other great powers, and would defend the Dutch and their possessions rather than allow their rivals to benefit from Dutch losses. There was rhetoric about justice and morality, but it was more a question of strategy, balance of power and realpolitik than about sentiment. The Anglo-Dutch alliance was not one between equals, and indeed the Dutch often felt very badly let down, especially over the Belgian Secession when the British publicly humiliated them. However, there were few alternative choices of partner, and the Dutch had to adjust to life as one of the UK's very junior allies. The psychology of the relationship was a difficult one for the Dutch, though, who were constantly seeking to assert themselves, and in diplomatic terms often showed signs of the behaviour typical of someone suffering from an inferiority complex.[48] In the negotiations on the colonies in particular, the Dutch repeatedly felt themselves very harshly treated,

---

[45] Kuiper, *Zelfbeeld*, 207–14; Van Koppen, *De Geuzen*, 162–5. The liberals were also involved: Te Velde, *Gemeenschapszin*, chapters 3 and 6.
[46] Kuitenbrouwer, *Nederland*, 176–8.
[47] Despatch of 25 February 1901, PRO London, printed in Smit, ed., *Bescheiden*, 168–9.
[48] In a manner not unlike the way in which the Dutch were continually apologizing for their lack of heavy industry. Schutte uses the word '*minderwaardigheidsgevoel*' in regard to Dutch national feeling at the time. Schutte, *Nederland en de Afrikaners*, 40.

and thought that the British did not afford them enough importance and would not sufficiently honour their dignity. Dutch attempts to get the British to take them seriously about matters which to them were very important proved on the whole to be in vain, and make up a painful tale. In the second half of the century there were constant reproaches about how the British were riding roughshod over Dutch rights and privileges in the East Indies. In the long-running dispute about control over North Borneo, in an incident concerning the botched rescue of the crew of the British ship *Nisero*, who were captured and held by a local potentate in northern Sumatra (Atjeh) in 1883, and in wranglings about renegotiating the 1824 Treaty between the two nations which regulated matters in South East Asia until 1871, the Dutch were preoccupied with their view that the British were constantly trying to put them in their place in colonial matters. London was always polite, but gave the Dutch no ground at all, and in the end knew precisely how to protect its interests in a sometimes rather venal way, especially in Borneo; in the face of this diplomatic deception and overwhelmingly superior power, the Dutch could do little more than bluster.[49] Behind this example of small-power diplomacy in a world dominated by global empires was the assertion of Dutch national feeling, using the overmighty foe as the 'other'. No wonder they sought outlets for cultural nationalism with other less problematic sparring partners. Another characteristic way the Dutch found of bringing their national identity to the attention of larger and more dominant partners was by claiming the moral high ground, for example by playing host to the international peace movement from the 1880s onwards.[50]

There were other external challenges and crises which drew the Dutch out of themselves, not least the relations with their German neighbours, especially after 1860, around the time of the invasion by Prussia and Austria of Danish Schleswig-Holstein, and the Franco-Prussian War. But the clearest manifestation of cultural assertion on the part of the Dutch was of course to be found in the regime imposed on their own colonies, and especially in the East Indies. On the occasion of Wilhelmina's accession to the throne in 1898, her mother the Queen-Regent Emma asked herself how else the Dutch as 'a small country could be great', if not through her colonies.[51]

There is a debate about whether the Netherlands was a full member of the imperialist movement at the end of the nineteenth century; as a small nation with restricted domestic resources the Dutch could not afford to defend their ancient colonial interests around the globe – in America,

---

[49] All this is the burden of Mead, 'Anglo-Dutch relations'. See also Reid, *The contest*, on the incident concerning the wreck of the ship *Nisero*.
[50] Te Velde, 'The debate', 93–4.   [51] Cited in Te Velde, 'The debate', 93.

Africa and Asia – in an age when all the European powers were 'scrambl-ing' not only for Africa but for every other corner of the globe. The verdict seems to be that the Dutch adopted a policy of 'limited imperialism', abandoning Africa altogether, and severely restricting their interests in the Caribbean, but squaring up with considerable commitment behind their interests in the Indonesian archipelago.[52]

As with other imperialist nations at the end of the nineteenth century, the whole gamut of expression of national feeling was there. Indeed, alongside its financial-capitalist and strategic aspects, the New Imperial-ism at the end of the nineteenth century was very much a cultural imperialism, representing a self-assurance (not without self-doubt) and a wish to export the culture of Western Europe to the rest of world, on the grounds that it was the best possible bounty that the metropole nations could offer to less fortunate people. This applied to the economy – capitalist production – but also to legal systems, infrastructure of all types, religion, education, social institutions and democracy. In the British Empire they even exported rugby and cricket, in an attempt to 'grind some grit' into the less disciplined races of the world. The Dutch may not have exported much of their sport, but they were highly active in national assertion through the attempted export of the rest of their culture. Van Tijn maintained that the Dutch were a little later than other imperialist nations in reaching this psychological stage of imperialism, but certainly by the 1870s they were hard at it.[53]

The self-assertion began in military and economic terms. The Achin War (1873–1914) and the Lombok expedition (1894), for example, showed the colony the strength of Dutch arms, and from the 1890s the Forward Movement was extending Dutch supervision and control to the more remote corners of the Indonesian archipelago. The Forward Move-ment involved the extension of first military, then civil, and finally econ-omic control over the Outer Provinces of the East Indies: Sumatra in the first place, Celebes, the Moluccas, Bali, New Guinea, Borneo and the rest. Between 1898 and 1911 no less than 300 previously self-governing states in the East Indies were brought under Dutch tutelage.[54] Military pacification was enforced, usually to clear the area of the often very real danger of pirates; the colonial officials would then move in, and when the coast was clear and the potential investment was safe, Dutch economic interests would follow, anxious to develop the mineral and agricultural

[52] Kuitenbrouwer, *Nederland* (translated as Kuitenbrouwer, *The Netherlands and the rise of modern imperialism*); and Groenveld and Wintle, eds., *State and trade*, 107–24.
[53] Van Tijn, 'Een nabeschouwing', 83–5. On Dutch cultural assertion in the East Indies after 1900, see Gouda, *Dutch culture overseas*.
[54] Hall, *A history* (1955), 499.

resources, and those of plentiful labour. The extension of Dutch shipping lines was aided and abetted by the Dutch and East Indies states, and represented an extension of political and economic control and influence in the face of foreign competition in the heyday of imperialism.[55] Then, from its launch in about 1900, the Ethical Policy was an archetypal and monumental example of culture assertion, granting the indigenous population of the colony the benefits of modest measures of Dutch-style politics, Dutch education and a Dutch-style money economy. (As we have seen in section 7.2, it failed.) And all the while the Dutch churches (the Protestants, and in particular the Catholics) were active in missionary work, especially in the colonies, spreading the word on Dutch religion and ethics.[56]

11.3   Conclusion

Surveying the various manifestations of national feeling both within the country and externally, there seems to have been a crescendo towards the end of the century which confirms in the Dutch case the association which Gellner and others have identified between modern capitalism, imperialism and nationalism. From the 1870s onwards, the activities of the emerging pillars in the domestic politics of the country, and the actions of government and various public opinion groups towards external stimuli to the Dutch nation, began to take on very similar attributes to those found in other European states with regard to the growth of nationalistic sentiments and policies, thereby confirming the Dutch place in the mainstream of North-West Europe. But the earlier development, prior to the last quarter of the century, should not be ignored. There were stirrings of national feeling all along, indeed from the later part of the eighteenth century, and the Dutch Patriot Movement of the 1780s had also been in a way nationalistic. Under the Republic, however, and especially away from the large towns and ports, the rest were probably more concerned with their regional environment, their religion, their kin and the like. But by the 1890s, more or less all the Dutch were fully integrated into the nationalism of the day, and the state, the nation and the individuals within them all had converged to an advanced degree.

The reforging of the Dutch state as a unitary structure in the years from 1795 to 1815 was heavily assisted by external events, many of them in

---

[55] See Wintle, 'Shipping and empire'; and Dick, *Indonesian interisland shipping*, 11.
[56] Van Rooden, *Religieuze regimes*, chapters 4 and 5, discusses the link between the expansion of Dutch (internal) missionary work towards the end of the eighteenth century and a rise in national consciousness at that time. The same link can be drawn between the cultural imperialism of the New Imperialist nations (including the Netherlands) a century later, and the explosion of religious proselytizing in their colonies.

Paris. The constitutions of 1813–15, 1840 and 1848 confirmed and cemented the unitary structure, drawing local and regional government ever more closely into the orbit of The Hague. There were continual state-building activities throughout the century, directed by succeeding governments, and augmented by an increasing national integration of the infrastructure and economy, as well as politics and social institutions.

At the same time, and to an extent as part of the same progress, the Dutch nation also grew apace. Here also there were external stimuli such as French, Belgian and British affronts to the national dignity, and, more positively, the chance to assert a Dutch national consciousness on various occasions. The main business of nation formation, however, took place within the Netherlands. By a variety of means, individuals were increasingly caught up in one form or another of national organization or institution. Civilization offensives, combined with a broadening of the impact of religion to affect politics, education and social life for large swathes of the populace, eventually effected an *embourgoisement* according to nationally defined behavioural patterns. But there were many forms of the nation: each group tended to define it by its own standards and in its own terms. The point was that most of the groups were national groups, which prised loose the ties which had bound men and women so closely to their local environment. The process was accelerated by the advance of communications, especially the press. During the second half of the century, the pillars of Dutch society took shape, building on earlier foundations but as essentially modern institutions, dependent on modern communications, mass politics, increasing democracy, modern economic growth, and a *national* recruitment base and organization. Each of them had its own brand of national feeling. The Dutch citizen was linked to his or her state through the nation, and to the nation through the national groupings, the largest of which were in the process of becoming pillars. It is no exaggeration to say that *verzuiling* and national consciousness in the Netherlands were part and parcel of the same set of developments.

12   Social groups

12.1   Introduction

In surveying the changing relationship between society and the individual, and between the state and the citizen, the last three chapters have adopted a thematic approach. The shoe is now placed on the other foot, and we look at the same issue of the interaction between people and their collectivity by examining the fortunes of certain specific groups in Dutch society. As a set of criteria for identifying them the following concepts are employed: class, ideology or *Weltanschauung*, gender or sexuality, and ethnicity. The latter category will include immigrants, gypsies and Jews, and also take stock briefly of the more significant regional identities, especially that of the Frisians.

The analysis in each section will differ in order to suit the subject matter in hand; there will be no dogmatically consistent set of questions levelled in turn at each group. But the general framework of the enquiry in this part of the book is to do with representation and location within the state. The state was manifested in a number of legal pronouncements about citizenship and the rights of various people living within its borders, and in the views and prejudices of the Dutch elite as it chose to interpret those laws and add its supplementary informal provisions. The changing relationship between on the one hand the state, and on the other the individuals with their shifting allegiances and identities, through the groups that they formed or which were formed for them, is therefore the theme of this chapter.

12.2   Social stratification

Social stratification in the modern period (since industrialization and the French Revolution) concerns 'class'. It has long been accepted that a class system is a system of changing relationships, rather than a fixed structure of discrete components. In the words of E. P. Thompson, 'class is a relationship, not a thing'.[1] One class cannot exist without another, for its existence is essentially its attitude or relationship to another class. It therefore follows that class does not meaningfully exist without class consciousness;[2] if class is a relationship, then one or more of the participants should have an awareness of it. This is little more than a recognition that a group's identity is at least partly formed by alterity, and that a class needs its 'other', just as individuals and nations do. The criteria determining class are not confined to access to the means of production, and have to do with social standing and status, and are also affected by other factors, like income level, profession, lifestyle, behaviour, status, religion and so on. A case study of Wormer (Noord-Holland) in the 1840s showed that income was the most important desideratum for social standing, but that profession, and behaviour like thrift, sobriety or avoidance of gambling, were also significant determinants.[3] Recent research into probate inventories has shown considerable variance in lifestyle and material culture between various parts of the Netherlands in the nineteenth century, but more especially between different 'classes'.[4] On the other hand, money always talks: in an investigation into the hiring out of church pews across the denominations and various locations over extended time periods, it was concluded that the determining criterion for social status and class was *income* (and to a lesser extent wealth).[5]

For a long time there was a debate in the Netherlands about a transition in social stratification from a pre-industrial fixed and closed system of *standen*, which translates as 'estates', 'orders' or (out of context) 'castes', to a modern and dynamic 'class' (*klasse*) system, much more tightly based on income and market position, but within which there was a degree of mobility.[6] I. J. Brugmans adapted the model to Dutch society and linked the changeover with what he saw as the Dutch 'Industrial Revolution' in the 1860s; prior to that, he maintained, there was a static social system of fixed estates with no middle class, and afterwards there was a dynamic and modern class system with entrepreneurs forming the new, vigorous bourgeoisie.[7] Before the mid-century, then, there were simply rich and poor. The thesis was easily refuted in a technical sense by demonstrating that there was indeed a middle class or bourgeoisie, and inter-class mobility, in existence before 1850, for example in Rotterdam, or Hoorn,[8] but the idea of 'two nations' – the 'haves' and the 'have-nots' – should not

---

[1] Thompson, *The making*, 11.   [2] Van Tijn, 'Voorlopige notities'.
[3] De Meere, 'Standen en klassen'.   [4] Schuurman, *Materiële cultuur*.
[5] Lucassen and Trienekens, 'Om de plaats'.
[6] For the classic formulation, see Van Heek, *Klassen- en standenstructuur*.
[7] E.g. Brugmans, *Welvaart*, chapter 9; and Brugmans, *Paardenkracht*, 190–1.
[8] Van Dijk, 'De beroepsmobititeit'; Leenders, *Benauwde verdraagzaamheid*, 72–96. For a review of the whole discussion, see Kooij, *Groningen*, 14–81.

be summarily dismissed. Once more, our own contemporary perspective is a distorting one: whatever the refinements of social stratification, Parts I and II have shown that for most of the nineteenth century, much of the population lived in penury to the point of malnutrition, with a quality of life cursed by chronic illness, constant uncertainty and shortage. The few who had enough resources to keep chance at bay were the upper class, and those who did not were the lower classes: that was the crucial division in society, and it was a heavily skewed one, for the vast majority of the populace fell into the second category. The king-maker Van Hogendorp had his finger on the pulse in 1813 when he issued a proclamation throughout the land to mark the end of the French occupation, with the following words: 'All important people (*aanzienlijken*) will have a hand in government . . . the people will have a holiday at public expense . . . Orange for ever!'[9]

Elites

The social system in the late Republic had been one characterized in economic terms by a small elite and a large, poor populace. Amongst the elite one could distinguish between a traditional patriciate of regent families with a local power base, who in oligarchic fashion divided up the public offices and related spoils between then, and a new moneyed class which was challenging the established position.[10] This situation survived many of the ravages of the French Revolutionary period, and in the 1840s, according to a study of urban society at the time which used contemporary 'physiologies' as its source material, there were four identifiable social groups, which could in their turn be bunched into two. First there was the elite, which consisted of the old regent families and aristocracy, challenged by a second group of *fatsoenlijken* ('decent', 'respectable'), who were wealthy and educated, but not part of the old establishment. Groups three and four formed the have-nots: the lower middle class (*kleine burgerij*, some of whom had possessions) and the lower classes, all of whom were more or less impecunious and politically counted for nothing.[11] In the countryside, the situation was not dissimilar: in the 1850s, H. J. Koenen spoke of a social division between a few gentlemen (whether farmers or otherwise) and the rest, who were (to one extent or another) poor.[12] So the idea of 'two nations' was by no means misplaced, though there were evidently nuances within each of the two. And this situation, before about 1850, would have been typical of most of Europe, certainly on the mainland.

[9] Quoted in De Wit, *De strijd*, 316.
[10] There are many studies: a classic one, of Drenthe, is Buning, *Het herenbolwerk*.
[11] Robijns, *Radicalen*, 59–63.   [12] Koenen, *De Nederlandsche boerenstand*, 113.

After the mid-century there were changes, as the economy grew and rising real wages carried some of the increasing prosperity part of the way down the social scale. Amongst the elite, the arrival of the Thorbeckian liberals in government represented the sharing of power at the highest level with the group of new blood – or a least new compared to the established position of the old regent elite which had run the country (and the towns) for time out of mind. The monographs of C. H. E. de Wit are the closest study of this century-long battle in high politics, between the forces of the Enlightenment and later liberalism on the one side, and the oligarchic control of the country by the Dutch equivalent of a blood aristocracy on the other: the old regent families (including the House of Orange).[13] In De Wit's words, 'Liberalism was primarily a struggle against the aristocracy, and against the estates system (*standenstaat*) which still dominated the Netherlands.'[14] The struggle had been long and hard. The cause of the new men, the meritocracy and the plutocracy, had been aided by the political doctrines of some of the French-inspired regimes during the Revolutionary period, and particularly by Napoleonic policies. King Willem I continued many of those policies, while not hesitating to make use of talent wherever he found it, and to play one group off against the other. The old elite was by no means routed in the nineteenth century – double-barrelled names often dominated governments and parliament even at the end of the century – but it had to make room for new blood. Either way, politics was for the elite before 1870, and that included the matter of voting.[15] What is more, that elite was concentrated geographically: as late as 1894 there were fewer than 78,000 people in the country who owned ƒ13,000 worth of property (under 2 per cent of the total population of more than 4.5m.). They were crowded into Amsterdam and The Hague, and to a lesser extent into Rotterdam and (lesser still) into Utrecht, Haarlem and Groningen. Those six cities contained 23 per cent of the population, 29 per cent of the assessed tax-payers and 42 per cent of the nation's wealth.[16]

Again, this profile was not unusual for Europe: the tiny top elite controlled the vast majority of resources in most countries, as it does to a slightly smaller degree still today. Perhaps the unusual feature of the Dutch experience was that ownership of large landed estates had not been the critical determinant for centuries, and the place of the titled land-owning aristocracy had long been taken over by an urban oligarchy. Titles were present in the Dutch elite (Willem I granted many of them after the 1815 Restoration), but nothing like to the extent that they were, for

---

[13] See De Wit, *De Nederlandse revolutie*; De Wit, *De strijd*; and De Wit, *Het ontstaan*.
[14] De Wit, *De strijd*, 314.   [15] Van Tijn, 'De wording', 590–1.
[16] Stoop, 'Interessante cijfers', 948–9, taken from government statistics for 1894.

instance, in high circles in Britain. It has been suggested that this may have been a reason for the liveliness of the liberal debate in the Netherlands in the nineteenth century: a traditional conservative aristocracy was not present to oppose it.[17]

Petite bourgeoisie

Shifting our attention to the *petite bourgeoisie* or lower middle class, for much of the century times were hard. Early studies had shown that urban populations of independent artisans, traders and shopkeepers declined heavily;[18] a recent monograph has confirmed that impression, and added the rural class of self-exploiters, the small independent farmers, to the list of casualties. Within agriculture, some 40 per cent of those involved were 'independent' in 1850, a figure which had fallen to 25 per cent by 1900. The decline in this class of small independents was partly due to increases of scale and improvements in markets, which cut out the small middleman and independent dealer, and partly due to intense pressure (especially towards the end of the century) in the countryside for fragmentation of land holdings or *morcellement*, in order to accommodate demand from below for small patches of land.[19]

However, while there was a decline on the part of what might be termed the 'old lower middle classes' for most of the nineteenth century, new armies of 'white-collar workers' were recruited as the century progressed, to attend to the burgeoning service sector as it outgrew and out-performed other parts of the economy. These people were civil servants, office workers, retail assistants and travelling sales personnel, and their numbers had risen from being negligible in 1850 to some 10 per cent of the workforce by 1900.[20] This group of workers – still male-dominated, but with increasing female participation – were not in any way an 'independent' middle class, and were all in employment, but represented an important new development linked to the changing economy after 1850.

The working class

A proletariat?   And what of the workers? Let us first deal with the issue of a proletariat; that is to say, of whether the gradual industrialization which was taking place across the Dutch economy was leading to the formation of large groups of people dependent solely on their ability to sell their unskilled or semi-skilled labour, completely cut off from control of the means of production, and alienated, casualized and class-conscious into

---

[17] Boschloo, *De productiemaatschappij*, 199–201.   [18] E.g. Van Dijk, *Rotterdam*.
[19] Wijmans, *Beeld en betekenis*, 71–7.   [20] Wijmans, *Beeld en betekenis*, 84–6 and 110–11.

the bargain. On the face of it such changes would be unlikely to have characterized the Netherlands in any special way, with its very limited mining, heavy industry and large-scale plant, at least until the very end of the century. On the other hand, the trend over the century as a whole was away from cottage industry, and agriculture in the sea-clay areas had long been commercialized and capitalized enough to generate a visible separation of capital and labour in some areas.[21] There is a running discussion about the continuity between the Republic and the nineteenth century here: Jan Lucassen has maintained that eighteenth-century Dutch workers' organizations (guilds) were clear prototypes for the first trade unions a century later, while Bert Altena has challenged that thesis.[22] To what extent, then, did a Dutch proletariat emerge or increase in the nineteenth century?

In the countryside, the structural crisis in the late 1820s and 1830s, and the crop failures of the 1840s, had not prevented a steady increase in population and therefore in demand for farms, which allowed land prices to drift upwards, while wages stagnated and unemployment rose. The resulting rural proletariat had perhaps all the classic attributes, except that of class consciousness: there is little evidence of anything but sporadic action or even self-awareness on the part of this group at this time.[23] As for its ensuing fortunes, in the capitalized sea-clay areas it continued;[24] however, these developments must be set in perspective. The relative prosperity of farming after 1850 for some twenty-five years alleviated many of the problems of the mid-century, and after 1860 the drift to proletarianization ran out of steam. At the time of the next structural crisis, in the 1880s, the problems were acute and caused alienation and casualization of agricultural labour in some farming areas, especially Friesland and Groningen. Nonetheless, the general solution to the national crisis in farming in the 1880s was sought and eventually found in a transfer of the population out of the farming sector to other parts of the economy, or to other farms across the oceans in America and elsewhere, and further in an intensification of agriculture. The latter involved smaller and smaller farms being worked by the proprietor and immediate family rather than by armies of day-labourers, and thus represented a reversal of

[21] Van Zanden, ed., *'Den zedelijken en materiëlen toestand'*, 6; and Paping, *'Voor een handvol stuivers'*, 64–119.

[22] In Davids and Lucassen, eds., *A miracle mirrored*, 367–409; and Altena, 'Continuiteit?'

[23] A study of income distribution speaks of 'proletarianization' in rural Overijssel at the beginning of the nineteenth century, but in this context the term means a rise in the inequality of income distribution, rather than class consciousness. Soltow and Van Zanden, *Income and wealth*, chapter 4, especially pp. 62–6.

[24] Gooren and Heger, *Per mud*, especially chapter 5; Staverman, *Volk in Friesland*, 165–6; Blok, *et al.*, eds., *Algemene geschiedenis der Nederlanden*, vol. XIII, pp. 296ff.; and Frieswijk, *Om een beter leven*.

the proletarianization trend. There were some areas which proved exceptions (much of the province of Zeeland, for instance), but for the most part Dutch agricultural labourers did not in the end become the army of alienated and class-conscious proletarians they had half-threatened to be at the mid-century, or around 1890.[25]

As for the towns, there seems to have been little evidence of a classic proletariat forming early in the century.[26] Later on, the picture was different. In the cyclical downswing from the mid-1870s to the early 1890s, a study of the Amsterdam labour market has revealed evidence of considerable casualization, deskilling and proletarianization.[27] From the 1880s, the entry of larger firms and factories to the production process and the influence of revolutionary ideology from abroad allowed a socialist and even anarchist movement to take off in the Netherlands.[28]

Interestingly, a major support group for libertarian socialism, or radical syndicalist anarchism, came from a rural area, Friesland and Drenthe, but was rooted not in agriculture but in extractive industry: peat cutting. Ferdinand Domela Nieuwenhuis (1846–1919) was the charismatic if unpredictable leader of the Dutch anarchists and other radical socialists, and indeed was a figure on the international stage of revolutionary socialism at the end of the nineteenth century. In 1881 he founded the Social-Democratic League (*Sociaal-Democratische Bond*, SDB), which was in its early years the national focus of socialism; Domela gradually moved away from parliamentarianism towards anarchism. His support came from factorized workers like the shipbuilding engineers in Vlissingen, but also in large numbers from the peat workers of the north-east. This physically demanding and semi-skilled work, in many ways akin to coal-mining, involved large numbers of men dependent entirely on their physical labour in harsh conditions, where the separation of capital and labour was as obvious as it would be in a conveyor-belt factory. The peat gangs of Drenthe and elsewhere were therefore one Dutch proletarian group which persisted throughout the century.[29]

The labour movement   In 1917 universal male suffrage was introduced, by which time there had been more than forty years of attempts to better the lot, in both socio-economic and political terms, of the working people of the Netherlands, just as there had been elsewhere. The most obvious organizations dedicated to that end were socialist ones, but they did not

[25] Van Zanden, *De economische ontwikkeling*, 326–44.
[26] Pot, *Arm Leiden*.   [27] Knotter, *Economische transformatie*.
[28] Altena, '*Een broeinest*', chapters 2 and 11.
[29] Van der Hoek, *Het bruine goud*, 109–15. Such proletarian traditions go back as far as the Middle Ages: see Lis, *et al.*, eds., *Before the unions*, especially pp. 171–94.

enjoy a monopoly on the working class. First, there was a distinct group of radical liberals who fought for the rights of ordinary people and supported the cause of labour laws and universal suffrage from an early stage. Many of them ended up merging with socialist organizations after 1900, but in the early decades, from the 1860s on, these were people not tarred with the brush of socialist subversion who were speaking within the parliamentary establishment for the cause of working people. They left the loose parliamentary party of the Liberal Union in 1892, forming the Radical League (*Radicale Bond*), which later became the Free-thinking Democratic League (*Vrijzinnig-Democratisch Bond*, VDB), in 1901. Its leader, M. W. F. Treub, was a sworn enemy of Marxism and socialism in general, but there was no more doughty champion in the Netherlands of the rights of the worker, and as a cabinet minister during the First World War, he and other radical liberals were in a position to achieve things the socialists could not.

Next came the confessional organizations, which also claimed to be concerned with the rights of ordinary people. They did so in specific opposition to socialism, and entirely rejected the very concept of class struggle in which the workers' interests were by definition inimical to those of the capitalist bourgeoisie. The Christian view, whether Catholic or Protestant, was that society was an organic whole, or corporate entity, which had common interests, and to divide workers against their employers was wrong and counter-productive for society's needs. From very patronizing, paternalist beginnings, the Calvinist and (eventually) the Catholic pillars developed a full range of institutions for the workers of their ideological persuasion.

And then there was socialism, in all its many forms, with the eventual triumph of the moderate parliamentary Social-Democratic wing. Active from the time of the First International in the 1860s, trade unions and political organizations were formed, reformed, abandoned and merged, all fighting for the rights of labour in the workplace and of the working man at the ballot. By the time of the First World War the moderate strand of socialist action was present in government deliberations and took full part in the power-sharing arrangements of corporatism and *verzuiling* for most of the twentieth century.[30]

From the 1860s onwards, therefore, increasing numbers of workers became actively involved in the business of the state by means of membership of or at least sympathy with one such organization or another, in a way which would have been unthinkable before the mid-century. This wide-

---

[30] The conformist, participatory character of Dutch trade unions, including the socialist ones, is emphasized in Visser, 'The politics of mediation'. A large number of the key texts of the Dutch labour movement are collected in Peet, *et al.*, eds., *Honderd jaar sociaal*.

scale mobilization and engagement of the Dutch masses (the adult males) was a defining feature of Dutch society towards the end of the century, as it was across Europe. The democratization of politics began to involve working men, especially towards the end of the century, and one of the issues with political potential concerned their working conditions. Thus the 'Social Question', or the political consequences of the social effects of industrialization, came to play a key role in the domestic politics of industrializing countries in the last decades of the nineteenth century.

Before the 1860s it is difficult to talk of an organized labour movement at all in the Netherlands. There were certainly sporadic protests and even strikes (which were illegal until 1872), usually against a perceived local outrage like mass redundancy, wage cuts or the substitution of foreign labour, but most were spontaneous and easily suppressed.[31] Some clubs and societies were formed by working men, for informal insurance and even social purposes, but there was very little evidence of any class consciousness, even on a local scale. From the 1860s there were embryonic artisan unions being formed in Amsterdam, and from 1864 the First International began publicizing the creed of socialism (the Dutch section was founded in 1869). From then on one can speak of four principal branches of the labour movement in the Netherlands: Protestant, Catholic, radical liberal and socialist.[32]

The Protestant labour movement was part and parcel of the orthodox Calvinist revival and 'emancipation', led by 'Anti-Revolutionary' politicians like Abraham Kuyper. Its attitude to labour issues was essentially anti-Marxist and anti-socialist; it was therefore a primarily reactive movement in the early decades.[33] The organization 'Patrimonium' was founded in 1877 as a splinter movement of orthodox Calvinists who, led by Klaas Kater (1833–1916), were unhappy with the secular policies of the emerging radical labour movement in the 1870s. Patrimonium admitted employers to its membership, and rejected any idea of a conflict of interest between capital and labour. It was against collective action, universal suffrage and labour legislation of any sort. This kind of paternalism was no longer sufficient by 1890 to retain the loyalty of Calvinist workers, and Kuyper held a conference on social issues in 1891 which signalled a change in orthodox Calvinist policy. A. S. Talma presided over the creation of a genuine Protestant labour movement with its own trade unions from the 1890s, which campaigned for labour laws and social reforms, many of which were introduced by confessional

---

[31] Maclean, 'Arbeidsconflicten'; Lis, *et al.*, eds., *Before the unions.*
[32] See Peet *et al.*, eds., *Honderd jaar sociaal.* For the earlier mutual societies, see section 6.4 above, on other services.
[33] See *inter alia* Windmuller, *Labor relations*, 9–11 and 20–1.

governments after 1901.[34] In 1900 the Christian Labour Secretariat (*Christelijk Arbeidssecretariaat*, CAS) was founded as a national confederation of all Protestant labour organizations in the country: it functioned as a Calvinist umbrella organization, and became in 1909 the Christian National Trades Union (*Christelijk Nationaal Vakverbond*, CNV), which still exists as the Calvinist federation today. The efforts of people like Talma between 1890 and 1914 were important in persuading Calvinist workers that their interests in the workplace could be represented in a meaningful way by Calvinist agencies, rather than by secular ones. After the First World War the Protestants would join the Catholics in developing important corporatist strategies which would help define the pillarized state right up to the 1960s and beyond, but before 1914 the Calvinist labour movement was in many ways driven by the need to keep Protestant workers out of the clutches of the socialists. When the CNV petitioned for some modest reforms such as a ten-hour day, free Saturday afternoons, and two days' paid holiday each year, they were told by their leader Paul van Vliet (1858–1941), who together with Talma had in 1901 become an MP, that they were no better than socialists.[35]

The Catholic labour movement in the Netherlands rather resembled a shadow of the Protestant one, much later and much slower. Papal teaching from the mid-century to 1890 was vehemently anti-socialist and even anti-liberal; any suggestion of democratic decision-making was anathema, in addition to the Christian corporatist rejection of any principle of conflict between employers and employees. The Dutch bishops installed at the restoration of the episcopal hierarchy in 1853 were of an extremely conservative stamp, and would not hear of any Catholic workers' organizations.[36] Because of late political emancipation combined with the delayed arrival of large factorized industry, Dutch Catholics had hardly begun to discuss the Social Question before the 1880s. L. J. Rogier remarked that the debate on these matters fought out across Europe by such Catholic social thinkers as Von Ketteler, Manning and Mermillod 'had apparently entirely eluded the Netherlands'.[37] Catholics were often too concerned with their specifically Catholic world in the Church and their schools to think about such universal matters as the workplace. However, the depression and misery of the 1880s affected the Catholic workers in the Netherlands as much as it affected anyone, and so in that decade various organizations cropped up to attend to the interests of the Catholic worker. The Roman Catholic People's League (*Volksbond*) was

[34] On Talma's efforts, see Altena, *'Een broeinest'*, chapter 4.
[35] Fogarty, *Christian democracy*, 301–2; Bornebroek, *De strijd*; and Bornebroek, *Gids voor de archieven*.
[36] See Windmuller, *Labor relations*, 21–4 and 35–8; and Wintle, 'Something for everyone'.
[37] Rogier, *Katholiek herleving*, 309–10. See also Perry, *Roomsche kinine*, 33–4; and Righart, *De katholieke zuil*, 219.

founded in 1888 as an association open to all classes, and was the product of diocesan social clubs based on 'estates' and under strict clerical control; it was not unlike the guilds of the *ancien régime*, and was the organizational form favoured by the bishops.

More progressive and politically astute Catholics, however, like the labour leader Alphonse Ariëns (1860–1928) and even the poet and statesman H. J. A. M. Schaepman (1844–1903), realized that, in order to provide a real alternative to socialism, it would be necessary to set up Catholic trade unions, exclusively for and devoted to the interests of working men and women.[38] In the 1880s Schaepman had been isolated in political circles, as had been Ariëns in social matters, for the episcopate favoured traditional integrated organizations. However, 1891 brought Leo XIII's *Rerum Novarum*, which shocked many of the Dutch church leaders by its willingness to embrace modern democratic forms of organization (like trade unions) in the fight against social and political evil.[39] By the mid-1890s, Schaepman had united the parliamentary forces of Catholicism behind him, with a social programme heavily based on *Rerum Novarum*, and genuine Catholic trade unions were under way. In 1909 a Bureau for Roman Catholic Trades Organizations was created, which was a national body to which trade unions could affiliate; it was, however, still very weak indeed. The episcopal frostiness persisted, and was only relaxed in the 1920s. The bishops were particularly alarmed by the prospect of 'Christian' unions in which Catholic and Protestant workers would fight for their rights alongside each other. A confessional textile workers' union in the east of the country, *Unitas*, was effectively banned by the bishops in 1906, and although the Dutch Catholics were eventually to be important partners in the construction of the corporatist edifice under *verzuiling* after World War One, the Catholic labour movement remained a sickly child before the 1920s.

It was the secular organizations which led the field in the Dutch labour movement, as they did in most countries.[40] In the 1860s in Amsterdam a number of professional clubs and associations began to form, and by

---

[38] This Dutch debate on the legitimate methods for Catholic organization was a microcosm of the international one played out between the various schools of social Catholicism in the 1880s, like the Fribourg and Liège groups. The encyclical *Rerum Novarum* was seen as an authoritative comment in the dispute, albeit one designed to alienate as few parties as possible. Rogier, *Katholiek herleving*, 327–8; Righart, *De katholieke zuil*, 223–4; and Roes, *Bronnen*, xxxvi.

[39] For the reactions in the Netherlands, see Wintle, 'Something for everyone'. On Dutch social Catholicism in the 1890s, see Blok, *et al.*, eds., *Algemene geschiedenis der Nederlanden*, vol. XIII, p. 454; Van de Giessen, *De opkomst*, 229–39; Rogier, *Katholiek herleving*, 289–93; Righart, *De katholieke zuil*, 224, 243, and 247–8; and Kossmann, *The Low Countries*, 351.

[40] For the following, there is a vast literature, much of it now rather dated. Windmuller, *Labor relations*, 6–34, is a good general guide.

1872 there were thirty-six local unions in the capital city. These were the highly skilled artisans: the printers, the diamond polishers and other tradesmen who wanted to protect their exclusive position on the labour market and who could afford to pay substantial union dues. In 1871 the General Netherlands Workers Union (*Algemeen Nederlandse Werklieden-verbond*, ANWV) was set up, as a neutral (non-denominational) radical liberal confederation to which local and trade unions could affiliate; it was neither socialist nor committed to the class struggle, and was not affiliated to the First International. These early stirrings of organized labour achieved some concessions, such as the right to strike in 1872, and the passing of Van Houten's Child Labour Act in 1874. As we have seen, the Calvinists left the ANWV at an early stage, and in due course the socialist groups did too. The Social-Democratic League (SDB) was set up in 1881 under Domela Nieuwenhuis, and it rapidly attracted the Marxist and other socialist organizations to it. As the charismatic leader drifted into anarchism, the SDB became too radical for more moderate socialists. In 1893 the National Labour Secretariat (*Nationaal Arbeidssecretariaat*, NAS) was set up on the initiative of the Second International, and in the Netherlands there rapidly arose a tension between the libertarian social-ism of Domela's SDB and the parliamentary social democracy of the NAS, to which the new Social-Democratic Labour Party (*Sociaal-Demo-cratische Arbeiderspartij*, SDAP) under P. J. Troelstra (1860–1930) was affiliated after 1894.[41] Several mutations later, in 1905 a new socialist trade union confederation called the Netherlands League of Trade Unions (*Nederlandse Verbond van Vakverenigingen*, NVV) was inaugur-ated with strong input from Social-Democrat politicians and the success-ful, efficient and effective diamond workers' union (ANDB) under Henri Polak (1868–1943). It soon eclipsed the NAS and formed links with the political party, the SDAP; the NVV co-ordinated socialist trade union interests in the Netherlands right up to 1975 when it merged with the Catholic federation. A major rail strike in 1903, when the confessional government under Kuyper clamped down hard, and was supported by the confessional unions, polarized matters among the socialists, and the eventual result was consolidation for the moderates, who eventually were to take their place in the pillarized Dutch state, and disarray for the libertarian radicals.[42]

It is an eloquent example of the way in which the labour movement, by and large, provided a means for locating working people within the public life of the nation as conformist contributors working within the system,

[41] See Hansen and Prosper, 'Transformation'.
[42] Blok, *et al.*, eds., *Algemene geschiedenis der Nederlanden*, vol. XIV, pp. 295–326; Bloemgar-ten, *Henri Polak*; Hofmeester, *'Als ik niet voor mijzelf ben'*; Rüter, *De spoorwegstakingen*.

rather than as excluded minorities. The libertarian socialist movement was significant, but after the First World War it came to play only a small role, and was much overshadowed by the parliamentary moderate wing of the socialist labour movement, although internal conflict continued, as it did everywhere else. Its phases of development were as follows: Dutch socialism awoke around 1870, underwent a confrontational period when parts of it were persecuted and it was all viewed with suspicion by the establishment until the First World War, after which it took important steps towards perceived responsibility inside the power-sharing system that was *verzuiling*.[43]

In 1920 the government's statistical agency reported that there were 683,000 'organized' workers in the country (out of a total workforce of 2.7 million, according to Table II.2). Of these, most were socialists: the moderate NVV had 248,000 adherents, while the more radical NAS had 52,000. The Catholic organizations had 141,000 members, while the Protestant CNV trailed well behind with 40,000.[44] These were small totals, and they did not rise very much before the Second World War, despite a massive population increase (in 1940 there was a total of 798,000 members, a 17 per cent increase on 1920, while total population rose by 29 per cent in the same twenty years). But the organizational aspects were important in giving the workforce a voice which would be listened to – according into its proportionate size within the emerging state system. The working class had found its place in the nation and state, and to a very large extent it was dispersed amongst three of the pillars.

Conclusion

In some ways social stratification in the Netherlands in the nineteenth century resembled a modern class system, and in others it definitely did not. The 'two nations', of the poor and the wealthy, or the 'haves' and the 'have-nots', remained the principal social division throughout the century. Nonetheless there were subdivisions and shifts of significance. Within the upper class there was something of a battle going on – alternatively it could be dubbed a process of positive dynamism – between the old and new elites. Meanwhile the traditional lower middle class – artisans and small independent farmers – tended to suffer from the economic changes taking place, but at the same time new intermediate groups were generated in the service industries, especially after the mid-century. In the poorer (and much larger) part of society, in the sea-clay

---

[43] See Heerma van Voss, *De doodsklok*.
[44] Blok, *et al.*, eds., *Algemene geschiedenis der Nederlanden*, vol. XIV, p. 232.

farming areas there was a tendency towards rural proletarianization in the years before 1850, and again in the 1880s and 1890s (especially in Friesland), caused by structural malaise in the farming economy. In the towns there was evidence of casualization and deskilling, but not until the last quarter of the century. From the 1870s to the First World War, the Dutch built up their institutions in the labour movement, with many different groups vying for control.

Such organizations and institutions were a direct means of locating increasing numbers of Dutch people in the public life of the state and nation. The representation of legions of the Dutch into labour-movement institutions was a preliminary means of raising political identity above the purely local level. In many ways much of the change in the social stratification system was very slow until the dramatic events of the crisis years of the 1880s and early 1890s, especially away from Amsterdam. A study of the provincial capital of Leeuwarden in Friesland revealed an almost stultified social system with only very slow change, up to the later 1870s at least, when the beast of lower-class consciousness began to raise its rather heavy head.[45] The increasing strength of the confessional movements interacted vigorously with the growth of a class system and a class consciousness. Siep Stuurman's seminal study of 1984 portrayed *verzuiling* as one of the strategies employed against the effects of democratization and socialism in order to maintain control for the traditional elites.[46] In this sense the characteristic feature of Dutch modern history – *verzuiling* – was intimately bound up with and indeed was a part of a more general European trend towards class formation.

12.3   The pillars and other ideological groups

We move now to consider the vertical groups in society, united by their shared ideological commitment or religious beliefs, as opposed to horizontal socio-economic groups. The foremost of these vertical groups were those which became fully fledged pillars. The evolution and development of these ideologically driven groups led towards the formation of a pillarized society in the twentieth century, where vertical social divisions seemed to be at least as important as the horizontal ones. In this the Netherlands was not perhaps unique, but has acquired the reputation of being the first among certain other equals. However, it should be remembered that the background forces in reaction to which *verzuiling* came about were universal in Western Europe in the nineteenth century: the coming of mass politics, and secularization. The unusual quality of the

---

[45] Van der Woude, *Leeuwarden*, especially chapter 6.   [46] Stuurman, *Verzuiling*.

Dutch situation lay therefore in the constellation of economic, social (and political) factors present in the Netherlands, rather than in the general forces of change which were at work in the country and elsewhere.

The coming of mass politics

Before the 1840s, the vast majority of Dutch people did not see politics – even local politics – as their business: it was simply left to the elite. After the First World War, however, Dutch public life was indubitably the concern of all Dutch men and women. The intervening watershed was the period in which the modern Dutch state evolved, as did the relationship of Dutch individuals to that state. The old social divisions – many of which had existed in one form or another since the Reformation – were refashioned in the second half of the nineteenth century, and the *volksdelen*, or parts of the nation, were reforged in a national image by powerful new leaders with control of modern techniques like the mass media.

One of the clearest manifestations of these vertical groupings based on ideology was in the formation of political parties. Up to the 1840s there was very little use for modern political parties, because before that time there was no mass politics. Parties in the sense of political interest groups or factions certainly existed before 1848, and indeed had riddled the politics of the Republic in the eighteenth century. Modern political parties, on the other hand, in the sense of formal associations dedicated to influencing the composition and political direction of representative bodies, with a programme and a national support organization to mobilize maximum voting power, were an irrelevance before 1848, and did not exist in the Netherlands before the 1870s.[47] Thorbecke's liberals brought these changes about (although they themselves clearly belonged to the old world of elite politics); their policies were feared and distrusted by much of the old elite, who wished nothing to do with a world where mass votes would carry the day. The political elite of the first half of the century was used to being left to discuss matters amongst itself, and to thrashing out policies without reference to manifestos and voters and other controlling factors. The stepped electoral arrangements in force before 1848, by which the tiny number of voters elected an electoral college, which then elected the Member of Parliament, meant that the politicians could remain almost entirely divorced from the electorate (let alone the people), and *vice versa*. In the changeover period of the 1860s and 1870s, 'party' became a dirty word for some of the old elite, who resented the slavish

---

[47] This definition of a modern political party is derived from Van Tijn, 'De wording'.

loyalty required and thought it robbed them of their independent judgement and their ability – indeed their mandate – to act as they thought fit on behalf of their constituents, but not at their beck and call. Pamphlet after pamphlet thundered out against ideological centralization and '*heerschzucht*' in the parties,[48] or what we might now call 'control freakery'. What the old guard objected to was the process of transforming them from representatives to delegates: as the former, a politician knew what was best for the people; as the latter, the party told him what to do. 'No general theories, no empty slogans, no word-screens [thundered an independent spirit in 1869] . . . Liberal – yes, we are in favour of that; we demand it! But not "liberal" as a slogan; not "liberal" in the sense that everything must be offered up to party dictates.'[49] In local politics, parties did not play a very important role before 1900,[50] although local clubs on party lines were highly active in national politics. But despite the opposition of the old elite, the extension of the franchise in direct elections to the Second Chamber made inevitable the onset of mass politics and mass political parties. These rapidly expanding party organizations were a dramatic force in the public life of the land after 1870, and they were an important contribution to the growth of a consciousness of national political affairs on the part of ordinary people as they gradually became enfranchised, and so integrated into the political life of the nation.[51]

In this move to mass politics and modern political parties, the press played a major role. Stamp Duty on newspapers was abolished in 1869, and we have already noted (in section 11.1) the importance which the neo-Calvinist leader Abraham Kuyper attributed to the power of the press in uniting like-thinking individuals across the nation. Before the age of mass politics there were three kinds of newspaper: government-subsidized conservative mouthpieces of the establishment; an opposition press run by liberals; and an ultra-radical democratic press, often in lilliput format to avoid the punitive Stamp Duty, and often openly subversive.[52] Examples of the latter, in the 1840s, were *De Tolk der Vrijheid* (The Mouthpiece of Freedom) and *De Star der Hoop* (The Star of Hope), both run by the maverick radical republican Eijlart Meeter (?1818–62), who spent several years in prison, was intimately involved in publicizing the court scandals which caused the collapse of King Willem II's authority in

---

[48] The word was used by the conservative liberal Frederik Nagtglas (1821–1902) in July 1869 to his local liberal association *De Grondwet* (The Constitution), in disgust at the fawning and unthinking loyalty shown by current liberal MPs to the leader Thorbecke. RAZ, Grondwet, no. 5 (*Ingekomen stukken* 1858–80).

[49] *Een nationaal getuigenis*, 7 and 15.   [50] Randeraad, 'Het geplooide land'.

[51] The role played by political parties in the 'unification' of the countries is expounded in Knippenberg and De Pater, *De eenwording*, 146ff.

[52] Robijns, *Radicalen*, 264.

1848, and died in exile.[53] None of these three sorts of media had anything significant to do with mass politics. The mass-circulation daily press, which became possible after 1869, was both cheap and respectable: truly popular political material did not need to be subversive. By about 1890, each emergent pillar had its national 'dailies', some of the more prominent among which were the following: *Recht voor Allen*, edited by Domela Nieuwenhuis for the socialists; *De Amsterdammer* for free-thinking independent liberals; the *Nieuwe Rotterdamsche Courant*, *Het Nieuws van de Dag*, the *Algemeen Handelsblad*, and the *Oprechte Haarlemsche Courant* for mainstream liberals; *De Standaard*, edited by Abraham Kuyper for the Calvinists; and *De Maasbode*, *De Tijd* and *Het Centrum* for various shades of Catholic opinion. In addition there were any number of weeklies and other periodicals directed at niche markets, including the pillars.

Also between 1870 and 1890, the period of the expanding electorate, we see the prototype party programmes or manifestos beginning to emerge, which were clear statements of the party line on a wide range of issues. They served to an extent as propaganda, instructing the rank and file how to think, but they were also promises to which politicians could be held when elected. The first was – typically – from the pen of Abraham Kuyper, for the neo-Calvinists (Plate 5). In the year of Groen's death, 1872, he set up *De Standaard* as a daily, and five years later in 1877 he revived *De Heraut* (The Herald) as a homiletic weekly for the *Gereformeerden* or orthodox Calvinist faithful. In 1878 the neo-Calvinist political leadership produced a twenty-one-point programme; in 1879 Kuyper published two hefty volumes based on extracts from the pronouncements in his two newspapers, under the title of *Ons Program* (Our Programme):[54] it has gone down as the first party political programme in the country. Others were obliged to follow suit, though not always wholeheartedly. The Catholics toyed with programmes at their national congresses in the early 1880s, and Schaepman produced a draft one in 1883.[55] (It took him another decade to complete the reform of the isolationist and defensive Catholic political machine: a more satisfactory programme was agreed under his leadership in 1896, and endorsed by the local associations a year later.) At their own annual conferences, the socialists hammered out their manifestos as well.

A new breed of leader emerged, typified by Kuyper himself: not merely a parliamentarian or someone who commanded the respect of the elite,

[53] Meeter, *Holland*, published in 1857 in exile in England, is an entertaining read and a good example in English of this kind of ultra-radical press.

[54] Kuyper, *Ons program*. Updates were published regularly thereafter.

[55] *Een katholieke partij: proeve van een program*, cited in Bornewasser, 'De katholieke partijvorming', 33.

but a man (and they were all men) able to move the masses, a master of propaganda, the spoken and written word, party organization and mass politics in general. Kuyper certainly fitted the bill; Domela Nieuwenhuis was the first socialist leader to do so, before Troelstra took over the mantle (after considerable shifts in direction) in the 1890s; and the priest-politician Schaepman was the political equivalent for those Catholics who accepted mass politics in the spirit of *Rerum Novarum*. The liberals were more difficult to cast in this mode: mass politics was less to their taste, except for the radicals, who often joined the socialists.

National organizations also followed, with regional electoral associations – Calvinist, Catholic, socialist and (reluctantly) liberal – being asked to sign up to the emerging programmes, in order to unify the nation-wide following behind a single leadership focussed on the Second Chamber of Parliament. The old elite, dominant in local politics, was less than enthusiastic, but the new organizations, driven by the confessionals, carried all before them.

In 1878 the Anti-Revolutionary Party (ARP) was inaugurated, formalizing a loose, long-standing grouping of conservative Calvinist political independents, opposed to the principles of the French Revolution, into a tight, national, grass-roots political organization. It had a programme, a range of media outlets, and local electoral associations; its organization drew heavily on the model of the Anti-Corn Law League which had been so successful in British politics some twenty-five years previously. The old guard of Calvinist politics, of distinctly patrician tendencies, was represented in the Christian Historical Union (*Christelijk-Historische Unie*, CHU) in 1908, which brought together those who had not agreed with the nature or at least the pace of Kuyper's populist mass politics, and were not in favour of any reckless enlargement of the franchise. It was the ARP, however, which dominated the powerful neo-Calvinist presence in national politics, and led the way in organizational reform for the new age.

Similar events took place in Catholic circles from the 1880s, but the implacable opposition of the bishops and some of the old aristocratic Catholic elite in the Second Chamber prevented a genuine national party from developing until the twentieth century (although the Catholics shared government with the ARP in 1888, and again in 1901). In 1904 there was a General League of Roman Catholic Electoral Associations formed (*Algemene Bond van Rooms-Katholieke Kiesverenigingen*), which effectively was the first national party (though a very weak one). There was a Roman Catholic People's Party formed in 1922, but the *Rooms-Katholieke Staatspartij* (RC State Party, RKSP), the precursor of the modern Party (the KVP, the *Katholieke Volkspartij*) had to wait until 1926 for the bishops to agree to a genuinely democratic political party in the name of Dutch Catholicism.

The socialists were quicker off the mark: after some local foundations had been laid in Amsterdam, the first national party was the Social-Democratic League, founded in 1882 and dominated by Domela. (The SDAP, the modern socialist party, followed in 1894.[56]) It too was a league of local electoral associations. The liberals produced a Liberal Union in 1885: it was a national umbrella organization for local liberal clubs, and commanded only partial allegiance. Even those who joined were too fond of their independence to have any stomach for a tight national organization, and their only points of agreement were their anti-clericalism and their support – of all things – for local autonomy. The national organization went through many transmutations in the years up to the First World War, with the left wing concentrating itself in the Free-thinking Democratic League (*Vrijzinnig-Democratische Bond*) after 1901. The liberals were in essence the old elite being challenged by these developments in mass politics, and so their hearts were not really in the new organizations.[57]

After 1870, in an age of the national political organization, it was rising real wages, rapidly proliferating communications and mass politics which gave the vertically aligned political movements their innovative quality. With an expanding electorate and an increasing culture of democracy, the pillars took shape in political institutions which were to mould the public life of Dutch men – and women – for the best part of the next century.

Secularization and religion

The other background force, against which the development of vertical, ideology-driven social groups must be seen, is secularization, which means the reduction over an extended period of the importance of religion in human existence. For a generation or more now it has been taken as read that secularization has been a feature of modern European culture for two centuries at least, resulting from the scientific revolution, the rise of rationalist thought, the Enlightenment, the French Revolution, the advance of science and modernization in general. As man has exerted more control over his environment and has achieved more material prosperity, longevity and safety from disease, he has had progressively less need of religion – so the secularization theories run. However, the secularization thesis has been heavily challenged, and Peter van Rooden has

---

[56] See section 12.2, on the labour movement.
[57] A good short guide to the organizational developments in the formation of all four pillars/parties is found in Lipschits, *Politieke stromingen*.

led a determined attack on its validity for the Netherlands.[58] His argument is that to view the religious part of modern Dutch history as a long, gradual, steady, 'secular' trend of declining importance is quite wrong, for Dutch society's relationship with religion has been marked by major discontinuities rather than by gradualness. Van Rooden's view, then, is that there were major changes in the function of religion in society – the onset of *verzuiling* being one of them – rather than a simple linear decline in its importance. It is of course true that, although secularism became more noticeable in the census figures, and certain intellectuals and even theologians 'came out' as unbelievers towards the end of the century, the importance of religion to the public life of the nation increased radically, as witnessed for instance by the confessional governments of 1888 and 1901. The 1994 'purple' coalition government of Labour and Liberals was the first administration in more than three quarters of a century not to contain ministers from the confessional parties. In the early 1980s, two American political scientists asserted (perhaps somewhat naively) that theories of secularization did not apply to the Netherlands, because traditional religion was still playing such an obviously important role in public life.[59] However, it will here be contended not only that secularization in its conventional sense was compatible with *verzuiling* and its forcing of religion to centre-stage, but that secularization was actually instrumental in causing *verzuiling*.

The national data are reproduced in Table I.7, and show that in 1899 only 2.25 per cent of the population were prepared to declare themselves atheist or agnostic. The provincial figures reveal regional variances: rural Friesland and Groningen, in the north, had high levels of agnosticism, as did Noord- and Zuid-Holland, with their urban concentrations.[60]

There was certainly an intellectual movement abroad in particular liberal circles which sought to reduce the influence of organized religion in public life. At the same time, within the religious establishment there were forces which (with hindsight) were contributing to the decline of the importance of religion in the minds and lives of the people, such as Dutch Modernism, led in its first phase by the theologian J. H. Scholten (1811–85), which sought to integrate Christianity with human reason. Some of the faithful went along with the Modernist trends, some left the Church (and smaller sects) in orthodox schisms, but others left the faith for good. At the very least the unity and therefore the authority of the churches was being diluted.[61]

[58] Van Rooden, *Religieuze regimes*, 10–45.
[59] Skillen and Carlson-Thies, 'Religious and political development', 45.
[60] The figures are reproduced in Staverman, *Volk in Friesland*, 29; and Kok, *Langs verboden wegen*, 76–9.
[61] On these secularizing influences, see Wintle, *Pillars*, chapters 2 and 4. Modernism's most famous work was its leader's masterpiece, Scholten, *De leer der Hervormde Kerk*.

In the face of increasing numbers of those claiming association with no church at all, of a reduction in the areas in which they operated as major players, and possibly of growing non-attendance at church and indifference to the pronouncements of institutionalized religion, the Dutch churches reacted in various ways. One of them was a concentration. Many of those who were lax members left for good, certainly north of the major rivers, and may thereby have strengthened the churches they left behind: smaller, but leaner and stronger. Accompanying this process of refinement or even purification, the cohesive influence which religion exerted on the local populace – helping to give it a sense of community – was arguably reduced. This further eroded the forces opposed to the powerful trends of national integration: the village as an isolated unit, united by its religion, was on its last legs. But most of all, the religious groups reacted defensively to secularization: they regrouped their forces, and took what action they saw fit to defend themselves. In this sense, *verzuiling* was primarily a defensive reaction on the part of the orthodox Calvinists and the Catholics to secularization and modernization; the socialists and liberals were obliged to follow suit and build their own pillars.[62]

Secular groupings

There were also vertical groups which grew into 'pillars', but which had secular ideologies, like socialism and liberalism. When looking at the labour movement we noted the growth of socialist institutions from the 1870s onwards (section 12.2). Socialism was certainly an ideology which pervaded virtually all spheres of life – and so qualifies as the life-philosophy, worldview, or *Weltanschauung* by and for which a 'pillar' lived; some sociologists have even defined it as a religion.[63] There are some problems with the social composition of the socialist pillar, for not surprisingly it was composed mainly of working-class people. But that was surely true of the religious pillars as well: around the time of the First World War, most of the country was working-class. There was a socialist leadership in the trade union movement, and a substantial presence of intellectuals, many of them from the middle classes. The social structure of the socialist pillar was therefore probably not much more skewed than the Calvinist or Catholic one. A greater problem was the nature of the belief-system itself. Socialism is an ideology with the horizontal divisions in society at its heart, and thus it is difficult to reconcile with a system, like *verzuiling*, which emphasizes the vertical fault-lines. There was no shortage of socialist organizations and institutions which, in time, could and

---

[62] Hellemans, 'Verzuiling', 44.   [63] E.g., Lenski, *The religious factor*, 298.

did become a kind of socialist sub-world, like those of the Calvinists and Catholics. But the idea that the workers should be allocated their own piece of society to do with as they please must rankle deeply with anyone who has even thought about the victory and dictatorship of the proletariat; it was not really until Dutch socialism espoused the revisionism and De Man Plan Socialism of the 1930s that it could bed down more comfortably in the principles of the system of *verzuiling*. Meanwhile, the socialist clubs, media and political organizations grew apace,[64] and socialism provided the route to participation in the public life of the state for many Dutch men and women by the time of the First World War.

The so-called 'liberal pillar' presents more serious problems. Liberalism – however vague, divided and disparate – was certainly an ideology applied to most spheres of life in the course of the nineteenth century (and indeed the twentieth). There were many political organizations with the label 'liberal' attached to them from the time of Willem I onwards. The problem lies in the fact that, as we have seen,[65] liberalism as a political force had little to do with mass politics (with the exception of the radical wing at the end of the century). Its membership was almost entirely of the upper-middle and upper classes (the elite), and after ruling the country for most of the century, in the age of mass politics it effectively became a small, loose collection of what was left of the old political classes, increasingly dominated by an entrepreneurial and free-market employers' interest group. In the crucial years at the end of the century, when the other three pillars were beginning to build walls around themselves in order to gain and consolidate powers, the liberals were being forced to break down their exclusive monopoly on power and share it with others. They did not need to fight for the establishment of their ideology: it had been dominant for decades (and arguably still is). Liberalism had dominated parliament for most of the century (it held fifty-seven of the hundred seats in 1894), but after the arrival of universal suffrage it never again won more than 20 per cent of the Second Chamber seats until after World War II (by which time the party – and Dutch society – had changed considerably). The liberals do not sit well in the *verzuiling* model as a pillar: their part of the vertical structure formed a combination of the remains of the old elite and anyone else who could not fit into the other three. It was mainly composed, however, of those who were entirely accustomed to location in the public life of the state and nation, and thus it did not perform that principal function of the other pillars. In the words of Göran Therborn, liberalism 'was an agglomerate of the enlightened wing of the urban bourgeoisie, provincial intellectuals and notables, and some sectors of the

---

[64] On socialists and social legislation, see Van Leeuwen, 'Trade unions'.
[65] In sections 9.3 and 12.2.

middle strata. This Liberalism constituted the bulk of the Establishment, against which the mass mobilizations of the late nineteenth century were most immediately directed.'[66]

The liberals, nonetheless, harboured some important groups of citizens formed around particular ideologies or at least ideas, and in this way they were crucial for the development of what was to become a Dutch 'civil society', in which the citizenry at large felt free to combine in like-minded groups to set up organizations and structures not necessarily sanctioned by government or even the establishment.[67] Some were purely social, cultural or academic in nature; some were mutually beneficial in an economic sense, and many were to one extent or another political. That freedom and toleration for the development of a civil society has been crucial to the evolution of Western democracy in general, but it is also at the heart of the Dutch variant of that Western consociational democracy, *verzuiling*. The golden age for the foundation of such societies was the latter part of the eighteenth century, but they continued to function in the nineteenth, and to introduce generation after generation to the public life of the country.

The earliest were general scientific and scholarly clubs, in the mid-eighteenth century, with establishment approval and participation by the political and ideological (clerical) elite.[68] Then came a wave of private but potentially political groups which did not necessarily enjoy official approval, like the Freemasons and some literary clubs, linked to the spectatorial press. Before and during the French period, a number of nationalist organizations were set up to promote patriotism and the fatherland, like the *Maatschappij tot Nut van 't Algemeen* (Society for the General Good) of 1784,[69] and the *Oeconomische Tak* (literally, the Economic Branch) of 1777. Then followed the early political clubs of the Patriot and Batavian period, which were oppositional and overtly political, and usually anti-establishment.[70] After the restoration of 1813–15, the political activity died down, and the liberal clubs turned to the arts and recreation; they were peopled by members of the local establishments, and were no longer oppositional. Later in the century many of the old societies took on a new lease of life, with programmes of lectures and readings, as the educated middle classes grew in number: a good example is the Rotterdam Batavian Society, which was founded in 1769, was heavily mixed up in

[66] Therborn, '"Pillarization"', 202–3.
[67] On the notion of civil society, see for example Keane, ed., *Civil society*; Cohen and Arato, *Civil society*; Hall, ed., *Civil society*; and Gellner, *Conditions of liberty*.
[68] For a typology, see Mijnhardt, 'Het Nederlandse genootschap'; and Mijnhardt, *Tot heil van 't menschdom*.
[69] On the *Nut*, see Mijnhardt and Wichers, eds., *Om het algemeen volksgeluk*.
[70] See also Prak, *Republikeinse veelheid*.

Freemasonry and politics, was suppressed, but revived as a scholarly and scientific society in the later nineteenth century, and still exists today.[71] After 1815, these clubs were no longer political. Dutch Freemasons, for example, never became the political force that they did in Belgium and other Catholic countries, and did not have the sometimes violently anti-clerical agenda that their brethren abroad did. Dutch Freemasonry by the late 1860s was very much an establishment affair (as it is now): the Grand Master was the heir to the throne, the Prince of Orange, while his deputies were an ex-Minister of Finance, E. C. U. van Doorn (1799–1882), and the romantic poet, popular novelist and nationalist Jacob van Lennep (1802–68). This was hardly a hotbed of conspiracy.[72]

Some clubs, however, could be highly political. There were free-thinkers' societies like the *Dageraad* (founded 1856), which was at times deist and atheist, but always a challenge to institutionalized religion. Liberal politicians were members of endless clubs and associations. The maverick liberal MP Daniël van Eck, who was one of the founders of the Liberal Union, was a member of the *Nut*, two agricultural societies, an educational society, a literary society and many more.[73] There were liberal political clubs in the major towns in the 1860s and 1870s which operated as caucuses for national elections.[74] Sometimes it was almost as if the members of these liberal clubs were just playing at public life, and it was easy to poke fun: there was a delightful pamphlet published about 1850 as a 'spoof' set of regulations for one of these myriad bourgeois societies, entitled *Regulations of the Bullshit Club established at Quick-Gout, under the sign, 'Chattering maketh the Chatterer'*:[75] the idea of the chattering classes endlessly forming clubs to discuss trivia obviously irritated some commentators (Plate 6). But it was an important role, often played out first within liberal ranks, which was an essential part of the development of civil society. It was emulated by the other emerging social and political groups, and led directly to the formation of political parties and other parts of the institutional paraphernalia of the pillars, which were the key to empowerment in Dutch society at the end of the nineteenth century, and continued to be so for much of the twentieth.

[71] Van Lieburg and Snelders, '*De bevordering*', Chapter 1.
[72] This according to a report commissioned in 1869 by Cardinal Barnabo, head of the *Propaganda Fide* in Rome, from the Nuntius in The Hague, Angelo Bianchi. ASV, Nunziatura, Busta 9, no. 24, on 'Protestants and Israelites'. On Dutch Freemasonry, see Van de Sande, *Vrijmetselarij*; and Van de Sande and Roosendaal, eds., '*Een stille leer-school*'.
[73] ARA, Van Eck, nos 5 and 6.
[74] A good example is *De Grondwet* (The Constitution) in Middelburg, active until 1880. See its archive, RAZ, Grondwet, especially no. 10 on the elections of the 1870s; and a commentary, Van Ommen, 'De liberale kiezersvereniging "De Grondwet"'.
[75] *Wet van het lul-collegie*.

N° 151   438 C 158

WET

VAN HET

LUL-COLLEGIE

GEVESTIGD TE PORT-FORT,

ONDER DE ZINSPREUK:

NUGANDO DISCIMUS NUGARI.

VLISSINGEN.

J. C. DE BUISONJÉ.

DRUKKER VAN HET COLLEGIE.

Plate 6 Title page of *Wet van het lul-collegie*, a spoof set of club regulations, *c.*1850. The title translates as *Regulations of the Bullshit Club established at Quick-Gout, under the sign, 'Chattering maketh the Chatterer'*. Towards the end of the century, clubs were formed for almost anything.

12.4   Groups based on gender and sexuality

Women

We come to the question of the relationship between the Dutch collectivity and those categories or groups in society defined by gender or sexuality. The last two decades have seen an explosion of research and publication on women's history in the Netherlands,[76] as is the case elsewhere, initially concentrating on the history of women themselves, and later on a 'gendered' approach, which has examined the position and relationship of women – or men – *vis-à-vis* others in society. Here our interest is in the way women saw themselves in society and the nation, their participation in public life, their economic function and their social position. Most women in the Netherlands were poor, as were most men. But they had additional problems. They had no vote until 1919; married women were virtually without status in law;[77] women received little education beyond primary school, and were paid much lower wages than men. Their physical condition was probably even worse than that of men because of the particularly gruesome state of gynaecology and obstetrics.[78] Women could sometimes enjoy high status and position amongst men, occasionally in the elite, and more generally throughout society as business-owning widows; but they were the exceptions to the rule. Certain changes had taken place to ameliorate some of these injustices by 1920, although many remained (and still do); the changes came about principally as a result of alterations in the role which women were perceived to fulfil in society, both by themselves, and by society at large (or men).

The bourgeoisie set the tone. Male and female roles in society were thought to be complementary; that is, different. Men were superior in civil law, and went out to earn money and run society; a woman's place was in the home, and her virtues were those of domesticity and motherhood. In the Netherlands there was a strong and early commitment to the ideal of the family provided for by the male breadwinner (alone).[79] After the mid-century there was a move to include 'caring' in the female repertoire, especially for the large numbers of unmarried women: the work of Florence Nightingale, and the trend fostered by the *Réveil* movement in the 1820s and 1830s towards practical social work as opposed to handouts to the poor, were important stimuli in that respect.

---

[76] For a brief overview, see Prak, 'De nieuwe sociale geschiedschrijving', 135–9. There is no section here on 'men', though the history of masculinity is making a start in the Netherlands. See for example Te Velde, 'Viriliteit en opoffering'.

[77] Except for numerous business-widows: Schrover, 'De affaire wordt gecontinueerd'.

[78] Shorter, *A history of women's bodies*, paints a horrifying picture. On the Dutch situation, see Schoon, *De gynaecologie*; and Kistemaker, ed., *Een kind*, chapter 1.

[79] Janssens, 'The rise and decline of the male breadwinner'; and Janssens, *Family*.

Nonetheless, domesticity continued to be the ideal, and child-raising the principal vocation in an essentially patriarchal society.[80] It was as if 'decent' women (for there were others) were almost asexual in their role as morally superior mothers, rather than sexual partners or actors.[81]

Out of this situation the first wave of the 'women's movement' was born (what has been dubbed 'the second wave' came in the 1960s).[82] Female suffrage was achieved relatively soon in the Netherlands, but otherwise the movement was not particularly advanced in its achievements in comparison to its European neighbours and America. In the 1860s and 1870s some of the (male) radical liberals and early socialists began to remark in public on the injustice of gender relations in Dutch society: the free-thinkers' groups were important in this respect. There had long been a small minority of independent and enlightened thinkers who questioned received opinion on the position of women in society, especially towards the end of the eighteenth century,[83] but with the liberal administrations of the mid-century the subject gained a partial respectability. It was Thorbecke who finally permitted the first woman to enter training for a medical degree in 1871, and, after qualifying, Aletta Jacobs (1854–1929) waged a campaign (in vain) in the 1880s to be permitted to vote in elections.[84] In the 1890s, numerous clubs and societies, exhibitions and events publicized the cause and radicalized the populace, discussing taboo subjects like divorce, birth control and even abortion. Finally the franchise was extended to Dutch women in 1919.

However, this version of a seemingly short and successful campaign tells only one part of the story. In the first place, it is probably misleading to think in terms of a unified, monolithic women's movement. The first-wave women's movement was relatively united, in terms of its membership and views, but that was because there were few working women involved in the high-profile movement; there were sometimes divisions along class lines.[85] The middle-class women's movement of the later nineteenth century grabbed most of the headlines, but there were also activists with a lower profile in the working-class movement, often in socialist organizations, which had quite different aims and agendas.[86] Perhaps the only target upon which most activists agreed was the vote,

---

[80] See Blok, 'Hemelse rozen'; Sevenhuijsen, *De orde van het vaderschap*; Van Heteren, 'De troost voorbij'; Fritschy and Toebes, eds., *Het ontstaan*, 209–13; and on the European bourgeoisie, Lasch, *Haven in a heartless world*, 5–6.

[81] Peeters, *et al.*, eds., *Vijf eeuwen gezinsleven*, 189.

[82] The major studies include Bosch, *Het geslacht van de wetenschap*; Braun, *De prijs van de liefde*; Jansz, *Denken over sekse*; and Grever, *Strijd tegen de stilte*.

[83] See Buisman, *Tussen vroomheid en Verlichting*, vol. II, chapter 9.

[84] De Wilde, *Nieuwe deelgenoten*; and Bosch, *Het geslacht van de wetenschap*.

[85] For example, ructions in the 1898 National Exhibition of Womens's Labour: Grever and Waaldijk, *Feministische openbaarheid*, 87–102. See also Jansz, *Denken over sekse*.

[86] Blok, *et al.*, eds., *Algemene geschiedenis der Nederlanden*, vol. XIII, pp. 297–8 and 316.

and even there the elite activists would hardly have been in favour of votes for *all* women. Although the women's movement before the First World War was dominated by the middle and upper classes, there were other women's groups with a rather different agenda.

The 'movement' was actually a series of actions and campaigns by different groups at different times. The political arena has received the most publicity, and it was dominated by the bourgeois strand. Radical liberals recruited women in the struggle to enlarge the franchise in the 1890s, and a targeted pressure-group called the Association for Female Suffrage (*Vereeniging voor Vrouwenkiesrecht*, VVV) was set up in 1894 to campaign expressly for votes for women; it was later run by Aletta Jacobs herself. Club after club was organized by aristocratic and middle-class women activists, working through the existing parliamentary system with the radical liberals, and concerned with rights and votes. The 1898 National Exhibition of Women's Labour, held in The Hague and timed to commemorate the accession of the young Queen Wilhelmina, was a crowning achievement of this period, patronized from on high, dispensing information, building international links, honing organizational skills, publicizing and making respectable the agenda.[87] It also gave untold numbers of Dutch women a new role in life – in public life – for the first time. These talented, motivated people were busy locating themselves in the nation and the state: they had objectives, structures, policies, events and support. The state saw them, and they eyed the state across their chosen battlefield. It may have involved only a small elite of the middle and upper classes, but the potential support was slightly more than half of the population. Along with its international siblings, this political and legal campaign gathered strength in the first decade of the twentieth century, was laid low by the diversion of the First World War, but claimed its main goal in 1919. It was a heroic achievement.[88]

Meanwhile, working-class women were active too. Several women's clubs and societies became affiliated in the 1880s to the socialist federation, the Social-Democratic League (SDB). In 1889 a Free Women's Association (*Vrije Vrouwen Vereniging*, VVV) was organized in Amsterdam in protest by Wilhelmina Drucker (1847–1925); linked to the Socialist Party (SDAP) there were more than eighty women's clubs and societies, which did not in the end exert very much influence, but they too supported votes for women, equal wages (in vain), work for women, and motherhood.[89]

---

[87] Grever and Waaldijk, *Feministische openbaarheid*.
[88] See also Posthumus-Van der Goot and De Waal, eds., *Van moeder op dochter*, 98–146.
[89] Dieteren and Peeterman, *Vrije vrouwen of werkmansvrouwen?*; and Outshoorn, *Vrouwenemancipatie*. For a more recent view with less emphasis on the working-class aspects, see Jansz, *Denken over sekse*.

Another branch of the 'movement' was concerned with gender relations in the workplace. Dutch women have traditionally worked less in the form of waged labour than their counterparts in neighbouring countries, though the statistics may have exaggerated the difference, which in any case has been declining in recent times. One estimate is that in the early years of the twentieth century, women's work accounted for some 25 per cent of all registered labour, so by any standards it was an important economic issue, as well as an ethical one.[90] Two particular points command our attention here: the question of skill, and the debate over married women's work.

Skill can mean 'trained dexterity', or knowledge of a craft; one can be skilled or unskilled at mending bicycles, for example. But skill can also be a social commodity or construct, or a means of differentiating between categories of people, and as such can change or be manipulated. In the process of industrialization, and especially of factorization, some traditional skills were down-graded – for instance those of the handloom weaver. New kinds of work were defined as – and rewarded as –' skilled', by force of a declaration on the part of the interested parties. This redefinition of skill in the face of economic change could also be applied along the gender divide in the workforce, and – inevitably – the women usually came off worst. Thus male work was (and is) often defined as 'skilled', meaning 'privileged' rather than 'requiring training or dexterity'. The classic example is the spinning of yarn. Spinning had always been women's work in the home, but when it was brought into the factory it was defined as 'skilled' and therefore a male preserve. The spinning 'mule' was commissioned in Lancashire to allow the substitution of the labour of women and children for that of men, but the strategy failed. In the words of two commentators on the European situation, 'from the late eighteenth century skill became a social construction more clearly related to gender than previously'.[91]

In the considerable new opportunities in office work and department stores which opened up for young women towards the end of the century, women's roles were rapidly defined as unskilled or at least less skilled than those of most men: power relations were clearly being constructed across the gender divide in the workplace.[92] Women had traditionally been marginalized on the labour market, for example by being largely excluded from the old guilds; as industrialization progressed across Europe and the

---

[90] Van Eijl, *Het werkzame verschil*, chapter 2. See also the review of the debate in Janssens, 'The rise and decline of the male breadwinner'.

[91] Goodman and Honeyman, *Gainful pursuits*, 110; see also De Groot and Schrover, eds., *Women workers*, 52.

[92] De Haan, *Gender and the politics*. See also Van Eijl, *Het werkzame verschil*, chapter 5, on the gendered division of labour in the Netherlands.

Netherlands, factory work became largely a new male preserve, and female factory labour tended to be confined to young, unmarried women: the mill girls. From 1859 right down to 1960, the occupational censuses in the Netherlands show that women never made up more than 20 per cent of factory workers; in 1859 it was 18.3 per cent, in 1889 15.3 per cent, and in 1909 18.2 per cent.[93] However, the impact of technology on gender divisions in labour was always complex, and differed widely on a local basis. In the cotton industry in Hengelo in the east, for example, both men and women worked on the machines; the deciding factor in this case seems to have been the customary sex of the machines' supervisors in the country of origin (for the machines were all imported, from England or Germany): some were male-tended, while others were looked after by women. Thus Hengelo was importing not only its heavy engineering, but also its gendered division of labour. In the food industry at the end of the nineteenth century, women were forced out of brewing by technological changes, brought into margarine production for a while and then eased out by technology, and used to replace men in the cocoa and chocolate factories when new machines were introduced. In the dairying industry, technological changes failed to dislodge women, but they were finally removed from the machines – ironically perhaps – by a law of 1889 on women and children in the workplace which prevented women from working on Sundays.[94] Local experience varied widely, then. Older women, however, worked as a rule in less regular employment, in temporary and unlicensed premises (sweated labour), from home, or in retail. This form of employment was erratic but flexible, and thus the older, married, working-class women performed a crucial service in Dutch industrialization by providing the *elastic* section of the labour supply, both in the countryside and in the more industrial towns.[95]

The 'Victorian' ideal of the family, with its 'angel' wife and mother, was a fitting rationalization of this economic need for flexible, unregulated labour: married women should not have regular jobs, for they were needed in the home.[96] In the Netherlands there was great hostility to the employment of married women.[97] The arguments put forward by patriarchal liberals and confessionals were to do with motherhood and morals, while the male-dominated unions were concerned more with a man's wage adequate to keep a family rather than an individual. Although the

[93] Leydesdorff, *Verborgen arbeid*, 18 and *passim*.
[94] De Groot and Schrover, eds., *Women workers*, chapter 4, pp. 52–66, and chapter 10, pp. 170–92.
[95] Peeters, *et al.*, eds., *Vijf eeuwen gezinsleven*, 230–2.
[96] Goodman and Honeyman, *Gainful pursuits*, 114–17.
[97] Janssens, 'The rise and decline of the male breadwinner'.

argument was seldom articulated, employers wanted flexible labour. As occurred in some other European countries with Christian Democrat majorities, in the 1920s the Dutch government actually went so far as to bar married women from jobs in the civil service, and in the 1930s the confessional-deflationary policies of Hendrik Colijn (1869–1944) and his governments decreed that women teachers had to resign when they became married.[98] In the new world of 'the office' too, there was hostility to female workers from male clerks, employers and government in the early decades of the twentieth century.[99]

However, not all was negative for women. There were considerable new opportunities for respectable employment, especially for unmarried women, in the new service industries and government-run activities like teaching and care; and in the family environment the concept of the 'complementarity' of the two partners in marriage and home meant that the woman did at least count for something. There were advances regarding opportunities and rights for women in education, law and public life, culminating in the vote in 1919. In the workplace some protection for women was forthcoming. (There was little joy on the equal wages front, and married women's work was beset with problems.) In addition, women participated in Dutch civil society through women's clubs and associations at all levels and in all sectors, although concentrated in the middle and upper classes; their votes were even solicited by the politicians. By the end of the First World War, Dutch women were still unjustly treated and seriously disadvantaged, but they had taken up a (contested) place in the nation and were beginning to play a modest part in the state.

Attitudes to sex

Several commentators have held that the people of Western Europe have – in fits and starts – been repressing many of their sexual urges since the sixteenth or seventeenth century.[100] The reasons were diverse – *embourgeoisement*, the spread of syphilis, or the moralism of the Reformation and Counter-Reformation. Within this secular trend, however, there have been periodic shifts or even lurches in Dutch attitudes to sex. Until the end of the eighteenth century matters were relatively relaxed, but then for the French period and most of the nineteenth century sex was increasingly

---

[98] Van Eijl, *Het werkzame verschil*, chapter 7; De Bruijn, *Haar werk*, chapters 2 and 3; Outshoorn, *Vrouwenemancipatie*, 50ff.
[99] De Haan, *Gender and the politics*.
[100] Peeters, *et al.*, eds., *Vijf eeuwen gezinsleven*, chapter 6.

seen as a 'burden' on mankind. As a result of civilization offensives, sex was more or less 'tamed' by the end of the century, and remained so until the 1960s, when freedom seemed to take over once more.[101]

The civilization offensives were certainly a reality: the Dutch bourgeoisie could be a powerful educational and moral force when it was in full cry. The timing tended to be from the 1850s onwards, and coincided with the early stages of the mobilization of confessional groups behind the barricades of education and poor relief. Since the closing stages of the eighteenth century there had been campaigns against sexual promiscuity and other forms of 'immorality', for example in the Catholic south,[102] but the 'offensives' gathered force as the century went on. Sexual promiscuity was not the only target: secularization, beggary and alcohol also came under censure. The reasons for 'this process of moralizing and disciplining' were perhaps to do with fear of the poor, fear of revolution (1848 and 1870), fear for falling real incomes in the 1850s and 1860s, and fear of the social effects of removing care functions from the churches.[103] It also was a part of the move towards pillarization. And what is more, it was effective: from the 1880s on, Dutch demographic behaviour began to differ noticeably from that of neighbouring countries, and it continued to do so until beyond the middle of the twentieth century. The Dutch reproduction rates began to soar as most of Europe settled down into a long-term decline in fertility. At the same time, Dutch illegitimacy rates were extremely low, premarital pregnancies declined rapidly, and cohabitation almost disappeared.[104] The Morality Act of 1911 was a milestone in this advance of the forces of righteousness, and even the activities of the Neo-Malthusian League, aimed at demystifying sexual matters and introducing contraception, were a force for the restriction of extra-marital sexual activity. It seems that the advance of secularization from the end of the eighteenth century sparked a number of reactions in the Netherlands, including *verzuiling* and civilization offensives. These reactions became so powerful that promiscuous behaviour was actually driven back for the best part of a century.[105]

As for homosexuality, public attitudes seem to have become more negative in the course of the nineteenth century, or so it would appear

---

[101] These phases are adopted by D. J. Noordam in Kistemaker, ed., *Een kind*, chapter 4.

[102] For a well-documented local example in eastern Noord-Brabant, see Rooijakkers, *Rituele repertoires*, 362–78.

[103] Peeters, *et al.*, eds., *Vijf eeuwen gezinsleven*, chapter 7, quotation from p. 205.

[104] Peeters, *et al.*, eds., *Vijf eeuwen gezinsleven*, chapter 8, pp. 221–2. Röling, 'Zedelijkheid', suggests that the effects of the campaigns were exaggerated; that may be so, but effects there certainly were.

[105] Peeters, *et al.*, eds., *Vijf eeuwen gezinsleven*, 224 and 227ff.; and Nabrink, *Seksuele hervorming*.

from the results of research into legal archives. While there had been violent campaigns against sodomy in the Republic,[106] the last execution for that 'crime' took place in 1803 because of changes in the law. But the number of prosecutions for public indecency increased, and 'ordinary people rejected and stigmatized the behaviour of sodomites more than in the previous period'.[107]

Another sexual matter receiving public attention was prostitution. In the 1811 penal code, prostitution was no longer listed as a criminal offence. In its policed sector, it took place in semi-regulated brothels. As a reflection of increasing *public* morality, the local regulations governing such houses were made more restrictive as the century went on, until the Morality Act of 1911 made them entirely illegal. After the Municipality Act of 1851, some thirty-six towns took the opportunity to introduce new regulations for their brothels.[108] There were thought to be some 300–400 prostitutes working in Rotterdam and Utrecht, and about a thousand in Amsterdam, where commerical sex was an important part of the labour market for lower-class women.[109] The religious revival movements were active campaigners on the causes and effects of prostitution. Hendrik Pierson (1834–1923) set up a Netherlands Association against Prostitution (*Nederlandsche Vereniging tegen de Prostitutie*) in 1878, which was a principal vehicle of the Protestant moral offensive.[110] There was increasing concern about contagious diseases, with the result that registered prostitutes were inspected with more regularity.[111]

Of course, much commercial sex took place outside the regulated sector, and it is very hard to estimate the real level of activity, as opposed to the public attitude. Prostitution outside the official brothels probably increased, as regulation and public disapproval chased it underground.[112] Furthermore, extra-marital sex and prostitution are highly complex matters: for example, some in the medical profession were in favour of regulated prostitution in order to protect other women – the motherly and wifely 'angels' – from the strain of too much exposure to the curse of male sexual urges.[113] The widespread internal missionary work directed at prostitutes surely reveals deep-seated needs for cultural assertion, as well as simple morality. But it is clear that public attitudes to 'deviant' sexual

[106] E.g., a campaign of 1730–2: Schama, *The embarrassment*, 602ff.; and Van der Meer, *Sodoms zaad*.
[107] Kistemaker, ed., *Een kind*, 155–6; see also Hekma, *Homoseksualiteit*.
[108] Stemvers, 'Prostitutie'; and Van Lieburg, 'De syfilitische patient'. See also De Vries, *Kuisheid*.
[109] Van de Pol, *Het Amsterdams hoerdom*; Kistemaker, ed., *Een kind*, 157.
[110] On Pierson, see Schram, *Hendrik Pierson*.
[111] For the regime in Groningen, see Kooij, 'Gezondheidszorg', 119.
[112] Kistemaker, ed., *Een kind*, 158–9.
[113] Sevenhuijsen, *De orde van het vaderschap*, 67ff.

behaviour tended to become more restrictive in the course of the nine-teenth century, and that they remained so for much of the early twentieth.

The family relationship

Dutch households became smaller in the course of the nineteenth cen-tury, and thus moved in the direction of the modern version. There were fewer live-in servants, fewer live-in relatives, and fewer children. On the other hand, families were often still large. Marriages in the late 1870s could be expected to produce between 7 and 8.5 live births (survival was another matter, of course), while forty years later, from 3.5 to 6 births could be reckoned on for weddings which took place between 1912 and 1916. Catholics had the most children, followed by the orthodox Calvin-ists. With the elderly living longer, three-generation households also continued, especially in the countryside, but also in industrial towns such as Tilburg.[114] But change was slow in these matters, and especially so in the Netherlands. The reasons for the changes were probably to do with economic modernization: industrialization, and social reactions to it. Those of a more 'progressive' turn of mind embraced the changes; many in the conservative bourgeoisie and the churches took action against them, as we have seen, with campaigns encouraging children within wedlock and condemning every other form of promiscuity. The Dutch family 'modernized' over the course of the long nineteenth century, but *verzuiling* ensured that the modernization from a mixed, extended family household to a modern nuclear one was gentle, and even slower than elsewhere. One of the distinctive features of the Dutch experience was the success of the confessional-conservative reaction, which was particularly manifested in the slow decline of marital fertility after 1900.[115]

In demographic terms, the Dutch marriage of the nineteenth century fell into the European pattern of relatively late wedlock, with a significant number of people not marrying at all.[116] As for numbers of children in the family, there was conflicting advice to be had. In the first half of the century in particular, the secular authorities were generally of the opinion that the poor (most of the country) bred too readily. The churches on the other hand encouraged procreation within marriage, and their blandish-ments became one with much of the political centre by the end of the century. As for what actually happened, as opposed to what people were

---

[114] Janssens, *Family*. On numbers of children, Kistemaker, ed., *Een kind*, 118; on house-holds, Van der Woude, 'Bevolking en gezin', 51–5. The household figures exclude those who lived alone.

[115] Peeters, *et al.*, eds., *Vijf eeuwen gezinsleven*, chapter 8, pp. 217–18; Kistemaker, ed., *Een kind*, chapter 3; and Kooy, *Gezinsgeschiedenis*, 198–9.

[116] For the details of the demography of marriage and divorce, see above, section 1.3; the standard work is Van Poppel, *Trouwen*.

urged to do, traditionally the mixed, extended and three-generational household had been a way of limiting the birth rate by restricting the number of people who actually married in order to form a procreative unit. The demographic 'modernization' process of the nineteenth century was essentially a slow breakdown of this convention, mainly as a result of the prosperity which allowed more people to marry and have children.

It was not, however, simply a matter of economic modernization generating the modern family: the structure of the family was influenced by complex cultural codes which were subject to exhortations from institutionalized religion and the example of the local elite.[117] The biological pressures on those who did not have the economic wherewithal to start a family were considerable, and so the practice of 'peasant bundling' or semi-licensed pre-marital sex was virtually universal across North-West Europe, including the Netherlands.[118] The percentage of Dutch marriages succeeded by a live birth within seven months ('shotgun weddings', as a result of pregnancy) fell steadily in the early nineteenth century, from about 21 per cent in the early 1820s to some 16 per cent in the late 1850s; interestingly, Calvinists had much higher levels of forced marriages than Catholics, but the general level declined.[119] A local study of Noord-Holland also showed the success of moralizing and economic improvement on pre-nuptial preganancies in the second half of the century.[120] Much of this refers to rural family life; in the towns, the tone was set by the 'Biedermeier' domestic style of the elite, with their culture of domesticity and devotion presided over by the benevolent father and angel-mother.[121] With all this devotion to family ideals, evidence has been found of a certain 'closing' of the family to outside influences, like the church, locality and extended family, with the complementary partnership being based on love or 'erotic idealization' of each other.[122] We shall examine further two particular aspects related to the family: illegitimacy and attitudes to children.

A study of illegitimacy in the province of Noord-Holland shows a steep

---

[117] See a study of family life in Noord-Brabant: Meurkens, 'Brabants familieleven'; and Janssens, *Family*.

[118] Stone, *The family*, 384. Of many local studies, see for example one on Noord-Brabant: Rooijakkers, *Rituele repertoires*, 360–2.

[119] Engelen and Meyer, 'Gedwongen huwelijken'. On ultra-orthodox Protestants and their attitudes to such things, see Miedema, 'The orthodox Protestants', which emphasizes the distance between the sacred and the profane in their world-view.

[120] Kok, 'Voorechtelijke verwekkingen'. The overall level changed little, but a greater differentiation between professional groups shows the same effect.

[121] On Biedermeier culture in the Netherlands, see Bank, *et al.*, *Delta*, 34ff.; on material bourgeois culture in the home, see Schuurman, *Materiële cultuur*; and Schuurman, *et al.*, eds., *Aards geluk*.

[122] Kooy, *Gezinsgeschiedenis*, 190–2.

decline in the percentage of illegitimate births between the 1820s and the 1880s, with the level remaining steady thereafter at between 1 and 2 per cent. Whereas bastardy rose across most of Europe from 1750 to 1850 at least, in the Netherlands it began to slow down earlier, and by the 1840s the moral offensives had a firm grip on the matter. The conclusion is drawn that illegitimacy is generally to be read as a symptom of economic deprivation and desperation, and that, despite widespread poverty, the Netherlands (Noord-Holland) was a relatively secure place where most women who became pregnant before marriage ended up in wedlock, and where people continued to believe in middle-class ideals of marriage, and were economically able to sustain their belief.[123] The province of Noord-Holland was a highly 'modern' and urbanized part of the country, with perhaps unusually rich economic opportunities; the national figures for bastardy continued to rise until the 1880s (when the message from the pillars really began to get across). Put in proportion, the problem of illegitimacy was virtually negligible, especially where religion held sway as it did in the Catholic south.[124] By about 1890, the changes in approaches to families can be said to have entered a 'pillarized' stage, with a Christian, bourgeois moral code based on the intimate domesticity of the family.[125]

As for attitudes towards children in the family, a number of theories about cultural attitudes to childhood have been applied to the past. Edward Shorter, for instance, maintained that parental love in its modern sense must have been virtually absent before 1800, not least because of the appalling levels of child mortality.[126] It has been posited that notions of child development through the various stages, like puberty and adolescence, only began to be conceptualized in the eighteenth century; before that children were viewed as small adults, for whose immaturity there was relatively little tolerance or indulgence. In the course of the nineteenth century more Romantic ideas about childhood went together with family ideals of devotion and domesticity: some well-to-do women at the end of the eighteenth century took a hand in the rearing of their own children, and might even suckle them – something which Wilhelmina, wife of the future King Willem I, chose to do in 1792.[127] A separate children's literature grew up, and it began to be thought that children should be sheltered from sexuality wherever possible, with nursery rhymes and stories subjected to Bowdlerization.

[123] Kok, *Langs verboden wegen*, 92–3, 141 and *passim*.
[124] See some local research into the Breda situation: Engelen and Hillebrand, 'Vruchtbaarheid'.
[125] Kistemaker, ed., *Een kind*, 116–22 and 160–2; and Kooy, *Gezinsgeschiedenis*, 172–81.
[126] Shorter, *The making of the modern family*. For what follows, see Peeters, *et al.*, eds., *Vijf eeuwen gezinsleven*, chapter 5 by J. Noordman and H. van Setten.
[127] Kistemaker, ed., *Een kind*, 114.

However, these new Enlightenment and then Romantic ideas remained to a large extent just that: ideas. They were of course confined to the moneyed elite, for most Dutch children lived in one form or another of poverty, and it was a harsh world in which (as we have seen) child labour was endemic. It does seem likely that more enlightened sections of the elite took on new attitudes towards their children from the late eighteenth century: whereas the bourgeoisie would decide the careers of their sons virtually without consultation in the Republic, this began to change in the nineteenth century, with young men being permitted and even expected to express a view about their lives.[128] Literary sources suggest that considerable discretion was afforded to nineteenth-century youths in Noord-Holland with regard to their sexual activities.[129] Education slowly changed childhood, as did the factory acts and labour laws. But for most Dutch children – as was probably the case elsewhere in Europe – it was well into the twentieth century before these changes took widespread effect. There was certainly no youth culture, and very little behaviour specific to childhood. There was undoubtedly parental affection, and certainly untold grief at bereavement, but the youth-centred world of the later twentieth century was almost entirely absent.

12.5   Ethnic groups

The Dutch did not harbour the same concerns for their ethnic minorities in the nineteenth century that they do today. The development of state and nation and the integration of most Dutch people in those structures inevitably had its casualties, and some of those were groups which did not fit into the concepts of 'the nation' or 'the state'. In nation formation, alterity is almost as important as identity, and the Dutch needed their 'others', some of whom were found abroad (section 11.2), and some at home. Certain members of what we would now term 'ethnic groups' were citizens of the Dutch state – like Frisians and Jews; others were not, because they were foreigners – like immigrant labour and gypsies. One of the prices to be paid for the formation of state and nation is, as we have noticed, the destruction of regional culture at home; another one was a degree of xenophobia.

'Foreigners' represented about 5 per cent of those resident in the Netherlands in 1800, falling to less than 2 per cent by the end of the century. The definitions changed over time: in the constitutions of the French period and 1813–15, a Dutch citizen had to be born within the

---

[128] See Schuurman and Spierenburg, eds., *Private domain*, 61–71.
[129] Kok, *Langs verboden wegen*, 67.

country – which made it hard for the children of diplomats, and several of Willem I's ministers accordingly needed to be naturalized. In the constitutional revisions of 1848 and 1887, and especially in the Aliens Act (*Vreemdelingenwet*) of 1892, the principle of descent or lineage, rather than place of birth, was acknowledged to be the principal determinant of nationality. Thus ethnicity or racial identity established precedence over locational geography. Many of the 'foreigners' were descendants of immigrants who had been both wealthy and welcomed by the indigenous Dutch at the time of their immigration, like the co-religionist Huguenots, and merchants and financiers from the towns of Flanders and Brabant in the southern Netherlands at the time of the Revolt. The Dutch had been glad to receive the original refugees, and as long as they placed no burden on the state their descendants were welcome to stay. These descendants of 'newcomers' were more or less invisible to the Dutch state,[130] except in certain religious forms, for instance with the Lutheran and foreign-language Calvinist congregations. In the nineteenth century, by means of the Aliens Acts of 1849 and 1892, policy on immigration probably became somewhat more restrictive, with an eye to excluding foreign vagabonds (especially in the 1840s) and politically active refugees from France and Germany around 1870.[131]

Two groups call for special comment in this respect: the Jews, and the gypsies. With the equal status granted to all churches in 1796, official anti-Jewish measures lapsed, and none was introduced again until the Germans occupied the country in the Second World War. However, according to some authorities there was considerable unofficial discrimination throughout the nineteenth century right up to 1940, though much depends on the definition.[132] In the light of other countries' experiences it would be unlikely that Jews in the Netherlands would be entirely exempted from the almost universal anti-Semitism of the age. The government followed policies of assimilation especially in education,[133] and by the end of the century Jewish distinctiveness was largely confined to their religious practices.[134] Their numbers rose from 36,800 in 1815 to 104,000 in 1899 (section 12.3 above, and Table I.7), but their share in the population was never more than 2 per cent, and declining.[135]

Gypsies, on the other hand, were the target of overt discrimination by government. The sources almost certainly confused true gypsies, who may

---

[130] Lucassen and Penninx, *Newcomers*, 29, 77–8 and 129.
[131] Leenders, *Ongenode gasten*.
[132] Michman, 'De emancipatie'; and for recent analysis and information, Berg, *et al.*, eds., *Venter*; and Hofmeester, *'Als ik niet voor mijzelf ben'*.
[133] See Te Velde and Verhage, eds., *De eenheid en de delen*, 135–76, chapters by R. Fuks-Mansfeld and K. Hofmeester.
[134] Kleerekoper, 'Het Joodse proletariat', 83–4; Reijnders, *Van 'Joodse natieën'*, 121–2.
[135] Boekman, *Demografie*, 17–19.

have originated in northern India,[136] with other nomadic groups, but in the seventeenth century there were organized 'gypsy hunts' in the east of the country, and persecution was merciless. It drove these people out of the country or into anonymity. In 1868 some colourfully dressed nomads (actually Hungarians and Bosnians) crossed the border near Almelo in the east, and after some confusion the government resumed its hostile attitude and excluded them on an increasingly systematic basis.[137] Kuyper himself pronounced that gypsies should be assimilated or disappear, but to an extent the government's attitude was formed by the policy of neighbouring states, especially Germany and Belgium, which kept putting the luckless gypsies over the Dutch border. A related group, the 'caravan-dwellers', began to be noticed around the turn of the century, perhaps partly because of the new Aliens Act of 1892, which was entrusted to the military police (*Maréchaussées*) for its implementation. These nomadic or at least transient people, living in caravans and houseboats, were not of gypsy stock; nonetheless the Dutch official mind could apparently not live with the thought of nomads in its ordered, pillarized, structured nation. The national government took action against them – there was a Caravan Act of 1918 – and this is reminiscent of the intolerance outside clearly defined parameters of acceptable variance, which was shown in the persecution of the anti-social families at about the same time (section 9.4).[138]

Another group which was viewed with suspicion tinged with occasional ethnocentricity was that of foreign workers. There were always gangs of Belgian navvies looking for work in the canal-digging and drainage sectors; often they were used by unscrupulous employers to undermine the wage claims of Dutch gangs of *polderjongens* or dike workers.[139] There were also many Belgian tradesmen, shopkeepers, farmers, clergymen and landowners in the border areas in the south, who were regularly the target of xenophobia, especially in the period after the Belgian Revolution and the stand-off in the 1830s.[140] No doubt similar feelings against the Germans flared up from time to time in the east. In the time of the Republic, Amsterdam had been a magnet for certain kinds of labour from all over Northern Europe, especially in the maritime trades; this international labour market seems to have practised little discrimination and did not lead to minority formation. However, much of its function had disappeared by the time of the nineteenth century.[141]

[136] Or may not: Willems, *In search of the true gypsy*.
[137] Lucassen and Penninx, *Newcomers*, 129–33.
[138] Lucassen, *'En men noemde hen zigeuners'*, chapters 3 and 4; and Cottaar, *Kooplui*.
[139] De Bruin, 'Over dijkgraven'. Some archival evidence is collected in Doedens, ed., *Autoriteit*.
[140] See Van Damme and Van Neste, 'Oost-Zeeuws-Vlaanderen', 142–4; Wintle, *Zeeland and the churches*, 146–8.
[141] Van Zanden, *The rise and decline*, chapter 3.

An important mechanism of *seasonal* labour migration existed for most of the nineteenth century, bringing temporary workers into the Netherlands for the harvest or other spring and summer work. Some 20,000 went back and forth each year, their summer destination being the coastal areas of the Netherlands and Belgium, while their winter bases were the inland areas of Belgium, northern France and especially Germany. Their summer work was in capitalized agriculture on the sea clays, infrastructural works, and some other industries like brickmaking in Groningen. The economic function of these workers was beneficial to the Netherlands, for they provided a flexible and seasonal labour supply which did not need to be maintained for the rest of year – during which time they went back to their smallholdings and cottage industries. The system declined in the second half of the nineteenth century, and was eclipsed by 1900, owing to industrialization in the economy of the areas where the migrants were based. As temporary residents they were never considered part of the state or nation, but meanwhile performed most useful economic functions, and possibly a cultural one by contributing towards the alterity necessary for the formation of the Dutch national consciousness.[142]

As we saw in Part I (section 1.6), there was an immigration surplus in the Netherlands before 1850, mainly from various parts of Germany. In the second half of the century the number of foreign residents fluctuated around 70,000, and in the twentieth century it began to rise fast. Again, half were German, and a quarter Belgian. In general, the groups of foreign origin, whether they were permanent or temporary visitors, were not ordinarily subjected to discrimination or violence, although it could flare up at any time. Religion had traditionally been an issue which could raise xenophobic hackles; in the nineteenth century it continued to be, with the Catholic Belgians, and perhaps the Jews. New features in the nineteenth century seem to be intensified competition on the labour market, as the economy became more internationalized and more capitalized with corresponding challenges to the indigenous workers, and emerging nationalist feelings.[143] The Belgian revolt certainly excited nationalistic emotion which could be and was directed against Belgian residents; the German workers may have been occasional recipients of similar feelings, especially around the time of Franco-German rivalry in the 1860s and 1900s, with vulnerable small countries like the Netherlands in between.

Other ethnic groups in the Netherlands resembled nations without a state, the most serious contender among which was the Frisian people.

---

[142] On all these points, see Lucassen, *Naar de kusten*; translated as Lucassen, *Migrant labour*. See also Van Zanden, *The rise and decline*, chapter 9.
[143] Lucassen and Penninx, *Newcomers*, 125–8.

The group was defined partly by its geographical location – within the province of Friesland – but mainly by its language, Frisian. It was spoken in its most distinctive form – the form most alien to Dutch – in the countryside, while in the towns a kind of pigeon Dutch-Frisian was usual. Dutch itself was also spoken. Government was perhaps not overtly hostile to the Frisian language, but its education policy struck at the culture's foundation, by replacing Frisian as the language of delivery in primary schools in 1806. As the nation moved towards further integration, young Frisian men performed their national service, Frisian labour unions liaised and affiliated with their brothers and sisters around the country, Frisian Calvinists joined forces with their co-religionists in other provinces, and political parties recruited Frisians to national organizations. The culture was under pressure, and it suffered;[144] typically, there was a Romantic reaction in the form of a Frisian Movement from the 1820s. Like many movements of its kind (especially the Flemish Movement in Belgium), it was primarily literary in its early phase, and was concerned with preserving the culture in the original language.[145] Magazines and periodicals were founded, and gradually Frisian found its way back into schools, and eventually even into church. There are now some 400,000 speakers of Frisian in the Netherlands, after a relatively successful post-war campaign.

The dominant trend in the nineteenth century, however, was for such regional identities to be broken down and replaced by the national ideal. Local and regional costumes held up quite well, especially in rural areas: they were expressions of a local community spirit where individual characteristics are subjected to the collectivity. As individual styles and tastes in clothing were adopted by the elite, the conservative dressers were the strict confessional groups; by 1920 the new trends had percolated to the *petite bourgeoisie* and working class, even in the countryside.[146] Frisian was the most prominent regional culture, but claims could also be made for Limburg or Brabant or Zeeland culture, to say nothing of the smaller local identities, based on islands or other geographically or historically distinct regions. Very few of them survived the integration processes of the nineteenth century in anything but folklore terms: local colour was welcome, but identity became national. As we have seen in the course of this part of the book, the cultural, political, economic and infrastructural changes of the nineteenth century ensured that the principal grounds for allegiance shifted from geographical locality to national ideology-based

---

[144] Knippenberg and De Pater, *De eenwording*, 169–71.

[145] See for example Feitsma, 'The Frisian movement'; and Jensma, *Het rode tasje*.

[146] See De Leeuw, *Kleding*; and Verhoeven, *Klederdracht*; and especially De Jong, 'Dracht en eendracht'.

criteria. As Gellner feared it would, this 'cultural revolution' marginalized local and regional cultural identity in the Netherlands, more or less for good.[147]

12.6   Conclusion

This chapter has dealt with a number of the more prominent social groups in the Netherlands, and the general approach has been through the perspective of the relationship between the individual and the state. Thematic concerns have been the changes in that relationship, and the shifting allegiances and identities of the Dutch people.

In some ways the class structure of the country changed only very slowly: there were still 'two nations' of rich and poor, and in the provinces the pace of change could be deadeningly slow. However, there were gradual changes, including new elites, white-collar groups, and a vigorous labour movement, which was of fundamental importance in empowering great swathes of working men – and many women – in membership of and representation through labour organizations and political parties. However, this mass-mobilization of the Dutch people took place in sections which were defined primarily by ideology as vertical divisions, rather than socio-economic ones. Secularization played a particular role, generating some of the institutionalization of the socialist and liberal pillars, but also exciting a reaction among orthodox Calvinists and Catholics which became the driving force of *verzuiling* across the country. In reviewing the various religious and secular vertical groups, it is remarkable perhaps that only four such groups emerged in the end as fully fledged pillars; the smaller religions and indeed secular societies never became politicized in the same way that the Catholics, the *Gereformeerden*, the socialists and (to a lesser extent) the liberals did.

Women also achieved a new place in society and the state in the course of the long nineteenth century. By a number of quite different routes, which sometimes interlaced, women of the elite and bourgeoisie, socialist women's groups and women in the workplace all agitated for recognition of their traditional and changing roles. This conglomeration of activity achieved a great deal, including the vote in 1919, and failed to achieve a great deal more; nonetheless, by 1920 women were indisputably involved in public life through their own associations and membership of general organizations in a way in which very few of them were in the first half of the century. Notions of 'civil society' have proved useful here: across all

---

[147] See his quotation in Gellner, *Nations and nationalism*, 57, printed in section 11.1 above. On the power of civilization offensives again local culture in Groningen, see Sleebe, *In termen van fatsoen*, chapter 6.

the social groups, those which were successful in the sense of achieving recognition in the state and the nation were those which engaged in all manner of formal and informal societies, clubs and associations, many of which eventually led to political organizations. The proliferation of such clubs, sponsored not by the state but by private and group initiatives, was an important apprenticeship for many on the road to political recognition, and made a fundamental contribution to the institutional culture of Dutch pillarized society. Not all were successful, though: certain groups of people defined by their sexuality or sexual activity fell foul of the civilization offensives of the second half of the century, and local culture was on the whole a casualty of increasing national integration. Some regional groups – like the Frisians – were able to organize a movement for cultural recognition which booked some successes, but most local characteristics were severely eroded by the standardization processes involved in nation and state formation. And while groups identified as 'aliens' were generally tolerated, nationalism and economic competition could cause xenophobia to rear its head. There were, therefore, some losers in the general progress towards the gradual empowerment of the Dutch people, as they became integrated, located and involved in the state and in the nation.

General conclusion

The transition to a modern society was substantially complete in the Netherlands by about 1920, right across the board. By that is meant that the most important structures of twentieth-century society were in place, and that change was advanced in all relevant fields. Some of them were virtually complete – like the extension of the franchise – while others still had some of their most important developments to come – as in the case of the welfare state. But most of the essential features of modern Dutch society of the twentieth century had emerged, and the transition period was essentially in the past by the end of the First World War.

The population had experienced astonishing growth, mainly owing to plummeting death rates. Fertility rates were very high, and were to remain so for some time. From the 1870s the environmental problems which had helped cause very high mortality were being brought under control, assisted by increasing levels of prosperity and improved nutrition after 1850. Cultural as well as economic factors were of importance in the demographic situation, especially those inspired by the churches. The Dutch diet in both quantity and quality had taken on distinctly modern characteristics in terms of nutrition and variety by the time of the First World War, and so assisted the fall in mortality and brought the causes of death more recognizably into line with those familiar in the later twentieth century.

In terms of the economy, it has recently been argued that the Dutch achieved 'modernity' in the seventeenth century, but that they apparently lost it again towards the end of the eighteenth.[1] Be that as it may, during the first half of the nineteenth century economic growth as measured by the rise in national income per capita was modest – as it was in most other places in the world at that time. In terms of the Kuznets definition of modern economic growth as sustained growth in national income per capita, accompanied by major population increase and structural change across all sectors, the Dutch had to wait until the mid-

---

[1] De Vries and Van der Woude, *Nederland 1500–1815*.

nineteenth century. After 1850 annual growth rates were stronger, with a relative slow-down around the 1880s but a return to higher rates at the end of the century. More to the point, the Dutch outperformed nearly all their neighbours, with the exception of Britain and (marginally) Belgium. They suffered few structural economic disadvantages, except lack of coal and ores; this needed to be compensated for (and was) by the ready availability of other factor inputs, and by an increasingly efficient infrastructure, especially after 1850. Dutch entrepreneurship and technology were not lacking in quality or vigour, and government policy was on the whole supportive of the economy (often more by luck than judgement), with even the very public failures of Willem I being balanced by the great success of his East Indies economic policy. While there was little wrong with Dutch manufacturing, it was not a dominant sector, and agriculture had reached too high a plateau by 1800 to advance very much further in the nineteenth century. The real motor of the transition to a modern economy, therefore, was the service sector, which by the time of the First World War dominated the economy in a way more characteristic of the second half of the twentieth century: in this respect the Dutch were very modern indeed.

The 1850s formed the crucial decade of transition in all economic sectors. The post-Napoleonic difficulties of the 1820s, the structural depression of the 1830s and the harvest failures of the 1840s were all shaken off in that decade, and more or less sustained per-capita growth set in across the field. The openness of the economy brought the Dutch some problems, for example in the Kondratieff slumps of the 1830s and 1880s (and indeed those of the 1930s and 1980s), but in many respects it was also their saviour: colonial demand came to the rescue in the 1830s, Britain's appetite for agricultural produce was always a life-line, and after 1850 the German market was an ever-increasing source of Dutch prosperity, by which time domestic demand was also beginning to play an increasing role. Certainly trade with other economies, alongside transport, was at the heart of the Dutch economic success. The Netherlands was part and parcel of the group of highly developed and industrializing countries of North-West Europe. It held its own against its neighbours, and indeed led most of them throughout the century. In this sense it played a full part in industrialization, even if manufacturing industry (or certain branches of it) was not its strongest suit.

In socio-political terms, with the benefit of hindsight the nineteenth century was one of constant revolution, although very little blood was shed in anger in the Netherlands. The country changed from an oligarchy to a democracy between 1780 and 1920, eventually with universal franchise; citizens were empowered, and the protection of the state guaranteed their interest groups and institutions. The state took on more and more responsibility for providing services to its people, forming the basis of what was to become the great edifice of the Dutch welfare state, replete with all its corporatist and pillarized elements. The Dutch became a nation in the modern sense of the word during the second half of the nineteenth century, with the nation-wide aspects of identity taking precedence for perhaps the first time in the minds and hearts of most ordinary Dutch people. Behavioural patterns altered as a national code was increasingly successfully sold to the populace by the bourgeoisie, aided and abetted by the pillars which were themselves fundamental to the process of nation formation in the Netherlands. Alongside small numbers of exclusions, the vast majority of adults in the Netherlands were integrated and located in the public life of the country as a whole in the course of the nineteenth century. The Dutch may arguably have been economically modern in the time of the Republic, but they became very much more so in the course of the nineteenth century. Certainly the Republic had not achieved the kind of demographic modernity manifested in Dutch behaviour by about 1900, and in the social and political terms outlined here it had hardly begun. That transition to modernity in the long nineteenth century in all fields has been the burden of this book.

The preceding chapters have not carved up the century into short periods, but have tackled the era as a whole. Nonetheless, periodicity has been a major concern in many parts of the study. In demography the critical decade was the 1870s, when death rates began to fall. In the economy the essential changes seem to date from the early 1850s, and, after a quarter-century of boom and a couple of decades of relative slow-down around the 1880s, the structural alterations came together and bore fruit in the 1890s. In socio-political terms, the legal changes which set the country on the road to modernity took place from 1848, with the new constitution followed by Thorbecke's 'organic laws', but it took the rest of the century and the beginning of the twentieth to work through to practical results for ordinary people. In fact that forms the general pattern: significant changes around 1850, with the appropriate preparation in preceding decades, allowed transition to take place over the next seventy years. The economy entered modern economic growth, and by the end of the century was beginning to see its benefits filter down to ordinary people in their real incomes, which was then reflected in their diet and consumption patterns. The democratic era was ushered in by the 1848 Constitution, but full participation by the people in the public life of the state and nation took another half-century and more to complete. By the end of World War I, however, the essential features of modern Dutch society in all its aspects were in place.

Since I. J. Brugmans produced his standard work on this subject in 1961, some of the strands of his analysis have come full circle. He believed in an 'industrial revolution' from 1850 to 1870; the results of the national accounts projects have confirmed that these were the crucial decades for change, although maturity in many sectors only arrived towards the end of the century. It has taken a long time for Dutch historians to abandon the idea of backwardness in the economy in the nineteenth century. The international comparative evidence now leaves no scope for not including the Dutch among the leaders of the economic pack; a spokesman for the national accounts project has pronounced that there was very little difference between the performance of the Dutch and the British, except that the former did not experience very early expansion in or domination by manufacturing industry.[2] It is now clear that the service sector was the mechanism by which the Dutch were able to compensate for all that heavy industry in Belgium and Britain: it was their trade and transport which set the Dutch apart, and set them ahead.

The Netherlands in the nineteenth century was very much part of the North-West European mainstream. The general parameters governing its evolution were common with those influencing its neighbours: industrialization, democratization, secularization and demographic transition. Its response to these and other forces was also similar to that of its neighbours. But there were of course differences, and they are interesting for their own sake, as well as for what they tell us about the detailed workings of these major formative influences in our contemporary world. For example, in the light of the Dutch experience, industrialization turns outs to have had relatively little to do with 'industry' in the sense of factorized manufacturing, and 'secularization' appears to have spawned a set of church-led moral offensives and socio-political structures which turned the Dutch into a religious and moral nation *par excellence* for the best part of a century. These are illuminating insights into these general processes, and the Dutch experience is full of them.

In some areas the Dutch have been quite distinctive. Naturally their own particular circumstances and resource base make their experience technically unique, but there are some aspects which stand out. One we have dealt with extensively: the importance of the service sector in economic development. Another worthy of mention in this general conclusion is *verzuiling*, which, despite recent attacks on its very validity as a concept, is still almost universally cited as the great Dutch distinguishing feature. Again, this Dutch solution was in reply to a set of challenges common across Northern Europe at the time, brought on by democratization.

---

[2] Burger, 'Dutch patterns', 165–6 and 176–7.

Because of gradually rising incomes, expanding political participation (the franchise), the social problems attendant upon industrialization, and the threat of revolutionary ideologies like socialism, the elites needed to make concessions and compromises, which eventually led to labour laws and the beginnings of the welfare state in most European countries.[3] In almost all of them – with the notable exception of Russia – the same elites remained in control, or at least the pace of change was gentle. The prosperity of the Netherlands helped it to be gentler than most, and the mechanism which evolved to allow the Dutch elite to continue in the saddle while involving more and more of the people in the public affairs of the nation was *verzuiling*. The strength and vigour of orthodox (but not other-worldly) Calvinism was important, as was the presence of a large minority of Roman Catholics, seeking out their own identity in the state and nation and available for alliance with the *Gereformeerden*. That particular religious mix is indeed one of those specific characteristics of the Netherlands which were influential in determining the Dutch answers to the universal challenges. A highly structured socio-political system was developed, where nearly everyone could be involved to one extent or another, according to the laws of proportional representation, in group formations which were more vertical than horizontal. The services of the elite were still required for negotiation, mediation, arbitration, regulation and distribution between the groups or pillars. The resources and authority devolved to the pillars seemed the reward for emancipation struggles, and the tradition of rather negative or defensive tolerance was an ideal enabling factor for the whole operation, as were the corporatist tendencies in Dutch society. Other countries – Belgium, Austria and Switzerland for example – came close to the same response to the general challenge, but the Dutch version was unique, and more highly systematized and regulated than elsewhere. That various forms of civil society were employed increasingly to locate people into the state and nation was a universal trend; the particularly pillarized form which it tended to take in the Netherlands was unusual.

Although this book has been schematically divided into three separate parts and twelve chapters, the divisions lose much of their meaning without the whole, and it has been a specific aim in these pages to integrate the various strands of the history of the Netherlands in the long nineteenth century: the demographic with the economic, the economic with the social, and everything with the political. Without necessarily espousing an agenda of integrated or 'integral' history-writing, the Dutch experience only makes sense, especially to 'outsiders', if it is seen in its

---

[3] These matters are explored in Altena, '*Een broeinest*', chapter 2.

entirety. The number of pages here devoted to the economy betray the importance which this author attaches to it, but at the same time the cultural and political determinants of economic activity are amongst the most potent in defining pathways to industrialization and modern economic growth. Political and social stability were crucial, tolerance was important, and the success of the civilization offensives was fundamental in delivering to the Dutch their economic success towards the end of the century and through into the twentieth. On the other hand, industrialization itself led to endless social and political consequences, the most distinctive of which in the Netherlands was *verzuiling*. Clearly, cultural factors were helping to determine demographic behaviour, particularly in its regional diversity, and the enormous population expansion itself was an economic factor of inestimable importance, influencing both the supply and demand sides. Political centralization, nation building and state construction were all critical for the economic surge from the 1850s onwards, and those socio-political factors joined together with industrialization to generate the state in service, or the welfare state, which again was to become a distinguishing feature of the Netherlands in the later twentieth century. All these aspects have been covered in this book, and they are all interrelated in an integral whole.

In the long nineteenth century, then, the Dutch were firmly locked into the economic miracle of the industrializing countries around them, and led the economic charge from the front rank, firing on all cylinders. To that extent, to see 'Dutch history as deviance from the general pattern' is an unrewarding approach. However, the unusual and even unique ways in which the Dutch reacted to general processes are equally worthy of study: their prestigious population growth, their fecundity, their mortality, their service sector, their empire, their tolerance, their *verzuiling*. Between about 1800 and 1920 this small country, in its own way, faced the challenges and stimuli of the age, and emerged after the First World War as a modern state in the demographic, economic and socio-political senses of the word.

Bibliography

ARCHIVE SOURCES

Algemeen Rijksarchief, The Hague
ARA, Van Eck.
  D. van Eck (1817–1895) and Th. G. van Eck (1862–na 1926), 1820–1930.
ARA, Goldberg.
  Jhr. J. Goldberg (1763–1828), 1578–1830.

Archivio Segreto Vaticano, Rome
ASV, Segreteria di Stato.
ASV, Nunziatura.
  Archivio della Nunziatura dell'Aja 1802–79.

Rijksarcief in Zeeland, Middelburg
RAZ, Grondwet.
  Kiezersvereniging De Grondwet te Middelburg, 1857–1880.

PRINTED WORKS

Adelman, I., and C. T. Morris, 'Patterns of industrialization in the nineteenth and early twentieth centuries: a cross-sectional quantitative study', *Research in Economic History*, 5 (1980), 1–83.
Akkermans, T., and P. W. M. Nobelen, eds., *Corporatisme en verzorgingsstaat* (Leiden, 1983).
Algera-Van der Schaaf, M. A.W., 'Quinine cultivation in the East Indies' (unpublished paper, Stolwijk, September 1991).
Altena, B., *'Een broeinest der anarchie'. Arbeiders, arbeidersbeweging en maatschappelijke ontwikkeling: Vlissingen 1875–1929 (1940)*, 2 vols. (Amsterdam, 1989).
  'Continuiteit of een nieuw begin? Gilden en vakbeweging in Dordrecht, 1798–1872', in M. Bruggeman, *et al.*, eds., *Mensen van de nieuwe tijd: een liber amicorum voor A. Th. van Deursen* (Amsterdam, 1996), pp. 462–82.
Altena, B., and D. van der Veen, 'Een onbekende enquête naar broodconsumptie in Nederland in 1890', *Tijdschrift voor Sociale Geschiedenis*, 12 (1986), 135–52.
Ark, B. van, and H. de Jong, 'Accounting for economic growth in the Netherlands', *Economic and Social History in the Netherlands*, 7 (1996), 199–242.

Armstrong, W. A., 'The use of information about occupation', in E. A. Wrigley, ed., *Nineteenth century society: essays in the use of quantitative methods for the study of social data* (Cambridge, 1972), pp. 191–310.

Atlas van Nederland, compiled by Stichting Wetenschappelijk Atlas van Nederland (The Hague, 1963–77, plus supplements).

Baart, K., *Een blik in de gemeenschappelijke woning* (Middelburg [1867]).

Westkapelle, hare bevolking, Westkapelsche dijk: geschiedkundig en karakteriseerend beschreven (Middelburg, 1889).

Bachiene, P. J., *Over een Nederlandsche hypotheekbank* (The Hague, 1855).

Baetens, R., *et al.*, ed., *Maritieme geschiedenis der Nederlanden*, vol. IV, *Tweede helft negentiende eeuw en twintigste eeuw, van 1850–1870 tot ca 1970* (Bussum, 1978).

Bairoch, P., 'Europe's gross national product: 1800–1975', *Journal of European Economic History*, 5 (1976), 273–340.

'The main trends in national economic disparities since the industrial revolution', in P. Bairoch and M. Lévy-Leboyer, eds., *Disparities in economic development since the industrial revolution* (London, 1981), pp. 3–17.

Bakker, H. de, *Major soils and soil regions in the Netherlands* (The Hague, 1979).

Bank, J. T. M., *Het roemrijk vaderland: cultureel nationalisme in Nederland in de negentiende eeuw* (The Hague, 1990).

Bank, J. T. M., *et al.*, *Delta: Nederlands verleden in vogelvlucht*, vol. III, *De nieuwste tijd: 1813 tot heden* (Groningen, 1993).

Barentsen, P. A. *Het oude Kempenland: een proeve van vergelijking van organisme en samenleving* (Groningen, 1935).

Baudet, H., 'The economic interest of the Netherlands in the Netherlands East Indies', in *Papers of the Dutch-Indonesian historical conference held at Noordwijkerhout, the Netherlands 19 to 22 May 1976* (Leiden, 1978), pp. 234–49.

'Nederland en de rang van Denemarken', *Bijdragen en Mededelingen betreffende de Geschiedenis der Nederlanden*, 90/3 (1975), 430–43.

Baudet, H., and C. Fasseur, 'Koloniale bedrijvigheid', in J.H. van Stuijvenberg, ed., *De economische geschiedenis van Nederland* (Groningen, 1977), pp. 309–50.

Baudet, H., and H. van der Meulen, eds., *Consumer behaviour and economic growth in the modern economy* (London, 1982).

Kernproblemen der economische geschiedenis (Groningen, 1978).

Bax, E. H., *Modernization and cleavage in Dutch society: a study of long term economic and social change* (Aldershot, 1990).

Bayley, D. H., 'The police and political development in Europe', in Charles Tilly, ed., *The formation of national states in Western Europe* (Princeton, NJ, 1975), pp. 328–79.

Beer, J. J. A. de, 'De levensstandaard in Nederland: voeding en gezondheid in de eerste helft van de negentiende eeuw', *Tijdschrift voor Sociale Geschiedenis*, 22/1 (1996), 24–52.

'Voeding, fysieke arbeidscapaciteit en productiviteit in Nederland, ca 1850–ca 1900', *NEHA-Jaarboek*, 61 (1998), 196–225.

Berg, H., *et al.*, eds., *Venter, fabriqueur, fabrikant: Joodse ondernemers en ondernemingen in Nederland 1796–1940* (Amsterdam, 1994).

Berger, J. A., *Van armenzorg tot werklozenzorg* (Amsterdam, 1936).

Bergink, A. H., *Samuel Senior Coronel: zijn betekenis voor de sociale geneeskunde in Nederland* (Assen, 1960).

'Samuel Senior Coronel: zijn strijd voor de afschaffing van de kinderarbeid in Nederland', *Sociaal Maandblad Arbeid* (1967), 754–62.

Bergman, M., 'The potato blight in the Netherlands and its social consequences (1845–1847)', *International Review of Social History*, 12 (1967), 390–431.

Berkel, K. van, *et al.*, *Spiegelbeeld der wetenschap: het Genootschap ter Bevordering van Natuur-, Genees- en Heelkunde 1790–1990* (Rotterdam, 1991).

Besouw, F. van, *et al.*, eds., *Balans en perspectief: visies op de geschiedwetenschap in Nederland* (Groningen, 1987).

Bie, R. van, der, *'Een doorlopende groote roes': de economische ontwikkeling van Nederland 1913–1921* (Amsterdam, 1995).

Bieleman, J., 'Dutch agriculture 1850–1920: responding to changing markets', *Jahrbuch für Wirtschaftsgeschichte*, 1 (1996), 11–52.

Geschiedenis van de landbouw in Nederland 1500–1950 (Meppel, 1992).

Bläsing, J.F.E., *Das goldene Delta und sein eisernes Hinterland 1815–1851: von niederländisch-preussischen zu deutsch-niederländischen Wirtschaftbeziehungen* (Leiden, 1973).

'Interne en externe oorzaken van de liberalisering der Nederlandse handels-politiek in het midden van de 19de eeuw', *Maandschrift Economie*, 40 (1976), 322–37.

Blink, H., *Geschiedenis van den boerenstand en den landbouw in Nederland: een studie van de ontwikkeling der economische, maatschappelijke en agrarische toestanden, voornamelijk ten plattenlande*, 2 vols. (Groningen, 1902–4).

Blockmans, W. P., and L. A. van der Valk, eds., *Van particuliere zorg naar openbare zorg, en terug? Sociale politiek in Nederland sinds 1880* (Amsterdam, 1992).

Bloemen, E. S. A., *Scientific management in Nederland 1900–1930* (Amsterdam, 1988).

Bloemgarten, S. E., *Henri Polak: sociaal democraat 1868–1943* (Amsterdam, 1993).

Blok, D. P. *et al.*, eds., *Algemene geschiedenis der Nederlanden*, 15 vols. (Haarlem, 1975–83).

Blok, J., 'Hemelse rozen door 't wereldse leven: sekse en de Nederlandse burgerij in de negentiende eeuw', in R. Aerts and H. te Velde, eds., *De stijl van de burger: over Nederlandse burgelijke cultuur vanaf de middeleeuwen* (Kampen, 1998), pp. 123–56.

Blok, L., and J. M. M. de Meere, 'Welstand, ongelijkheid in welstand en census-kiesrecht in Nederland omstreeks het midden van de 19de eeuw', *Economisch- en Sociaal-Historisch Jaarboek*, 41 (1978), 175–293.

Blom, J. C. H., 'Pillarization in perspective' (paper delivered to the Second European Social Science History Conference, Amsterdam, March 1998).

Boekman, E., *Demografie van de joden in Nederland* (Amsterdam, 1936).

Boelmans Kranenburg, H. A. H., 'Visserij', in R. Baetens, *et al.*, eds., *Maritieme geschiedenis der Nederlanden*, vol. IV, *Tweede helft negentiende eeuw en twintigste eeuw, van 1850–1870 tot ca 1970* (Bussum, 1978), pp. 272–301.

Boissevain, G. M., 'De omvang en de verdeeling van het stoffelijk vermogen in

Nederland', *De Economist* (1883), part II, 692–700.

Bonaparte, Louis, *Historical documents and reflections on the government of Holland*, 3 vols. (London, 1820).

Boogman, J. C., and C. A. Tamse, eds., *Emancipatie in Nederland: de ontvoogding van burgerij en confessionelen in de negentiende eeuw: 27 teksten over emancipatie in Nederland* (The Hague, 1978).

Boonstra, O. W. A., *De waarde van een vroege opleiding: een onderzoek naar de implicaties van het alfabetisme op het leven van inwoners van Eindhoven en omliggende gemeenten, 1800–1920*, A.A.G. Bijdragen 34 (Wageningen, 1993).

Boonstra, O. W. A., and A. M. van der Woude, 'Demographic transition in the Netherlands: a statistical analysis of regional differences in the level and development of the birth rate and of fertility 1850–1890', *A.A.G. Bijdragen*, 24 (1984), 1–58.

Bornebroek, A. H., *De strijd voor harmonie: de geschiedenis van de Industrie- en Voedingsbond CNV 1896–1996* (Amsterdam, 1996).

Gids voor de archieven van de christelijke vakbeweging in Nederland (Amsterdam, 1998).

Bornewasser, J. A., 'In 1845 een Nederlandse Ronge? Vervlogen illusie en denkbeeldig gevaar', in H. F. J. M. van den Eerenbeemt, *et al.*, eds., *Voor Rogier: een bundel opstellen van oud-leerlingen de hoogleraar bij zijn afscheid aangeboden* (Hilversum, 1964), pp. 223–39.

'De katholieke partijvorming tot de eerste wereldoorlog', in L. W. G. Scholten, *et al.*, *De confessionelen: ontstaan en ontwikkeling van de christelijke partijen* (Utrecht, 1968), pp. 23–40.

Bos, H. C., 'Economic growth of the Netherlands: a summary of findings' (unpublished paper, Rotterdam, 1959, presented to the sixth European Conference of the International Association for Research in Income and Wealth, Portoroz (Yugoslavia), 23 August to 1 September 1959).

'Long-term demographic development in the Netherlands: a statistical survey' (unpublished paper, Rotterdam, 1956).

Bos, N. J. P. M., 'Vermogensbezitters en bevoorrechte belastingbetalers in de negentiende eeuw', *Bijdragen en Mededelingen betreffende de Geschiedenis der Nederlanden*, 105 (1990), 553–77.

Bos, R. W. J. M., *Brits-Nederlandse handel en scheepvaart, 1870–1914: een analyse van machtsafbrokkeling op een markt* (Wageningen, 1978).

'Industrialization and economic growth in the Netherlands during the nineteenth century: an integration of recent studies', *Low Countries History Yearbook*, 15 (1982), 21–58.

'Kapitaal en industrialisatie in Nederland tijdens de negentiende eeuw', *A.A.G. Bijdragen*, 22 (1979), 89–107.

'Van periferie naar centrum: enige kanttekeningen bij de Nederlandse industriële ontwikkeling in de negentiende eeuw', in P. A. M. Geurts and F. A. M. Messing, eds., *Economische ontwikkeling en sociale emancipatie: 18 opstellen over economische en sociale geschiedenis*, 2 vols. (The Hague, 1977), vol. II, pp. 68–92.

'Remarks upon long-term economic fluctuations: industrialization and economic growth during the nineteenth century', in D. Petzina and G. van Roon, eds., *Konjunktur, Krise, Gesellschaft: wirtschaftliche Wechsellagen und soziale Entwicklung im 19. und 20. Jahrhundert* (Stuttgart, 1981), pp. 36–41.

'Techniek en industrialisatie: Nederland in de negentiende eeuw', *A.A.G. Bijdragen*, 22 (1979), 59–88.

Bos, S. B., *'Uyt liefde tot malcander': onderlingse hulpverlening binnen de Noord-Nederlandse gilden in internationaal perspectief (1570–1820)* (Amsterdam, 1998).

Bosch, C. W., *Het geslacht van de wetenschap: vrouwen en hoger onderwijs in Nederland 1878–1948* (Amsterdam, 1994).

Bosch, I. G. J. van den, *et al.*, 'Rapport van het voorstel tot afschaffing der tienden', *Verslag van het Verhandelde op het Landhuishoudkundig Congres*, 2 (1847), 28–83.

Bosch Kemper, J. de, *Inkomsten en uitgaven van den staat* (Amsterdam, 1860).

'Statistiek van Nederland: grondgebied, bevolking, middelen van bestaan', in J. de Bosch Kemper and L. Mulder, *De aardrijkskunde in het algemeen en die van Nederland en zijne koloniën in het bijzonder* (Amsterdam [1869]), pp. 1–40.

Boschloo, T. J., *De productiemaatschappij: liberalisme, economische wetenschap en het vraagstuk der armoede in Nederland 1800–1875* (Hilversum, 1989).

Bosschaert, D., *De stad Utrecht als medisch ontwikkelingsgebied* (Rotterdam, 1969).

Bouman, P. J., *Geschiedenis van den Zeeuwschen landbouw in de negentiende en twintigste eeuw en van de Zeeuwsche Landbouw-Maatschappij 1843–1943* (Wageningen, 1946).

'Landbouworganisaties', in Z. W. Sneller, ed., *Geschiedenis van den Nederlandschen landbouw 1790–1940* (Groningen, 1943), pp. 252–68.

'De tuinbouw', in Z. W. Sneller, ed., *Geschiedenis van den Nederlandschen landbouw 1790–1940* (Groningen, 1943), pp. 385–403.

Braun, M., *De prijs van de liefde: de eerste feministische golf, het huwelijksrecht en de vaderlandse geschiedenis* (Amsterdam, 1992).

Bree, L. W. de, *Het platteland leert lezen en schrijven: het lager onderwijs op het platteland in de eerste helft der 19e eeuw* (Amsterdam, s.a. [c. 1955]).

Breman, J. C., *Taming the coolie beast: plantation society and the colonial order in Southeast Asia* (Delhi, 1989).

Brink, E. A. B. J. ten, *De geschiedenis van het postvervoer* (Bussum, 1969).

Brinkman, H. J., *et al.*, 'Lichaamslengte en reëel inkomen: een nieuwe schattings-methode voor historische inkomensreeksen', *Economisch- en Sociaal-Historisch Jaarboek*, 51 (1988), 35–79.

Brinkman, H. J., *et al.*, 'The representativeness of the Dutch military registers as a source for quantitative history', *Economic and Social History in the Netherlands*, 1 (1989), 149–70.

Broecke, J. P. van den, *Beschermd door dijk en duin: bladzijden uit de geschiedenis van de Zeeuwse strijd tegen het water* (Delft, s.a. [c. 1970]).

Broecke, W. van den, *Financiën and financiers van de Nederlandse spoorwegen 1837–1890* (Zwolle, 1985).

Broek, J. O. M., *Economic development of the Netherlands Indies* (New York, 1942).

Broes van Dort, K., *Bijdrage tot de kennis van de sterfte der gemeente Goes, en van den gemiddelden en waarschijnlijken levensduur harer inwoners, gedurende het 30 jarige tijdvak (1830–1859)* (Goes, 1861).

Broeze, F. J. A., 'Atlantic rivalry: the struggle for the Dutch tea market 1813–1850', *Low Countries History Yearbook*, 11 (1978), 94–127.

'Laat mercantilist of selectief vrijhandelaar? Koning Willem I en zijn economische politiek aangaande de Nederlandse handel met China', in Joh. de Vries, *et al.*, eds., *Ondernemende geschiedenis: 22 opstellen geschreven bij het afscheid van mr. H. van Riel als voorzitter van de vereniging Het Nederlandsch Economisch-Historisch Archief* (The Hague, 1977), pp. 220–40.

Brouwer, H., 'Malaria in Nederland in de achttiende en negentiende eeuw', *Tijdschrift voor Sociale Geschiedenis*, 9 (1983), 140–59.

Brugmans, I. J., *Begin van twee banken 1863: uitgegeven ter gelegenheid van het eeuwfeest van de Rotterdamsche Bank en de Nationale Handelsbank* (s.l. [1963]).

'Economic fluctuations in the Netherlands in the nineteenth century', in F. Crouzet, *et al.* eds., *Essays in European economic history 1789–1914* (London, 1969), pp. 128–54.

'Nederlands overgang van onderontwikkeld gebied tot industrieland', *De Economist*, 117 (1969), 73–85.

Paardenkracht en mensenmacht: sociaal-economische geschiedenis van Nederland 1795–1940 (The Hague, 1961).

Tachtig jaar varen met de Nederland 1870–1950 (Den Helder, 1950).

Welvaart en historie: tien studiën, second edition (The Hague, 1970).

Bruijn, J. de, *Haar werk: vrouwenarbeid en arbeidssociologie in historisch en emancipatorisch perspectief* (Amsterdam, 1989).

Bruin, M. P. de, 'Dr. Coronel en zijn tijd', *Zeeuws Tijdschrift*, 9 (1959), 29–37.

'Over dijkgraven en polderjongens', *Archief Zeeuws Genootschap* (1970), 100–14.

Bruin, M. P. de, and M. H. Wilderom, *Tussen afsluitdam en deltadijken*, vol. I, *Noord-Beveland: geschiedenis van strijd, nederlaag en overwinning op het water*, second printing (Middelburg, 1971).

Brunt, L., 'Over gereformeerden en kleine luyden: enige kanttekeningen bij de voorstelling van zaken m.b.t. de afkomst en samenstelling van het huidige gereformeerde volksdeel', *Sociologische Gids*, 19 (1972), 49–58.

Bruwier, M., and J. Dhondt, 'The industrial revolution in the Low Countries 1700–1914', in C. M. Cipolla, ed., *The emergence of industrial societies*, Fontana Economic History of Europe 4, 2 vols. (Glasgow, 1973), vol. I, pp. 329–66.

Büch, B., 'Proeve van een inleiding tot het drug- en medicijngebruik in het 19e-eeuwse Nederland', *Negentiende Eeuw*, 1 (1977), 66–76.

'De verziekte revolutie van 1848: gezondheidstoestand van de Nederlandse bevolking', *Negentiende Eeuw*, 1 (1977), 193–9.

Buis, J., *Historia forestis: Nederlandse bosgeschiedenis*, 2 vols., A.A.G. Bijdragen 26 and 27 (Wageningen, 1985).

Buisman, J. W., *Tussen vroomheid en Verlichting: een cultuurhistorisch en -sociologisch onderzoek naar enkele aspecten van de Verlichting in Nederland (1755–1807)*, 2 vols. (Zwolle, 1992).

Buissink, J. D., 'Regional differences in marital fertility in the Netherlands in the second half of the nineteenth century', *Population Studies*, 25 (1971), 353–74.

Buning, L., *Het herenbolwerk: politieke en sociale terreinverkenning in Drenthe over de periode 1748–1888* (Assen, 1966).

Burema, L., *De voeding in Nederland van de middeleeuwen tot de twintigste eeuw* (Assen, 1953).

Burger, A., 'Dutch patterns of development: economic growth and structural change in the Netherlands, 1800–1910', *Economic and Social History in the Netherlands*, 7 (1996), 161–80.

Burger, A., and J. P. Smits, 'A benchmark comparison of service productivity between Europe and the United States for 1910', *Economic and Social History in the Netherlands*, 7 (1996), 133–60.

Burger, A., and A. Vermaas, 'Dutch industrial wage development in an international perspective, 1850–1913', *Economic and Social History in the Netherlands*, 7 (1996), 109–32.

Butter, I. H., *Academic economics in Holland 1800–1870* (The Hague, 1969).

Buyst, E., and J. Mokyr, 'Dutch manufacturing and trade during the French period (1795–1814) in a long term perspective', in E. Aerts and F. Crouzet, eds., *Economic effects of the French Revolutionary and Napoleonic Wars*, Proceedings of the Tenth International Economic History Congress, Leuven 1990, Session B-1 (Leuven, 1990), pp. 64–78.

Buyst, E., *et al.*, 'National accounts for the Low Countries, 1800–1990', *Scandinavian Economic History Review*, 43/1 (1995), 53–76.

Caland, A., *Beschouwingen over den gezondheidstoestand van Nederland en in het bijzonder van Middelburg* (Middelburg, 1857).

Caldwell, M., *Indonesia: an alternative history* (Sydney, 1979).

Cameron, R., *et al.*, *Banking in the early stages of industrialization: a study in comparative economic history* (London, 1967).

Camijn, A. J. W., *Een eeuw vol bedrijvigheid: de industrialisatie van Nederland, 1814–1914* (Utrecht, 1987).

Carter, A. C., *The Dutch Republic in Europe in the Seven Years War* (London, 1971).

Carter, A. C., ed., *Getting, spending and investing in early modern times: essays on Dutch, English and Huguenot economic history* (Assen, 1975).

'Centralisatie en staatkundige vrijheid', *Tijdschrift voor Staathuishoudkunde en Statistiek*, 22 (1862), 417–40, and 23 (1863), 1–24, 115–35 and 411–38.

Charité, J., *De Sociaal-Democratische Bond als orde- en gezagsprobleem voor de overheid (1880–1888)* (The Hague, 1972).

Clemens, A., P. Groote, and R. Albers, 'The contribution of physical and human capital to economic growth in the Netherlands, 1850–1913', *Economic and Social History in the Netherlands*, 7 (1996), 181–98.

Cohen, J. L., and A. Arato, *Civil society and political theory* (Cambridge, Mass., 1992).

Colenbrander, H. T., *Koloniale geschiedenis*, 3 vols. (The Hague, 1926).

Coopmans, J. P. A., 'Van beleid van politie naar uitvoering en bestuur 1700–1840', *Bijdragen en Mededelingen betreffende de Geschiedenis der Nederlanden*, 104 (1989), 579–91.

Coronel, S., *De gezondheidsleer toegepast op de fabrieksnijverheid: een handboek voor industriëlen, genees- en staathuishoudkundigen* (Haarlem, 1861).

Middelburg voorheen en thans: bijdrage tot de kennis van den voormaligen en tegenwoordigen toestand van het armwezen aldaar (Middelburg, 1859).

'De ziekten der calicot-wevers', *Nederlandsch Tijdschrift voor Geneeskunde*, 4 (1869), 497–506.

Cottaar, A., *Kooplui, kermisklanten en andere woonwagenbewoners: groepsvorming en beleid 1870–1945* (Amsterdam, 1996).

Couwenberg, S. W., ed., *De Nederlandse natie* (Utrecht, 1981).

Crafts, N. F. R., 'GNP in Europe 1870–1914: some new estimates', *Explorations in Economic History*, 20 (1983), 387–401.

'Patterns of development in nineteenth-century Europe', *Oxford Economic Papers*, 36 (1984), 438–58.

Daal, J. van, and A. Heertje, eds., *Economic thought in the Netherlands: 1650–1950* (Aldershot, 1992).

Dahl, R. A., ed., *Political opposition in Western democracies* (New Haven, 1966).

Damme, J. van, and N. van Neste, 'Oost-Zeeuws-Vlaanderen in de status-quo periode 1830–1839' (unpublished doktoraalskriptie, K.U. Nijmegen, 1983).

Davids, K., 'Shifts of technological leadership in early modern Europe', in K. Davids and J. Lucassen, eds., *A miracle mirrored: the Dutch Republic in European perspective* (Cambridge, 1995), pp. 338–66.

Davids, K., and J. Lucassen, eds., *A miracle mirrored: the Dutch Republic in European perspective* (Cambridge, 1995).

Davids, K., J. Lucassen and J. L. van Zanden, *De Nederlandse geschiedenis als afwijking van het algemeen menselijk patroon: een aanzet tot een programma van samenwerking* (Amsterdam, 1988).

Deprez, P., 'The Low Countries', in W. R. Lee, ed., *European demography and economic growth* (London, 1979), pp. 236–83.

Dercksen, A. and L. Verplancke, *Geschiedenis van de onmaatschappelijkheidsbestrijding in Nederland, 1914–1970* (Meppel, 1987).

Derksen, J. B. D., 'De groei van het reële nationale inkomen in Nederland en in een aantal andere landen, 1900–1955', *Statistische en Econometrische Onderzoekingen* (1957), 150–64.

'Long-term changes in growth in the Netherlands since the middle of the nineteenth century', in D. Petzina and G. van Roon, eds., *Konjunktur, Krise, Gesellschaft: wirtschaftliche Wechsellagen und soziale Entwicklung im 19. und 20. Jahrhundert* (Stuttgart, 1981), pp. 23–35.

Derksen, J. B. D., and J. Tinbergen, 'Berekeningen over de economische beteekenis van Nederlandsch-Indië voor Nederland', *Maandschrift van het C.B.S.* (1945), 210–16.

Dick, H. W., *The Indonesian interisland shipping industry: an analysis of competition and regulation* (Singapore, 1987).

Dieleman, P., 'Inleiding', in D. R. Mansholt, *De waterschapslasten in de provincie Zeeland* (The Hague, 1940), pp. 9–52.

De Zeeuwsche Landbouw Maatschappij 80 jaar: historische rede (s.l. [1923]).

Dierikx, M., 'De positie van Nederlands-Indië in de internationale burgerluchtverkeer, 1981–1942', in P. Luykx and A. F. Manning, eds., *Nederland en de wereld 1870–1950* (Nijmegen, 1988), pp. 121–39.

Dieteren, F., and I. Peeterman, *Vrije vrouwen of werkmansvrouwen? Vrouwen in de*

Sociaal-Democratische Bond (1879–1894) (Utrecht, 1984).

Dijk, H. van, 'De beroepsmobititeit in Rotterdam in de negentiende eeuw', in J. van Herwaarden, ed., *Lof der historie* (Rotterdam, 1973), pp. 187–210.

Rotterdam 1810–1880: aspecten van een stedelijke samenleving (Schiedam, 1976).

The three seaports of the Low Countries in the nineteenth century: Amsterdam, Antwerp and Rotterdam (Rotterdam, 1980).

Wealth and property in the Netherlands in modern times, Centrum voor Maatschappijgeschiedenis Mededelingen 8 (Rotterdam, 1980).

Doedens, A., ed., *Autoriteit en strijd: elf bijdragen tot de geschiedenis van collectief verzet in de Nederlanden, met name in de eerste helft van de negentiende eeuw* (Amsterdam, 1981).

Doorn, J. A. A. van, 'Schets van de Nederlandse politieke traditie', in J. W. de Beus, *et al.*, *De ideologische driehoek: Nederlandse politiek in historisch perspectief* (Meppel, 1989), pp. 11–60.

Douwes, P. A. C., *Armenkerk: de hervormde diaconie te Rotterdam in de negentiende eeuw* (Rotterdam, 1977).

Drukker, J. W., *Waarom de crisis hier langer duurde: over de Nederlandse economische ontwikkeling in de jaren dertig* (Amsterdam, 1990).

Dudink, S., *Deugdzaam liberalisme: sociaal-liberalisme in Nederland 1870–1901* (Amsterdam, 1997).

Dussen, J. W. van der, 'Financial relations between central and local government in the Netherlands: why are they different?', *Local Government Studies*, 18/4 (1992), 94–105.

Eeckhout, P. van den, and P. Scholliers, 'De hoofdelijke voedselconsumptie in België, 1831–1939', *Tijdschrift voor Sociale Geschiedenis*, 9/31 (1983), 273–301.

Eekelen, A. van, *Naar een rationele zuigenlingenvoeding: voedingsleer en kindergeneeskunde in Nederland (1840–1914)* (Nijmegen, 1984).

Eerenbeemt, H. F. J. M. van den, 'Armoede in de "gedrukte" optiek van de sociale bovenlaag in Nederland, 1750–1850', *Tijdschrift voor Geschiedenis*, 88 (1975), 468–500.

Bedrijfskapitaal en ondernemerschap in Nederland 1800–1850: rede (Leiden, 1965).

Ontwikkelingslijnen en scharnierpunten in het Brabants industrieel bedrijf 1777–1914 (Tilburg, 1977).

Eijl, C. van, *Het werkzame verschil: vrouwen in de slag om arbeid, 1898–1940* (Hilversum, 1994).

Ellemers, J. E., 'Pillarization as a process of modernization', *Acta Politica*, 19 (1984), 129–44.

Empel, M. van, and H. Pieters, *Zeeland door de eeuwen heen*, 2 vols. (Middelburg, 1935 and 1959).

Engelen, T., and H. Hillebrand, 'Vruchtbaarheid in verandering: een gezinsreconstructie in Breda, 1850–1940', *Tijdschrift voor Sociale Geschiedenis*, 11 (1985), 248–89.

Engelen, T. L. M., and J. A. Hillebrand, 'De daling van de vruchtbaarheid in de negentiende en twintigste eeuw: een historiografische overzicht met bijzondere aandacht voor Nederland', *Bijdragen en Mededelingen betreffende de*

Geschiedenis der Nederlanden, 105 (1990), 354–67.

Engelen, T. L. M., and M. M. Meyer, 'Gedwongen huwelijken op het Nederlandse platteland, 1812–1862', *A.A.G. Bijdragen*, 22 (1979), 190–220.

Engels, P. H., *De belastingen en de geldmiddelen van den aanvang der Republiek tot op heden* (Utrecht, 1862).

'Ervaringen onzer arbeidsinspectie: verslagen van de Inspecteurs van den Arbeid over 1899 en 1900', *Tijdschrift der Nederlandsche Maatschappij ter Bevordering van Nijverheid*, new series, 6 (1902), 12–18.

Evans, R. J., *Death in Hamburg: society and politics in the cholera years 1830–1910* (Oxford, 1987).

Evers, J. C. G., *Bijdrage tot de bevolkingsleer van Nederland* (The Hague, 1882).

Everwijn, J. C. A., *Beschrijving van handel en nijverheid in Nederland*, 3 vols. (The Hague, 1912).

Eyck van Heslinga, E. S., *Van compagnie naar koopvaardij: de scheepvaartverbinding van de Bataafse Republiek met de koloniën in Azie 1795–1806* (Amsterdam, 1998).

Faludi, A., and A. van der Valk, *Rule and order: Dutch planning doctrine in the twentieth century* (Dordrecht, 1994).

Fasseur, C., *Kultuurstelsel en koloniale baten: de Nederlandse exploitatie van Java 1840–1860* (Leiden, 1975).

Feitsma, A., 'The Frisian movement in European perspective', *Dutch Crossing*, special issue on Frisian Studies, 18/2 (1994), 137–64.

Fijnaut, C., *Opdat de macht een toevlucht zij? Een historische studie van het politieapparaat als een politieke instelling*, 2 vols. (Arnhem, 1979).

Filarski, R., *Kanalen van de koning-koopman: goederenvervoer, binnenscheepvaart en kanalenbouw in Nederland en België in de eerste helft van de negentiende eeuw* (Amsterdam, 1995).

Fischer, E. J., *Fabriqueurs en fabrikanten: de Twentse katoennijverheid en de onderneming S. J. Spanjaard te Borne tussen circa 1800 en 1930* (Utrecht, 1983).

Stroom opvaarts: de electriciteitsvoorziening in OverIJssel en Zuid-Drenthe tussen circa 1895 en 1986 (Zwolle, 1986).

Fischer, E. J., and R. E. M. A. de Peuter, 'Winstontwikkeling en kapitaalvorming in de Twentse katoennijverheid: de firma S. J. Spaniaard, 1833–1900', *Economisch- en Sociaal-Historisch Jaarboek*, 43 (1980), 194–244.

Flinn, M. W., *The origins of the industrial revolution* (London, 1966).

Fockema Andreae, S. J., 'De landaanwinning in Nederland, historisch bezien', *Economisch-Statistische Berichten*, 27 (1942), 580–1.

Fogarty, M. P., *Christian democracy in Western Europe, 1820–1953* (London, 1957).

Fokker, A. P., 'De volksvoeding in Zeeland', *Nederlandsch Tijdschrift voor Geneeskunde*, 13/2 (1877), 195–240.

Frank, A. G., *On capitalist underdevelopment* (Bombay, 1975).

Frieswijk, J. A., *Om een beter leven: strijd en organisatie van de land-, veen- en zuivelarbeiders in het noorden van Nederland (1850–1914)* (Leeuwarden, 1989).

Frijhoff, W., 'Identiteit en identiteitsbesef: de historicus en de spanning tussen verbeelding, benoeming en herkenning', *Bijdragen en Mededelingen betreffende de Geschiedenis der Nederlanden*, 107 (1992), 614–34.

Fritschy, W., and J. Toebes, eds., *Het ontstaan van het moderne Nederland: staats-en natievorming tussen 1780 en 1830* (Nijmegen, s.a. [1996]).

Furnivall, J. S., *Netherlands India: a study of plural economy* (London, 1939).

Galema, A., *Frisians to America 1880–1914: with the baggage of the fatherland* (Groningen, 1996).

Gales, B. P. A., and J. L. J. M. van Gerwen, *Sporen van leven en schade: een geschiedenis en bronnenoverzicht van het Nederlandse verzekeringswezen* (Amsterdam, 1988).

Gales, B. P. A., and K. E. Sluyterman, 'Outward bound: the rise of Dutch multinationals', in G. Jones and H. G. Schröter, eds., *The rise of multinationals in continental Europe* (Aldershot, 1993), pp. 65–99.

Gellner, E., *Nations and nationalism* (Oxford, 1983).

Genabeek, J. van, *Met vereerende kracht risico's verzacht: de plaats van de onderlinge hulp binnen de negentiende-eeuwse particuliere regeling van sociale zekerheid* (Amsterdam, 1999).

Geneeskundig Jaarboekje voor het Koningrijk der Nederlanden en zijne Overzeesche Bezittingen, 2 (1865).

Geneeskundig Jaarboekje voor Nederland, 1 (1882) to 62 (1943).

Gerding, M. A. W., *Vier eeuwen turfwinning: de verveningen in Groningen, Friesland, Drenthe en Overijssel tussen 1550 en 1950*, A.A.G. Bijdragen 35 (Wageningen, 1995).

Gerretson, C., *The history of the Royal Dutch*, 4 vols. (Leiden, 1953–57).

Gerschenkron, A., *Economic backwardness in historical perspective: a book of essays* (Cambridge, Mass., 1966).

Gerwen, J. van, and M. H. D. van Leeuwen, eds., *Studies over zekerheidsarrangementen: risico's, risicobestrijding en verzekeringen in Nederland vanaf de middeleeuwen* (Amsterdam, 1998).

Geschiere, A., *Het leven van den Walcherschen boer gedurende de laatste twee eeuwen historisch geschetst* (Bruinisse [1933]).

Geuze, M. A., 'Bij een eeeuwfeest: Maatschappij de Bathpolders bestond honderd jaar', *Zeeuws Tijdschrift*, 6 (1956), 131–6.

Giessen, J. van de, *De opkomst van het woord democratie als leuze in Nederland* (The Hague, 1948).

Gladdish, K., *Governing from the centre: politics and policy-making in the Netherlands* (London, 1991).

Goldberg, J., 'Journaal der reize van den agent van nationale oeconomie der Bataafsche Republiek (ao. 1800)', *Tijdschrift voor Staathuishoudkunde en Statistiek*, 18 (1859), 194–217, 241–54, 313–37, 377–92 and 441–59 (and 19 (1860)).

Goldstein, R. J., *Political repression in 19th century Europe* (London, 1983).

Goodman, J., and K. Honeyman, *Gainful pursuits: the making of industrial Europe 1600–1914* (London, 1988).

Goor, J. van, *De Nederlandse koloniën: geschiedenis van de Nederlandse expansie 1600–1975*, second edition (Amsterdam, 1997).

Gooren, H. M. C., and L. J. B. Heger, *Per mud of bij de week gewonnen: de ontwikkeling van beloningssystemen in de Groningse landbouw, 1800–1914*, Historia Agriculturae 26 (Groningen, 1993).

Gorter, R. A., and C. W. de Vries, 'Gegevens omtrent de kinderarbeid in Nederland volgens de enquetes van 1841 en 1860', *Economisch-Historisch Jaarboek*, 8 (1922), 1–262.

Gouda, F., *Dutch culture overseas: colonial practice in the Netherlands Indies, 1900–1942* (Amsterdam, 1995).

Goudsblom, J., *Dutch society* (New York, 1967).

Goulmy, P. J. L. M., *Nederland naar het Vaticaan: wat aan de tijdelijke zending naar den H. Stoel voorafging, haar vergezelde en volgen moet* (Nijmegen, 1915).

Grever, M., *Strijd tegen de stilte: Johanna Naber (1859–1941) en de vrouwenstem in de geschiedenis* (Hilversum, 1994).

Grever, M., and B. Waaldijk, *Feministische openbaarheid: de Nationale Tentoonstelling van Vrouwenarbeid in 1898* (Amsterdam, 1998).

Griffiths, R. T., *Achterlijk, achter of anders? Aspecten van de economische ontwikkeling van Nederland in de 19de eeuw: rede* ([Amsterdam, 1981]).

'The creation of a Dutch national economy', *Tijdschrift voor Geschiedenis*, 95 (1982), 513–37.

'Economische ontwikkeling in industrieel Europa', in F. van Besouw, *et al.*, eds., *Balans en perspectief: visies op de geschiedwetenschap in Nederland* (Groningen, 1987), pp. 147–66.

'Eyewitnesses at the birth of the Dutch cotton industry 1832–1839', *Economisch- en Sociaal-Historisch Jaarboek*, 40 (1977), 113–81.

'Industrial retardation in the Netherlands: 1830–1850' (PhD thesis, 1976).

Industrial retardation in the Netherlands 1830–1850 (The Hague, 1979).

'The role of taxation in wage formation in the Dutch economy in the first half of the nineteenth century', in Joh. de Vries, *et al.*, eds., *Ondernemende geschiedenis: 22 opstellen geschreven bij het afscheid van mr. H. van Riel als voorzitter van de vereniging Het Nederlandsch Economisch-Historisch Archief* (The Hague, 1977), pp. 260–71.

Groen van Prinsterer, G., *Ongeloof en revolutie: een reeks van historische voorlezingen*, fourth edition (Amsterdam, 1940) [original edition 1847].

Groenveld, S., and M. J. Wintle, eds., *State and trade: government and the economy in Britain and the Netherlands since the Middle Ages*, Britain and the Netherlands 10 (Zutphen, 1992).

Under the sign of liberalism: varieties of European liberalism in past and present, Britain and the Netherlands 12 (Zutphen, 1997).

Groot, G. de, and M. Schrover, eds., *Women workers and technological change in Europe in the nineteenth and twentieth centuries* (London, 1995).

Groote, P., *Kapitaalvorming in infrastructuur in Nederland 1800–1913* (Capelle, 1995).

Groote, P., R. Albers, and A. Clemens, 'Dutch rail- and tramways in a comparative perspective, 1838–1913', *Economic and Social History in the Netherlands*, 7 (1996), 41–56.

Groote, P., and V. Tassenaar, 'Infrastructurele vernieuwing en de levensstandaard in Drenthe, 1821–1904: een regionale toetsing van de moderniseringsparadox', *NEHA-Jaarboek*, 60 (1997), 69–95.

Haan, F. de, *Gender and the politics of office work: the Netherlands 1860–1940* (Amsterdam, 1998).

Hall, D. G. E., *A history of South-East Asia* (London, 1955).

A history of South-East Asia, fourth edition (London, 1981).

Hall, J. A., ed., *Civil society: theory, history, comparison* (Cambridge, 1995).

Hansen, E., and P. A. Prosper, 'Transformation and accommodation in Dutch socialism: P. J. Troelstra and Social Democratic political theory, 1894–1914', *European History Quarterly*, 27 (1997), 475–503.

Hart, M. 't, J. Jonker, and J. L. van Zanden, *A financial history of the Netherlands* (Cambridge, 1997).

Hart, P. D. 't, *Utrecht en de cholera 1832–1910* (Zutphen, 1990).

Hartog, A. P. den, 'De beginfase van het moderne voedselpatroon in Nederland: voedsel en voeding in de jaren 1850–1914', *Voeding*, 41 (1980), 334–42 and 348–57.

Headrick, D. R., *The tentacles of progress: technology transfer in the age of imperialism, 1850–1940* (New York, 1988).

The tools of empire: technology and European imperialism in the nineteenth century (New York, 1981).

Heek, F. van, *Het geboorte-niveau der Nederlandse rooms-katholieken: een demografisch-sociologische studie van een geëmancipeerde minderheidsgroep* (Leiden, 1954).

Klassen- en standenstructuur als sociologische begrippen (Leiden, 1948).

'Het Nederlandse geboortepatroon en de godsdienstfactor gedurende de laatste halve eeuw', *Mens en Maatschappij*, 38 (1963), 81–103.

Heerding, E., *Een onderneming van vele markten thuis*, Geschiedenis van de N. V. Philips' Gloeilampenfabrieken 2 (Leiden, 1986).

Het ontstaan van de Nederlandse gloeilampen industrie, Geschiedenis van de N. V. Philips' Gloeilampenfabrieken, 1 (The Hague, 1980).

Heere, W. R., 'De tegenwoordige en toekomstige demografische situatie in Nederland', *De Economist*, 97/1 (1949), 1–34.

Heeren, H. J., and P. van Praag, eds., *Van nu tot nul: bevolkingsgroei en bevolkingspolitiek in Nederland* (Utrecht, 1974).

Heeringa, K., 'Zeeland', in G. J. W. Koolemans Beijnen, ed., *Historisch gedenkboek der herstelling van Neêrlands onafhankelijkheid in 1813*, 4 vols. (Haarlem, 1913), vol. III, pp. 411–501.

Heerma van Voss, L., *De doodsklok voor den goeden ouden tijd: de achturendag in de jaren twintig* (Amsterdam, 1994).

Hegeman, J. G., 'Darwin en onze voorouders: Nederlandse reacties op de evolutieleer 1860–1875: een terreinverkenning', *Bijdragen en Mededelingen betreffende de Geschiedenis der Nederlanden*, 85 (1970), 261–314.

Heide, H. ter, *Binnenlandse migratie in Nederland* (The Hague, 1965).

Heijden, C. G. W. P. van der, *Het heeft niet willen groeien: zuigelingen- en kindersterfte in Tilburg, 1820–1930. Omvang, oorzaken en maatschappelijke context* (Tilburg, 1995).

Kleurloos, reukloos en smaakloos drinkwater: de watervoorziening in Tilburg van het einde van de negentiende eeuw (Tilburg, 1995).

Heijden, M. C. A. van der, ed., *Werkmansboekje: sociale bewogenheid in de literatuur rond 1900* (Utrecht, 1971).

Hekma, G., *Homoseksualiteit, een medische reputatie: de uitdoktering van de homo-*

seksueel in negentiende-eeuwse Nederland (Amsterdam, 1987).

Hellemans, S., 'Verzuiling en ontzuiling van de katholieken in België en Nederland: een historisch-sociologisch vergelijking', *Sociologische Gids*, 35/1 (1988), 43–56.

Hemels, J. M. H. J., *Op de bres voor de pers: de strijd voor de klassieke persvrijheid* (Assen, 1969).

Hemerijk, A., 'The historical fragility of Dutch corporatism' (unpublished paper, MIT, Boston, 1990).

Hendrickx, F. M. M., *'In order not to fall into poverty': production and reproduction in the transition from proto-industry to factory industry in Borne and Wierden (the Netherlands), 1800–1900* (Amsterdam, 1997).

Hendriks, J., *De emancipatie van de gereformeerden: sociologische bijdrage tot de verklaring van enige kenmerken van het gereformeerde volksdeel* (Alphen, 1971).

Henkes, B., *Heimat in Holland: Duitse dienstmeisjes 1920–1950* (Amsterdam, 1995).

Heringa, A., *Free trade and protectionism in Holland* (London, 1914).

Herinneringen en beschouwingen betreffende den landbouw en het tiendregt: met bijvoeging van een eenvoudig plan om de tiendvorderingen op te heffen (Amsterdam, 1857).

Heteren, G. van, 'De troost voorbij: medische instructie voor het kinderlijk leven in de negentiende eeuw', in W. de Blécourt, *et al.*, eds., *Grenzen van genezing: gezondheid, ziekte en genezen in Nederland, zestiende tot begin twintigste eeuw* (Hilversum, 1993), pp. 203–52.

Hill, C., *Reformation to industrial revolution* (Harmondsworth, 1969).

Hobsbawm, E. J., *Nations and nationalism since 1780: programme, myth, reality* (Cambridge, 1990).

Hoek, S. van der, *Het bruine goud: kroniek van de turfgravers in Nederland* (Amsterdam, 1984).

Hofmeester, K., *'Als ik niet voor mijzelf ben…': de verhouding tussen joodse arbeiders en de arbeidersbeweging in Amsterdam, Londen en Parijs vergeleken, 1870–1914* (s.l., 1999).

Van Talmoed tot statuut: joodse arbeiders en arbeidersbewegingen in Amsterdam, Londen en Parijs, 1880–1914 (Amsterdam, 1990).

Hofstee, E. W., *De demografische ontwikkeling van Nederland in de eerste helft van de negentiende eeuw: een historisch-demografische en sociologische studie* (Arnhem, 1978).

'De demografische ontwikkeling van Nederland sinds 1800', in H. J. Heeren and P. van Praag, eds., *Van nu tot nul: bevolkingsgroei en bevolkingspolitiek in Nederland* (Utrecht, 1974), pp. 36–75.

'De groei van de Nederlandse bevolking', in A. N. J. den Hollander, *et al.*, eds., *Drift en koers: een halve eeuw sociale verandering in Nederland*, third printing (Assen, 1968), pp. 13–84.

Korte demografische geschiedenis van Nederland van 1800 tot heden (Haarlem, 1981).

Hollander, A. N. J. den, *et al.*, eds., *Drift en koers: een halve eeuw sociale verandering in Nederland*, third printing (Assen, 1968).

Holthoon, F. L. van, ed., *De Nederlandse samenleving sinds 1815: wording en samenhang* (Assen, 1985).

Homan, G. D., 'Catholic emancipation in the Netherlands', *Catholic Historical Review*, 52 (1966–67), 201–11.

Hoogland, J., *Landbouwcoöperatie, in het bijzonder coöperatieve aankoop van landbouwbenoodigheden in Nederland* (Leeuwarden, 1923).

Horlings, E., *The economic development of the Dutch service sector 1800–1850: trade and transport in a premodern economy* (Amsterdam, 1995).

Horlings, E., and J. P. Smits, 'A comparison of the pattern of growth and structural change in the Netherlands and Belgium, 1800–1913', *Jahrbuch für Wirtschaftsgeschichte*, 2 (1997), 83–106.

'Private consumer expenditure in the Netherlands', *Economic and Social History in the Netherlands*, 7 (1996), 15–40.

Houten, S. van, *Maatschappelijike en wettelijke stelling der vrouw: verspreide opstellen*, new edition (The Hague, 1918).

Houtte, J. A. van, 'Economic development of Belgium and the Netherlands from the beginning of the modern era', *Journal of European Economic History*, 1 (1972), 100–20.

An economic history of the Low Countries 800–1800 (London, 1977).

Economische en sociale geschiedenis van de Lage Landen (Zeist, 1964).

Houtte, J.A. van, *et al.*, eds., *Algemene geschiedenis der Nederlanden*, 12 vols. (Utrecht, 1949–58).

Houwaart, E. S., *De hygiënisten: artsen, staat and volksgezondheid in Nederland 1840–1890* (Groningen, 1991).

Huizinga, D. S., 'De invloed van het onderwijs en van de wetenschap op den landbouw', in Z. W. Sneller, ed., *Geschiedenis van den Nederlandschen landbouw 1795–1940* (Groningen, 1943), pp. 235–51.

Huysmans, G. W. M., 'Het landbouwcrediet in Nederland', *De Economist*, 90 (1941), 369–401.

'De industrie in Nederland', *Economisch-Statistische Berichten*, 26 (1941), 64–7.

Israel, J. I., *Dutch primacy in world trade, 1585–1740* (Oxford, 1989).

The Dutch Republic: its rise, greatness, and fall 1477–1806 (Oxford, 1995).

Jaarcijfers voor het Koninkrijk der Nederlanden, Rijk in Europa (1881–1921) (The Hague).

Jacquemyns, G., *Histoire de la crise économique des Flandres (1845–1850)* (Brussels, 1928).

Jansen, P. C., and J. M. M. de Meere, 'Het sterftepatroon in Amsterdam 1774–1930: een analyse van de doodsoorzaken', *Tijdschrift voor Sociale Geschiedenis*, 8/26 (1982), 180–223.

Janssens, A., *Family and social change: the household as process in an industrializing context. Tilburg 1840–1920* (s.l., 1991).

'The rise and decline of the male breadwinner family? An overview of the debate', *International Review of Social History*, 42 (1997), 1–23.

Jansz, U., *Denken over sekse in de eerste feministische golf* (Amsterdam, 1990).

Jappe Alberts, W., and A. G. van der Steur, *Handleiding voor de beoefening van lokale en regionale geschiedenis*, second revised edition (Weesp, 1984).

Jenkins, H. M., 'Report on the agriculture of the Kingdom of the Netherlands', *Parliamentary Papers, Reports from Commissioners, Inspectors, and Others*

(1881), vol. XVI, 638–713.

Jensma, G., *Het rode tasje van Salverda: burgerlijk bewustzijn en Friese identiteit in de negentiende eeuw* (Leeuwarden, 1998).

Jobse-Van Putten, J., *Eenvoudig maar voedzaam: cultuurgeschiedenis van de dagelijkse maaltijd in Nederland* (Nijmegen, 1995).

Jong, A. de, 'Dracht en eendracht: de politieke dimensie van klederdrachten, 1850–1920', in D. Verhoeven, *et al.*, eds., *Klederdracht en kleedgedrag: het kostuum Harer Majesteits onderdanen, 1898–1998* (Nijmegen [1998]), pp. 67–82.

Jong, F. de, 'Verzuiling in historisch perspectief', *Socialisme en Democratie*, 14 (January 1957), 2–10.

Jong, H. de, 'Ondernemerschap in Nederland 1840–1940: succes en falen van ondernemers in Nederland vanuit markttheoretisch perspectief', *Jaarboek voor de Geschiedenis van Bedrijf en Techniek*, 5 (1988), 53–71.

Jong, H. J. de, and R. M. Albers, 'Industriële groei in Nederland, 1913–1929: een verkenning', *NEHA-Jaarboek*, 57 (1994), 444–90.

Jonge, J. A. de, *De industrialisatie in Nederland tussen 1850 en 1914* (Nijmegen, 1976).

'De industriele ontwikkeling van Nederland 1850–1914 gezien in het licht van enkele facetten van de theorie van Rostow', in P. W. Klein, ed., *Van stapelmarkt tot welvaartstaat* (Rotterdam, 1975), pp. 75–93.

'The role of the outer provinces in the process of Dutch economic growth in the nineteenth century', in J. S. Bromley and E. H. Kossmann, eds., *Metropolis, dominion and province*, Britain and the Netherlands 4 (The Hague, 1971), pp. 208–25.

Jonker, J., *Merchants, bankers, middlemen: the Amsterdam money market during the first half of the nineteenth century* (Amsterdam, 1996).

Kamerling, R. N. J., ed., *Indonesië toen en nu* (Amsterdam, 1980).

Kanter, J. de, and J. ab Utrecht Dresselhuis, *De provincie Zeeland* (Middelburg, 1824).

Kautz, E. A., *Der Hafen von Vlissingen: seine Stellung und Entwicklungsaussichten im internationalen Verkehr* (Jena, 1933).

Keane, J., ed., *Civil society and the state: new European perspectives* (London, 1988).

Kenwood, A. G., and A. L. Lougheed, *The growth of the international economy 1820–1980: an introductory text* (London, 1983).

Kint, P., and R. C. W. van der Voort, 'Economische groei en stagnatie in de Nederlanden 1800–1850', *Economisch- en Sociaal-Historisch Jaarboek*, 43 (1980), 105–53.

Kint, T. L. M., 'Industriële lonen in de pre-industriële negentiende eeuw', in P. Boomgaard, *et al.*, eds., *Exercities in ons verleden: twaalf opstellen over de economische en sociale geschiedenis van Nederland en koloniën 1800–1950 aangeboden aan prof. dr. W. J. Wieringa* (Assen, 1981), pp. 6–26.

Kistemaker, R., *Een kind onder het hart: verloskunde, volksgeloof, gezin, seksualiteit en moraal vroeger en nu* (Amsterdam, 1987).

Kleerekoper, S., 'Het Joodse proletariat in het Amsterdam van de negentiende eeuw', *Studia Rosenthaliana*, 1/1 (1967), 97–108; and 1/2, 71–84.

Klein, P. W., 'Het bankwezen en de modernisering van de Nederlandse volkshuishouding tijdens de tweede helft van de 19e eeuw', *Economisch- en Sociaal-historisch Jaarboek*, 36 (1973), 131–45.

Kluit, M. E., *Het Protestantse Réveil in Nederland en daarbuiten 1815–1865* (Amsterdam, 1970).

Knappert, L., *Geschiedenis der hervordme kerk onder de Republiek en onder het Koninkrijk der Nederlanden*, 2 vols. (Amsterdam, 1911–12).

Knibbe, M., *Agriculture in the Netherlands 1851–1950: production and institutional change* (Amsterdam, 1993).

Knippenberg, H., 'De demografische ontwikkeling van Nederland sedert 1800: een overzicht', *Geografisch Tijdschrift*, 14 (1980), 54–76.

Knippenberg, H., and B. de Pater, *De eenwording van Nederland: schaalvergroting en integratie sinds 1800* (Nijmegen, 1988).

Knotter, A., *Economische transformatie en stedelijke arbeidsmarkt: Amsterdam in de tweede helft van de negentiende eeuw* (Zwolle, 1991).

Knotter, A., and H. Muskee, 'Conjunctuur en levensstandaard in Amsterdam 1815–1855: een onderzoek op basis van plaatselijke accijnzen', *Tijdschrift voor Sociale Geschiedenis*, 12 (1986), 153–81.

Koenen, H. J., *De Nederlandsche boerenstand historisch beschreven* (Haarlem, 1858).

Voorlezingen over de geschiedenis der nijverheid in Nederland (Haarlem, 1856).

Kok, J., *Langs verboden wegen: de achtergronden van buitenechtelijke geboorten in Noord-Holland 1812–1914* (Hilversum, 1991).

'The moral nation: illegitimacy and bridal pregnancy in the Netherlands from 1600 to the present', *Economic and Social History in the Netherlands*, 2 (1990), 7–35.

'Voorechtelijke verwekkingen in Noord-Holland in de negentiende eeuw', *Bevolking en Gezin*, 18 (1989), 49–81.

Kok, J. A. de, *Nederland op de breuklijn Rome-Reformatie: numerieke aspecten van protestantisering en katholieke herleving in de noordelijke Nederlanden 1580–1880* (Assen, 1964).

Koning, N., *The failure of agrarian capitalism: agrarian politics in the UK, Germany, the Netherlands and the USA, 1846–1919* (London, 1994).

Kooij, P., 'Gezondheidzorg in Groningen 1870–1914', *Tijdschrift voor Sociale Geschiedenis*, 8/26 (1982), 111–55.

Groningen 1870–1914: sociale verandering en economische ontwikkeling in een regionaal centrum (Assen, 1987).

'Stad en platteland', in F. L. van Holthoon, ed., *De Nederlandse samenleving sinds 1815: wording en samenhang* (Assen, 1985), pp. 93–115.

Koolmees, P. A., *Symbolen van openbare hygiëne: gemeentelijke slachthuizen in Nederland 1795–1940* (Rotterdam, 1997).

Koopmans, C., *Dordrecht 1811–1914: een eeuw demografische en economische geschiedenis* (Hilversum, 1992).

Kooy, G. A., ed., *Gezinsgeschiedenis: vier eeuwen gezin in Nederland* (Assen, 1985).

Koppen, C. A. J. van, *De Geuzen van de negentiende eeuw: Abraham Kuyper en Zuid-Afrika* (Wormer, 1992).

Kossmann, E. H., *De Lage Landen 1780–1980: twee eeuwen Nederland en België*, 2 vols. (Amsterdam, 1986), vol. II, *1914–1980*.

The Low Countries 1780–1940 (Oxford, 1978).

Politieke theorie en geschiedenis: verspreide opstellen en voordrachten (Amsterdam, 1987).

'Some questions concerning Dutch national consciousness', *Dutch Crossing*, 34 (April 1988), 1–14.

Een tuchteloos probleem: de natie in de Nederlanden (Leuven, s.a. [1994]).

Kraemer, P. E., *The societal state: the modern osmosis of state and society as presenting itself in the Netherlands in particular: a case study of a general trend* (Meppel, 1966).

Kroef, J. M. van der, 'Abraham Kuyper and the rise of Neo-Calvinism in the Netherlands', *Church History*, 17 (1948), 316–34.

Kruif, J. de, 'De prijs van de armenzorg: de financiering van de armenzorg in Den Bosch', *Tijdschrift voor Sociale Geschiedenis*, 20 (1994), 24–51.

Kruijt, J. P., 'Mentaliteitsverschillen in ons volk in verband met godsdienstige verschillen', *Mensch en maatschappij*, 19 (1943), 1–28 and 65–83.

'Sociologische beschouwingen over zuilen en verzuiling', *Socialisme en Democratie*, 14 (January 1957), 11–29.

Kruithof, B., *Zonde en deugd in domineesland: Nederlandse protestanten en problemen van opvoeding, zeventiende tot twintigste eeuw* (Groningen, 1990).

Kuiper, R., *Zelfbeeld en wereldbeeld: Antirevolutionairen en het buitenland, 1848–1905* (Kampen, 1992).

Kuitenbrouwer, M., *Nederland en de opkomst van het moderne imperialisme: koloniën en buitenlandse politiek 1870–1902* (Amsterdam, 1985).

The Netherlands and the rise of modern imperialism: colonies and foreign policy, 1870–1902 (Oxford, 1991).

Kuperus, J. A., 'Honderd jaar bedrijfsresultaten van de Wilhelminapolder (1814–1913)', *Historia Agriculturae*, 6 (1962), 117–273.

Kuyper, A., *Ons program*, 2 vols. (Amsterdam, 1879).

'De rede van dr. Kuyper (1897)', in J. C. Boogman and C. A. Tamse, eds., *Emancipatie in Nederland: de ontvoogding van burgerij en confessionelen in de negentiende eeuw: 27 teksten over emancipatie in Nederland* (The Hague, 1978), pp. 176–82.

Labrijn, A., *Het klimaat van Nederland gedurende de laatste twee en een halve eeuw* (The Hague, 1945).

Laing, S., *Notes of a traveller, on the social and political state of France, Prussia, Switzerland, Italy, and other parts of Europe, during the present century* (London, 1842).

Landes, D. S., *The unbound Prometheus: technological change and industrial development in Western Europe* (Cambridge, 1969).

Langer, W. L., 'American foods and Europe's population growth 1750–1850', *Journal of Social History*, 8 (Summer 1975), 51–66.

Langeveld, H. J., *Hendrikus Colijn: dit leven van krachtig handelen*, vol. I (Amsterdam, 1998).

Lasch, C., *Haven in a heartless world: the family besieged* (New York, 1977).

Lee, W. R., ed., *European demography and economic growth* (London, 1979).

Leenders, J., *Benauwde verdraagzaamheid, hachelijk fatsoen: families, standen en kerken te Hoorn in het midden van de negentiende eeuw* (The Hague, 1992).

Leenders, M., *Ongenode gasten: van traditioneel asielrecht naar immigratiebeleid,*

1815–1938 (Hilversum, 1993).

Leerssen, J. T., and M. van Montfrans, eds., *Borders and territories, Yearbook of European Studies*, 6 (Amsterdam, 1993).

Leeuw, K. de, *Kleding in Nederland 1813–1920* (Hilversum, 1992).

Leeuwen, M. H. D. van, 'Armenzorg 1800–1912: erfenis van de Republiek', in J. van Gerwen and M. H. D. van Leeuwen, eds., *Studies over zekerheidsarrangementen: risico's, risicobestrijding en verzekeringen in Nederland vanaf de middeleeuwen* (Amsterdam, 1998), pp. 276–316.

Bijstand in Amsterdam, ca. 1800–1850: armenzorg als beheersing- en overlevingsstrategie (Zwolle, 1992).

'Trade unions and the provision of welfare in the Netherlands, 1910–1960', *Economic History Review*, 50 (1997), 764–91.

Leeuwen, W. L. M. E. van, *Honderd jaar Nederland 1848–1948: uitgegeven ter gelegenheid van het vijftigjarig regeringsjubileum en de troonafstand van H. M. Koningin Wilhelmina* (Hengelo, 1948).

Lenski, G., *The religious factor: a sociological study of religion's impact on politics, economics, and family life* (New York, 1961).

Lente, D. van, 'Ideology and technology: reactions to modern technology in the Netherlands 1850–1920', *European History Quarterly*, 22 (1992), 383–414.

Letters from Flushing: containing an account of the expedition to Walcheren, Beveland, and the mouth of the Scheldt, under the command of the Earl of Chatham: to which is added a topographical and statistical account of the islands of Walcheren and Beveland. By an officer of the Eighty-First Regiment (London, 1809).

Lewe, A., *'Invoer te lande verboden': een verkenning van de handel over landwegen tussen Nederland en de Pruisische provincies Rheinland en Westfalen, 1836–1857* (Hilversum, 1995).

Leydesdorff, S., *Verborgen arbeid vergeten arbeid: een verkenning in de geschiedenis van de vrouwenarbeid rond negentienhonderd* (Assen, 1977).

Lieburg, M. J. van, *Bronovo 1865–1990: van 's-Gravenhaagsche Diakonessen-Inrichting tot Ziekenhuis Bronovo* (Kampen, 1990).

Het Coolsingelziekenhuis te Rotterdam (1839–1900): de ontwikkeling van een stedelijk ziekenhuis in de 19e eeuw (Amsterdam, 1986).

'De syfilitische patient in de geschiedenis van het Nederlandse ziekenhuiswezen vóór 1900', *Tijdschrift voor Sociale Geschiedenis*, 8/26 (1982), 156–79.

Lieburg, M. J. van, and H. A. M. Snelders, *'De bevordering en volmaking der proefondervindelijke wijsbegeerte': de rol van het Bataafsch Genootschap te Rotterdam in de geschiedenis van de natuurwetenschappen, geneeskunde en techniek (1769–1988)* (Amsterdam, 1989).

Lijphart, A., *The politics of accommodation: pluralism and democracy in the Netherlands* (Berkeley, 1975; first edition 1968).

Lindblad, J. T., 'The economic relationship between the Netherlands and colonial Indonesia, 1870–1940', in J. L. van Zanden, ed., *The economic development of the Netherlands since 1870* (Cheltenham, 1996), pp. 108–19.

Lintsen, H. W., *et al.*, eds., *Geschiedenis van de techniek in Nederland*, 6 vols. (Zutphen, 1992–95).

Lipschits, I., *Politieke stromingen in Nederland: inleiding tot de geschiedenis van de Nederlandse politieke partijen* (Deventer, 1977).

De protestants-christelijke stroming tot 1940: ontstaansgeschiedenis van de Nederlandse politieke partijen, vol. I (Deventer, 1977).

Lis, C., *et al.*, eds., *Before the unions: wage earners and collective action in Europe, 1300–1850*, *International Review of Social History*, 39 (1994), Supplement 2 (Cambridge, 1994).

Livi-Bacci, M., *Population and nutrition: an essay on European demographic history* (Cambridge, 1991).

Loo, L. F. van, *Armelui: armoede en bedeling te Alkmaar 1850–1914* (Bergen, 1986).

Lucassen, J., *Dutch long distance migration: a concise history 1600–1900*, IISG Research Papers 3 (Amsterdam, 1991).

'Labour and early modern economic development', in K. Davids and J. Lucassen, eds., *A miracle mirrored: the Dutch Republic in European perspective* (Cambridge, 1995), pp. 367–409.

Migrant labour in Europe 1600–1900: the drift to the North Sea (London, 1987).

Naar de kusten van de Noordzee: trekarbeid in Europees perspektief, 1600–1900 (Gouda, 1984).

'The Netherlands, the Dutch, and long-distance migration in the late sixteenth to early nineteenth centuries', in N. Canny, ed., *Europeans on the move: studies on European migration, 1500–1800* (Oxford, 1994), pp. 153–91 and 297–302.

Lucassen, J., and R. Penninx, *Newcomers: immmigrants and their descendants in the Netherlands 1550–1995* (Amsterdam, 1997).

Lucassen, J., and G. Trienekens, 'Om de plaats in de kerk: een onderzoek naar maatschappelijke ongelijkheid voornamelijk in de negentiende eeuw', *Tijdschrift voor Sociale Geschiedenis*, 12 (1978), 239–304.

Lucassen, J., and E. J. Zürcher, 'Conscription as military labour: the historical context', *International Review of Social History*, 43 (1998), 405–19.

Lucassen, L., *'En men noemde hen zigeuners'. De geschiedenis van Kaldarasch, Usari, Lowara en Sinti in Nederland: 1750–1944* (Amsterdam, 1990).

Luurs, J. R., 'De aanleg van verharde wegen in Drenthe, Groningen en Friesland, 1825–1925', *NEHA-Jaarboek*, 59 (1996), 211–37.

Maarseveen, J. G. S. J. van, 'Gemeentelijke belastingen in de twintigste eeuw', in W. Fritschy, *et al.*, eds., *Doel en middel: aspecten van financieel overheidsbeleid in de Nederlanden van de zestiende eeuw tot heden* (Amsterdam, 1995), pp. 167–96 and 263–6.

Maas, J. van der, and L. Noordegraaf, 'Smakelijk eten: aardappelconsumptie in Holland in de achttiende eeuw en het begin van de negentiende eeuw', *Tijdschrift voor Sociale Geschiedenis*, 31 (August 1983), 188–220.

Maclean, J., 'Arbeidsconflicten in de periode 1813–1872: gegevens uit het Kabinet des Konings', *Tijdschrift voor Sociale Geschiedenis*, 16 (1979), 293–312.

Maddison, A., *Dynamic forces in capitalist development: a long-term comparative view* (Oxford, 1991).

Maitra, P., *The mainspring of economic development* (London, 1980).

Man, J. C. de, *Bijdrage tot de kennis der sterfte in Zeeland* (s.l. [*c.* 1850]).

'Het sterftecijfer in de onderscheidene gemeenten van Zeeland, met uitsluiting van de levensloos-aangegevenen, gemiddeld berekend over dertig jaren (1831–1860)', *Nederlandsch Tijdschrift voor Geneeskunde*, 7 (1863), 49–53.

Mandemakers, K., and O. Boonstra, eds., *De levensloop van de Utrechtse bevolking in de 19e eeuw* (Assen, 1995).

Mansvelt, W. M. F., *Geschiedenis van de Nederlandsche Handel-Maatschappij: uitgegeven ter gelegenheid van het honderdjarig bestaan*, 2 vols. (Haarlem [1924–26]).

Mare, H. de, and A. Vos, eds., *Urban rituals in Italy and the Netherlands: historical contrasts in the use of public space, architecture and the urban environment* (Assen, 1993).

Maris, C. H. J., 'De beleggingen van 25 Utrechtenaren aan de hand van de memoriën van aangifte voor het recht van successie, in 1879' (unpublished doctoraalscriptie, RU Utrecht, 1984).

Mathias, P., and J. A. Davis, eds., *Innovation and technology in Europe from the eighteenth century to the present day* (Oxford, 1991).

Mead, Y. M., 'Anglo-Dutch relations in the age of imperialism: three case studies focussing on the Anglo-Dutch relationship' (unpublished PhD thesis, University of Hull, 1998).

Meer, T. van der, *Sodoms zaad in Nederland: het ontstaan van homoseksualiteit in de vroegmoderne tijd* (Nijmegen, 1995).

Meere, J. M. M. de, *Economische ontwikkeling en levensstandaard in Nederland gedurende de eerste helft van de negentiende eeuw; aspecten en trends* (The Hague, 1982).

'Long-term trends in income and wealth inequality in the Netherlands 1808–1940', *Historical Social Research*, 27 (July 1983), 8–37.

'Standen en klassen in een Noordhollands dorp. De gemeente Wormer in 1844: de visie van een tijdgenoot', *Tijdschrift voor Sociale Geschiedenis*, 15 (1979), 245–63.

Meeter, E., *Holland: its institutions, its press, its kings and prisons* (London, 1857).

Meier, G. M., *Leading issues in development economics: selected materials and commentary* (New York, 1964).

Meier, G. M., and R. E. Baldwin, *Economic development: theory, history, policy* (New York, 1957).

Messing, F. A. M., *Geschiedenis van de mijnsluiting in Limburg: noodzaak en lotgevallen van een regionale herstructurering* (Leiden, 1988).

Meulen, H. van der, 'Nederlanders en hun voeding 1852–1977', *Economisch- en Sociaal-Historisch Jaarboek*, 48 (1985), 48–70.

Meurkens, P., 'Brabants familieleven (1850–1910): over gezinsvorming en verzuiling' (unpublished paper, Heelsum, 1979).

Michman, J., 'De emancipatie van de joden in Nederland', *Bijdragen en Mededelingen betreffende de Geschiedenis der Nederlanden*, 96 (1981), 78–82.

Middendorp, C. P., *Ideology in Dutch politics: the democratic system reconsidered 1970–1985* (Assen, 1991).

Miedema, N., 'The orthodox Protestants in the Netherlands and enforced marriage', *Annual Review of the Social Sciences*, 3 (1979), 213–36.

Miellet, R., *Honderd jaar grootwinkelbedrijf in Nederland* (Zwolle, 1993).

Miert, J. van, 'Confessionelen en de natie, 1870–1920', in D. J. Wolffram, ed., *Om het christelijk karakter der natie: confessionelen en de modernisering van de maatschappij* (Amsterdam, 1994), pp. 89–112.

'Nationalisme in de lokale politieke cultuur, Tiel 1850–1900', *De Negentiende Eeuw*, 16 (1992), 59–85.

'Verdeeldheid en binding: over lokale, verzuilde en nationale loyaliteiten', *Bijdragen en Mededelingen betreffende de Geschiedenis der Nederlanden*, 107 (1992), 670–89.

Mijnhardt, W. W., 'Natievorming in het revolutietijdvak', *Bijdragen en Mededelingen betreffende de Geschiedenis der Nederlanden*, 104 (1989), 546–53.

'Het Nederlandse genootschap in de achttiende en vroege negentiende eeuw', *De Negentiende Eeuw*, 7 (1983), 76–101.

Tot heil van 't menschdom: culturele genootschappen in Nederland, 1750–1815 (Amsterdam, 1988).

Mijnhardt, W. W., and A. J. Wichers, eds., *Om het algemeen volksgeluk: twee eeuwen particulier initiatief 1784–1984. Gedenkboek ter gelegenheid van het tweehonderdjarig bestaan van de Maatschappij tot Nut van 't Algemeeen* (Edam, 1984).

Milward, A. S., and S. B. Saul, *The development of the economies of continental Europe 1850–1914* (London, 1977).

Minderhoud, G., 'De landbouwindustrie', in Z. W. Sneller, ed., *Geschiedenis van den Nederlandschen landbouw 1790–1940* (Groningen, 1943), pp. 404–25.

Mitchell, B. R., *European historical statistics 1750–1970*, abridged edition (London, 1978).

Moes, J., 'Absenteïsme van grondbezitters in Friesland en Zeeland 1850–1890', in H. Diederiks, *et al.*, eds., *Het platteland in een veranderende wereld: boeren en het proces van modernisering. Opstellen aangeboden aan Prof. dr. H. de Vries* (Hilversum, 1994), pp. 255–76.

Mokyr, J., 'Capital, labor and the delay of the industrial revolution in the Netherlands', *Economisch- en Sociaal-historisch Jaarboek*, 38 (1975), 280–99.

'The industrial revolution in the Low Countries in the first half of the nineteenth century', *Journal of Economic History*, 34 (1974), 365–91.

'Industrialization and poverty in Ireland and the Netherlands', *Journal of Interdisciplinary History*, 10 (1979–80), 429–58.

Industrialization in the Low Countries, 1795–1850 (New Haven, 1976).

The lever of riches: technological creativity and economic progress (Oxford, 1990).

Money, J. W. B., *Java; or, how to manage a colony: showing a practical solution of the questions now affecting British India*, 2 vols. (London, 1861).

Multatuli [E. Douwes Dekker], *Max Havelaar of de koffieveilingen der Nederlandse Handelmaatschappij* (Antwerp, 1970).

Multatuli, *Max Havelaar or the coffee auctions of the Dutch Trading Company*, introduced by D. H. Lawrence (London, 1967).

Myrdal, G., *Economic theory and underdeveloped regions* (London, 1957).

Nabrink, G., *Seksuele hervorming in Nederland: achtergronden en geschiedenis van de Nieuw-Mathusiaanse Bond (NMB) en de Nederlandse Vereniging voor Seksuele Hermorming (NVSH), 1881–1971* (Nijmegen, 1978).

Nater, J. P., *Vigelerende vrouwen, gedienstige meiden: seksualiteit in Nederland in de negentiende eeuw* (Amsterdam, 1986).

Een nationaal getuigenis: een woord aan de kiezers van Zeeland (Middelburg, 1869).

De Nederlandsche landbouw in het tijdvak 1813–1913 (The Hague [1914]).

Netherlands, OECD Economic Surveys 1989/90 (Paris, 1990).

Netherlands, OECD Economic Surveys 1991/1992 (Paris, 1991).

Nierop, L. van, 'Een enquête in 1800: eene bijdrage tot de economische geschiedenis der Bataafsche Republiek', *De Gids*, 77/3 (1913), 71–106 and 293–323.

Noordegraaf, L., and G. Valk, *De gave Gods: de pest in Holland vanaf de late middeleeuwen* (Bergen, 1988).

Noordegraaf, L., and J. L. van Zanden, 'Early modern economic growth and the standard of living: did labour benefit from Holland's Golden Age?', in K. Davids and J. Lucassen, eds., *A miracle mirrored: the Dutch Republic in European perspective* (Cambridge, 1995), pp. 410–37.

Notestein, F., 'Population: the long view', in T. W. Schultz, ed., *Food and the world* (Chicago, 1945).

Nusteling, H., *Welvaart en werkgelegenheid in Amsterdam 1540–1860: een relaas over demografie, economie en sociale politiek van een wereldstad* (Amsterdam, 1985).

De Rijnvaart in het tijdperk van stoom en steenkool 1831–1914: een studie van het goederenverkeer en de verkeerspolitiek in de Rijndelta en het achterland, in verband met de opkomst van de spoorwegen en de concurrentie van vreemde zeehavens (Amsterdam, 1974).

O'Brien, P. K., 'Do we have a typology for the study of European industrialization in the XIXth century?', *Journal of European Economic History*, 15 (1986), 291–333.

O'Brien, P. K., ed., *The industrial revolution in Europe*, 2 vols. (Oxford, 1994).

Ommen, A. F. van, 'De liberale kiezersvereniging "De Grondwet" te Middelburg van 1858 tot 1880', *Archief Zeeuws Genootschap* (1981), 1–128.

Onderzoek naar het verbruik van sommige voedings- en genotmiddelen, Bijdragen tot de Statistiek van Nederland 2 (The Hague, 1895).

'Onderzoek naar het verbruik van sommige voedings- en genotmiddelen 1892–1918', *Maandschrift van het CBS*, 15 (1920), 1e aflevering, 1e bijvoegsel.

Oostveen, G. J. van, *De economische ontwikkeling van Dordrecht 1795–1945: gedenkboek uitgegeven bij gelegenheid van het 150-jarig bestaan der Kamer van Koophandel en Fabrieken te Dordrecht* (Dordrecht, 1946).

'De opbrengst van de rijks-, de provinciale en de gemeentelijke belastingen van 1841 tot 1940', *Maandschrift van het C.B.S.*, 37 (1942), 750–7.

Otterloo, A. H. van, *Eten en eetlust in Nederland 1840–1990: een historisch-sociologische studie* (Amsterdam, 1990).

Oud, P. J., *Honderd jaren: een eeuw van staatkundige vormgeving in Nederland 1840–1940*, 5th printing (Assen, 1971).

Oude, D. de, *Neêrlands behoud: of plan tot het invoeren van eene belasting op de inkomsten, ter vervanging van al de thans ten behoeve van den staat geheven wordende belastingen* (Middelburg, 1849).

Outshoorn, J., *Vrouwenemancipatie en socialisme: een onderzoek naar de houding van de SDAP ten opzichte van het vrouwenvraagstuk tussen 1894 en 1919* (Nijmegen, 1973).

'Over de oorzaken van de landverhuizing der Nederlanders naar de Vereenigde Staten', *Tijdschrift voor Staathuishoudkunde en Statistiek*, 26 (1866), 87–102.

Overmeer, P. C. H., *De economische denkbeelden van Gijsbert Karel van Hogendorp (1762–1834)* (Tilburg, 1982).

Overzicht van marktprijzen van granen te Middelburg, pachtprijzen van landerijen en polderlasten in den polder Walcheren in de jaren 1801–1900, Bijdragen tot de Statistiek van Nederland, Nieuwe Volgreeeks 46 (The Hague, 1904).

Papers of the Dutch-Indonesian historical conference held at Noordwijkerhout, the Netherlands, 19 to 22 May 1976 (Leiden, 1978).

Paping, R. F. J., *'Voor een handvol stuivers'. Werken, verdienen en besteden: de levensstandaard van boeren, arbeiders en middenstanders op de Groninger klei, 1770–1860* (Groningen, 1995).

Peet, J. M., *et al.*, eds., *Honderd jaar sociaal: teksten uit honderd jaar sociale beweging en sociaal denken in Nederland 1891–1991* (Amsterdam, 1998).

Peeters, H., *et al.*, eds., *Vijf eeuwen gezinsleven: liefde, huwelijk en opvoeding in Nederland* (Nijmegen, 1988).

Pennings, P., 'Verzuiling: consensus en controverse', in U. Becker, ed., *Nederlandse politiek in historisch en vergelijkend perspectief*, second edition (Amsterdam, 1993), pp. 97–120.

Perry, J., *Roomsche kinine tegen roode koorts: arbeidersbeweging en katholieke kerk in Maastricht 1880–1920* (Amsterdam, 1983).

Petersen, W., 'The demographic transition in the Netherlands', *American Sociological Review*, 25 (1960), 334–47.

Planned migration: the social determinants of the Dutch-Canadian movement (Berkeley, 1955).

Pfeil, T. J. E. M., 'Het Nederlandse bezuinigingsbeleid in de Bataafs-Franse tijd (1795–1810): illusie en werkelijkheid', in W. Fritschy, *et al.*, eds., *Doel en middel: aspecten van financieel overheidsbeleid in de Nederlanden van de zestiende eeuw tot heden* (Amsterdam, 1995), pp. 133–50 and 256–61.

Pilat, D., *Dutch agricultural export performance (1846–1926)*, Historia Agriculturae 19 (Groningen, 1989).

Pol, L. van de, *Het Amsterdams hoerdom: prostitutie in de zeventiende en achttiende eeuw* (Amsterdam, 1996).

Pols, K. van der, 'De introductie van de stoommachine in Nederland', in Joh. de Vries, *et al.*, eds., *Ondernemende geschiedenis: 22 opstellen geschreven bij het afscheid van mr. H. van Riel als voorzitter van de vereniging Het Nederlandsch Economisch-Historisch Archief* (The Hague, 1977), pp. 183–98.

Pons, G., *De bakens verzet: een analyse van de Hollandse pekelharingvisserij met kielschepen in de periode 1814–1885* (Halsteren, 1996).

Poppel, F. van, 'De differentiële vruchtbaarheid in Nederland in historisch perspectief: de invloed van de sociale status', *Bevolking en Gezin*, 2 (1974), 223–47.

'Religion and health: Catholicism and regional mortality differences in nineteenth-century Netherlands', *Social History of Medicine*, 5 (1992), 229–54.

De 'statistieke ontleding van de dooden': een spraakzame bron? (Nijmegen, 1999).

Trouwen in Nederland: een historisch-demografische studie van de 19e en vroeg-20e eeuw, A.A.G. Bijdragen 33 (Wageningen, 1992).

Popta, K. B. van, 'Staatsschuld en consolidatiebeleid in Nederland in de periode 1814–1994', *NEHA-Jaarboek*, 57 (1994), 159–205.

Posthumus-Van der Goot, W. H., and A. de Waal, eds., *Van moeder op dochter: de maatschappelijke positie van de vrouw in Nederland vanaf de franse tijd* (Nijmegen, 1977).

Postma, J. K. T., 'Sociale zekerheid als onderdeel van de publieke financiën', in W. Fritschy, *et al.*, eds., *Doel en middel: aspecten van financieel overheidsbeleid in de Nederlanden van de zestiende eeuw tot heden* (Amsterdam, 1995), pp. 197–212 and 266–8.

Pot, G. P. M., *Arm Leiden: levensstandaard, bedeling en bedeelden, 1750–1854* (Hilversum, 1994).

Prak, M., 'De nieuwe sociale geschiedschrijving in Nederland', *Tijdschrift voor Sociale Geschiedenis*, 20 (1994), 121–48.

Republikeinse veelheid, democratisch enkelvoud: sociale verandering in het Revolutietijdvak, 's-Hertogenbosch 1770–1820 (Nijmegen, 1999).

Priester, P. R., *De economische ontwikkeling van de landbouw in Groningen 1800–1910: een kwalitatieve en kwantitatieve analyse*, A.A.G. Bijdragen 31 (Wageningen, 1991).

Geschiedenis van de Zeeuwse landbouw circa 1600–1910, A.A.G. Bijdragen 37 (Wageningen, 1998).

Provinciaal Blad van Zeeland (Middelburg, 1845).

Punch, M., ed., *Control in the police organization* (Cambridge, Mass., 1983).

Raalte, E. van, *The Parliament of the Kingdom of the Netherlands* (London, 1959).

Raedts, P., 'Katholieken op zoek naar een Nederlandse identiteit 1814–1898', *Bijdragen en Mededelingen betreffende de Geschiedenis der Nederlanden*, 107 (1992), 713–25.

Ramaer, J. C., 'Middelpunten der bewoning in Nederland, voorheen en thans', *Tijdschrift van het Koninklijk Nederlandsch Aardrijkskundig Genootschap*, second series, 38 (1921), 1–38 and 174–214.

Randeraad, N., 'Het geplooide land', essay for inclusion in volume on *Pillarization*, edited by J. C. H. Blom (Amsterdam, 2000, forthcoming).

Randeraad, N., ed., *Mediators between state and society* (Hilversum, 1998).

Rasker, A. J., *De Nederlandse Hervormde Kerk vanaf 1795: haar geschiedenis en theologie in de negentiende en twintigste eeuw* (Kampen, 1974).

Razzell, P., *The conquest of smallpox: the impact of inoculation on smallpox mortality in eighteenth century Britain* (Firle, 1977).

Edward Jenner's cowpox vaccine: the history of a medical myth (Firle, 1977).

Reid, A., *The contest for North Sumatra: Atjeh, the Netherlands and Britain 1858–1898* (London, 1969).

Reijnders, C., *Van 'Joodse natiëen' tot Joodse Nederlanders: een onderzoek naar getto-en assimilatieverschijnselen tussen 1600 en 1942* (Amsterdam, 1969).

Reinsma, R., 'De West-Indische Maatschappij (1828–1863)', *Tijdschrift voor Geschiedenis*, 73 (1960), 58–74.

Renkema, W. E., *Het Curaçaose plantagebedrijf in de negentiende eeuw* (Zutphen, 1981).

Renooy, D. C., 'De Nederlandsche Handel-Maatschappij en het emissie-bedrijf', in *Economisch-historische opstellen geschreven voor prof. dr Z. W. Sneller* (Amsterdam [1947]), pp. 153–66.

Ribberink, A. E. M., 'Van Ghert; achtergronden van een falen', *Archief voor de*

Geschiedenis van de Katholieke Kerk in Nederland, 10 (1968), 329–42.

Ridder, J., *Een conjunctuur-analyse van Nederland 1848–1860* (Amsterdam, 1935).

Righart, H., *De katholieke zuil in Europa: een vergelijkend onderzoek naar het ontstaan van verzuiling onder katholieken in Oostenrijk, Zwitserland, België en Nederland* (Meppel, 1986).

Rijken van Olst, H., 'De ontwikkeling van de macro-economische statistiek in Nederland', *Economisch-Statistische Berichten*, 34 (1949), 11–12.

Riley, J. C., 'The Dutch economy after 1650: decline or growth?', *Journal of European Economic History*, 13 (1984), 521–69.

International government finance and the Amsterdam capital market 1740–1815 (Cambridge, 1980).

'That your widows may be rich: providing for widowhood in Old Regime Europe', *Economisch- en Sociaal-historisch Jaarboek*, 45 (1982), 58–76.

Robijns, M. J. F., *Radicalen in Nederland (1840–1851)* (Leiden, 1967).

Roes, J., ed., *Bronnen van de katholieke arbeidersbeweging in Nederland: toespraken, brieven en artikelen van Alphons Ariëns 1887–1901* (Nijmegen, 1982).

Rogier, L. J., *Katholiek herleving: geschiedenis van katholiek Nederland sinds 1853* (The Hague [1956]).

Röling, H. Q., *'De tragedie van het geslachtsleven'. Dr J. Rutgers (1850–1924) en de Nieuw-Mathusiaansche Bond* (Amsterdam, 1987).

'Zedelijkheid en struisvogelpolitiek', in P. Luykx and H. Righart, eds., *Van de pastorie naar het torentje: een eeuw confessionele politiek* (The Hague, 1991), pp. 147–54.

Rooden, P. van, *Religieuze regimes: over godsdienst en maatschappij in Nederland 1570–1990* (Amsterdam, 1996).

'Studies naar locale verzuiling als toegang tot de geschiedenis van de constructie van religieuze verschillen in Nederland', *Tijdschrift voor Theoretische Geschiedenis*, 20 (1993), 439–54.

Rooij, P. de, 'Zes studies over verzuiling', *Bijdragen en Mededelingen betreffende de Geschiedenis der Nederlanden*, 110/3 (1995), 380–92.

Rooijakkers, G., *Rituele repertoires: volkskultuur in oostelijk Noord-Brabant 1559–1853* (Nijmegen, 1993).

Roovers, J. J., *De plaatselijke belastingen en financiën in den loop der tijden: een historische schets* (Alphen, 1932).

Rostow, W. W., 'Rostow on growth: a non-Communist manifesto', *The Economist*, 192 (15 August 1959), 409–16.

'Ruffles on the calm; a survey of the Dutch economy', *The Economist* (30 January 1982), 1–26.

Rullman, J. C., *Kuyper-bibliografie*, 3 vols. (The Hague/Kampen, 1923–40).

Rüter, A. J. C., *De spoorwegstakingen van 1903: een spiegel der arbeidersbeweging in Nederland* (Nijmegen, 1978).

Rutten, W., *'De vreeslijkste aller harpijen': pokkenepidemieën en pokkenbestrijdingen in Nederland in de achttiende en negentiende eeuw: een sociaal-historische en historisch-demografische study*, A.A.G. Bijdragen 36 (Wageningen, 1997).

Said, E. W., *Orientalism*, revised edition (London, 1995).

Sande, A. van de, *Vrijmetselarij in de Lage Landen: een mysterieuze broederschap zonder geheimen* (Zutphen, 1995).

Sande, A. van de, and J. Roosendaal, eds., *'Een stille leerschool van deugd en goede zeden': vrijmetselarij in Nederland in de 18e en 19e eeuw* (Hilversum, 1995).

Sas, N. C. F. van, 'De mythe Nederland', *De Negentiende Eeuw*, 16 (1992), 4–22.

'Varieties of Dutchness', in A. Galema, *et al.*, eds., *Images of the nation: different meanings of Dutchness 1870–1940* (Amsterdam, 1993), pp. 5–16.

Sas, N. C. F van, ed., *Vaderland: een geschiedenis vanaf de vijftiende eeuw tot 1940* (Amsterdam, 1999).

Schama, S., *The embarrassment of riches: an interpretation of Dutch culture in the Golden Age* (London, 1987).

Patriots and liberators: revolution in the Netherlands 1780–1813 (London, 1977).

Schiff, E., *Industrialization without national patents: the Netherlands, 1869–1912, Switzerland, 1850–1907* (Princeton, 1971).

Schilstra, W. N., *Vrouwenarbeid in landbouw en industrie in Nederland in de tweede helft der 19e eeuw* (Amsterdam, 1940)

Schmal, H., ed., *Patterns of European urbanisation since 1500* (London, 1991).

Schmal, J. J. R., *Tweeërlei staatsbeschouwing in het Réveil* (The Hague, 1943).

Schmidt, J., *From Anatolia to Indonesia: opium trade and the Dutch community of Izmir, 1820–1940* (Leiden, 1998).

'Three decades of Dutch opium trade in the Levant, 1825–1855', in D. Panzac, ed., *Histoire économique et sociale de l'Empire Ottoman et de la Turquie (1326–1960)* (Paris, 1995), pp. 263–8.

Schöffer, I., 'Verzuiling, een specifiek Nederlands probleem', *Sociologische Gids*, 3 (1956), 121–7.

Scholliers, P., ed., *Real wages in 19th and 20th century Europe: historical and comparative perspectives* (Oxford, 1989).

Scholten, J. H., *De leer der Hervormde Kerk in hare grondbeginselen uit de bronnen voorgesteld en beoordeeld*, 2 vols. (Leiden, 1848–50).

Schoon, L., *De gynaecologie als belichaming van vrouwen: verloskunde en gynaecologie 1840–1920* (Zutphen, 1995).

Schot, J. W., 'Het meekrapbedrijf in Nederland in de negentiende eeuw nader bezien in het licht van het industrialisatiedebat', *Economisch- en Sociaal-Historisch Jaarboek*, 50 (1987), 77–110.

Schram, P. L., *Hendrik Pierson: een hoofdstuk uit de geschiedenis van de inwendige zending* (Kampen, 1968).

Schrover, M., '"De affaire wordt gecontinueerd door de weduwe": handelende vrouwen in de negentiende eeuw', *Jaarboek voor Vrouwengeschiedenis*, 17 (1997), 55–74.

Het vette, het zoete en het wederzijdse profijt: arbeidsverhoudingen in de margarine-industrie en in de cacao- en chocolade-industrie in Nederland 1870–1960 (Hilversum, 1991).

Schutte, G. J., *Het Calvinistisch Nederland: rede* (Utrecht, 1988).

'Nederland: een Calvinistisch natie?', *Bijdragen en Mededelingen betreffende de Geschiedenis der Nederlanden*, 107 (1992), 690–702.

Nederland en de Afrikaners: adhesie en adversie (Franeker, 1986).

Schuttevaer, H., and J. G. Detiger, *Anderhalve eeuw belastingen* (Deventer, 1964).

Schuurman, A. J., *Materiële cultuur en levenstijl: een onderzoek naar de taal der dingen op het Nederlandse platteland in de negentiende eeuw: de Zaanstreek, Oost-Groningen, Oost-Brabant,* A.A.G. Bijdragen 30 (Wageningen, 1989).

Schuurman, A., *et al.,* eds., *Aards geluk: de Nederlanders en hun spullen van 1550 tot 1850* (Amsterdam, 1997).

Schuurman, A., and P. Spierenburg, eds., *Private domain, public inquiry: families and life-styles in the Netherlands and Europe, 1550 to the present* (Hilversum, 1996).

Sevenhuijsen, S. L., *De orde van het vaderschap: politieke debatten over ongehuwd moederschap, afstamming en huwelijk in Nederland 1870–1900* (Amsterdam, 1987).

Shorter, E., *A history of women's bodies* (Harmondsworth, 1984).

The making of the modern family (London, 1976).

Skillen, J. W., and S. W. Carlson-Thies, 'Religious and political development in nineteenth-century Holland', *Publius,* 12/3 (1982), 43–64.

Sleebe, V. C., *In termen van fatsoen: sociale controle in het Groningse kleigebied 1770–1914* (Assen, 1994).

Slicher van Bath, B. H., *Bijdragen tot de agrarische geschiedenis* (Utrecht, 1978).

Een samenleving onder spanning: geschiedenis van het platteland in Overijssel (Assen, 1957).

Sluijk, B. C., 'Meekrap', *Jaarverslag Stichting Textielgeschiedenis* (1958), 17–38.

Smit, C., *Diplomatieke geschiedenis van Nederland: inzonderheid sedert de vestiging van het Koninkrijk* (The Hague, 1950).

Smit, C., ed., *Bescheiden betreffende de buitenlandse politiek van Nederland 1848–1919, 3e periode 1899–1919,* vol. VI, *Buitenlandse bronnen 1899–1914,* RGP 128 (The Hague, 1968).

Smit, H. J., 'De armenwet van 1854 en haar voorgeschiedenis', in *Historische opstellen aangeboden aan J. Huizinga op 7 december 1942 door het Historisch Gezelschap te 's-Gravenhage* (Haarlem, 1948), pp. 218–46.

Smith, A. D., *National identity* (London, 1991).

Smits, J. P., 'The size and structure of the Dutch service sector in international perspective, 1850–1914', *Economic and Social History in the Netherlands,* 2 (1990), 81–97.

Economische groei en structuurverandering in de Nederlandse dienstensector, 1850–1913: een bijdrage aan het proces van 'moderne economische groei' (Amsterdam, 1995).

Smits, J. P., E. Horlings and J. L. van Zanden, 'Sprekende cijfers! De historische nationale rekeningen van Nederland, 1807–1913', *NEHA Jaarboek,* 62 (1999), 51–110.

The measurement of Gross National Product and its components: the Netherlands, 1800–1913 (Utrecht, 1997).

Smits, J. P., J. L. van Zanden, and B. van Ark, 'Introduction: the study of historical national accounts in the Netherlands', *Economic and Social History in the Netherlands,* 7 (1996), 7–14.

Sneller, Z. W., 'Anderhalve eeuw in vogelvlucht', in Z. W. Sneller, ed., *Geschiedenis van den Nederlandschen landbouw 1795–1940* (Groningen, 1943), pp. 37–124.

Soltow, L., and J. L. van Zanden, *Income and wealth inequality in the Netherlands 16th–20th century* (Amsterdam, 1998).

Staatkundig en Staathuishoudkundig Jaarboek[je] 1 (1849) to 36 (1884) (Amsterdam).

Statistiek van de scheepvaart over het jaar 1898 (The Hague, 1899).

Statistisch Jaarbooekje voor het Koninkrijk der Nederlanden (1851–1868) (The Hague; in 1856 becomes *Statistisch Jaarboek*).

Statistisch Zakboek (The Hague, 1899 onwards).

Staverman, R. J., *Volk in Friesland buiten de kerk* (Assen, 1954).

Stel, J. C. van der, *Drinken, drank en dronkenschap: vijf eeuwen drankbestrijding en alcoholhulppverlening in Nederland. Een historisch-sociologische studie* (Hilversum, 1995).

Stemvers, F. A., 'Prostitutie, prostituées en geneeskunde in Nederland 1850–1900', *Spiegel Historiael*, 18 (June 1983), 316–23.

Stokvis, P. R. D., 'Nederland en de internationale migratie, 1815–1960', in F. L. van Holthoon, ed., *De Nederlandse samenleving sinds 1815: wording en samenhang* (Assen, 1985), pp. 71–92.

De Nederlandse trek naar Amerika 1846–1847 (Leiden, 1977).

Stone, L., *The family, sex and marriage in England 1500–1800*, abridged edition (Harmondsworth, 1979).

Stoop, J. A., 'Interessante cijfers', *De Economist*, 45 (1896), 944–54.

Stuijvenberg, J. H. van, 'Economische groei in de negentiende eeeuw: een terreinverkenning', in P. W. Klein, ed., *Van stapelmarkt tot welvaartsstaat: economisch-historische studiën over groei en stagnatie van de Nederlandse volkshuishouding 1600–1970* (Rotterdam, 1970), pp. 52–74.

Stuijvenberg, J. H. van, and J. E. J. de Vrijer, 'Prices, population and national income in the Netherlands 1620–1978', *Journal of European Economic History*, 11 (1982), 699–712.

Stuurman, S., *Verzuiling, kapitalisme, en patriachaat: aspecten van de ontwikkeling van de moderne staat in Nederland* (Nijmegen, 1984).

Wacht op onze daden: het liberalisme en de vernieuwing van de Nederlandse staat (Amsterdam, 1992).

Suttorp, L. C., 'Nederland en het Vaticaan in de negentiende en twintigste eeuw', *Christelijk Historisch Tijdschrift*, 24/1–2 (1979), pp. 1–38.

Swaan, A. de, *In care of the state: health care, education and welfare in Europe and the USA in the modern era* (Cambridge, 1988).

Swart, K. W., *The miracle of the Dutch Republic as seen in the seventeenth century* (London, 1969).

Swellengrebel, N. H. and A. de Buck, *Malaria in the Netherlands* (Amsterdam, 1938).

Swierenga, R. P., '"Exodus Netherlands, promised land America": Dutch immigration and settlement in the United States', *Bijdragen en Mededelingen betreffende de Geschiedenis der Nederlanden*, 97 (1982), 517–38.

Swierenga, R. P., ed., *The Dutch in America: immigration, settlement, and cultural change* (New Brunswick, NJ, 1985).

Swierenga, R. P., and H. S. Stout, 'Socio-economic patterns of migration from the Netherlands in the nineteenth century', *Research in Economic History*, 1

(1976), 298–333.

Tamse, C. A., and E. Witte, eds., *Staats- en natievorming in Willem I's koninkrijk* (Brussels, 1992).

Taverne, E., and I. Visser, eds., *Stedebouw: de geschiedenis van de stad in de Nederlanden van 1500 tot heden* (Nijmegen, 1993).

Taylor, A. J., ed., *The standard of living in Britain in the industrial revolution* (London, 1975).

Teijl, J., 'Nationaal inkomen van Nederland in de periode 1850–1900: tasten en testen', *Economisch- en Sociaal-Historisch Jaarboek*, 34 (1971), 232–62.

Teuteberg, H. J., ed., *European food history: a research review* (Leicester, 1992).

Therborn, G., '"Pillarization" and "popular movements". Two variants of welfare state capitalism: the Netherlands and Sweden', in F. G. Castles, ed., *The comparative history of public policy* (Oxford, 1989), pp. 192–241.

Thompson, E. P., *The making of the English working class* (Harmondsworth, 1968).

Thomson, D., *Europe since Napoleon*, second edition (London, 1962).

Thurlings, J. M. G., 'The case of Dutch Catholicism: a contribution to the theory of a pluralistic society', *Sociologia Neerlandica*, 7 (1971), 118–36.

Tijdschrift ter bevordering van Nijverheid, 1 (1833–) (Haarlem, etc.).

Tijdschrift voor Geschiedenis, special issue on immigration, 100/3 (1987), 319–490.

Tijn, T. van, 'Een nabeschouwing', *Bijdragen en Mededelingen betreffende de Geschiedenis der Nederlanden*, 86 (1971), 79–89.

'De negentiende eeuw', in J. H. van Stuijvenberg, ed., *De economische geschiedenis van Nederland* (Groningen, 1977), pp. 201–60.

'Voorlopige notities over het ontstaan van het moderne klassebewustzijn in Nederland', in P. A. M. Geurts and F. A. M. Messing, eds., *Economische ontwikkeling en sociale emancipatie: 18 opstellen over economische en sociale geschiedenis*, 2 vols. (The Hague, 1977), vol. II, pp. 129–43.

'De wording van de moderne politieke-partij-organisaties in Nederland', in G. A. M. Beekelaar, *et al.*, eds., *Vaderlands verleden in veelvoud* (The Hague, 1975), pp. 590–601.

Tinbergen, J., 'Kapitaalvorming en conjunctuur in Nederland, 1880–1930', *Nederlandsche Conjunctuur*, 4 (1932), 8–16.

Toonen, T. A. J., 'On the administrative condition of politics: administrative transformation in the Netherlands', *West European Politics*, 19/3 (1996), 609–32.

Trienekens, G. M. T., *Tussen ons volk en de honger: de voedselvoorziening 1940–1945* (Utrecht, 1985).

Tuma, E. H., *European economic history: tenth century to the present, theory and history of economic change* (New York, 1971).

Uitkomsten van het onderzoek naar den toestand van den landbouw in Nederland, ingesteld door de Landbouwcommissie benoemd bij K.B. van 18 september 1886, no. 28, 4 vols. (The Hague, 1890).

Unger, R. W., 'Energy sources for the Dutch Golden Age: peat, wind and coal', *Research in Economic History*, 9 (1984), 221–53.

Valk, L. van der, 'Poor Law and social security legislation in the Netherlands', *Economic and Social History in the Netherlands*, 3 (1991), 99–118.

'Zieken- en begrafenisfondsen in de negentiende eeuw: traditie en vernieuwing', *NEHA-Jaarboek*, 59 (1996), 162–210.

Valkhoff, J., 'Vermaatschappelijking van recht en staat', in A. N. J. den Hollander, et al., eds., *Drift en koers: een halve eeuw sociale verandering in Nederland*, third printing (Assen, 1968), pp. 265–86.

Vandenbroecke, C., F. W. A. van Poppel, and A. M. van der Woude, 'De zuigelingen- en kindersterfte in België en Nederland in seculair perspectief', *Tijdschrift voor Geschiedenis*, 94 (1981), 461–91.

Vandenbroecke, R., 'Voedingstoestanden te Gent tijdens de eerste helft van de 19de eeuw', *Revue Belge d'Histoire Contemporaine*, 4 (1973), 109–69.

Veenendaal, A. J., *De ijzeren weg in een land vol water; beknopte geschiedenis van de spoorwegen in Nederland 1834–1958* (Amsterdam, 1988).

Slow train to paradise: how Dutch investment helped build American railroads (Stanford, 1996).

Velde, H. te, 'The debate on Dutch national identity', *Dutch Crossing*, 20/2 (1996), 87–100.

Gemeenschapszin en plichtbesef: liberalisme en nationalisme in Nederland 1870–1918 (The Hague, 1992).

'Viriliteit en opoffering: "mannelijkheid" in het Nederlandse politieke debat van het fin-de-siècle', *Tijdschrift voor Vrouwenstudies*, 14 (1993), 421–33.

Velde, H. te, and H. Verhage, eds., *De eenheid en de delen: zuilvorming, onderwijspolitiek en natievorming in Nederland 1850–1900* (Amsterdam, 1996).

Venema, A., 'Proeve eener berekening van de koopwaarde der gronden bij den landbouw en de veehouderij in gebruik', *De Economist*, 46 (1897), 801–52 and 897–908.

Verberne, L. G. J., *Geschiedenis van Nederland*, edited by H. Brugmans, 7 vols. (Amsterdam, 1937), vol. VII, *Nieuwste geschiedenis*.

De verbetering van den bakerstand: een woord ter behartiging voor vrouwen en moeders, door de Vereeniging voor Genees- en Heelkundigen, in Zeeland (Middelburg, 1851).

Verbong, G., *Technische innovaties in de katoendrukkerij en -ververij in Nederland 1835–1920* (Amsterdam, 1988).

'Verbruik van veraccijnsd gedistilleerd 1913', *Maandschrift van het CBS*, 15 (1920), 1e aflevering, 2e bijvoegsel.

Verdoorn, J. A., *Het gezondheidswezen te Amsterdam in de 19e eeuw*, new edition (Nijmegen, 1981) [original edition 1965].

Verhallen, H. J. G., et al., eds., *Corporatisme in Nederland: belangengroepen en democratie* (Alphen, 1980).

Verhoeven, D., et al., eds., *Klederdracht en kleedgedrag: het kostuum Harer Majesteits onderdanen, 1898–1998* (Nijmegen [1998]).

Verhoog, P., *De ontwikkeling van onze scheepvaart en havens* (Amsterdam, 1959).

Vermeulen, W. H., *Den Haag en de landbouw: keerpunten in het negentiende-eeuwse landbouwbeleid* (Assen, 1966).

Verrips, J., *En boven de polder de hemel: een anthropologische studie van een Nederlandse dorp 1850–1971* (S.l. [1977]).

Verslag der eerste algemeene vergadering van Nederlandsche vrijdenkers, gehouden 12 september 1869 te Amsterdam (Amsterdam, 1869).

Verslag omtrent den toestand der 'Nijverheids-vereeniging' gevestigd te Middelburg: 1 juli 1874–30 juni 1877 (Middelburg [1877]).

Verslag omtrent den toestand van den Landbouw en de Veeteelt in Zeeland, en van de Maatchappij tot Bevordering van Landbouw en Veeteelt in dat gewest (1863–1880) (Zwolle, etc.).

Verslag van [from 1879: *over*] *den Landbouw in Nederland* (1851–1960) (The Hague).

Verslag van den Staat der Nederlandsche Zeevisscherijen (1858–1910) (The Hague).

Verslag van het Verhandelde op het Nederlandsch Landhuishoudkundig Congres, 1 (1846) to 47 (1894) (Groningen, etc.).

Verstegen, S. W., 'Een der dragelijkste middelen: de politieke discussie in de Tweede Kamer over de belasting op het recht van successie in de periode 1817–1878', in W. Fritschy, *et al.*, eds., *Doel en middel: aspecten van financieel overheidsbeleid in de Nederlanden van de zestiende eeuw tot heden* (Amsterdam, 1995), pp. 151–66 and 261–3.

Verstegen, W., 'National wealth and income from capital in the Netherlands, 1805–1910', *Economic and Social History in the Netherlands*, 7 (1996), 73–108.

Visser, J., 'The politics of mediation: trade unions in the Netherlands 1910–1930', in N. Randeraad, ed., *Mediators between state and society* (Hilversum, 1998), pp. 41–56.

Vleggeert, J. C., *Kinderarbeid in Nederland 1500–1874: van berusting tot beperking* (Assen, 1964).

Vlissingen, P. van, 'Huishoudelijke budjets van gezinnen van werklieden te Amsterdam', *Tijdschrift voor Staathuishoudkunde en Statistiek*, 13 (1856), 229–34.

Vogelzang, I., *De drinkwatervoorziening in Nederland voor de aanleg van de drinkwaterleidingen* (Gouda, 1956).

Voort, J. P. van de, 'Dutch capital in the West Indies during the eighteenth century', *Low Countries History Yearbook*, 14 (1981), 85–105.

'De Nederlandse Maatschappij voor Nijverheid en Handel (1777–1977) en de bevordering van de zeevisserij', in Joh. de Vries, *et al.*, eds., *Ondernemende geschiedenis: 22 opstellen geschreven bij het afscheid van mr. H. van Riel als voorzitter van de vereniging Het Nederlandsch Economisch-Historisch Archief* (The Hague, 1977), pp. 199–219.

De Westindische plantages van 1720 tot 1795: financiën en handel (Eindhoven, 1973).

Voort, R. H. van der, *Overheidsbeleid en overheidsfinancien in Nederland 1850–1913* (Amsterdam, 1994).

Vooys, A. C. de, 'De regionale verscheidenheid in de geboortefrequentie in de tweede helft der 19e eeuw', *Tijdschrift van het Koninklijk Nederlandsch Aardrijkskundig Genootschap*, second series, 81 (1964), 220–32.

'De sterfte in Nederland in het midden der negentiende eeuw: een demogeografische studie', *Tijdschrift van het Koninklijk Nederlandsch Aardrijkskundig Genootschap*, second series, 68 (1951), 233–71.

Voskuil, J. J., 'De verspreiding van koffie en thee in Nederland', *Volkskundig Bulletin*, 14/1 (1988), 68–93.

'De weg naar luilekkerland', *Bijdragen en Mededelingen betreffende de Geschiedenis der Nederlanden*, 98 (1983), 460–82.

Het vraagstuk der gemeente-classificatie: rapport uitgebracht door de commissie (The Hague, 1951).

Vrankrijker, A. J. C. de, *Een groeiende gedachte: de ontwikkeling der meningen over de sociale kwestie in de 19e eeuw in Nederland* (Assen, 1959).

Vries, A. de, *Geschiedenis van de handelspolitieke betrekkingen tusschen Nederland en Engeland in de negentiende eeuw (1814–1872)* (The Hague, 1931).

Vries, B. W. de, *De Nederlandse papiernijverheid in de negentiende eeuw* (The Hague, 1957).

Vries, H. de, 'Absenteisme van grootgrondbezitters in Nederland 1850–1890', *Economisch- en Sociaal-historisch Jaarboek*, 38 (1975), 109–23.

'The labour market in Dutch agriculture and emigration to the United States', in R. P. Swierenga, ed., *The Dutch in America: immigration, settlement, and cultural change* (New Brunswick, NJ, 1985), pp. 78–101.

Landbouw en bevolking tijdens de agrarische depressie in Friesland (1878–1895) (Wageningen, 1971).

Vries, Jan de, 'Barges and capitalism: passenger transportation in the Dutch economy, 1632–1839', *A.A.G. Bijdragen*, 21, (1978), 33–398.

'The decline and rise of the Dutch economy, 1675–1900', *Research in Economic History*, Supplement 3 (1984), 140–89.

The Dutch rural economy in the Golden Age, 1500–1700 (New Haven, 1974).

'Regional economic inequality in the Netherlands since 1600', in P. Bairoch and M. Lévy-Leboyer, eds., *Disparities in economic development since the industrial revolution* (London, 1981), pp. 189–98.

Vries, Jan de, and A. van der Woude, *The first modern economy: success, failure and perseverance of the Dutch economy, 1500–1815* (Cambridge, 1997).

Nederland 1500–1815: de eerste ronde van moderne economische groei (Amsterdam, 1995).

Vries, Joh. de, 'Het censuskiesrecht en de welvaart in Nederland 1850–1917', *Economisch- en Sociaal-Historisch Jaarboek*, 34 (1971), 178–231.

De economische achteruitgang der Republiek in de achttiende eeuw (Leiden, 1968).

'Economische groei en industrialisatie in Nederland 1815–1914', *Maandschrift Economie*, 33 (1968), 118–28.

Hoogovens IJmuiden 1918–1968 (IJmuiden, 1968).

'De problematiek der Duits-Nederlandse economische betrekkingen in de negentiende eeuw', *Tijdschrift voor Geschiedenis*, 78 (1965), 23–48.

'De twintigste eeuw', in J. H. van Stuijvenberg, ed., *De economische geschiedenis van Nederland* (Groningen, 1977), pp. 261–308.

Vries, P. A. de, *Kuisheid voor mannen, vrijheid voor vrouwen: de reglementering en bestrijding van prostitutie in Nederland, 1850–1911* (Hilversum, 1997).

Wet van het lul-collegie gevestigde te Port-Fort, onder de zinspreuk: nugando discimus nugari (Vlissingen, s.a. [c. 1850]).

Wielen, H. G. W. van der, 'Sociale toestanden ten plattelande', in Z. W. Sneller, ed., *Geschiedenis van den Nederlandschen landbouw 1790–1940* (Groningen, 1943), pp. 426–66.

Wijmans, L., *Beeld en betekenis van het maatschappelijke midden: oude en nieuwe middengroepen 1850 tot heden* (Amsterdam, 1987).

Wijtvliet, C. A. M., *Expansie en dynamiek: de ontwikkeling van het Nederlandse handelsbankwezen 1816–1914* (s.l., 1993).

'De Nederlandse Handel-Maatschappij; van handelsonderneming naar bankbedrijf', *Jaarboek voor de Geschiedenis van Bedrijf en Techniek*, 6 (1989), 96–118.

Wilde, I. E. de, *Nieuwe deelgenoten in de wetenschap: vrouwelijke studenten en docenten aan de Rijksuniversiteit Groningen, 1871–1919* (Assen, 1998).

Willems, W., *In search of the true gypsy: from Enlightenment to final solution* (London, 1997).

Willemse, R., 'Orde en rust in het Land van Cadzand: een historisch sociologische bijdrage tot de geschiedenis van westelijke Zeeuws-Vlaanderen in het midden van de vorige eeuw' (unpublished paper, Biervliet, 1979).

Wilson, C. H., 'Dutch investment in eighteenth-century England: a note on yardsticks', in A. C. Carter, ed., *Getting, spending and investing in early modern times: essays on Dutch, English and Huguenot economic history* (Assen, 1975), pp. 53–9.

Economic history and the historian: collected essays (London, 1969).

The history of Unilever: a study in economic growth and social change (London, 1954).

Windmuller, J. P., *Labor relations in the Netherlands* (Ithaca, 1969).

Winter, P. J. van, 'De Nederlanders in de Zuid-Afrikaansche Republiek', in H. van Riel, *et al.*, eds., *Zeventien studiën van Nederlanders verzameld door de vereniging Het Nederlandsch Economisch-historisch Archief ter gelegenheid van haar vijftigjarig bestaan 1914–1964* (The Hague, 1964), pp. 74–100.

Wintle, M. J., 'Agrarian history in the Netherlands in the modern period: a review and bibliography', *Agricultural History Review*, 39/1 (1991), 65–73.

'"Dearly won and cheaply sold": the sale and purchase of agricultural land in the province of Zeeland in the nineteenth century', *Economisch- en Sociaal-Historisch Jaarboek*, 49 (1986), 44–99.

'De economie van Zeeland in 1808: een rapport van landdrost Abraham van Doorn over de economie in Zeeland in het najaar van 1808', *Archief Zeeuws Genootschap* (1985), 97–136.

'The liberal state in the Netherlands: historical traditions of tolerance, permissiveness and liberalism', in S. Groenveld and M. J. Wintle, eds., *Under the sign of liberalism: varieties of European liberalism in past and present*, Britain and the Netherlands 12 (Zutphen, 1997), pp. 116–32.

'Modest growth and capital drain in an advanced economy: the case of Dutch agriculture in the nineteenth century', *Agricultural History Review*, 39/1 (1991), 17–29.

'Natievorming, onderwijs en godsdienst in Nederland 1850–1900', in H. te Velde and H. Verhage, eds., *De eenheid en de delen: zuilvorming, onderwijspolitiek en natievorming in Nederland 1850–1900* (Amsterdam, 1996), pp. 13–28.

'The Netherlands economy', in *Western Europe 1989* (London, 1988), pp. 356–64.

'Pillarisation, consociation, and vertical pluralism in the Netherlands revisited: a European view' (paper delivered to the Second European Social Science History Conference, Amsterdam, March 1998).

Pillars of piety: religion in the Netherlands in the nineteenth century (Hull, 1987).

'"Plagerijen, hatelijkheden en onregt": Dutch tithing in the nineteenth century, with special reference to Zeeland', *Economisch- en Sociaal-Historisch Jaarboek*, 44 (1982), 224–46.

'Policing the liberal state in the Netherlands: the historical context of the current reorganization of the Dutch police', *Policing and Society*, 6 (1996), 181–97.

'Positive and negative motivation in Dutch migration to North America: the case of the province of Zeeland in the nineteenth century', in R. Hoefte and C. Kardux, eds., *Connecting cultures: the Netherlands in five centuries of transactive exchange* (Amsterdam, 1994), pp. 135–53.

'Push-factors in emigration: the case of the province of Zeeland in the nineteenth century', *Population Studies*, 46 (1992), 523–37.

'Shipping and empire: Dutch contacts with Asia and the world, 1850–1939', *Dutch Crossing*, 19/2 (1995), 118–41.

Zeeland and the churches: religion and society in the province of Zeeland in the nineteenth century (Middelburg, 1988).

Wintle, M. J., ed., *Culture and identity in Europe: perceptions of diversity and unity in past and present* (Aldershot, 1996).

Wit, C. H. E. de, *De Nederlandse revolutie van de achttiende eeuw 1780–1787: oligarchie en proletariaat* (Oirsbeek, 1974).

Het ontstaan van het moderne Nederland 1780–1848 en zijn geschiedschrijving (Oirsbeek, 1978).

De strijd tussen aristocratie en democratie in Nederland 1780–1848: kritisch onderzoek van een historisch beeld en herwaardering van een periode (Heerlen, 1965).

Wit, O. de, *Telefonie in Nederland 1877–1940: opkomst en ontwikkeling van een grootschalig technisch systeem* (Amsterdam, 1988).

Woud, A. van der, *Het lege land: de ruimtelijke orde van Nederland 1798–1848* (Amsterdam, 1987).

'Ondergang en wederopstanding van de neogotiek in Nederland', *Ons Erfdeel*, 39/5 (1996), 737–45.

Woude, A. M. van der, 'De alfabetisering', in D. P. Blok, *et al.*, eds., *Algemene geschiedenis der Nederlanden*, 15 vols. (Haarlem, 1975–82), vol. VII (1980), pp. 257–64.

'Bevolking en gezin in Nederland', in F. L. van Holthoon, ed., *De Nederlandse samenleving sinds 1815: wording en samenhang* (Assen, 1985), pp. 19–70.

Woude, R. E. van der, *Leeuwarden 1850–1914: de modernisering van een provinciehoofdstad* (Leeuwarden, 1994).

Wright, H. R. C., *Free trade and protection in the Netherlands 1816–1830: a study of the first Benelux* (London, 1955).

Wrigley, E. A., *Industrial growth and population change: a regional study of the coalfield areas of North-West Europe in the later nineteenth century* (Cambridge, 1961).

Zainu-ddin, A., *Indonesia* (Victoria, 1975).

Zanden, J. L. van, 'Een debat dat niet gevoerd werd: over het karakter van het proces van pre-moderne economische groei', *NEHA-Bulletin*, 8/2 (1994), 77–92.

'The development of government finances in a chaotic period, 1807–1850', *Economic and Social History in the Netherlands*, 7 (1996), 57–72.

'The Dutch economy in the very long run: growth in production, energy consumption and capital in Holland (1585–1805) and the Netherlands (1805–1910)', in A. Szirmai, *et al.*, eds., *Explaining economic growth* (Amsterdam, 1993), pp. 267–83.

The economic history of the Netherlands 1914–1995: a small open economy in the 'long' twentieth century (London, 1998).

'Economische groei in Nederland in de negentiende eeuw: enkele nieuwe resultaten', *Economisch- en Sociaal-Historisch Jaarboek*, 50 (1987), 51–76.

De economische ontwikkeling van de Nederlandse landbouw in de negentiende eeuw, 1800–1914, A.A.G. Bijdragen 25 (Wageningen, 1985).

De industrialisatie in Amsterdam 1825–1914 (Bergen, NL, 1987).

'Industrialization in the Netherlands', in M. Teich and R. Porter, eds., *The industrial revolution in national context: Europe and the USA* (Cambridge, 1996), pp. 78–94.

'Kosten van levensonderhoud en loonvorming in Holland en Oost-Nederland 1650–1850', *Tijdschrift voor Sociale Geschiedenis*, 11 (1985), 309–24.

'Op zoek naar de "missing link": hypothesen over de opkomst van Holland in de late middeleeuwen en de vroeg-moderne tijd', *Tijdschrift voor Sociale Geschiedenis*, 14 (1988), 359–86.

'Regionale verschillen in landbouwproduktiviteit en loonpeil in de Lage Landen aan het begin van de negentiende eeuw: een toetsing van de Mokyr-hypothese', *NEHA-Jaarboek*, 57 (1994), 271–86.

The rise and decline of Holland's economy: merchant capitalism and the labour market (Manchester, 1993).

The transformation of European agriculture in the 19th century: the case of the Netherlands (Amsterdam, 1994).

Zanden, J. L. van, ed., *The economic development of the Netherlands since 1870* (Cheltenham, 1996).

'Den zedelijken en materiëlen toestand der arbeidende bevolking ten platten lande': *een reeks rapporten uit 1851*, Agronomisch-Historische Bijdragen 14 (Wageningen, 1991).

Zanden, J. L. van, and R. T. Griffiths, *Economische geschiedenis van Nederland in de 20e eeuw*, Aula Series (Utrecht, 1989).

Zappey, W. M., 'Het Fonds voor de Nationale Nijverheid 1821–1846', in P. Boomgaard, *et al.*, eds., *Exercities in ons verleden: twaalf opstellen over de economische en sociale geschiedenis van Nederland en koloniën 1800–1950 aangeboden aan prof. dr. W. J. Wieringa* (Assen, 1981), pp. 27–42.

Zee, T. van der, 'Armoede en cholera in 1832', *Economisch-Historisch Jaarboek*, 22 (1943), 196–250.

Zeeuw, J. W. de, 'Peat and the Dutch Golden Age: the historical meaning of energy-attainability', *A.A.G. Bijdragen*, 21 (1978), 3–31.

Zeventig jaren statistiek in tijdreeksen: 1899–1969, C.B.S. (The Hague, 1970).

Zon, H. van, *Een zeer onfrisse geschiedenis: studies over niet-industriële verontreiniging in Nederland, 1850–1920* (The Hague, 1986).

Zuidema, J. R., 'Economic thought in the Netherlands between 1750 and 1870: from commercial mercantilism towards the true principles of political economy', in J. van Daal and A. Heertje, eds., *Economic thought in the Netherlands: 1650–1950* (Aldershot, 1992), pp. 29–74.

Index